W9-DHU-600

International Law
and National Behavior

International Law and National Behavior

a behavioral interpretation of contemporary international law and politics

Ahmed Sheikh

Western Illinois University

John Wiley & Sons, Inc.

New York • London • Sydney • Toronto

Library of Congress Cataloging in Publication Data:

Sheikh, Ahmed, 1934–
    International Law and national behavior.

    Bibliography: p.
    1. International relations.   2. International law.   I. Title.

JX1395.S44   341   73–19922
ISBN 0-471-78229-7
ISBN 0-471-78230-0 (pbk.)

Printed in the United States of America

10 9 8 7 6 5 4 3

To Nargis, Nalni,
and the memory of my father

preface

The subject of this text book is the relationship between international law and national behavior in the international system. I have employed an interdisciplinary approach based on some of the newer social science concepts whose utility is no longer in doubt. Specifically, I have attempted to integrate the traditional pursuits of jurisprudence per se and the descriptive concerns about international law with the interests and research of the "behavioral approach." For example, this approach was used in exploring answers to specific questions about a nation's behavior vis à vis international law compliances or violations. This task was aided by several case studies. Finally, this book is a result of my concern that an introductory course in international law today must acquaint students not only with the abstract description of existing laws that the pure theory of law has always emphasized, but also with the many substantive and conceptual concerns about the dynamic relationship between international law and world politics. I have also gone beyond the popular view that perceives international law simply as a *set of rules* and relegates it entirely to the realm of the "normative." International law does not consist merely of a static body of pronouncements. On the contrary, it has a sociopolitical aspect and (even if viewed primarily as a set of rules) it is often an outcome of sociopolitical processes that men make and that unmake law. Indeed, it is more dynamic than frequently realized.

I am indebted to several people who contributed to the thinking that has gone into this book. I thank specially Samuel P. Huntington of Harvard University, who read the initial proposal for this book and provided valuable advice and encouragement. Another colleague, William D. Coplin of the Maxwell School of Citizenship and Public Affairs at Syracuse University, has read the entire manuscript with immense benefit to every chapter and the book as a whole. Some of the earlier work was commented on by the late Wolfgang Friedman of Columbia University, whose tragic loss will be felt by all of us for a long time. I also thank Walter S. Jones of Northeastern University for his valuable suggestions and graduate assistants James Currier and Allen Yeh for their research assistance. I am also grateful to my wife Nargis. Without her help this book would not have been possible. The much-needed funds for the secretarial help were provided through a research grant by Western Illinois University.

Ahmed Sheikh

contents

section III
International Law and
National Behavior in
Different Area Issues

section IV

International Law and
Patterns of Compliance
and Noncompliance

section V
Conclusion

section I
Introduction to the Study of International Law and Politics

chapter 1
points of concern

A concern with the study of international law

A generation of young people that must live with the knowledge of two recent world wars, characterized by widespread international lawlessness, appalling savagery and destruction, followed by so-called regional wars, bloodier than ever, cannot be denied its criticism of the effectiveness of the contemporary international order. Young minds who not only continue to see a very high proportion of their national resources devoted to national armaments, but also are painfully aware that employment of these weapons can destroy, at any moment all past and future, as well as the present, find no satisfaction in technical answers concerning international law. Yet answers must be provided if international law is still to be taught as a worthwhile subject. There is little doubt that the study of international law in the classroom is in deep trouble. It is a subject that increasingly has faced a classroom audience that is apparently convinced of its irrelevance to much of what transpires today in the real world of international politics. Some people in the audience tend to reject international law as "law" altogether, on the oversimplified premise that it does not have "all those qualities" that are attributed to "real" law, meaning domestic law. Many tend to be simply skeptical or confused. Then, there are others who want to believe in international law but are apparently disillusioned by the present state of what they call "general lawlessness" in international affairs. Driven by a sense of their own idealism, inspired by such notions as "a world without war," "world government through world law," etc., they tend to regard the present state of international law as a broken promise that was made in the immediate years following World War II. Stanley Hoffmann has characterized the circumstances of this betrayal in this way:

> The permanent plight of international law is that, now as before, it shows on its body of rules all the scars inflicted by the international state of war. The tragedy of contemporary international law is in that of a double divorce: First, between the old liberal dream of a world rule of

law, and the realities of an international system of multiple mini-dramas that always threaten to become major catastrophies; second, between the old dream and the new requirements of moderation, which in the circumstances of the present system suggest a downplaying of formal law in the realm of peace-and-war issues, and an upgrading of more flexible techniques, until the system has become less fierce.[1]

Unwilling to give up all hopes of a future world of law, these students prefer to believe that the role of law in today's world can be better understood as an ideology that promises a panacea that eludes implementation because of the nature of the contemporary international system. They hope that someday when nations have finally terminated an era of bloody confrontations, renounced the illegal use of force as a means of solving international disputes, and settled down to a life of international justice, law, and order, the study of international law will be more meaningful. But almost all of these students see international law primarily as an esoteric subject conducive to academic speculation and little more.

What has gone wrong? What can be done to overcome a sense of futility that many students feel when studying international law? It is quite clear that both scholars and teachers are at least partly responsible for the current disillusionment with international law. For instance, it is a field that has suffered considerably in recent years from the claims of what Louis Henkin has called both "too much" and "too little" concerning its role in the present affairs of nations.[2] On the one hand we have the utopians who conceive international law as a cure-all for the world's ills, a magic formula for international justice and peace, needing only to be accepted and put into effect by the international society. On the other hand, the cynics, the so-called political realists, first reject the moralistic-legalistic approach to international affairs as unrealistic, then argue that what is passed as international law is no law at all; rather, it is a clever scheme sometimes to cover and at other times to justify the use of brutal force in the international system. Utopians have erred in insisting that the role of international law in world affairs must be viewed generally in the context of legal doctrines, institutions, and procedures. This has meant an unfortunate neglect of the dynamics of the international system in which law obviously must operate, mold, and be molded by its impact. The cynics have incorrectly attempted to show international law as noth-

[1]Stanley Hoffmann in L. Scheinman and D. Wilkinson (eds.) *International Law and Political Crises* (Boston: Little, Brown), 1968, pp. xiiv–xix.

[2]Louis Henkin, *How Nations Behave: Law & Foreign Policy* (New York: Praeger), 1968. Read the introductory chapter.

ing more than an international norm that is successful only when it is actually observed; thus, its violations must be equated with its failures.

Need for a shift in emphasis

Most students of international politics who approach the subject of international law today are caught in the middle of a contest between the well-meaning idealist, who continues to argue for a lawful world as the best solution to such problems as the arms race, war, national insecurities, and injustice and the so-called hard-boiled realist, who is seemingly convinced that what has passed as international law is nothing more than an unsuccessful attempt to hide the anarchy that prevails in the international arena. Whether a student chooses to dream with the idealists about the law that really never existed or to scoff with the realists about the law that cannot be, in neither case has he found something to study. Obviously, both schools of thought have taken positions based more on their respective temperaments than as a result of analytical judgment.

There is, however, a considerable difference between the mythical law that will prevail over national interests and, in fact, will abolish international politics, and the fictitious law that unsuccessfully conceals the stark realities of international politics. This is the realm of international law that is intertwined with international politics and, therefore, can be best studied in the context of international politics. It reflects the paramount political interest of nations. It registers the dynamics of international politics that are both consensual and conflictive and takes note of the systemic adjustments. It expresses in its stability and instability the political demands for order and predictability and for rapid change. It is the real international law. It makes no promises to transform the international system overnight; nor does it provide a mask for states to disguise the realities of that system. It establishes channels through which states may achieve tentative accommodation between their simultaneous urges for freedom of action based on notions of sovereignty, (i.e., a nation's right to be unpredictable) and their need to act in predictable patterns to be able to deal with the major catastrophies that always seem ready to erupt in the international system. It attempts to conciliate between their strong desires for the ruthless pursuit of national self-interest and for the collective enjoyment of a relatively peaceful life of coexistence that can only come through settled international relationships.

International law, understood in this context, is not expected to abolish international politics, prevail over politics, or be subservient to it. *It is simply an integral part of the political process and should be studied in the same manner.* Conceived as the exploration of the middle ground between the dreams of the idealist and the cynicism of the realist the study of international law can be most interesting to the student and rewarding to the scholar.[3]

Viewed from this perspective it quickly becomes apparent to the scholar that international law is a field where development of new conceptualizations, approaches, models of analysis, and the general task of theory building has been largely neglected on its most important aspect, that is, its relationship to *national behavior in the international system.* This relationship can be best explained by two distinct yet not mutually exclusive processes: (1) the influence of national attitudes and behavior on the role of international law, which should include an attempt at systematic analysis of several pertinent independent variables, both domestic and international, that account for a nation's foreign policy conduct as it affects international law, and (2) the influence of international law itself on many aspects of national behavior in the international arena, some of which are not so obvious and thus subject to neglect by a casual observer.

More specifically, in this *law-politics relationship* theorizing can be quite fruitful to our understanding of (1) various acts of national compliance and/or violations of existing international norms, and (2) various processes of international bargaining and consensus formation prior to the development of new laws. Apart from theorizing any insights on such crucial questions as to "how," "why," "when," and to "what effect" nations feel impelled to develop new laws, abolish old ones, and use international law as a tool of foreign policy, and why they gladly comply with existing laws in some circumstances and yet choose to ignore them in others (as if they were neither a guide nor a restraint) in the study of law-politics relationship should be of immense interest to all—students of international law and foreign affairs, diplomats, and practicing international lawyers.

Students of international law must break fresh ground in the social and natural sciences in order to find new approaches, methods, points of view and, most importantly, data that will broaden our understanding of the law-politics relationship and, therefore, of law. International law is concerned, at least by implication, with a very broad range of national behavior in international politics. This behavior may range from that of an

---

[3]In support of this "middle ground" between the idealists and realists, see an interesting article by Richard A. Falk, "The Relevance of Political Context to the Nature and Functioning of International Law: An Intermediate View" in K. W. Deutsch and Stanley Hoffman (ed.), *The Relevace of International Law*, (Cambridge, Mass.: Schenkman), 1968, pp. 133–152.

individual decision maker, to that of a state, affecting the lives of many millions of people, or an international organization, representing dozens of states. At various points of analysis, social-psychological, anthropological, economic as well as military-technical considerations impinge on international law. International law, because it includes a codification of behavioral norms, depends for its observance on the truth of a great many assumptions about the ways individuals and collectivities behave. It seems important, therefore, to investigate some of these assumptions upon which the efficiency of international law depends, even if this may at times lead us to some normative considerations and speculative thinking. *Just as a viable theory must be empirically verified to establish its utility, so a legal system must bear some direct relationship to the behavior of those it wishes to regulate.* To the extent social sciences draw out, sharpen, and test the assumption on which international legal norms depend, they help to identify the law-politics relationship and its significance to our understanding of international law.

The task of interpreting the true relationship between contemporary international law and national behavior should be carried out in a theoretical scheme that is designed to give continuity and integration to the material presented. Such a scheme must provide flexibility to permit constructive speculation and criticism unrestricted by an author's bigotry. This task can be best completed by *an interdisciplinary approach that uses some of the more recent social sciences concepts whose utility is no longer subject to serious doubts.* More specifically, it can be carried out by integrating the traditional pursuits of jurisprudence per se and the descriptive concerns about international law with the interest and research of the behavioral approach, at least where it is found to be useful, for example, in analyzing the law-politics relationship and in answering some of the "how," "why," "when," and "to what effect," questions with regard to nations' behavior *vis à vis* international law. It should be obvious to everyone that answers to some of these questions will be extremely difficult to arrive at. The motivations of national decision makers are frequently complex, often unclear to others and sometimes even to themselves. Clearly, not all of foreign policymaking is systematic and deliberate. Sometimes it just happens, as an abrupt by-product of many forces, both domestic and international, that are difficult to assimilate into an intelligible conceptual framework and much harder to draw any casual inferences from. The task of analysis is further complicated because national leaders, even in relatively democratic societies, do not submit to cross-examination by social scientists. Even if some success is achieved in identifying and classifying sets of variables that contribute to a country's foreign policy (and we find international law among them) the problem of measuring the degree of its influence is sure to come back to haunt the scholar.[4] To go a step further, even if the problem of measurement was also resolved and some influence of international law in a select group of foreign policy decisions was shown, any generalizations drawn from it will still be suspect given the unavoidable inadequacy of sampling. Obviously, we cannot, in the always limited space of a book analyze all the confrontations between international law and national behavior of all nations in order to develop a comprehensive understanding of law violations and observances. What is being suggested here is that to a substantial degree our conclusions about the relationship between international law and national behavior should be regarded as a priori, somewhat speculative, certainly less than scientific, and impressionistic.

A conceptual framework for the study of international law and politics

Any study of international law and national behavior bears its own conceptual and methodological burdens. The classical writers of international law have developed over the years convenient frameworks and methods of their own. If for the moment we lump all the old methods together, we shall find them in fundamental opposition to the viewpoint of the social sciences. This is a serious charge; nonetheless it is true. Although we have heard a great deal about jurisprudence being the "science of law," it really has always been insulated from the scientific method. As one scholar has put it, "the past theoretical approaches of the legal profession have involved logical manipulation of a legal corpus more often than the empirical study of patterns of human behavior."[5] This being so, the concerns of a social scientist with the study of international law and legal problems require conceptual frameworks and methodologies that *will move the study beyond what Richard Falk has called "impressionism" of earlier approaches.*[6] The present is generally acknowledged as a *time* for increasing interdisciplinary research, which in itself is a judgment on the diminishing boundary lines not only within the social sciences but also between them and international law.

[4]For a very interesting discussion of some of these problems see Louis H. Henkin, *How Nations Behave,* Introduction.

[5]Michael Barkun, *Law Without Sanctions* (New Haven: Yale University Press), 1968, p. 3.

[6]Richard A. Falk, "New Approaches to the Study of International Law" in Morton A. Kaplan (ed.), *New Approaches to International Relations* (New York: St. Martins Press), 1968, pp. 357–380.

A conceptual framework is needed for the study of the functions of international law in the international system. More specifically, the framework should allow us to concentrate on the *interaction* of the law-politics processes, with the expectation of learning systematically the law's influences in the modification of state behavior and the state's attempts to redefine existing international legal norms, to make new laws and discard old ones, and most importantly, to either observe international law, ignore it, or violate it in specific instances. I believe that the components of this interaction are accessible to empirical study if social science indicators are used. These indicators, for instance, may include (1) concensus and process of consensus formation among states prior to the development of new international law through international treaties, (2) a systematic study of cost-reward implications for a state with regard to law observance or violation, (3) a probing of the international law-observance *habit* of states in the sense of "doing what comes naturally," and (4) an observance of state behavior in a *historical* and, on some occasions, in a *comparative* context, to establish a degree of concurrence between existing international law, the prevailing state expectations, and the actual observance of law in the everyday international life of the states.

A social science conceptual framework, emphasizing its interdisciplinary virtues and the tools of behavioral persuasion appears to be the answer for the study of functions of international law in international politics. When a decision is made to use such a framework with its approaches and skill, it is not always sufficient to consider methodology alone. There is no doubt that building methodological bridges is an important task, but what we presently need most in our understanding of international law is a bridge that will allow us to bring the two disciplines (i.e., international law and international politics) closer by permitting us to develop bridge topics and pose bridge questions connecting the two fields of interaction such as law and politics. This task, if could be accomplished even partially, at the textbook level in the field of international law, is a worthwhile effort, because this will undoubtedly enrich the study of both fields for the students, lawyers, and diplomats alike. Without each other's cooperation neither the lawyer nor the behavioral scientist can help the student thoroughly in his understanding of international law. For example, in a bargaining situation where the states are huddled together in negotiations in order to develop a new international law, the lawyer may emphasize the formal power of negotiations, and behavioral scientist may concentrate on the strategies and tactics of international bargaining. But, quite conceivably, both may fail, without the cooperation of each other, to convey the complete picture to the student or produce a bridge.[7] The product of

[7]For an elaboration of this point, see W. L. Gould, "Laboratory, Law, and Anecdote: Negotiations and the Integration of Data," *World Politics, 18* (1965), 92–104.

their labors, although significant for perhaps other purposes here will remain discrete items of scholarship that are likely to leave the students of politics and law dissatisfied. In this circumstance the study of international law will suffer more than the study of international politics because it is behind in the development and use of law concepts and techniques. In other words, if today in the study of the functions of international law, we refrain from using an interdisciplinary framework, shy away from using the tools of modern social sciences, or refuse to look at the study from a behavioral perspective, the eventual development of a new science of the functions of international law will be further postponed. In the meantime, the disillusionment with the role and the study of international law will probably continue.

The framework that is suggested here is not entirely new or radical in its concerns. If we analyze the writings in the field of sociology of law, we see that the possibilities for developing bridge topics, asking, and answering bridge questions have existed for some time now either implicitly or explicitly. The present textbook at least implicitly, is concerned with the bridge questions between law and politics.

Utility of a behavioral perspective

Perhaps the greatest utility in using a behavioral interpretation with social science methods, in the study of legal phenomenon through bridge questions concerning the law-politics relationship, is to probe the pathology of national behavior in the international system and the role of international law in it. This can be done by developing several provocative, but not too complicated conceptual schemes to *unify* the thinking of the theorists beyond what the so-called pure theory of international law will permit, or some of the traditional theorists of international relations will permit for that matter.

For example, let us consider the possible utility of a structural-functional variant of systems analysis in our understanding of international law-making process. Structural-functional analysis has been with us for a long time, although it received its major boost only recently in the 1950s and 1960s by several contemporary social scientists. Recently perhaps one of the most useful contributions to structural functionalism for our purposes was made by Gabriel Almond in his application of Marion J. Levy's structural-functional requisites analysis.[8] Very briefly, Almond's contribution is based on the analysis of the functions of social structures that are found in all

[8]See first M. J. Levy, *The Structure of Society*, (Princeton: Princeton University Press), 1952; G. Almond, "A Developmental Approach to Political Systems," *World Politics*, 17 (1965), 183–214; and Almond and G. B. Powell, Jr., *Comparative Politics: A Developmental Approach* (Boston: Little, Brown), 1966.

political systems, including the international system. Using the general systems theory he constructs a theory of political development through a systematic comparative analysis of structures and functions in various states. His functional categories include interest aggregation, interest articulation, information, at the input level and rule making, rule application, and rule adjudication at the output level. This particular typology that was primarily intended for the comparative studies of complex (industrial) and simple (agregarian) political systems has helped in the construction of developmental theories. But this can also help us in our task. Surely not too many experts in developmental politics would disagree that this approach does attempt to bridge the systems of domestic law and economics as well as other areas of study. At the domestic level it can help us in the *analysis of interaction of political units (through international law) with the international community*. At the international level it can certainly help us to the extent relevant, in the understanding of (to use Almond's own terms) lawmaking, law application, and law adjudication.

Utility of systems theory has already been proven in the study of international relations. Its application in international relations started with Morton Kaplan's well-read work, *Systems and Processes in International Politics*. Today, several scholars, such as Charles McClelland, Andrew Scott, Karl Deutsch, and J. David Singer, have contributed to its development.[9] In the study of international law this approach was also first suggested by Morton A. Kaplan.[10] Since then its utility as an analytical tool in the understanding of the law-politics relationship has been verified by the works of Richard A. Falk, Stanley Hoffmann, and Saul Mendlovitz.[11]

Kaplan, along with Katzenbach, suggested that "the international system" can be relied on to be the fundamental concept by which the systemic data relevant to the role of international law in world affairs could

[9]Charles A. McClelland, *Theory and International Systems* (New York: Macmillan), 1966; Andrew M. Scott, *The Functioning of the International System* (New York: Macmillan), 1967; Morton A. Kaplan, *System and Process in the International Politics* (New York: Wiley), 1964; J. David Singer (ed.), *Quantitative International Politics* (New York: The Free Press), 1968; James N. Rosenau (ed.), *Linkage Politics* (New York: The Free Press), 1969; Karl W. Deutsch, *The Analysis of International Relations* (Englewood Cliffs, N.J.: Prentice-Hall), 1968; and Bruce M. Russett (ed.), *Economic Theories of International Politics* (Chicago: Markham), 1968.

[10]Morton A. Kaplan and Nicholas de B. Katzenbach, *The Political Foundations of International Law* (New York: Wiley), 1961.

[11]Stanley Hoffmann *The State of War*, (New York: Praeger), 1965; Richard A. Falk and Cyril E. Black, *The Future of International Legal Order* (Princeton: Princeton University Press), 1969; and Richard A. Falk and Saul Mendlovitz, *The Strategy of World Order*: Vol. I, *Toward a Theory of War Prevention*; Vol. II, *International Law*; Vol. III, *The United Nations*; Vol. IV, *Disarmament and Economic Development* (New York: World Law Fund), 1966.

be organized and, on the basis of this data, the future role of international law predicted. The rationale for this approach is that the international systemic context is relevant to the study of law and that this relevance can be established through the specification of a rather small number of crucial independent variables whose impact on international law can be assessed. Two variables, *power* and its distribution among the various members of the system, and the *costs* involved in pursuing various courses of action by these members in conflict situations, seem most important to Kaplan in the study of law. In other words, the nature of the international system determines the strengths and weaknesses of international law in any given period of history. Kaplan's writings effectively demonstrate the value of this approach by their very interesting, although at times speculative, analysis of the multiple norms of intervention or nonintervention that states follow in the balance of power and loose bipolar international systems.

Other scholars, particularly Stanley Hoffmann, have attempted to use the systems approach to international law in the context of historical sociology.[12] He constructed an international system, which was sensitive to the international conflicts of the past, and then correlated these conflictive patterns of the past with the prevailing social structures operating in the international society to discover the true place of international law in world affairs. I believe Kaplan's work also stimulated the thinking of Richard Falk and Saul Mendlovitz. These gentlemen posited a future international system along the lines of the Clark-Sohn model[13] of a disarmed world subservient to the international authority of a greatly revitalized United Nations. Falk and Mendlovitz' efforts were directed toward looking into future international conflicts and the present social structures to assess empirically the work of law in the present and near future. Instead of concentrating on the past as Hoffmann does or on the distant future as Clark and Sohn do in their utopian model, these authors felt data should be organized to emphasize the prospects for law in the present and immediate future. Their efforts brought law-politics analysis to the grips of what the present author considers to be another of the hardest problems in this area, that is, a correct assessment of political attainability of a vastly improved legal order.

Because international lawyers frequently use such systemic terms as "legal order" and "legal system" in the exposition of their formal "theories" of law, they should be only too eager to accept systems theory

[12]Stanley Hoffmann, "International Systems and International Law" in Klaus Knorr and Sidney Verba (eds.), *The International System* (Princeton: Princeton University Press), 1961, pp. 205–237.

[13]Grenville Clark and Louis B. Sohn, *World Peace Through World Law*, 3rd edition (Cambridge: Harvard University Press), 1966.

in their midst. They will find it handy in empirically observing the place of law in human dealings. Its use will certainly help the scholar avoid arbitrarily suggesting that a hierarchial structure exists in legal norms, on a a priori basis. Up to the present time neither the monoist school of international law (whether it accords supremacy to the national or international legal order) nor the dualist school have exhibited sufficient analytical energy to help us understand and describe the law-politics relationship. In all likelihood the systems approach will tell us more about this relationship than any other concept at the present time. Under its analytical arrangement we can accept the course of diplomatic history, its accidents, and other unplanned and unforeseeable happenings that may well account for a good deal of foreign policymaking in the world today. This type of foreign policymaking just happens as the result of many forces that create among states actions, reactions, and interactions that were not deliberately planned by the decision maker. The study of international law should employ an open systems approach that will allow the scholar to take into account the law's interactions with nonlegal systems.

In the use of analytical frameworks in social sciences, the comparative approach has been found to be quite useful in the understanding of various relationships. It can be used variously in the analysis of the law and politics relationship as well in such areas as attribute surveys, trend analysis of states' attitude and behavior concerning international observance of or lack of it during certain periods of their diplomatic history, cross-unit testing of behavior vis à vis international law hypotheses, and many more cross-national uses now common to behavioral techniques.

A communication approach to the study of international law might be quite useful at the present. An attempt to use the methods and findings of communication research in the social sciences may well tell a great deal to the student about the legal processes and functions in the international system. If nothing else, this approach can certainly help us to construct models of communications for the purpose of organizing the material and measuring the degree of common understanding of international legal norms, perhaps also the degree of common acceptance, and prediction of behavior among some 140 sovereign states in the present international system. Let us not forget, after all, the international system is decentralized and its membership relies primarily upon self-interpretation of international law in their use. International law itself is an important instrument of communication. Its success can be measured first according to how well it has communicated its own norms. Once again, the notion of "communication" also should not be alien to the international lawyers. Indeed, even in some of the most traditional textbooks on international law one can easily identify normative communication generally carried out by such authoritative communicators as jurists, law scholars, and arbitrators. This is particularly true of customary international law where the need for communications is greater. Surely, a communication approach to the study of international law can tell us the *reasons* for specific distortions, modifications, and multiple interpretations of the law by states. It can also tell us what it will take to improve law observance in a world of states with different cultural, economic, social, religious, and linguistic backgrounds and above all with different priorities in foreign and domestic affairs. It could help us minimize the problem of different perceptions of decision makers particularly when they are pursuing conflicting national interests. A communications approach could be used in simulation as a teaching tool in international law, as has been true in international relations for some time now. It is not unreasonable to suggest that simulation can further enrich the old and useful teching device called moot court experience. Simulation structures and patterns can be further developed to allow a focus on the functions of international law in the conduct of interstate relations; or a focus on the *true* functions of a legal advisor to national governments, the so-called "norms twister."

I have made an implicit attempt to follow broadly a systems framework and, wherever possible, to raise bridge questions concerning the relationship between international law and international politics. The emphasis is on the behavioral perspective within the concerns of social sciences. In recent years students of international relations in general have become increasingly aware of the wide utility of behavioral concepts and models as well as viewpoints and methods in their discipline. A great deal of effort has been devoted to explaining what behavioral persuasion is all about,[14] applying it to concrete international problems, and defending it.[15] Some

[14]Robert A. Dahl, "The Behavioral Approach in Political Science: Epitaph for a Monument to a Successful Protest," *American Political Science Review*, LV (December 1961); J. David Singer, "The Relevance of the Behavioral Sciences to the Study of International Relations," *Behavioral Science*, VI (October 1961); Heinz Eualu, *The Behavioral Persuasion in Politics* (New York: Random House), 1963; David Easton, "The Current Meaning of Behavioralism," in James C. Charlesworth (ed.), *Contemporary Political Analysis* (New York: The Free Press), 1967; Malford Q. Sibley, "The Limitations of Behavioralism," in Charlesworth. More citations to the fairly extensive literature can be found in the works cited here.

[15]Earon M. Kirkpatrick, "The Impact of Behavioral Approach on Traditional Political Science," in Austin Ranny (ed.), *Essays on the Behavioral Study of Politics* (Urbana: University of Illinois Press), 1962; Michael Haas, "Bridge Building in International Relations: A Neo-Traditional Plea," *International Studies Quarterly*, XI (December 1967); James N. Rosenau, "Games International Relations Scholars Play," *Journal of International Affairs*, XXI (1967); Kenneth W. Thompson, "The Internationalists' Dilemma: Relevance and Rigor," *International Studies Quarterly*, XII (June 1968); Arthur L. Kalleberg, "Concept Formation in Normative and Empirical Studies: Toward Reconciliation in Political Theory," *American Political Science Review*, LXIII (March 1969).

people have attempted to reconcile it with more traditional approaches,[16] and others have simply dismissed it as unacceptable.[17] For our purposes it has a utility that hopefully will become clear as we proceed.

Some other contemporary approaches to the study of international law

A systematic analysis of current literature reveals that there are three, maybe four, new conceptual and methodological orientations to the study of international law. Time and space does not permit a comprehensive analysis of these approaches and the scholarly pros and cons of each of them. However, they will be briefly described, and their most important supporters in the discipline acknowledged. These orientations are not mutually exclusive. All of these are concerned with studying law in its social and political setting, which includes perceptions, interests, values, and objectives of the participants in the international arena and the impact of these variables on the nature and character of current laws and future law development. The presence of these orientations and their concern with law-politics analysis has initiated the liveliest debate yet in this discipline among the people who continue to observe "legal data" (e.g., judicial decisions, treaties, and formal diplomats' correspondence) dispassionately in a social and political vacuum and the people who have introduced the "new realism" in law by avoiding some of the wishful thinking of the past. These new approaches are given below.

Policy sciences approach

Several scholars, including Harold D. Lasswell and Daniel Lerner, have contributed to the development of this particular analytical orientation in the social sciences.[18] In the study of international law this approach is

[16]A good example of this will be Morton A. Kaplan, "The New Great Debate: Traditionalism vs. Science in International Relations," World Politics, XIX (October 1966).

[17]Hendley Bull, "International Theory: The Case for a Classical Approach," World Politics, XVIII (April 1966); Francis D. Wormuth, "Matched Dependent Behavioralism: The Cargo Cult in Political Science," Western Political Science Quarterly, XX (December 1967); See also the collection of articles in Charles A. McCoy (ed.), Apolitical Politics: A Critique of Behavioralism (New York: Crowee), 1967.

[18]Daniel Lerner and Harold D. Lasswell (eds.), The Policy Sciences (Stanford: Stanford University Press), 1951.

attributed to the work of Myres S. McDougal and his associates.[19] When applied to law-politics analysis some of its most significant attributes appear to be: (1) an emphasis on the sophistication of various *methodologies* used in the analysis of decision-making processes concerning foreign policy objectives and their implementation; (2) a detailed study of *findings* for the purpose of predicting future policy processes and outcomes; (3) Application of specific findings in various disciplines to the *solutions* of contemporary problems.

In law this approach represents the thinking of the American school of legal realists.[20] According to McDougal the approach enables the investigator to assess the utility and effectiveness of international law in the context of two important variables: *factual events* as they appear to the observer in many international processes (these, I suspect, will include both positive and negative factors for international law) and the important *role of the national decision maker* in the foreign policy decision-making and execution process. To the policy scientists this process includes (1) a clarification of the national objectives to be pursued; (2) a systematic and thorough evaluation of the international situation to be faced; (3) selection of a particular course of action after considering the probable consequences of other alternatives; (4) determination of optimum means to successfully carry out the action.[21]

With the assistance of other scholars, McDougal considers all the variables that he thinks necessary for a fully rational decision. These variables include a host of socioeconomic, political and cultural, military and strategic, and several psychological factors relating to the past experiences of a nation, its present circumstances, and its future aspirations in international politics. Thus the decision is usually made on grounds other than legal ones, and the international lawyers are then required by the decision maker simply to provide legal justification for the decision. In this context, McDougal argues that past legal rules and precedents serve a purpose only when they can be used to "legalize" a nation's actions. Viewed from the perspective of a decision maker, McDougal's contention

---

[19]Myres S. McDougal and Associates, *Studies in World Public Order* (New Haven: Yale University Press), 1960; see particularly "Impact of International Law upon National Law: A Policy Oriented Perspective," pp. 157–236, in the same volume. See also Myres S. McDougal and Florentino P. Feliciano, *Law and Minimum Public Order* (New Haven: Yale University Press), 1962; Myres S. McDougal and William Burke, *The Public Order of the Oceans* (New Haven: Yale University Press), 1963; Myres S. McDougal, Harold D. Lasswell and Ivan Vlasie, *Law and Public Order in Space* (New Haven: Yale University Press), 1964.

[20]The realist school stands in basic contradiction to the earlier thought in law as represented by scholars such as Hans Kelson, *The Principles of International Law* (London: Stevens), 1944.

[21]Daniel Lerner and Harold D. Lasswell (eds.), *The Policy Sciences*, p. ix.

amounts to saying that there is available a plausible legal argument for almost any type of decision that a leader cares to make and it all depends on the caliber and ingenuity of his lawyers to come up with the "right" legal justification for it.

McDougal's emphasis on the role of the decision maker apparently stems from his perception of the international system, which he considers as essentially decentralized and particularly devoid of a specific legal order. Therefore, the most important role is performed by the decision maker; as such, he is the most appropriate focus within law-politics analysis. To McDougal, he is the man with whom power and authority rests and is looked upon by his people to be the person who will assert claims on their behalf in the international system. I suspect that this participation in the claiming process gives rise to situations where international law becomes *relevant* for McDougal, in the sense that it is twisted and shaped to support a preferred policy goal.

Thus, for McDougal and his associates, the crucial test of legality, that is, whether an action is in accordance with law, is the degree to which that action conforms to relevant community expectations. This, of course, is tantamount to saying that only the laws of consensus that reflect a community of interests have a chance to survive as "laws." This is indeed a far cry from the test of laws as "laws" in the past. The great advantage of this particular approach, according to its supporters, is that it reflects realistically both the decisive role of the decision maker and the limits of decision making in defining the requirements of international law. In other words, what constitutes law and its role is determined primarily by examining the decisions made by the people who are in a position of authority and who through their decisions ultimately define the content and role of law. Law is also determined by the expectations of the community in reaction to these decisions.

If international law today expects to play an effective role in the foreign affairs of nation-states, it must, according to the various spokesmen for this approach, identify itself more closely with the community expectations and thus create a much wider consensus for its norms. It must also promote such values as human dignity, equality, and impartiality. Supposedly it is possible for law to achieve these goals, and supposedly this constitutes realism. This framework of inquiry has been instrumental in the efforts of McDougal and his associates to reconstruct major portions of international law. Their approach has been used particularly in the fields of outer space, laws of the seas, and laws governing the use of force.

Functionalist approach

Again several scholars, including David Mitrany, Ernest Haas, and James Sewell, have contributed to the development of this analytical tool in international relations and organization.[22] This particular approach addresses itself to those "functional" aspects of international organizations or that mass of organized international activity that is related directly to economic, social, technical, and humanitarian problems of the world. It is supposedly a nonpolitical, pragmatic, and a service-oriented approach to international cooperation. The assumption is that cooperation among various states is more likely in nonpolitical areas. It is essentially an assertion and defense of the contention that an ever-increasing interdependence among states in economic, social, and technical areas will eventually resolve political conflicts and eliminate war. David Mitrany has argued that the major problem today is not how to keep nations peacefully apart but how to bring them actively together.

Functionalists in their proposals for international cooperation attempt to link authority to a specific socioeconomic or technical activity rather than to a definite territory. They argue that in an age of increasing international complexities the old concepts of state sovereignty (a nation's right to be unpredictable) cannot be overcome by simply signing international treaties, but they can be overcome through a "function" designed to satisfy a basic international need. A few examples of such functional international organizations are the International Postal Union, Permanent Central Opium Board, International Labor Organization, and the International Congress on Vineyards and Wine.

In the study of international law, however, this orientation is associated with such esteemed names as Percy Corbett, Wolfgang Friedman, C. Wilfred Jenks, and Julius Stone.[23] These scholars believe that the domain of international law can be extended and its effectiveness improved if we were to correlate closely the development and study of law with the satisfaction of certain socioeconomic needs or the attainment of nonpolitical (e.g., noncontroversial) goals in the international system. Their assumption is that in many nonpolitical areas some states are perfectly willing to entrust the attainment of their national interests to the "rule of Law" and whatever institutional arrangements that may be created for that purpose.

This particular view of the role of international law that emphasizes

---

[22]David Mitrany, A Working Peace System (Chicago: Quadrangle Books, Inc.), 1946; Ernest Hass, Beyond the Nation-State (Stanford: Stanford University Press), 1964; and James Sewell, Functionalism and World Politics (Princeton: Princeton University Press), 1966.

[23]Percy E. Corbet, Law in Diplomacy (Princeton: Princeton University Press), 1959; Wolfgang Friedman, The Changing Structure of International Law (New York: Columbia University Press), 1964; C. Wilfred Jenks, Law, Freedom and Welfare (Dobbs Ferry, N.Y.: Oceana Publications), 1964; and Prospects of International Adjudication (Dobbs Ferry, N.Y.: Oceana Publications), 1965; and Julius Stone, Legal Controls of International Conflict (London: Stevens), 1959.

service and satisfaction of needs (rather than an authority image above international politics) finds merit among many law supporters, even among some law critics who have always doubted international law's capacity to regulate interstate behavior by use of force. Functionalism is not at the present a comprehensive framework of inquiry as compared with, for example, policy science orientation. It is instead a specific approach, because it addresses itself to certain aspects of law and its development. However, it does have a potential. The utility of this approach will certainly increase if the present trend toward rapid international interdependence in noncontroversial areas continues.

Case study approach

Many scholars have at one time or the other used this approach in social sciences. In international law it has been used by Brainerd Currie, Richard A. Falk, and recently by Lawrence Scheinman and David Wilkinson.[24] This approach emphasizes depth analysis of single cases; it helps the scholar to relate his findings to the broader structure of international law. One needs to be extremely careful in using this approach because it requires a jurisprudential rationale. A unit of analysis is acceptable for the purpose of broader generalizations so long as the validity of the sample as used in other situations can be partially established.

[24]Brainerd Currie, *Selected Essays on the Conflict of Laws* (Durham: Duke University Press), 1963; Richard A. Falk, *The Role of Domestic Courts in the International Legal Order* (Syracuse: Syracuse University Press), 1964; IQ, "The Shimada Case: A Legal Appraisal of the Atomic Attacks Upon Hiroshima and Nagasaki," *American Journal of International Law* (1963), 759–793; Lawrence Scheinman and David Wilkenson, *International Laws and Political Crises*.

section II
Background Factors and Conditions in the Relationship of International Law to National Behavior

chapter 2
present climate
of international politics—
the dynamics
of the system

In recent years international law has been passing through a severe crisis concerning its relevance. Much of the disillusionment with its role in world affairs is caused by the nature of contemporary international system that it attempts to regulate. Thus, a systematic study of international law and national behavior should first of all assess the dynamics of this system.

The sweeping changes

A revolution of vast proportions is in progress in world politics.[1] Foreign policy decisions of states now flow in numerous directions, currents, cross-currents and pressures, not readily susceptible to a thorough inquiry by the social scientist. Several forces continue to divide the participants in the system, making international cooperation politically difficult, and raising the possibility of further conflicts of varying magnitude. There have been fundamental changes in the social, economic, and political structure of the world. The number of independent and sovereign states has almost tripled in a relatively short period of time, thus increasing the domain of international law but not necessarily its observance. As new

[1]Consider, for instance, the following literature: Kurt London, *The Permanent Crises* (London: Blaisdell), 1968, 2nd edition; Linda B. Miller (ed.), *Dynamics of World Politics: Studies in the Resolution of Conflict* (Englewood Cliffs, N. J.: Prentice-Hall), 1968; Evan Luard, *Conflict and Peace in the Modern International System* (Boston: Little, Brown), 1968; and, John W. Spanier, *World Politics in an Age of Revolution* (New York: Praeger), 1967.

states continue to join the society of nations without giving up portions of their own disparate value systems (some of which are in basic contradiction to several cherished principles of customary international law) and while vigorously pursuing their own national interests, the traditional concepts of the state system tend to fall in disrepute. So has some aspects of international law, which is tradition bound and has a Western character in an increasingly non-Western world. Meanwhile differences among the great powers, despite some meeting of minds between the Soviet Union and the United States, go unresolved. While many of the newer states adhere to policies of neutralism and nonalignment in an East-West contest, thus increasing their influence disproportionately, the influence of the politically mature middle powers has continued to diminish in the World Organization and elsewhere.[2]

A revolution of even greater magnitude is occurring in the natural sciences and technology. Recent developments in nuclear science and in military, space, and communications technology have added new dimensions to the policies of nations; the expanding world population and the growing distance between the big rich, the little rich, and the very poor nations to which the new technology has contributed have also affected national policies. The ability of man to project scientific devices beyond the earth's atmosphere and tap the resources of the ocean floor and the seabed is symbolic of the changes that are occurring in world affairs. Study of international law cannot remain indifferent to those changes. Among these changes, forces are at work attempting to focus on new forms of international cooperation that are partially due to an awareness among states of increasing interdependency for developmental and security purposes.[3] Much of this cooperation centers around regional groupings, organizations, and other arrangements.

There are other changes that are taking place in the international system that we need to be aware of if the true place of international law in world affairs is to be determined. Here the social scientist can be of great help because he is uniquely equipped to comprehend and gauge the dynamics of specific international changes. Some of these are (1) changes in the international objectives and strategies of nations; (2) changes in their relative capabilities to affect in desired ways the behavior of other nations; (3) changes in the modes of conducting international bargaining and in the processes of foreign policy decision making; (4)

[2]See John G. Stoessinger, *The United Nations and the Superpowers* (New York: Random House), 1965; and Jack C. Plano and Robert E. Riggs, *Forging World Order: The Politics of International Organization* (New York: Macmillan), 1967.

[3]A good collection of statements on international interdependence and cooperation among states is *An Anthology, International Political Communities* (New York: Doubleday), 1966.

changes in the relative utilities and disutilities of military weapons and nonmilitary instruments and techniques; (5) changes in the political roles and operational modes of the United Nations and other international organizations; and (6) changes in the physical, social, economic, political, and psychological environment to which the actions and accomplishments of nations are related.[4]

The comprehension of those changes is both challenging and sobering to serious-minded students of international politics who see them as having created three major problems for the national decision maker: first, how to preserve the institutions that embody established national values as nations adapt to a constantly changing world; second, when and how to enhance these values through foreign policy goals with a minimum of cost incurred; and third, how to shape the world environment to a more stable and secure international order? These and other changes and the concomitant problems have inevitably and significantly affected the role and content of international law, given the entire subject a new and more practical importance, and have presented new challenges to the student of international law. Above all, these changes have produced an acute realization that international law today can no longer be treated *as simply a description of what states have done in the past in the form of a complex intellectual construction.* We also realize that some of its traditional institutions that were consecrated by philosophical systems and political circumstances that are unlikely to be repeated should be called in question. The historical evolution of these institutions, indeed their very utility, is now being subjected to an analytical scrutiny that is unprecedented in legal and political scholarship. International law and its study need to face up to the host of challenges and opportunities that the contemporary international system has created.

However, before probing into the role of international law, we need to understand in *detail* the dynamics of international politics and its sources. I believe that useful insights can be gained if we study our subject in the general context of what is frequently called the international environment and within that, from the perspective of complex, often confusing processes that are responsible for its form and substance. For instance, if the decision makers today, as it is often charged by international law scholars, are indeed inclined to act politically instead of legally in a given international situation, their very nature then must be shaped and moulded by the socioeconomic, military and political circumstances of their states. The student of international law is therefore better off if he analyzes states' behavior from several points of view. He should, of course, analyze the domestic and international institutional

---

[4]See, for instance, Jack C. Plano, *Forging World Order.*

arrangements responisble for this behavior. However, beyond the institutions and even the personalities of individual leaders themselves, he should consider the societal factors that these institutions and individuals govern and that are influenced by them. Surely, international politics today is not simply governance; it is a way in which nations organize their lives in an ever-increasing web of interdependence according to a hierarchy of their own national interests and objectives. Consider, for instance, national survival. It is reasonable to say that this is the most important objective in the minds of most national leaders. If this is true, as some scholars have argued, thinking about how to survive means, to a great extent, thinking about international politics. It is a correct assumption, although the past is not very far removed from our memories in which other considerations, such as economics and domestic affairs loomed larger in the daily concerns of people than what were called "foreign affairs." This is particularly true of the United States and the Soviet Union. However, today questions concerning survival have become extremely crucial in an era in which the threat of nuclear catastrophy hangs everywhere. In international politics events producing rapid changes now govern the very basis of almost everything else, whether these are threats to the survival of the human race in the literal physical sense of the term or many other crises. What is being suggested here is that the study of international politics and the concomitant facts, explanations, and solutions is no longer mere philosophizing, but it is a study of the art of "survival" that is sought by each state.

In the field of international politics, considerations of elite perception, the politics of mass deception, role behavior, legitimization and decision making along with analyses of national interests, ideological preferences, and transactions that cut across state boundaries have begun to bring into focus new approaches to the study of international politics. Some of these approaches are also useful to the study of the role of international law in international politics. To understand the political processes the student must also comprehend the reality of rapid changes that are taking place in the world today. It is a truism to say that the world society and the interaction of its member states have undergone constant change throughout much of man's known history, but the post-world War II period is unique because never before has such fundamental, rapid, and dynamic changes occurred in such a relatively short period of time. What is also unique is that these changes have had almost instantaneously a profound effect not only on the nature of world politics and the conduct of foreign policy, but also have had a direct impact on the daily life of every individual. Increasingly the individual, through mass media, is generally forced to learn about world news and thus acquires a sense of empathy, yet the great irony of our times is that he also feels increasingly helpless and unable to influence the great revolutions sweeping the globe. He has gotten very close to the rest of the world in terms of his knowledge of his fellowman and their plight, yet he is very far away in terms of his capacity to affect his own nation's foreign policy, to say nothing of world politics, in order to bring about desired changes.

To carry or not to carry a "big stick"

Probably every generation in history is accustomed to view the international problems of its own times as unique, bewildering, and defying commonsense solutions. Yet the characterization of international politics as "complex" and "dangerous" was never more accurately used to describe the human predictment as it is today. This is not to imply that foreign affairs in the past were simple matters. But in the past we never had to deal with the presence of weapons of mass destruction and the international systemic convulsions caused by political and social revolutions that have already transformed the face of three continents in a very short period of time. It is not that the present generation is unaware that the world has changed; probably no generation has talked so often about the revolutionary impact of nuclear weapons, the complexities of national liberation fronts and guerrilla warfare, the growing gap between the "have" and "have not" nations, etc. Certainly no generation has faced so frankly the conclusion that a possibility of a nuclear war, either by design or by accident, threatens the continuity of civilization and of human life itself. How then are the people, for instance, of the United States, as members of a relatively free society, to account for a public policy that continues to rely so heavily on armed might abroad and frequently belittles small voices of dissension against international violence at home? Would not one assume that sane men, to say nothing of free men, would give the most serious and soul-searching thought to whether the traditional techniques of power politics are rationally appropriate to a world in which for the first time men have acquired the power to eliminate mankind? Might it not be supposed that such a radical alteration in the conditions for international rivalry should raise some basic questions in the minds of responsible men about the relevance and validity of such traditional concepts as "national security," "retaliation," "balance of armed might," and "deterrence" and make them reevaluate their thinking in regard to old conditions of peace and new causes of war? Are there no alternatives to the use of violence in international affairs as the most significant instrument of attaining peace? Is the shallow cynicism that defines the politics of nations as the raw struggle for power, in which the ultimate arbiter is the preponderance of instruments of violence, really a realistic analysis of the failures and successes in the contemporary international contest? Can the policy of "massive retaliation" under conditions of thermonuclear destruction be rationally justified? The first thing the present generation needs to be very clear about is that the issue is not only the question what assumptions are to guide their foreign and military policy, be it Russian or American policy. It is most immediately the question of whether Americans or Russians as a nation have any choice in this matter.

The policy in the past on each side of the iron curtain has been frequently predicated on the proposition that we really have no choice, that international communism, as the American would say, or bourgeois capitalism, according to the Russians, has choosen the weapons and made the rules; consequently, however much our basic moral impulses might lead us to want to play by other rules, such options are not open to us. To relax our defenses, either side claims, is to invite the "enemy" to attack and to ensure the defeat of freedom (defined by both sides in their own terms) around the globe. This is a particularly comfortable view of the world that both sides prefer to maintain. It shifts all the responsibility for violence and general lawlessness in international affairs on to the "other" side and, thus, it relieves both sides of any responsibility for their *own* role in the game of international anarchy. However, the truth seems to be that both countries *are* responsible for varying degrees of lawlessness in several international crisis situations in the post-War era and that both sides have made choices based on selfish national interests and some of these choices have been tragically incompatible with the long-range maintenance of peace and security in the world.

Military power is not the only deterent to which both the United States and Russia are sensitive. In addition, there is a significant body of world law and the powers of international organizations, the common interests in the maintenance of the status quos in the international system that benefit both nations, and above all, the moral force of the opinions and aspirations of masses of humanity the world over. To assert this is not to engage in idealistic dreams of what the world might be or ought to be, but to describe a significant aspect of the fundamental revolution in the character of international politics that has been recurring since the end of the War. For the first time in the history of the nation-state system the smallest, and militarily the weakest, nations can be considered sovereign in the full sense of that word. This has rendered such national slogans as "carry the big stick and speak softly" quite irrelevant.

Concurrent revolutions

The nature of our task, that is, understanding the development and execution of foreign policies and the possible role of international law in it, can be further comprehended if we view international politics as taking place in the midst of several major concurrent revolutions each of which has succeeded in creating complex issues that bewilder the policy-makers and also the students of international law and politics.

Systemic structural changes— current perspective in a historical context

The most important of all the revolutions are the structural changes that have taken place in the international system itself. After playing a leading role in world politics and the development of international law for centuries, Western Europe disintegrated during the Second World War as a center of diplomatic influence and military power. The post-War period brought the United States to the forefront of international politics; it was quickly joined by the Soviet Union. Prior to the War, for a long time, international politics was largely conducted by and among the Western European states, mostly to their own benefit, and frequently to the detriment of what is known today as the "Third World." The United States during this period, that is, during the first century and a half of its national existence, followed a policy of self-imposed isolationism; therefore it had little influence in world politics of that time. Similarly, Russia was considered part of European political arena, somewhat reluctantly by Western European states. Nonetheless, for long periods of time it played no significant role in world politics or in the making of international law. Much of the rest of the world prior to the War was either part of European overseas empires or, with the exception of Japan, had no significant status in international politics and, as such, played no significant role in it. By the end of the War, European leadership in world politics transformed into rapid decline. There were several reasons for this, most of them well documented in history books. The one most readily accepted is that because of the War Western Europe had exhausted its human and material resources. The massive mobilizations, a prolonged war, staggering wartime expenditures, and the widespread destruction of the countries all took their toll. Western Europe after the War simply did not have sufficient capacity to remain the center of world politics. The repercussions of the Western European collapse were revolutionary both inside and outside the European arena. Most importantly it triggered the disintegration of the colonial empires. Independence movements long in ferment surfaced throughout the colonies. Dozens of new states subsequently entered the international system as independent units creating power vacuums as well as new political forces. New nations, new politics, and new problems have contributed significantly to the momentum of this structural revolution in the nature of the international system. Collapse of Western Europe also brought about a sudden dampening of

European nationalism. This had an immediate negative effect but also what now clearly appears to be a long-term positive impact. On the more immediate negative side, public confidence in their governments diminished, expressions of despair and disgust with old-style politics and diplomacy were commonplace, and one could observe a general emotional drift toward anarchy. On the more positive side, rejection of narrow nationalism and the realization of the futility of war paved the way for and then set the rapid pace of rising aspirations for Western European unity, cooperation, economic development, and eventual integration. European cooperative achievements, integrative movements, and a high regard for the rules of international law in their international relations today are not only very much a part of the contemporary international environment, but also are more hopeful examples for other regions to follow.

The collapse of Western Europe also prompted the rise of the United States to the military and political leadership of the world. This leadership was gained by default. There is sufficient evidence in history to suggest that neither the American policymakers nor the people had any particular ambitions, let alone designs for the world leadership or to play the role of world policemen in the immediate post-War years. In fact one does not even find any great desire in the United States at that time to maintain and further develop the weapon systems that were forged during the war. In short, the United States entertained no illusions concerning its role as guarantor of international stability, peace, and development. Yet of all the nations that shed blood in the war, only the United States emerged physically undamaged. This is not to say that the Americans did not pay a heavy price during the War in terms of lives lost, but since war was not fought on American soil, no American cities were destroyed, no economic facilities were devastated, and no post-War reconstruction cost involved (even though the United States generously paid for Europe's reconstruction) that stifled American economic, political, and military growth, as was true in Europe. The United States emerged from the War uniquely affluent, technologically advanced, and militarily prepared, as no other state was, to continue her active role in world politics. But the military and economic preparedness that pushed the United States to a status of world prominence was equally matched by its inexperience in world affairs, which has caused the American people much grief in the post-War years, most recently in the Indo-China episode. In any case, with the American rise to preeminence, international politics became American international politics, world problems became American problems, and world stability, freedom, and economic development became an American responsibility. The United States' rise to superpower status further revolutionized the international system. It Americanized it. The United States ran the show in the United Nations and in many other international organizations around the world.

Of course, the Americanization of world affairs after the War did not go very long unchallenged by another emerging giant, the Soviet Union. After the War it really did not take very long for the Allied coalition with Russia to fall apart. It was a marriage of convenience against a common enemy and did not have the usual common, positive purposes. It was based largely on the old saying, "an enemy of my enemy is my friend." The result was the dissolution of the marriage shortly after the War and the emergence of a cold war period between two sides. As the Eastern European states fell under Communist domination, the Soviet Union expanded its influence outwardly both militarily and ideologically. In the Far East it forged an alliance with China that by now had a Communist government. At the same time Soviet military technology and economic development moved ahead rapidly to keep pace with the growing Soviet influence in world affairs. By mid-fifties, it is fair to say, the U.S.S.R. politically, economically, and ideologically dominated large areas of the world stretching from Berlin to Hanoi. It became a second superpower, the second most highly industrialized nation in military and economic power, second only to the United States. Today some two decades later in specific areas of military capability the Soviets have either achieved parity or are in fact ahead of the United States.

Space here does not permit a detailed analysis of the consolidation of Western efforts for mutual security and peace in the face of Communist challenge. The development of security communities (e.g., the North Atlantic Treaty Organization, South East Asia Treaty Organization, and the Central Treaty Organization), John Foster Dulles and the policy of brinkmanship and containment, and an intense cold war atmosphere in Europe, all of these events are also well documented in history books. It is more important here to remember that American ascendance and absolute military predominance in world affairs was short-lived, and with the rise of Soviet power the world quickly moved into a tight bipolar international system, thus changing the nature of international politics once again. The tight bipolar system later became the loose bipolar system that indicated the loosening of Soviet and American grip on their respective allies and regions of influence.

In the contemporary scene of international politics the structure of international system has begun to change radically once again. We are now witnessing a rapid loosening of the bipolar environment. Several factors explain this change. Relationships between the superpowers and their allies were always marked with some strains and a general resentment of the "big brother" role of the two superpowers. What is new, at least in Western Europe, is that the coming of European prosperity, unity, and self-identity, when coupled with a mutual Soviet and American troop cuts there, will allow the European nations to create a new pole of world politics. Both superpowers recognize this eventuality. The hierarchical structures of both poles are being modified currently. Changes within the Western bloc are much more apparent than in the Communist bloc, although the potential for change in relationships in the Communist bloc is far greater because the resentment against Soviet domination by force is greater. In all probability the Soviet bloc will loosen very rapidly just as soon as the Soviet Union relaxes their military control of their satellite nations. Western Europe is no longer economically dependent on the United States. In the process of achieving tremendous economic success through the European Common Market and through other arrangements, Western European Nations are now asserting political independence from the United States. Some of the signposts along this path of independence are French attempts to play a neutral and thus moderating role between the two superpowers; West Germany's new and moderately successful efforts to normalize relations with Eastern Europe, particularly with East Germany, and the support of this policy by the people of West Germany, as indicated in the 1972 general election; and most importantly, an attitudinal change among the people of Great Britain that they are a *European* nation and thus need to move closer to the continent and away from the so-called time honored "special" Anglo-American bonds. There are other changes worth noting: for instance, serious conflicts within the NATO membership have appeared over the sharing of nuclear weapons; France has withdrawn from the integrated NATO command; and increasingly, the United States, under domestic pressure and for political and economic considerations, has decided to negotiate seriously with the Soviet Union for mutual cuts in force levels in Europe. There has been a general lessening of a military threat to the security of Western Europe, thus reducing its once strong military dependence on the United States. The conclusion seems clear. The Western alliance system led by the United States has indeed loosened considerably, both militarily and politically.

The Communist bloc, despite its forced interdependence and the still harsh attitude of Soviet Union against the liberalization of relationships among the socialist fraternal order, is loosening. Even the 1968 Czechoslovakian episode, when the Soviet Union along with four of its allies invaded this country under the provisions of the Warsaw Pact to which the Czechs also belong and forcefully imposed its hierarchical control, cannot overshadow other developments. Consider, for instance, the fact that the Sino-Soviet split is for all practical purposes now permanent. Rumania can no longer be counted on by the Soviet Union always to support the Communist bloc in the United Nations. In addition, it has successfully moved out of the Soviet Union's dominated economic organization COMECON. Recently this small country has frequently criticized several Soviet policies from within the bloc, thus causing the Russians to react in irritation. Albania, another Communist country in Eastern Europe, has followed a policy of moving closer to the People's Republic of China and away from the Soviet Union. The independent role that Yugoslavia has played in the Socialist camp for some time is quite apparent now even to the Soviet Union that has generally accepted the Yugoslav's neutral position in world affairs. In short, movements for the strong reassertion of national self-interest are responsible for the rapid loosening of both alliance systems.

Another factor that marks the beginning of this current bipolar international environment is the growing influence of the People's Republic of China in world affairs. This country may very well become a new pole of power. The Chinese always had the potential for a superpower status, and they are now realizing this potential. Economically, they are making every effort, with some success, to industrialize. Politically, they have been more successful. They are no longer dependent on Russia and, in fact, are in competition with it in many countries of the "Third World." They have joined the "nuclear club," and after reaping the usual political benefits from this membership, they have encouraged political revolutions in some parts of the world. Their inexperience in world affairs has caused them some headaches in this area, particularly in Africa. In recent years they have belittled the Soviet Union for making accommodations with the number one capitalist country of the world, meaning the United States, at the expense of Marxism. However, very recently they seem to have been following the Soviet path by inviting an American President and by attempting to "normalize" relations with the same number one enemy, the United States. Their entry in the United Nations and their diplomatic recognition by several new countries have given them further preeminence in world affairs. Militarily, Chinese are rapidly becoming a first-rate military power; having developed the "bomb," they appear now to be concentrating on the delivery system. As the war in Indo-China winds down with the American pullout, one cannot escape the conclusion that the Chinese have successfully challenged the United States in Southeast Asia, an area that the Chinese have traditionally regarded as their sphere of influence. Also, it seems that China will be soon ready and willing to claim a superpower status, thus altering the structure of the international system still further.

Revolution in science and military technology

Another revolution that is currently affecting the nature of international politics is the revolution in science and military technology. It is hardly news to most people in the world today that the present generation lives in an intensely scientific age. The word "science" and "technology" invokes, respect whenever used, even in some of the most backward areas in the world. In the Western world one can go as far back as the seventeenth century and find an air of respectability about science among the general popululation. However, the "explosion" in scientific knowledge, great discoveries in the natural and physical sciences, and their application to civil and military use is a more recent phenomenon. The military application of technology, particularly the use of nuclear energy in this area since the War, has been the most awsome, fearful, and ominous signpost of this revolution. In the civilian usage this revolution has equally affected automation, communication, and space exploration. The momentum and depth of this revolution is still increasing.

Specifically, our immediate concern here is to determine the impact of this revolution on world politics, since the Second World War in particular. In the field of nonmilitary application, science and technology have very rapidly enhanced the physical capabilities of humans to communicate and to affect each others' lives. It is a technological world, and international affairs are also affected by it. For instance, as a result of what technology can do, there had been a revolution of rising expectation concerning the satisfaction of material wants in poor countries. This faith in technology and in its pursuit has now superseded religious and even ideological goals as a guiding force in world politics. The demise of absolute military security and a growing national interdependence in economic affairs are the products of advancements in technology. The superpower status of the Soviet Union and the United States is based solely on their military and industrial advancements because of technology, rather than on superior moral, religious, or social philosophies that they might possess. Europe became dominant in world affairs and was able to colonize much of the world largely because of its technological superiority. It is quite likely that in the future the non-Western world may combine its nationalism and the restless energy of its masses along with its untapped resources of its land and develop its industry. This can be expected to make a significant impact on world affairs. Surely China and Japan are already moving in this direction.

Very briefly, the impact of technology in international affairs can be divided in five broad categories. First, the advancement of technology has constantly changed the significance of various national objectives by changing the assumptions that were originally responsible for the formulation of these objectives. However, one of the major problems that appears here is that the revolutionary effect of technological advancement is not always understood at the time. Consequently, at any given time a nation may be following a foreign policy that may no longer be in its best interest or at least may be unnecessary because of its advancement in technology. A few examples here will help clarify this proposition. For instance, the United States abandoned its traditional "isolation" policy at the time when it needed this policy most: that is, when the threats to its national security became more real because of the advancements in military technology in Europe. Another example, technology has made winning wars extremely costly in terms of the human suffering that terrible weapons can inflict and the risks of a general nuclear war that are involved; yet we have not, as a result, given the prevention of wars the first priority in the agenda of national goals. Second, technology influences the objective factors in international relations, such as considerations of international trade and economics, the importance of geographic strategic relations, and the problems of population. For instance, oil-producing areas of the world have been traditionally regarded as strategically important, but with the development of atomic energy for peaceful purposes their importance may be slowly diminishing. The same is true of strategic territories abroad, which were used as military bases. With the production of long-range bombers, the ICBMs and missile-laden nuclear-powered submarines, these strategic areas have lost their significance. The United States and its allies constructed military bases in what were deemed to be the most strategically important areas in the non-Communist world at the height of the cold war. Many of these bases are now being dismantled because they are no longer needed for national security. Consider, for instance, the role of science and technology in contributing to the population explosion. The advancement of medical science has contributed to this situation by cutting down the infant mortality rate considerably and by pushing the life expectancy average further by several years. Yet it's the same science and technology that we expect will solve the problem of food shortages to feed the new millions. Third, technology has affected the content of foreign policy itself and a host of its supporting programs. In many subject areas of foreign policy discussions, the technological considerations are paramount. Consider, for instance, the highly technical nature of arms control and disarmament negotiations, and technical assistance programs. Even the development of international law is influenced by technological considerations, particularly in the frontier areas of law such as legal norms concerning outer space, moon, and other celestial bodies, the ocean floor, and the seabed. Fourth, technology is now considered by almost all nations as the primary instrument for economic development, industrialization, and what is popularly known in the developing countries as "nation building." In international relations the technologically more advanced countries have a tremendous advantage because of their capacity to create and export capital to the poor parts of the world, with strings attached of course. In the developing societies, technology is a major part of their capacity to absorb this capital to arrive at the so-called "take-off" point in their drive for rapid industrialization. Fifth, and last, technology has had an almost revolutionary effect on the methods of conducting foreign policy: for instance, the use of radio, T.V., instant communications between foreign offices, propaganda techniques, intelligence and espionage, technical exchanges and other projects, all of which are the result of advancement in technology. All of these provide an efficient means to conduct foreign policy.

Nuclear weapons—a note of civility and mutual respect among major powers

Perhaps the greatest impact of science and technology in international politics has been in the field of modern weaponary systems and their delivery vehicles. The development of nuclear weapons has fantastically escalated the coercive capabilities of the states that belong to this so-called "nuclear club." It is extremely difficult for most people even to imagine the results of a nuclear holocaust. Apart from the megatonage of nuclear bombs and the complete destruction based on this factor alone, there are other factors that can contribute to the spread of devastation that will be caused by these bombs. Consider, for instance, the many contingencies concerning the attacker's strategic planning: the warning time, which is constantly being reduced in the face of developing new and more sophisticated, efficient weapons; weather conditions; and extent of elaborate and effective defense preparations. All of these factors make it difficult to predict accurately the loss of life and property should a nuclear attack be initiated. Strategic experts have made rough guesses concerning the results of various kinds of nuclear attacks on the United States. These range from 40 to 180 million dead on the first strike—a surprise attack. The second strike capability of the Soviet Union will result in tens of millions dead. Estimates of the time necessary for economic revitalization, that is, if it were possible to revitalize the economy, range from 20 to 150 years.

Nuclear weapons have radically modified the nature of international politics by enormously increasing the risks of mass destruction. The nuclear powers are confronted by the alternatives of initiating a nuclear catastrophe through political miscalculations or of gradually losing their influence in world affairs because of the fear of assuming great risks. Since the highest stake in the contemporary international conflict is the total destruction of mankind or at least the crippling of whole nations, nuclear weapons have had a paradoxical political effect. The nuclear powers, which have at their command destructive weapons that man has never known before in his turbulent history, are compelled by the very existence of these weapons to tread on the international stage with a caution never known to great military powers in the past. The high risks of using military force even affect the relations of nuclear powers to smaller nations. The most immediate result has been a resolve of both superpowers not to get drawn into a nuclear war. This resolve, along with the continuing conflict between the two superpowers, has provided the small countries, particularly the nonaligned nations, with a vicarious power that allows them to speak more brashly, to maneuver among the big powers more freely, and to reap in the process far greater benefits than could have been achieved by these states if a nuclear stalemate did not exist.

Beyond this stalemate there seems to be no general agreement among the two superpowers forbidding the use of most sophisticated conventional weapons, some of which have a greater destructive capacity, if used in a large quantity, as compared with small, low-yield, nuclear bombs. In fact many people have suggested that the United States has already tried out and perfected a host of these weapons successfully in the Indo-China war. Clearly, avoidance of a direct and possibly nuclear conflict between the United States and the Soviet Union has not meant elimination of conflict between these two countries at lower levels, that is, indirect conflict in underdeveloped countries. Wars by proxy, as some have suggested, continue to take place between these two in various regions of the world. The only improvement one can expect in this area, particularly after the stalemate in the Vietnam conflict, is that both powers will show a greater tendency in the future to accommodate one another to the extent possible, without seriously hurting their national aspirations, instead of going out of their way to "get involved" or frustrate each other in each and every international crisis situation, as they did during the cold war period. They may also continually postpone or circumvent the national aspirations that provoke the other side into a military collision course. For example, the kind of aspiration that Russia exhibited when it decided to place missiles in Cuba in 1962; this act provoked the United States to erect a Cuban blockade which almost led to military confrontation with Russia. Another example is the American U-2 episode, which infuriated the Soviets and destroyed the subsequent Soviet-American summit in Paris.

Reducing the chances of a nuclear war is not the only political outcome of the present nuclear stalemate. The threat of an uncontrollable catalytic war, the accidental or deliberate starting of a war by a staff officer and, of great importance, the extremely high cost of weapons have forced the adversaries to cooperate with each other and to achieve arms control and disarmament. After all, common interest in survival is strong enough to overcome ideological incompatabilities. For all of its dreadfulness, the balance of terror has given the world a reasonable chance to move toward a more lawful world based on reason and mutual respect even if this respect arises from a common fear of the total annihilation of mankind. Moreover, the existence of these weapons has started in some quarters of the world a revolution in thinking about international affairs, resulting in the changes of military strategic planning for the future as well as a reappraisal of national objectives and how they can be best pursued through nonmilitary means. War, for instance, is regarded a very poor means for the successful attainment of national objectives. This conclusion is based on the assumption that a nuclear war will be suicide and that conventional wars, the so-called regional conflicts, or the "preventive" wars designed to prevent larger conflicts, all of these tend to have negative effects. Consider "preventive" wars, for instance. These conflicts, given the contemporary nature of international politics, end up achieving exactly the opposite results, that is, instead of preventing major conflict later on, they escalate into major conflicts, for example, the Vietnam war. The logic of the situation here seems to be that as soon as a major power gets involved in a regional or local civil-war type of conflict, the other major powers simply feel they cannot leave unchallenged the appearance of their major rival. So the conflict enlarges, acquiring an international status and risking a possible nuclear war. Only after discarding wars as a suitable means to achieve national objectives, the superpowers can shift their attention toward the development of new diplomatic techniques, bargaining strategies, and a greater use of international norms in mediation, third-party intervention, and pacific settlement. Indeed, this process has in some instances already started.

While modern military technology has *injected a note of civility and mutual respect, largely based on fear, into major powers,* the same does not appear to be the case with the minor "Third World" countries. In their international relations, particularly when they are dealing with each other, these countries are often guided by their own brand of all-encompassing ideologies, fervent nationalism, traditional disputes, and at times what appears to be an exaggerated sense of national pride, rather than considerations of the possibility of war and its effects on all aspects of life in their countries. In most instances they possess fairly sophisticated conventional weapons provided to them by major powers under one pretext or the other. Consequently, there have been relatively frequent, unusually bloody, if not always prolonged wars among the smaller countries. Most of these wars, which have occurred since the Second World War, could have been avoided or contained, their destruction limited, had it not been the national ambitions of major powers in the conflicted areas. Some of these wars were purely civil wars and could have been left alone to take their own course by the major powers, but obviously no such luck.

Spectacular as it certainly is, the introduction of weapons of massive destruction is only one of the many contributions of modern science and technology to the science of warfare. Just as impressive and deadly have been technological advancements in speed, usage of remote control techniques, accuracy of the delivery systems, and breakthroughs in biological, radiological, and gas weapons of warfare. To this list one can easily add improvements in electronic devices for purposes of military intelligence gathering, reconnaissance gathering from orbiting satellites, which provide the data for the strategic deployment and successful targeting of the latest weapons. Sophisticated computers have literally taken over the task of submarine and antisubmarine warfare. Today's counterinsurgency operations frequently use such devices as sound amplifiers, odor detectors, infrared gunsites, and photographic equipment and techniques to detect enemy movement. Most of these devices have been used by the United States in the Indo-China war, along the Ho Chi Minh trail, quite successfully, or at least that is what the government has consistently claimed. When one adds to these advancements the fantastic logistical capabilities of the superpowers in airlifting massive armies within a few hours to any part of the world and maintaining them effectively for long periods of time, it becomes quite apparent that these powers are uniquely capable of making their wrath felt on the rest of the world anytime they so choose. But there is also a limiting aspect to the tremendous military capabilities of the superpowers. I believe that for the first time military power can be regarded as a distinct liability in the struggle for world influence and prestige. Today, the most powerful nations vie with one another for the title of peacemaker by seeking to assure the rest of the world, along with their own people, that their military exists *solely as a guarantee to peace.* There is no more dramatic proof of the impact of this emergent political consciousness on the character of international politics than contemporary history itself. If we seek to evaluate the fluctuations of the fortunes of both superpowers in this struggle, perhaps the most significant determinent of gains and losses is the use of force, but with consequences exactly opposite from those that have prevailed heretofore in the affairs of the state. The major gains on each side have been a consequence of the other side's resorting to the use of military power. Can any one deny that the recitation of the aggression of Soviet arms is at the same time a list of our own greatest gains and *vice versa?* Second, neither the Soviet Union nor the United States can continue to build new weapons because of the extraordinary cost involved which is perhaps lucky for the rest of the world. The national resources in both countries are sorely needed for other more productive civilian projects.

A revolution of sinking expectations in the poor countries

The third revolution that is currently affecting international politics is the revolution in sinking expectations of poor yet sovereign countries of the "Third World." This revolution has been variously described as the failure of the desired and expected leap of African, Latin American, and Asian nations into the Western-dominated modern world of industrialization and technological innovations. It is a revolution in sinking expectations because these societies wished to modernize their economies, satisfy the basic needs of their citizens and, in the process, try to gain international status and prestige. They have not succeeded in their goals. Although they have managed to get rid of, for the most part, their unscrupulous colonial masters, their plight is far from over. They are rapidly giving in to apathy. Most of these countries lack dedicated leadership, a developmental elite, and the minimum amount of political stability necessary for socioeconomic development. There seems little doubt that the direction taken by these states in their quest for nation building will significantly change both the nature of international politics and the role of international law in it.

Those of us who live in the more advantaged parts of the world realize that accelerating the process of social and economic development in these less priviledged rural areas of the world is of paramount importance. The great upsurge of interest in the developing areas[5] in recent years lends testimony to this fact. The main problem is widespread poverty, and the dominant manifestation of this improverishment is instability and chaos for the affected political systems.

Many of the developing societies today are led by Western-educated or trained elites that frequently tend to be anti-Western for several reasons, some real, some imagined, yet these same elites very much wish to see their nations westernize, that is, industrialize. Their apparent anti-Western stand has some psychological advantages both for them and for the masses they lead. First, it tends to boost their feelings of indigenous nationalism, because this brand of nationalism originally led to their independence from the West. Now it is badly needed again to unite the masses and to motivate them to become mobilized for rapid development without, at the same time, demanding immediate benefits for their labors.

---

[5]To speak of countries as "developing," "emerging," "transitional," or "underdeveloped" is possible only if these terms have no more than paradigmatic meaning. Riggs has made a strong case for using the term "prismatic" society to suggest a transitional society or one that lies between the extremes of fused (traditional) and diffracted (modern) societies. See Fred Riggs, *Administration in Developing Countries: The Theory of Prismatic Society* (Boston: Houghton Mifflin), 1964. Two years later, however, Riggs expressed dissatisfaction with this formulation that he regards as implying that development proceeds along a deterministically unilineal path. His new formulation, which provides a different frame of reference, is illustrated and explained in an article, "Administrative Development: An Elusive Concept," in John D. Montgomery and William J. Siffin (eds.), *Approaches to Development: Politics, Administration and Change* (New York: McGraw-Hill), 1966, pp. 241–243.

Second, anti-Westernism can be, and is often used, in the formerly Western-dominated countries, as a "scapegoat" for the elites' failure to deliver the "promised goods" to their people. For instance, there is a tendency to blame the colonial past for elites' shortcomings.

This national awakening of dozens of developing nations of the non-Western world, when combined with the Western colonial retreat, has resulted in the further decentralization of international decision-making centers. The number of states whose actions and reactions must be considered in the international system is constantly increasing without any assurance that all of them have a reasonable chance of surviving the internal and external threats to their existence. Their national self-assertion in world politics today and their demands for changes to suit their temperament have no relationship to their extremely limited powers. Rather, the real source of their authority comes from the propitious circumstance that the rift between the great powers has created. Since this self-assertion comes in the wake of the slow but sure termination of Western domination and an ever-increasing Communist influence in these countries, it has unavoidably an anti-Western character. Thus the Soviet Union and the People's Republic of China seem to be filling the political vacuums created by the West *at no great cost to themselves.* Yet the same national self-assertion of the developing countries might not *forever* favor the Communists. For the time being, the Chinese and the Russians may reap the benefits from the disputes between the West and the developing countries by playing the role of the counterbalancer of the West. However, the differences between the West and the developing countries are of a *temporary* nature, arising from the past when the West exploited these nations. Should these differences be buried, there is a good chance that the two shall find a new *modus vivendi.* When this happens, the same national self-assertion will certainly find it difficult to accommodate itself to Communist domination, sugarcoated in lofty ideological goals of socialist fraternalism, which have never really been practiced thus far even within the Socialist camp itself. Above all, it must be remembered that national aspirations today, particularly in the "Third World," which has recently achieved its independence, are bound to run counter to *any* foreign domination whether it be Western or Communist.

Continuing civil wars, *coup d'etats,* and other forms of civil disturbances in the developing societies have in the past and will probably continue to influence the course of international politics by inviting intervention from the outside, either for pragmatic or ideological reasons. The economic intervention of major powers in these societies through various technical and other assistance programs is already an accepted fact both by the prospective recipients and donor states. In fact, the emerging international welfare philosophy in the world has already been accepted with some reservations by most nations. Very simply, this philosophy emphasizes that states that enjoy a high standard of living and a self-perpetuating rapid economic growth are under *some moral obligation* to assist the other less fortunate nations who constitute the majority of minkind. The exact implication of this rather vague new obligation has not yet been clarified, although the demands of poor countries for help have become louder in recent years. However, rich nations still give aid mainly according to political considerations. Thus when these considerations change, so does the giving of the aid; it may increase, decrease, or even completely cease. A new international political order will most likely evolve some new standard of distributing foreign aid to needy nations, its source may become independent of political considerations, and its amount and direction may be determined solely on the need and capacity of the recepient nation to use it effectively. We shall have to wait and see.

The ideological revolution

The fourth revolution is the ideological revolution. The present century has brought back the ideological conflicts waged by nation-states in the past. To be sure, there were other eras in man's history when ideological conflicts were frequent, such as the period of religious wars, the era of Christian-Moslem struggles or, still earlier, the Peloponnesian War. What is new about the contemporary ideological conflict is its wider impact in world affairs and the general confusion that surrounds the ideological differences and their interpretation. Influences of ideology on international behavior are not clearly understood. There are scholars who simply refuse to recognize ideology as a motivating factor in international politics. Consequently, they argue political ideology is not much of a guide to a nation's behavior in the international system. On the other hand, an impressive number of writers continue to insist that ideology is a major determinent not only of a nation's behavior but also of what objectives a nation is likely to follow in its foreign policy.

Among people who agree that ideology influences international relations, there is a broad disagreement on how it does so and how this influence can be measured. For instance, many experts and laymen still believe that the Marxist-Leninist ideology is still being followed religiously by the Soviet Union and the Chinese; therefore both states are still committed to the dictatorship of the proletariat all over the world. Other scholars regard Marxism-Leninism as nothing more than a tool for serving Russia's and China's traditional national goals. When it comes to an interpretation of an ideology, the exponents of conflicting ideologies disagree strongly in interpreting their *own* ideology and also the ideology of their *opponents*.

For example, Communists have consistently argued that Marxism-Leninism is a democratic creed. It is based on principles of human equality, dignity and respect by the state, and it is anti-imperialistic. Western nations continue to regard Marxism-Leninism as suppressive, aggressive, and inherently authoritative. They view it essentially antidemocratic. On the other hand, Communists have usually contended that Western "democracies" are nothing more than bourgeois capitalism, and as such they necessarily breed war and imperialism. Western nations look at their democratic ideology as supporting human dignity and freedom, and find it conducive to peace and international cooperation.

In actual practice, each side deviates frequently from the dictates of its ideology in international politics, regretfully, because of the "threat" of the "other" side. For instance, Americans see their country engaged in power politics with the Soviet Union. There have been several bloody clashes between the countries, one of which was supported by the United States and the other by the Soviet Union. Because of the threat of international Communism, Americans feel they have no choice but to face the challenge regardless of their democratic norms and aspirations, some of which clearly run contrary to American military involvements abroad. The Soviet Union cannot permit the true Socialist philosophy to be practiced in the country, allow the state to "wither away," and set up a dictatorship of the proletariat because of the constant threat of "capitalist aggression."

A student of international politics finds it fairly difficult to arrive at some satisfactory conclusions concerning the role of ideology in international politics. Nonetheless, there is general agreement that ideology's full impact on the international scene is yet to be assessed. The problem of assessment is aggravated, first, by the nature of ideologies themselves, their complexities, and internal contradictions. Second, there is the problem of the "predictability gap" between the espousal of an ideology and its translation into public or foreign policy. Third, there is the complex problem of attempting to measure the relative weight of several influences that are responsible for a state's behavior in international politics, of which ideology is only one. Fourth, there is the extreme, impassioned, and often divergent claims that are made for, and against particular ideologies.

To be sure, regardless of the problems in understanding the role of ideologies in international politics, their role has increased greatly since the Second World War. Looking at the developments in this century one finds several reasons for this increase. *First*, and perhaps the most visible reason, is the emergence of a number of very powerful states officially espousing nondemocratic ideologies and challenging the very basis of Western-type democracies, which were developed in the tradition of nineteenth-century liberal, democratic philosophy. For instance, the

Bolshevik Revolution in Russia and the emergence of the Soviet Union, Fascist Italy, National Socialism in Germany, and Marxism-Leninism-Maoism in China, all have challenged the idea of Western democracy. *Second*, ideology since the War has become extremely important in foreign affairs because of the growing influence of the masses (the man in the street) on the foreign policy decision-making process. Increasingly, foreign affairs affect the citizens in a most intimate way; consequently, most states, democratic or otherwise, are being influenced in their foreign policy decisions by public opinions. For example, foreign policy is no longer the business of a handful of "experts" in foreign offices. *Third*, the developing societies and their leaders (for several reasons) have adopted strong ideological predispositions, at least verbally, and their ideological preferences at times do dominate their view of the rest of the world. Inasmuch as the superpowers are competing for the loyalties of these countries, their ideological dispositions become important for the superpowers to understand. On the other hand, the superpowers often give aid to these countries on the basis of their ideological affinity with the superpowers rather than on their genuine need for aid.

The growth of various incompatible ideologies has caused new splits among nations, thus affecting the nature of international politics considerably. Consider, for instance, the impact of the "cold war" era or the "Sino-Soviet split" on world politics. These developments clearly suggest that the nature of interstate relations is now in several ways affected by domestic social and political norms and structures that nations develop. This realization has led several political scientists to develop "linkage theories" that explain the internal determinents of international behavior and *vice versa*. What is also new concerning the impact of ideology in foreign affairs is that ideology has penetrated the structure of what was always known as the pragmatic world of international politics. Today it has succeeded in creating a highly emotionally charged atmosphere.

The Communist states are officially committed to the ideology of Marxism-Leninism, which they would like to extend to the whole world. Therefore, by definition, they are not supposed to be at home with the present political, economic, and social arrangements in the non-Communist states of the "Third World." Americans, often having enjoyed the fruits of democracy for a long time, are convinced they have a moral duty to remake the world so that it is more conducive to the acceptance of their brand of democracy. Both sides, convinced of the rightness of their ideologies, find it difficult to resist the temptation of converting other states to their belief systems. Under the circumstances neither side is willing to accept the concept of "limited goals," which, after all, was the fundamental principle of the balance of power system.

A concluding remark

To conclude, it is admitted that given the many problems, international politics today has become more dire and deadly. There is sufficient ground for despair. Today, when the power of destruction is beyond imagination, when a common language of diplomacy and a common terminology of simple human concerns apparently have failed us, we feel more helpless to influence the history of our own times. It seems we have been tossed at the mercy of uncontrollable, uncalculable, and often unforeseeable international events. In these circumstances can foreign policy of a nation do more than to simply prepare for successive crises? Has our obsession with the fear of the worst in international arena preempted our capacity to think and act in more positive ways in order to create a more livable world?

While some despair is unavoidable, a great deal of soul-searching on the part of all nations is also needed. The goal of a peaceful and lawful world can still be achieved. In fact, in the midst of revolution and instabilities there are *elements of predictability and signs of hope, and international law is one of them.* The next chapter will explain the nature of contemporary international law.

chapter 3
nature of contemporary international law

As we begin to understand the true nature of international law several questions come to mind. Is international law really important to our future existence? Is there no way to measure its utility in terms of what a nation "gets out of it?" Is it merely a product of a multitude of relations among nations, and therefore falls in disrepute when these relations change? Can it be used as an instrument to build a more lawful world? Can one detect a feedback from the practice of international law that could be used by decision makers in their efforts to move the world away from international anarchy, where law itself becomes a victim, and toward the nonviolent management of international conflict? Is law so bogged down in individual cases and multiple interpretations of specific treaties that it cannot capture the imagination of today's masses? Is there no opportunity to use law to upgrade significantly aggregative justice among nations? Can national self-realization be achieved today at the expense of abandoning international law? Is it possible for nations to still be able to use their "old techniques" of diplomacy in their relations with each other, but within a framework of commonly accepted international law, techniques such as shrewd bargaining, propaganda, alliance formation, and political manipulation? All of these are important questions that have been posed by social scientists, and an exposition of the nature of international law should help us in the answers.

First, international law is a constantly evolving body of norms that are, contrary to the popular view, generally consistently observed by states. These norms, it is widely accepted today, confer certain responsibilities and privileges not only on states but also on international organizations and individuals. In other words, states are not the only entities having rights and responsibilities under international law. Efforts, particularly since the Second World War, have been made to broaden the scope of international law to include public international organizations, and to a lesser degree, the individual.[1] Therefore, international law today governs the relations between individuals and states or international organizations, between these organizations and states and, of course, the relations between states. Any elaboration of its nature must recognize these facts.

Some of its distinctive features are: (1) It is a legal phenomenon but heavily dependent on political considerations, because it is generally the outcome of a successful political process. To elaborate further, its development is the result of many forces of consensus and cooperation that can be found in the international system, despite the widespread conflict that rages in international politics. Unlike domestic law, it is not created by a single state. (2) Its development throughout the history has also been influenced by technical and procedural considerations that arise from everyday transactions between states. (3) It consists of "customary" and "conventional" "rules," but it is more than that, because it also includes general principles of law. (4) It is no longer, perhaps never was, a mere "body of rules" and should not be characterized as such. (5) It is more of a *process* than anything else, subject to frequent changes and interpretations at the time when it is being applied to concrete acts of states. (6) Its respect and success are to a certain extent closely tied to its continued ability to remain relevant, that is, its ability to conform to the prevailing political context and, at the same time, to influence the international environment to acquire a more lawful character.

In the Western societies, international law is commonly defined as a body of principles, rules, and norms, generally observed by the members of the international society in their international relations or when they are dealing with international organizations or citizens of other states. It is believed that international law provides the legal basis for the orderly management of world affairs. There are a variety of terms used in textbooks in place of the notion "international law." For instance, many scholars in the past have emphasized the term "law of nations," a translation of *droit des gens*. Others have a distinct preference for the term "international public law" to underline the clear distinction from "international private law" or what is called by some "the conflict of laws." A number of distinguished writers have adopted the term "transnational law," including *all* law that is responsible for regulating all forms of interstate behavior. However, the most commonly used term in the West and elsewhere remains international law. To be sure, there are several

[1]In support of this position see Reparation for Injuries Suffered in the Service of United Nations. Advisory opinion, 1949. *International Court of Justice* Reports No. 174. For a balanced view, see also W. Friedman, *The Changing Structure of International Law* (New York: Columbia University Press), 1964, pp. 221–249.

definitions of international law in the West, but in reality the differences
are in phraseology rather than substance.

Contrary to the popular view, the Soviet Union's and its allies' definition of international law is not too different from the Western definition.
It is admitted, however, that the similarity in the definition of law per se
has not produced similar attitudes toward law. Furthermore, there is no
clear agreement among the Communist jurists and scholars themselves on
the nature and functions of international law. Nonetheless, Soviet official
textbooks on international law do contain a definition. Cosider the following quote from a Soviet textbook.[2]

> International law can be defined as the aggregate of rules governing
> relations between states in the process of their conflict and cooperation,
> assigned to safeguard their peaceful coexistence, expressing the will of
> the ruling classes of the states and defended in case of need by coercion
> applied by states, individually or collectively.

The above definition of international law will perhaps be not acceptable
to many writers in the West, and the problem is largely the way the
Soviets have phrased it. What the Soviet jurists seem to be emphasizing
is that one of the major purposes of contemporary international law is to
promote peaceful coexistence through cooperation between all states regardless of their social and political systems. No one in the West could
disagree with this view of international law. However, the more pertinent
question is whether the Soviet Union's concept of "peaceful coexistence"
really means what it suggests: to coexist peacefully. More important, will
this notion be able to overcome other Communist ideological goals such
as "world revolution," a goal hardly compatible with the philosophy of
peaceful coexistence?

The People's Republic of China has also relied on its own brand of
the concept of "peaceful coexistence" in its definition of international
law. Some Chinese scholars have argued that there are two systems of
international law, one applicable to socialist states only in their own
international relations, and the other for the relations with the capitalist
states. The Chinese view of peaceful coexistence differs from the Soviet
view. They have endorsed, at least theoretically, the famous five principles
of peaceful coexistence embodied in the 1954 Sino-Indian Agreement
as the main basis for international law. These are: (1) respect for territorial integrity and sovereignty; (2) nonaggression; (3) noninterference in
domestic affairs; (4) equality among nations; and (5) mutual benefit and
coexistence. On the surface these principles are basically in harmony with

[2]Quoted in W. L. Tung, International Law in An Organizing World (New York:
Crowell), 1968, p. 4.

the role of international law as perceived by the Western states. However, China's attitudes in world affairs and therefore her conduct is guided by several important factors, both past and present, domestic and international, that are peculiar to China alone. Therefore their view of international law, notwithstanding the harmony of their principles of peaceful coexistence, is different than the Soviet or Western view of the law. Chinese and Soviet views of international law are discussed in a later Chapter.

To probe further into the true nature of contemporary international law and some of its more dynamic aspects, it can be argued that in the broadest sense, the function of law, both municipal and international, is to serve the interests of its citizens by normalizing, that is, standardizing, their relationships. International law attempts to do just that. Moreover, in a social sense, it attempts to foster a community of interests and values by providing the maximum satisfaction of desired ends for a vast majority with a minimum inconvenience, sufferings, or deprivations for the minority. In an economic sense, international law attempts to limit the choice of alternatives available, along with the scope and intensity of conflicting interests of nations in the competitive pursuits of their national goals. Most important, international law, in a political sense, performs several crucial functions: as suggested elsewhere, it enhances cooperation among states through standardizing techniques and patterns aimed at limiting interstate conflict, that is, it attempts to serve as an impartial framework for the process of international decisions. In a decentralized and heterogenous world of multiple states, it serves as an instrument of communications by providing a common language and a common frame of reference. In the process of foreign policy decision making it frequently serves as a tool because states do indeed use legal arguments to protect or enhance their positions. It is, also, used as a tool to condemn the adversary's position as "illegal."

All of this is essentially done by using international law as a means of pressuring an adversary through mobilization, for example, of international opinion and other forces of law and order, and thus internationalizing a national interest. But at the same time it is only fair to point out that the inherent ambiguities in international law and the perennial problem of multiple interpretation of its norms provide an opportunity to the policymakers to dismiss at times international law altogether as irrelevant in other situations, as if it were neither a guide nor a restraint.

One of the major weaknesses of international law is that it does not have a truly impartial character, or at least so it seems to many observers outside the Western society of nations. Its dictates and its existence, they argue, tend to favor the West, who are after all solely responsible for its creation and growth up until very recently. They further point out that not only is there a general lack of *effective* legal institutions that could serve as impartial arbiters of interstate disputes, but also law itself has become tainted with value-laden overtones. Many Western scholars such as McDougal, Goldie, Burke, and Lauterpacht have viewed international law in terms of "reasonableness." But is it not true that what seems a reasonable norm, policy, or national interest to one nation may not appear at all reasonable to other nations?

There is some truth in the above criticism of international law. It *is* cloaked in the values of the historically stronger nations, values, some of which most of the weaker, newer nations of today simply do not share. Consequently, if one of the "Third World" states is not satisfied with a legal interpretation of its rights and obligations under a particular law, it proceeds to choose definitions that suit its needs and that it considers "morally" justified in professing. Since the Second World War, in several former colonies of the Western European powers we have witnessed a rash of illegal nationalizations on moral and economic grounds of foreign property usually belonging to these European powers. Consider, for instance, current states' actions with regard to the doctrine of continental shelf: Chile, Ecuador, Peru, Costa Rica, and Panama claim a continental shelf area up to 200 miles from their national borders; the United States and all states on the North Sea, also find justification for expansion of their national jurisdictions. Thus, in this situation, as indeed in many other areas, one is faced with a lack of consensus both on the procedure and substance of international law. Before proceeding we should have a clear idea of the development of international law in a *historical perspective* and some of the present sources of the development of international law.

Development of international law in a historical perspective

Most writers agree the history of international law is long and varied. The length of its existence in one form or the other and the variety of its background are still debated today among the Western scholars, the Socialist writers, as well as the Third World writers. Whatever the outcome of the controversy, one thing seems certain. Much of the modern international law as we understand it today is essentially the brainchild of Western civilization. On its body of rules it indeed shows the unmistakable impressions of the last three to five hundred years of European thought. It is, however, possible to go much futher back in the history of man and find some of its earliest roots. A broader picture of its creation and development in a historical perspective allows two tentative conclusions: first, it is practically impossible to link the rudimentary legal practices of Ancient Greece or China directly to the development of modern international law; second, some of these ancient practices were remarkably similar to some of our present legal customs and concerns.

The Chinese, Indians, and Egyptians

Some authors have unsuccessfully attempted to link the modern law with the gentle and often complicated legal customs and transactions of the "silk people," the ancient Chinese. They have argued impressively, but inconclusively, that rudimentary norms regulating interstate relations did exist in ancient China[3] and in several other states, notably India. But they fail to make their case when it comes to the problem of "linkage" between the ancient and the modern. According to some scholars from the Soviet Union, the birthplace of international law was decidedly China, India, and Egypt, rather than the states of the Mediterranean basin. Speaking on the contributions of Ancient China, one writer suggests Chinese legal norms existed as early as 2500 B.C.[4] Several other writers concluded that on the basis of all the information that is available, "international law" probably developed simultaneously in the Ancient East and the West.[5] More significant than the controversy on the early beginnings of law seem to be the fact that some of the earliest papers and documents of man's recorded history, describing the relations between nations, contain evidence of the existence of legal norms that are still very much operative in the contemporary international law. For instance, Professor Gerhard Von Glahan points out that a treaty was concluded in the very dawn of man's written history, around 3100 B.C., between the rulers of Lagash and Umma, two Mesopotamian communities. It was concerning a settlement of a boundary dispute through arbitration, and both sides took a solemn oath in advance that they would abide by the decision.[6] A thousand years later many treaties appeared that dealt with

[3]Many Chinese scholars have painfully gathered the documents and reproduced the information concerning the practice of customary rules of international law during the Chou Dynasty from 1122–249 B.C. See Cheng Te-Hsu, "International Law in Early China," Chinese Social and Political Science Review, (1) (1927), pp. 38–56 and (2), 257–270. See also, W.A.P. Martin, "Treaties of International Law in Ancient China," International Review (January 1883), 63–77.

[4]See, J. J. G. Syatouw, Some Newly Established Asian States and the Development of International Law (The Hague), 1961, p. 36.

[5]For details on this position see C. Phillipson, The International Law and the Custom of Ancient Greece, (London: Macmillan) 2 Volumes, 1911 and 1915. See also S. V. Visharath'a Aiyar, International Law in Ancient India (London), 1925.

[6]G. Von Glahan, Law Among Nations: An Introduction to Public International Law (New York: Macmillan), 1965, p. 36.

such contemporary subjects as the settlement of boundaries between feuding states, extradition of individuals wanted by their governments, creation of vassal states by their more powerful neighbors and, of course, military alliances. An analysis of the little written diplomatic history of the ancient Hindu, Chinese, Assyrian, Hebrew, and Babylonian empires indicate that policymakers then were just as eager to instill predictability into their international relations as their modern counterparts are today. International legal norms have always attempted to create order and predictability by their very nature.[7]

Information gathered concerning the presence of legal norms in various ancient societies and our knowledge of the practice of international relations in those early times do not lead us to conclude that there is any link between the fragmentary laws of the ancient past and the modern international law. Earlier civilizations simply had no concept of such notions as "society of men" or "sovereign equality of states" or "Concerns" that emerge only out of international interdependency, as we know them today. These notions seem to be important prerequisites for the development of a true system of international law. Most of these civilizations were self-centered, and were convinced of the superiority of their own culture, power, and style of life. Thus, most of their energy and imagination was used to develop their own culture, language, laws, morality, and religion. There were no such things as "international affairs" or "foreign policies" per se to worry about, as we know them today. It is true that the inevitable contact with bordering states created headaches, sometimes wars, there was a need to sign treaties and exchange diplomats, and some trade also existed, but even the slightest sense of "international community" did not exist.

The Greeks

Even the great civilization of Greek city-states, with all of its varied accomplishments did not contribute much to the growth of modern international law. The Greeks did develop international legal arrangements among their sovereign city-states, and some of these norms have contributed to the mainstream of Western civilization. Some of our contemporary concerns in law were their concerns too. They apparently acquired several broad principles and norms concerning diplomatic immunities and privileges based on the principle of reciprocity. They signed many trade agreements between the sovereign cities.[8] Greeks were conscious of, for

[7]For details on this point see F. M. Russel, *Theories of International Relations* (New York: Appleton-Century-Crofts), 1936, Chapters 1–4.

[8]For an interesting discussion of the ancient customs of Greece and Rome, see C. Phillipson, *The International Law and the Custom of Ancient Greece.*

example, common bonds of race, language, and religion among the people of the city-states. They also frequently developed enmities toward those who were not of Greek origin and called them "barbarians," not worthy of association. This particular outlook alone was a detriment to the development of international law, which could conceivably standardize conduct of behavior between the Greeks and the others as equals. Along with this problem, the temperament of Greeks always favored local independence and a love for the self-control of their own affairs. Both of these factors appears to have dampened the chances of a united and well-integrated international system of Greek city-states and their colonies around the shores of the Mediterranean sea, a system that certainly would have contributed to the development of an international law. Instead of creating an appropriate body of law to suit their unique situation in history, they simply depended on their mutual feelings of kinship, common customs, and understanding to create stability and predictability in their inter–city-state relations. Consequently, whatever similarities that may exist today between the practices of ancient Greeks and aspects of modern international law cannot be regarded as any more than mere accident. The Greeks, too, like the ancient civilizations of the East, had no mental conceptual framework of the international society as it exists today.

The Romans

In contrast to the lack of impact of early Eastern and Greek civilizations, the Roman contributions to modern international law are impressively extensive. Their international law was not the kind of law applicable to interstate relations in the contemporary sense of the term, although Rome at the height of its glory wielded tremendous power, and considered itself *the* civilization. As such there was no question of developing an international law *equally* applicable to several independent and sovereign states of which Rome would be one. Rather, in keeping with its conquests and glory, Rome developed an elaborate system of "intergroup" law or a sort of private international law that was practiced throughout the Roman Empire. It was called the *jus gentium*. It should not be confused with *jus civile*, a system of law that initially developed in the early Roman history and applied only to Roman citizens, but that later merged with *jus gentium*.

This legal system entitled *jus gentium* or a sort of private international law was extensively used throughout the Roman Empire. Under this legal system the government appointed its "legal official" who was a mixture of attorney general, a judge, and more. He had the authority to appoint judges, interpret the international law as applicable to various private and commercial disputes within the Empire, and between the citizens of various territories. The official was called *praetor peregrinus*. The first major philosophical contribution of the Romans to the growth of modern international law is in their articulation of the concept of "universalism." This attitude of universality contrasts sharply with Greek emphasis on their decentralized system of municipal sovereignties. The Romans were able to bypass if not overcome the forces of narrow provincialism, which still beset many states today, by emphasizing notions of equality under law and virtues of belonging to a powerful Empire. In the success of their drive for the above they must have been considerably helped by their enlightened policy of imposing only moderate controls or restraints over the inhabitants of the areas they conquered. Roman conquest frequently brought the material benefits of Roman superior civilization, thus providing some satisfaction to the natives. More than anything else, Roman rule brought Roman laws and Roman military protection against other invaders and that must have had a positive impact on many of these areas under their rule.

As the Roman Empire grew, the earlier law called *jus civile*, which was only applicable to a handful of early Romans living on nearby hills, became inadequate. The increasing contact with the outside world and with foreigners created problems in the administration of justice in the absence of an international law. Thus, the rights of aliens were recognized as early as 242 B.C. by the creation of this "official" mentioned earlier. Under this institution the development of *jus gentium* took place. It had a more liberal and broader legal philosophy than *jus civile*. With the passage of time as we enter the period of imperial Rome, the two legal systems became one and thus one system of law governed the conduct of citizens and aliens alike living within the Roman Empire. Roman writers emphasized the wider appeal of *jus gentium* and argued that it was applicable to all *even by reason*. Its observance created a common element between all civilized states. These arguments on behalf of Roman international law made an impact on the writers of the Middle Ages who were interested in "discovering" the presence of a universal law that could be applied to all states.

The Middle Ages

It is possible to view this period as a continuity of Roman era in the philosophy of universalism. The attitudes of the elites of this era were influenced by the legal developments of the Roman period. But the political makeup and the temperaments of this period were vastly different. It was characterized by political instability in which authority became increasingly decentralized. The only source of unified power was the Church and the Holy Roman Empire. This source was used on the side of the forces of good and law and order. But, nonetheless, other smaller political units of decision making became dominant in European politics, thus making international law more transnational.

Development of international law in this period was also influenced by the notion of "laws of nature," *jus naturale*, that was originally discovered about 150 B.C. by Roman philosophers from the Greek Stoic thinkers. The law of nature or "the natural law" as it came to be known later on was supposedly given to man by nature so that he could comprehend "justice" that was valid for all men and for all times. It was there in every man, waiting to be discovered by him through the powers of "right reasoning." In this era the disintegration of Western empire was followed by a period of anarchy and widespread brutality of man to his fellowman. It was a period man probably had never known before. This period was essentially offensive to the practice or growth of international law. However, in the midst of the so-called establishment of "Barbarian" kingdoms in the "civilized" world of the past, Roman law was preserved and supplemented by the laws invaders brought with them. As time passed, the two legal systems merged frequently resulting into a synthesis such as Frankish laws, Neustrian laws, and Bargdian laws.

Contrary to the common belief the period of the Middle Ages did contain some of the seeds of modern international law. The following factors of the past were important in this respect: the existence of a single religion, the powerful role of the church further buttressed by the fact that it had the powers of excommunication, the centralized administrative institutions, a single set of laws called the canon laws applicable to all of the Church's believers irrespective of their race, nationality, or place of birth. The "ecclesiastial law," as it was also called, had a profound impact in many areas considered today under the domain of modern international law, areas such as observance of treaties, territorial boundry agreements, the right to make war with the approval of the Church, and the role of Papacy in the arbitration of international disputes. During this period the repeated but unsuccessful attempts of the church to abolish private wars altogether and to mitigate the evils of the so-called legitimate international conflict were the high points for the forces of law and order.

The layman "lawyers" during this period rediscovered Roman law and also made some contributions to the growth of modern international law. They argued that Roman law was the law of Christian Western world because of the "fact" that the emperor was the lineal successor of the Roman emperors. More significant than such dubious reasoning was the remarkable development of international commercial laws many of which remain in force today; for example, by the use of binding legal norms developed through treaties, businessmen living in foreign countries were accorded some privileges, and the "most favored nation" clause was developed. In other words, there were significant developments in the norms of private international law. For the first time legal codes of the sea, such as the Rhodes, Amalfi, Barcelona, and the Hanseatic League were developed and practiced.[9] Detailed rules governing the diplomatic conduct were enacted.[10] Toward the close of the period of the Middle Ages the modern states begun to appear in Italy and in other parts of Europe, thus undermining the political authority of the Church, a process that rapidly escalated in part because of the Reformation. Then came the period of religious wars and the infamous Thirty Years War that set new standards of brutality and ruthlessness in armed conflicts, which prompted many writers of law to admit that international law is "dead" and that man has forsaken the principles of "right" and "fairness" in war. Even the father of modern international law, Hugo Grotius, himself expressed deep concern about the future of law.[11]

Early modern era

The roots of modern international law historically took hold some time in the sixteenth century, but it was not until middle of the seventeenth century that they begun to bear fruit. Just about this time the medieval international system begun to crumble and with it the traditional units of Christendom and the role of the papacy as an arbiter of secular disputes among states. As the modern nation-states system emerged full-blown first in the shape of England, France, and Spain, the secular rulers refused to recongnize the authority of the Pope in the political affairs of their states, which included international affairs and the role of international law in it. Just about the same time a growing number of scholars begun to write about international law. *Perhaps the most significant event of the century was the beginning of secularism in European politics and its impact on the growth of modern international law*

In fact, the contemporary theory of international law had its beginnings in the emergence of this secularism in the shape of nation-state system and its evolution since then to the present times. This development of secularism and international law can be viewed in three distinct phases of history. The *first* phase lasted from the Renaissance to the Con-

[9]For an interesting discussion in this area see the work of J. H. Wigmore, A *Panorama of the World's Legal System* (St. Paul, Minn.: West), 1929, pp. 875–929.

[10]These rules generally are still with us today. See, for instance, G. H. Stuart, *American Diplomatic and Counselor Practices* (New York: Appleton-Century-Crofts) second edition, 1952, pp. 118–123.

[11]Hugo Grotius, *The Classic of International Law*, translated by F. W. Kelsey, (Oxford, England: Clarendon), 1925, 2 volumes.

gress of Vienna. The *second* phase roughly from 1815 to the First World War, and the *third* phase from the First World War to the present. We shall consider all three of these phases in detail.

International law before 1815. It was a period of natural law and the laws of nations. In this period philosophers desperately searched for a *unifying theory of human relations* to replace the already crumbling, once unifying theory of the institutions of Christianity. They found this in the universal laws of nature. During this period three significant considerations had their impact on the development of international law.

First, international law was regarded as an essential part of universal law of nature. There was no systematic creation of a legal order based on the philosophy of natural law as usually was the case with domestic legal systems, but as the old Christian-oriented political systems broke down, writers of those times sought to legitimize new developments by rationalizing the existence of secular states. Important legal (political) questions were asked: for instance, by what authority and right do the monarchs rule? What are their obligations to other monarchs, to the Church, to God, and to their subjects? This was one of the most fascinating periods of European history. Language and thought increasingly became secular, religious conflicts became national conflicts, concerns with otherworldly values became concerns with world values and, most important, the *a priori* reasoning that characterized the church thinking for a long period of time finally gave way to a rapidly developing faith in empiricism. Thinkers of late Renaissance and the Age of Reason sought universally valid legal norms on which not only the modern international law but *all* law could be based. The sacred duty to obey the king became the sacred duty to revolt against arbitrary rules, an interesting notion that was later formalized in the political theories of "consent" and "right of revolution." In international affairs Hugo Crotius translated these concepts into notions of "just wars" versus "unjust wars." The fundamental point here is the prevailing belief of this time that the law of nations that was based on reason among all men should be equally observed by all states. *Thus natural law became international law.* It was immutable.

Second, during this period much of domestic and international law was based upon customs and common conceptions of morality. In other words, not too many laws at this time were deliberately created to implement society's values. Most laws simply grew out of custom, usage, and habit. Obviously, the processes through which laws could be constructed were not highly formalized or even rationalized. The bureaucratic procedures as we know them today in law-making process were simply unheard of. This was also the age of European colonialism. Laws governing colonial claims and possessions were developed reflecting essentially the attitudes of major colonial powers. Laws of the seas were developed pretty much under the supervision of Britain, which in reality ruled the seas through much of the modern period. The United States and then later England pressed for laws guaranteeing the freedom of the seas, which were subsequently established.[12] A great many of the writings in international law during this period, dealt with the rules of warfare.

Finally, the precious little institutional context of law that existed in this period should be remembered. In the field of foreign affairs the monarchs' exclusive right to make and conduct foreign policy was generally accepted. Politics was the business of very few people and international politics of still fewer. International law required that states in their mutual relations always act *justly, morally* and, above all, with *reason*. In a real sense the role of the scholars and jurists was more than just interpreting existing legal norms. They played a sort of legislative role. They discussed customs, derived principles from the past practices, and developed new norms through analogy and reason and frequently advised the king on legal matters. Thus during this period the "laws of nations" were essentially viewed as a part of "laws of nature," and the men of knowledge simply based their existence on reason, a universal moral code, and the necessities of their times.

International law from the Congress of Vienna to the First World War. During this period of roughly 100 years from 1818 to 1914, the "law of nations" became the "international law" according to most scholars; that is, many aspects of its universal system of justice were translated into particular rules of international law governing the relations of sovereign states. There were several factors that contributed to this change. The Congress of Vienna is a generally accepted convenient point of departure because it symbolized what was to come. In this Congress major nations, mostly European, assembled to legislate new international laws not just for Europe, but for the entire world. Thus, the Congress marked the formal recognition of an international system based around European powers that was central to world politics until the Second World War. International law in this period, naturally, had to fit the circumstances of European international politics or risk neglect. In terms of new laws, nothing that could not satisfy the needs of European system could possibly emerge as international law.

The above restriction on the development of international law imposed two conditions that are still very much reflected on the body of its rules today. First, international law had to recognize the nature of the Euro-

---

[12]See A. Pearce Higgins and C. J. Colombas, *The International Law of the Seas* (London: Longmans, Green), 1943, pp. 37–57.

pean international system and be compatible with it. It was a political system in which a selected number of states operated. These states were competitive, highly suspicious of each other and were quite opportunistic in their political alignments with each other. It was a system commonly known as the "balance of power" system. Second, international law also had to be compatible with the value system these states shared. In both of these respects, *international law became Europeanized*. Its European-ization was made clear by several nineteenth-century writers. A clear emphasis developed that international law was the law of "civilized nations." Many early American scholars made use of such phrases as the "law of Christian Nations," meaning, again, "civilized nations." Time and again it was made clear that the application of law was limited to the people of Europe and people of their origin, which included the white dominions of the British Empire and, of course, the United States.

Certainly, international law was *always* of European origins *in reality*, but under the natural law theory it had maintained this charade of being "universal," equally applicable to all men and nations alike. But now, perhaps for the first time, the rest of the world learned in no uncertain terms of the racist aspect of European international law. The European custom and race-based international law was superimposed by force or fiat on other nations and thus it became "internationalized" *in a sense*.

In this period there were several other significant developments that contributed to this transformation of the "law of nations" to "inter-national law." The first and most obvious development was the rapid *growth of nationalism* and the tendency of the state to consider itself the sole recipient of citizens' loyalties and in return the sole provider of their security, social solidarity, and "happiness." As a result of the growth of nationalism, the strong concept of *consent* emerged. It was argued that state being the supreme body could not be forced into accepting any international law that has not been willed, acknowledged, or consented to by the state. Second, there was the growth in *democratic ideology and practice* in one form or the other, resulting in an increased participation of people in politics and in the demands of various groups for more pre-dictability in their relations with each other. This had a dramatic impact on the growth of legal institutions both national and international. Vari-ous businesses and other interest groups insisted that states create new laws concerning international trades, prices, tariffs, cartels, etc., and develop means to enforce them. Third, the industrial revolution caught on, bringing more demands for the development of new laws and the codification of existing norms. To conclude, during this period of roughly 100 years, international law formally became Europeanized with racial overtones and became a conscious and deliberate process. It acquired structure and rules or principles. In other words, it became more than simply indulging into right reasoning and doing justice, and much more than looking to various customs, precedents, and common morality for the purpose of resolving disputes.

During this period the positivist school of international law became prominent. This school believed that laws are manmade and are arrived at through consent. This school called these laws volitional laws, which later came to be known as positive law. The positivist school is divided into two subschools called the dualist and the monoist. The dualists contend that domestic and international laws have separate sources. With regard to domestic law they argue it has a source in "higher" legal authority such as a legislator or in the case of interpretation of customary laws, the courts. With regard to international law, they contend that states are essentially sovereign and, as such, they are above the law. Only *through their consent* they become bound by the dictates of laws. This position on consent has caused several problems. If consent is an important factor concerning the acceptability of international law, then do the new states coming into the society of nations really consent to accept international law? There are a number of states that were carved out of the territories of older states, for example, Pakistan, Israel, Indonesia, Malaysia, and Libya. If they do consent, then to what laws and what is the evidence of such consent? In the past there were occasions when nations, because of political-military circumstance, were in fact forced to conclude treaties against their will. As a result of these unequal treaties international law had the opportunity to grow further. Are the laws of these treaties binding? What if a state wishes to withdraw its consent?

The monoist school believes that all law, both domestic and international, has a common source, and this common source may be what is called "right," which according to one author in this school is an *innate psychological quality of man*. Another monoist sees the international law flowing from the *sentiment of social solidarity*. The logic here is that rules are followed because they are necessary for the existence of the social group. Still another monoist has advanced what is called a "pure theory of law" suggesting that all law has its source in an axiom or first legal principle that is outside the formal body of law. This argument amounts to suggesting that custom is the most important law creating source. On the question of sovereignty the monoists say it is simply a legal "right" or "freedom" that is given to states by international law or, to put it another way, what the international law does not forbid states to do, it permits them to do, and this is the area of national sovereignty.

During this period under the impact of positivism there was a general rejection of ethical jurisprudence. Although the positivists did not reject "custom" as a proper source of law, they insisted on several qualifications. For instance, a custom to become law must have a *wide acceptance*. With regard to the precedents of the past they argued that before these could become a source of law, they must be based on a *binding legal norm.* Needless to say, this requirement, conceptually related to notions of consent and contract, makes it extremely difficult to know in the absence of a treaty or a formal agreement which custom reflects international law and which does not.

Partly because of the above reasons put forward by the positivists and partly because of the impact of domestic laws that were at this time increasingly based on more formal and precise norms, the latter part of the nineteenth century saw a rapid formalization of international law. This was the beginning of an ever-increasing complex of formal international agreements or legislation. As international affairs became more institutionalized, elaborate treaties were negotiated and signed with regard to trade, navigation in international waterways, diplomatic protocol, and rights and privileges and immunities to aliens under international law. As a result of these developments, new treaties and interpretation of old treaties became one of the most important sources of international law. Since more treaties are negotiated on political grounds than on any other consideration, at the close of this period international law became a matter of *formal political consensus and not of universal moral principles.*

International law since 1914. In the past half century the formal concepts and sources of international law have changed far less dramatically than has the nature of international politics, as indicated earlier. Today, we are still accustomed to thinking of international law as principles governing the conduct of sovereign states who have agreed to international obligations under these principles and, in the absence of principles in other areas, these states are free to act as they please. The "legality" of many of the past norms is in doubt today because there are many new non-European nations under the domain of law. Today, more than ever, the international society is made up of theoretically equal, independent, and sovereign states. Even though the international politics of these non-Western states and their supporting institutions have created many challenges to existing international legal norms, the response of international law has been slow, but the unmistakeable signs of changes and new developments in law are already here. Efforts are already well underway toward devising new legal theories, approaches and conceptual frameworks, and the appropriate legal institutions along with, of course, the presence of revised and new norms.

Perhaps the "failure" of international society to create an entirely new and appropriate system of norms and legal institutions to insure a better management of international affairs is not a failure at all. Instead, it is the fantastic speed of change in international politics that is the real culprit that makes all progress in the area of law and institutions look insignificant. There is no doubt the dynamics of international politics has succeeded in overshadowing the considerable progress that has been made in the development of international law in the past 50 years. Today, among other things, we have a variety of international bodies that constantly redefine the boundaries of an expanding international system and thus contribute to international law. For example, any theory of international relations that views the contemporary international system as the exclusive domain of nation-states, at the exclusion of individuals and many international organizations, no longer reflects the realities of international life. It is a theory that has already been left behind in the history.

Perhaps Woodrow Wilson was not a dreamer after all as some "realists" have said. International politics and law have followed in recent decades the direction he outlined in his Fourteen Points. For instance, there has been a reemergence of strong moral convictions suggesting that the problems of humanity are world problems. There has been a reemergence of eighteenth-century faith in reason in the form of "world public opinion." Today's international law reflects some of these recurring trends in international affairs. It is a curious mixture of eighteenth-century reason and nineteenth-century democractic belief as translated into its body of rules, suggesting, for instance, that peace can be built not so much on *power relations* but on the *unreasonableness of war* and that all nations of the world should be free from outside domination not because they are *capable of politically and economically governing their affairs* but because they have the *right of self-determination* and national independence.

Today, as it will be indicated in details in the next chapter, the nature of contemporary international politics has made international law a positive instrument of public policy. International law has once again become concerned with human values. It is an instrument of social engineering, a method of distributing and redistributing world resources, a protection of individualism and human rights. It has, in fact, become a dynamic *process* instead of a body of *formal, static rules* in the midst of world affairs.

Present sources of international law

There are several meanings attached to the term "sources" of international law. Several scholars have used it to emphasize the theoretical foundations of international law in general. Others have used the term to describe the more contemporary "sources" of specific rules, embracing "evidences" of international law. It is desirable, however, to distinguish between "source" and "evidence." The first concept refers to the *original establishment* of a norm while the latter simply points to the fact that *proof* exists or does not exist concerning the validity of the norm. The mergence of the two sometimes in court's decisions does take place.

Furthermore, a common difficulty is experienced by the students of international law and judges in locating the specific norms of international law that may be applicable to an international dispute at hand. Despite many efforts made by individual scholars and some success achieved by the United Nation's International Law Commission to compile codes of law on specific subjects, the difficulty remains. One is still confronted with an overabundance of legal material written in languages one may not know, even if he simply wishes to locate the sources of the existence of a legal norm, to say nothing about the task of actually determining the proper rule that may apply to a particular dispute. For the determination of various sources of international law for our purposes, Article 38 of the Statute of International Court of Justice is of some help. According to this Article there are three major sources of international law and two subsidiary means for the determination of the rules of law. The listing in this Article is by no means exhaustive. In any case, some of the pertinent present sources of law are discussed in following sections.

International custom

Customary international law consists of legal norms that came into existence through general usage and practice over fairly long periods of time. It is difficult to set a specific number on years that must lapse before a custom or practice becomes a law. The real test seems to be its political acceptability by sufficient number of states. It must receive sanction of the members of the international society. This principle is illustrated in the famous *The Paquete Habana and the Lola, 1900* case, where the United States Supreme Court ruled that the ancient custom of exempting the coastal fishing vessels together with their cargo as prize of war has been commonly practiced by *many* nations for a *long* period of time and, therefore, it deserves recognition as a rule of international law. Notice that even the Communist nations recognize the existence of custom as an important source of law.

The major disadvantage in using custom as a source of international law is that here law develops very slowly. Besides, in order to acquire a secure status in the body of law, quite frequently, a customary international law has to wait until it is formally recognized through treaties or courts decisions. On the other hand, there have been more recent instances where customs were rapidly solidified in law. Consider, for instance, the principle of national sovereignty over territorial air space, or the custom of national sovereignty over the continental shelf. In both of these instances the interest of the international community developed so quickly that appropriate laws, based on custom, were readily developed. One of the most widely quoted international laws that has its origins in custom is *pacta Sunta servanda*, meaning that there is a long-standing state obligation, based on custom, to abide by the terms of agreements. That is, when treaties have been agreed to, and ratified, all parties have a legal obligation under customary rules to uphold them. Custom as a source of international law is still very much with us.

International treaties and conventions

International treaties and conventions are also major sources of international law. There are hundreds of formal agreements among states, establishing the rules and obligations that they must observe in their mutual relationships. Treaties may be signed by two or more states resulting either in particular international laws, if fewer states have signed them, or in general international laws, if many states have agreed to them. Some scholars have referred to treaties as a source of conventional law. However, while some treaties do contribute to the growth of international law, a great many do not. For instance, a commercial treaty signed by the People's Republic of China and Pakistan, a military assistance alliance between the United States and Turkey, or an extradition treaty, possibly between Cuba and the United States will not create new international law. These treaties strengthen the existing laws by using them. These treaties are, more correctly, testimonials to the *existence* of international law.

Only multilateral treaties either signed or ratified, by *large* number of sovereign states can be regarded as lawmaking treaties. These treaties tend to have, by virtue of their significance, worldwide or nearly worldwide implications. The Non-Proliferation of Nuclear Weapons Treaty, Limited Nuclear Test Ban Treaty, the Arctic and Antarctic Treaties, and treaties forbidding the placing of weapons of mass destruction in outer space, on the ocean floor, and on the seabed are good examples of lawmaking treaties. These treaties are unique because they are used as an instrument through which a substantial number of sovereign states declare their understanding and accept a set of particular conduct that in the future will have the force of law. This set of conduct may abolish some existing custom or law, or modify it, or add an entirely new law to the existing body of law. Usually, only through such treaties, are the norms of conventional international law created. Initially, the norms embodied in these treaties are binding only on those states who have either signed them or ratified them at a later date. If the initial number of countries agreeing to one of these treaties is small, the treaty creates norms of particular international law, applicable perhaps to a region or the disputants involved in a particular controversy. With the passage of time more states may ratify this treaty, and this treaty may contribute to the development of general international law. A formal acceptance by all nations is not necessary, however. Even if there has been an increasing acquiescence to its principles by additional states, it tends to become part of general international law. But, it should be remembered, if a state *specifically* refuses to accept the provisions of this treaty or even refuse to acquiesce to it, this state will not *normally* be bound by the norms the treaty creates.

Treaties are the best instrument for continuously updating the rules of international law. The main reason is that unlike court decisions or custom, treaties can be legislated and the underlying political process can be completed relatively quickly, somewhat like the process of domestic lawmaking and unmaking. This is, of course, not to imply that international "legislative" process can be equated with the domestic legislative process. There are marked differences. For example, in the international arena the "majority rule" as applied to the enactment of laws in the domestic political system (at least in democracies) and a binding obligation to uphold the laws once enacted, whether one disagreed with them or not, *simply does not exist*. Some scholars in their zest to find similarities between the domestic and international lawmaking process have gone too far in comparing the states in the international society with the legislators in a democratic domestic society. This appears to be true, particularly when we consider the present illegal practices, attitudes, and general standards of behavior in foreign affairs of some of these states.

History of the growth of international law indicates during the past 150 years many remarkable lawmaking treaties have appeared in the international system that have broadened the scope of international law.[13] These treaties can be divided roughly into three categories: (1) Many of these treaties, as pointed out earlier, transfer the existing customary norms or the norms developed by one of the many judicial organizations, into statutory international laws.[14] (2) Some lawmaking treaties simply interpret and apply existing norms to specific disputes, issues, or the content

[13]A comprehensive list of these treaties, for example, will include the famous 1960 Vienna Convention of Diplomatic Privileges and Immunities, the United Nations Charter, the Geneva Conventions of 1949 (regulation of certain aspects of war, including the treatment of prisoners of war, etc.) and 1958 Agreement on the Law of the Sea, etc.; please see the works of Charles De Visscher, *Theory and Reality in Public International Law* (Princeton, N.J.: Princeton University Press), 1957, pp. 44–46.

[14]A good example of this will be the Final Act of the Congress of Vienna in 1815, Articles 108, 117, and 118. The rules governing freedom of navigation on international waterways were codified here, and the principles relating to diplomatic representation were classified.

of an older treaty, and in the process of interpretation and application of the norm, they sometimes *add new dimensions* to the existing law through emphasis or deemphasis of the past norms. This is done essentially without creating new principles of international law.[15] (3) Many lawmaking treaties combine two or more of the above functions.[16]

Here, a brief comment should also be made concerning the impact of a multitude of various resolutions and declarations passed by many international organizations and other bodies endowed with a legal character concerning the growth of international law. There is no clear consensus in the writings of leading scholars concerning their role. A major part of the problem seems to be that resolutions and declarations require no formal ratification by states and as such cannot be favorably compared with treaties. On the other hand, they do represent a consensus among states, a meeting of minds, and an understanding. At least in one region of the world they are taken so seriously that they are regarded as having the binding force of the law. This is the case in Latin America, where one finds them in abundance. Because of this unusual and remarkable development in this part of the world, I can only conclude that if consensus among the states of a region concerning the binding nature of resolutions and declarations exists, they can be regarded as contributing to regional or particular international law. It is reasonable to speculate that many of present-day international laws may have been initially created through such method.

Decisions of the courts

Court decisions, popularly known as "landmark" decisions, are regarded as a third major source of international law. Decisions of this nature, depending on the authority and jurisdictions of the court, may well be binding in the specific cases in which the court was involved. But they have an impact beyond these cases. Such decisions set precedents for future cases. The assumption is that once the precedent is set, the court has an obligation to adhere to this precedent. These precedents later get translated into law.

Some judicial systems conform rather closely to precedents; others do not. There are, of course, several types of courts involved in decision making in this area. Some cases are decided upon in national courts but, because of their overlapping content, they have definite implications for

[15]A few examples of these types of treaties would be: The Convention concerning the international circulation of motor vehicles, signed in 1909, the International Opium Convention of 1912, and the Convention on International Civil Aviation.

[16]The famous four Geneva Conventions of 1949 and an earlier convention on laws and customs of war are fair examples of multipurpose treaties.

international law. Many cases are decided upon by international courts of adjudication. A few are settled in arbitration tribunals. Regardless of the court involved, precedent is used in varying degrees in all courts. An analysis of the records of the International Court of Justice certainly indicates that its contemporary thinking is considerably influenced by its earlier decisions. It will be only fair to suggest that the advisory opinions of the past Permanent Court of International Justice and the present International Court of Justice have made a profound impact on the growth of international law. Besides these two courts, the judgments and the awards of the Permanent Court of Arbitration, the Mixed Claim Commission, and several other international tribunals have also in varying degrees, influenced the development of international law. On the domestic scene, the United States Supreme Court has played an impressive role in influencing the course of international law.

Decisions of "courts" fall into two areas: first, decisions of national courts of major powers and, second, decisions of international courts. The domestic courts' decisions, while primarily concerned with municipal law, do influence international law through their interpretation of points in international law, which may have a bearing on the case at hand. For instance, the American casebook method of teaching international law, now not so common, was frequently based on analysis of domestic cases with international significance. The decisions of international courts can be divided into two categories: (1) adjudication and (2) arbitration. In both situations states agree in advance, first, that the dispute be submitted to a court and, second, that the decisions be applicable only to the case involved.

Writings of leading scholars and jurists

Over the years men of judicial training and knowledge have exerted considerable influence on the development of international law. Their judgments and interpretations in the non-Communist societies are generally taken seriously by courts and by the policymakers. Their approach is essentially this: persuasion through arguments, presentation of evidence, development of analogies, etc. In court cases, the opinions of leading international law scholars are quoted as an authoritative source and pertinent evidence. Their opinions at times have influenced the thinking of national leaders and thus altered the course of foreign affairs. Usually, scholarly writings either clarify or confirm international laws of customs. These writings may offer interpretations of various treaties and court decisions. But on other occasions their writings have broken fresh ground, raised controversies within the discipline, and forged new directions in legal thinking. At times this has been done through conjecture and analogy without breaking away from the past. Other times, entirely new, somewhat revolutionary, positions have been adopted under the impact of "new realism" in the study of international law.

Other sources and evidences of law

During early period in the history of development of modern international law, there was a frequent reliance on "principles" as the true source of international law. For instance, in the rather colorful history of that time the great scholars and statesmen alike used the principle of "natural law." It was argued strongly, that "right" and "justice" existed in the nature of things, and all that was needed is to discover them and apply them in the relations of men. This raised questions concerning the "how" of discovery. The answer was simple enough; all that was needed, it was suggested once again, was the use "right reasoning." Anyhow the notion of "principles" played an extremely significant role in the works of Hugo Grotius.

Another use of the term "principles" of international law refers to the adoptions of fundamentals of Roman laws to the urgent needs of the international society. International society's reliance on the Roman law at the time was understandable because it needed more legal norms to function satisfactorily. Principles of Roman law, by this time, were fairly well developed and had international legal implications. They were also, it was generally believed, based on, or synonymous with, the principles of natural law. So it was only logical that this source be used for the development of early modern international law.

Another source of international law is official government documents, for example, the State Department's "White Papers," explanatory notes, diplomatic correspondence, decisions of the Attorney General, and key statements of international actors. All of these sources have some influence on the direction that international law takes. For instance, if an official correspondence, a public statement by an international leader, or a significant policy pronouncement is accepted or supported by several other states, even if this acceptance is based only on purely political considerations, at some future date this acceptance may acquire the force of law.

Still another source is the draft conventions sponsored by leading law schools, proposals of various international law societies and organizations, for the creation of new legal norms, united expression of several countries of what they believe to be a customary international norm with binding quality. All of these sources, for example, conventions, proposals, symposiums, draft resolutions, which may never get ratified, are not of course international law per se. Yet they have an impact on international law, which is admittedly difficult to measure. In any case, they usually are the best available and most current expression of customary law and, thus, have a persuasive influence on international law.

Realities of political acceptability

The above listing of many sources of international law will certainly be incomplete without discussing the *political* sources of international law. It is clear that the application of legal rules must be politically acceptable. This may entail several things, for example, special acceptance of a treaty, an implied or expressed act of "giving in" for whatever political reason, to a custom, or a principle or practice, and supporting a political act that has implications for the development of legal norms, such as a United Nations peacekeeping operation. Since international law cannot be simply viewed or analyzed in terms of its technical construction alone, it is important to understand its political sources. It is also just as important that political considerations should not be given such a significance where violations of international law, for whatever political reasons, are regarded as failures of international law.

A concluding remark

Obviously, the commonality of attitudes, national interests, and value systems play a determining role in the making and unmaking of international law. However, a characterization of law as a dynamic process with developmental potential through foreign policy decision making, should not overshadow the fact that there are portions in the body of legal norms that are relatively stable and specific. These portions contain central norms, and most decision makers would not dare violate them. At the same time, these central norms are just that, "central." They are not a "body of static rules," a notion that has increasingly failed us in our attempts to understand the law-politics relationship.

While much of international law operates in the midst of a highly politically charged environment, many of its "other" norms are well established and continuously observed. Many of these norms are procedural or business norms. Hence, the legal nature and the obligatory force of these norms is well recognized by men responsible for their nation's international affairs. This common recognition by policymakers of the binding nature of law makes it more than mere "right standards of behavior." Standards of behavior may have their sources in international ethics or morality and, as such, they do not create a recognized legal obligation to uphold them unless they are translated into international law. The binding nature of international law also distinguishes it from what is called international comity, which is nothing more than a set of practices that two states follow in their mutual relationship as a matter of courtesy or necessity. For example, the United States allows Canadian citizens to enter and travel freely in its territory without a passport for short periods of time and vice versa, but neither side extends this privilege to citizens of other states. Apart from the significance of a successful political process, the nature of international law and its development are also conditioned by its international sociological environment. An analysis of its development in a historical context reveals how strongly the character of international society during various historical periods has impressed itself on international law.

International law is concerned, either directly or by implication, with a wide range of national activity. These activities may range from that of an individual to that of a state or a public international organization, encompassing millions of lives. It is therefore not a static abstract concept, or an artificial judicial proceeding isolated from the dynamics of power politics. When properly understood with all its commitments and procedures, international law offers a continuous formulation and reformulation of policies.

International law has been justifiably subjected to abuse by some states; it has been challenged and attacked. But it is also true that many states have often religiously followed it whatever their reasons. However, despite a lot of idle talk about peaceful settlements of international disputes and offers of peaceful coexistence that the superpowers have made to each other, wars have broken out, and some of the most fundamental precepts of international law have been violated. In contrast, some members of the international community do submit their disputes to impartial third-party adjudications either by the International Court of Justice or by Arbitral Tribunals. Although some international crises can be best resolved by political solutions alone, this is nothing new. In the past there were always such disputes, but law was not going through a period of "crisis." In any case, despair over the role of law in today's world is not justified. Certainly, there has been some intensification of lawless tendencies in specific areas of international relations, but in most of these instances the international laws that are frequently violated are the laws of the past, whose existence is being challenged by radical changes in the international system, including the entry of many new states. Although we cannot condone law violations, in these instances we can have a greater understanding of the problems involved and maybe even an appreciation of the need for more just laws.

In our present mood of disillusionment it is extremely important that we resist the temptation to minimize the role that international law plays in world affairs and the role that it could easily play with a stronger commitment by its most important subjects, for example, nation-states, to uphold its main values. At least part of the "crisis" of international law is nothing more than the "growing pains" of a relatively under-developed system of law. In fact, there are good reasons to be hopeful about the future of international law. Consider, for instance, its remark-able expansion in a relatively short period of time into the so-called "frontier areas" of law (e.g., outer space, the ocean floor and the seabed) in the United Nations peacekeeping operations, and currently in the field of arms control and disarmament. Consider also the widespread and sustained efforts that are being made on its behalf to clarify the un-certainties of its past laws and resolve one of its age old dilemmas, for example, conflicting interpretations of its rules.

It is a mistake to say "if law is law," all of it must be observed; otherwise there is no law at all. It is a greater mistake to equate the failures of certain nations at certain times to observe certain laws with the failure of law itself, or to suggest that the law no longer exists. It is also a mistake to put too much emphasis on the fact that without the enforcement mechanism a law is useless. The truth is that no system of law regardless of how advanced or primitive, simple or complicated it may be, whether domestic, regional, or general international law, depends *entirely* for its effectiveness on the use of force or the fear of punishment. Coercion is only a very small part of the *incentive* that is needed to per-suade an individual an organization, or a state to observe law. Surely the benefits derived by a state in observing a law, whether immediate or long term, are bound to figure more heavily in the minds of decision makers than a fear of punishment, when they face the question to observe or not to observe a particular law in a specific situation.

International Law and National Behavior in Different Area Issues

chapter 4

international law
and the management
of violence

The present era of international politics is characterized by many fervent hopes for a more peaceful world and yet a perennial fear of a possible nuclear war. It is an era of extremely rapid international actions and reactions that characterize the everyday process of making foreign policy and implementation—a process that is not entirely understood by the policymakers themselves and is still less under their full control. The logic of the present era is perhaps best expressed in the language of political conflict. The era is slowly being transformed by increasing competition among states and occasional active cooperation because they are not yet linked by a strong consensus or a central common authority.

International law recognizes these "facts of life" and works through the dynamics of these and the many other forces to be found in the international system. As a result of its association with international politics it carrys in its body of rules some scars inflicted by the general persistence of war. But at the same time it has succeeded in no uncertain terms in harnessing and channeling some of the uncontrollable forces that are released by the interaction among states in the international arena.

This chapter considers the dynamics of law-politics relationship in the management of international conflict in several contexts. Before these contexts are described and analyzed we might keep in mind a number of points about this relationship. First, there is little doubt that how a particular state decides to act in regard to an issue on which international law has some bearing is in part determined by the conditions and status of the law itself. Law and politics are not always at odds with each other, and they are not mutually exclusive. In fact, international law is the by-product of international politics and because of its deep political conception, neither politics nor law are insentitive to each other.

Much of the business of foreign offices and their embassies and consulates is essentially a noncrisis business, and is regularly conducted without much fanfare by the application of norms and procedures of international law. Many important activities of the international system, without which the world as we know it today simply could not exist (e.g., international trade, travel, economic assistance programs, diplomacy, and international communications) are effectively regulated by international law. This does not imply that foreign policy invariably is determined by legal factors alone; political, economic, military, and other factors often work to minimize the role that law plays, but in almost all issues legal norms do matter and the extent of their influence is determined by the nature of issues involved.

At the same time, the authority of international law, its respect, and relevance, if not its survival, depends on its ability to address itself frequently to the needs of its times. Law has changed in recent eras and will certainly respond to the current political system that is marked by revolutionary transformations and ideological conflicts, that have challenged some of its traditional norms as irrelevant, falling in disrepute, and expendable to make room for new norms. Regardless of these challenges and the capacity of international law to accommodate them, one thing is clear: contrary to all the dire predictions of law critics, it has not folded up, gone under, or been rendered useless. It is still very much in the business of regulating interstate behavior.

Our purpose here is to analyze several significant present trends in the law-politics relationship in the management of conflicts that are made necessary by the dynamics of the international system. We shall conduct our analysis by concentrating on the trends or functions of law that seem important: the functions through which international law currently plays, has begun to play or could play an important role (with some international systemic changes) in the management of conflict. These functions are (1) instilling an attitude of dissillusionment mixed with a rapidly emerging hope concerning the role of law in conflict management; (2) present techniques and mechanisms in the management of conflict; (3) the role of the United Nations peacekeeping operations in the management of conflict.

These are some of the more important contexts in which international law by virtue of its own dynamics, has exhibited a concern through its norms and procedures, and seeks to impose a framework of "law management," the legal structure of which is derived through international consensus. By the term "law management" it is not meant that law can be a supranational governmental control that can manage conflict. More simply, the term is intended to mean the establishment, through legal processes, of *patterns of predictability and expectations* by states in their international conduct. Remember that law and politics do not confront each other in a vacuum. They operate within the international system that contains many "other" forces including several global value goals.[1] Both law and politics attempt to satisfy these goals and sometimes in the process conflict with each other, and at other times, compliment each other, but most of the time they do influence each other. The actual processes by which international politics and international law interact in the complexities of the international system are complex themselves. However, the outcome is clear. Out of this interaction, on the one hand, new modes of state behavior emerge that change the nature of international politics, on the other hand, a mixture of revised and new norms of law may also emerge that change the content of international law and make it more relevant to the needs of its times.

International law and management of international conflict—a mixture of disillusionment and rising hopes

Management of international conflict, or its resolution, is one of the most important problems of contemporary international society and thus of international law. Criticism has been consistently levied against international law both in the public press and within the discipline to the effect that "once again law has failed to deter armed conflict." Indeed, in an international society that is armed with nuclear weapons and thus forced to live under a constant threat of war, the success or failure of the management of conflict seems to be the most important yardstick by which all attempts to create a more peaceful world have been measured. This yardstick has been applied to the activities of the United Nations and its peacekeeping initiatives, to the ongoing disarmament and arms control negotiations at various levels, and to the role of international law in conflict management. There seems to be a fundamental consensus among all concerned on at least one job that international law must do successfully—that at the very minimum it must eliminate the possibility of nuclear and general warfare and manage conflict at local and regional levels.

Beyond this fundamental consensus on its role, various spokesmen for

---

[1]Some of the global goals are: (1) A universal desire for national security. It is an urge in part, to escape the perils of a nuclear war that the weapons of mass destructions have made it a possibility. (2) A desire for the material improvement of the present standards of living. (3) A desire to maintain a global environment free of various kinds of pollution so that the human race could continue to live on this planet, etc.

law differ only in either overstating or understating the future potential and present capabilities of law in the contemporary international arena. In this area international law has suffered considerably from the hands of both types of well-meaning scholars and statesmen. Consider, for instance, the overstatement of the potential of law in curtailing international violence. Plan after plan for world disarmament has been presented in which international legal institutions occupy a prominent place. According to most of these proposals the present orthodox system of the maintenance of peace through military might is to be replaced with a system of law that will not only maintain peace and security but also create a world order with stability. It will be a system not devoid of force; instead, the element of force will be rooted in legal doctrines and institutions to locate disputes among states and impose sanctions through the use of a police force. The only problem with these plans is that none of them has ever been accepted by the superpowers or by other major powers. Governments have not yet developed sufficient confidence in alternatives to armed conflict for resolving all of their mutual differences. Note also that while nothing radical has happened to increase the possibility of "reliance on law" in international relations, the familiar rhetoric at many peace conferences concerning the control of violence through law has increased. Even the Soviet Union, which has a history of exhibiting suspicion and skepticism toward international organizations with even a moderate amount of independent authority (e.g., a U.N. with an international peacekeeping force with enforcement capability), has also presented disarmament proposals containing reliance on certain international laws, such as laws of coexistence and nonintervention. Many members of our profession have consistantly stressed the urgent need to move from a world of arms and power politics to a more peaceful world of law and order. It is sometimes argued that all we need are habits of obedience to the law throughout the international community, based on the development of an international political culture. But despite the rhetoric of public statements by national leaders or the submission of disarmament proposals and scholarly writings, the fact remains that more powerful states continue to run the show by claiming both the legal and political rights to make a greater number of decisions with more far-reaching consequences than has been true in the past three to four centuries. Both superpowers have invaded countries without the declaration of war and in what appears to be flagrant violation of international legal norms. Both sides have on occasions threatened a nuclear war and have taken it upon themselves to make unilateral decisions without regard to and in violation of the law, affecting the politics, economics, indeed, the very existence of many other smaller countries. The superpowers' behavior and their extravagant claims for the inherent right of self-judgment in every aspect of international life and society have damaged the chances for the development of a climate more conducive to the obedience of international law. The reality of our times seems to be that we continue to live under the shadow of two world wars and in the midst of all kinds of regional, local, and internal armed conflicts. Korea, Indo-China, the Middle East, and South Asia are only some of the more obvious arenas of international violence.

Ironically, there is another side of the picture that is sometimes overlooked in our current disillusionment with the apparent incapacity of law and politics to manage international conflict. For instance, while the superpowers have made the task of legal control of international violence more difficult, their mutual relations at the same time also show an emerging stability and predictability that can only be sustained through favorable legal expectations in the international system. As we prepare to enter the last quarter of this rather turbulent century there is some evidence (as it will be shown elsewhere) that the great power conflict that was responsible for two world wars is being resolved more rationally. At the same time there is relative stability at the superpower level because of the awareness that the nuclear weapons have been developed at a staggering cost to both nations in terms of the utilization of resources badly needed in other areas. This stability, based on a system of mutual deterrence, demands from its participants extreme caution, rational responses to fear, the ability to understand each other's threats and, above all, an ability to stabilize the mechanisms of deterrence during periods of regional crises when national interests make the temptation to "get directly involved" very strong. In order to meet the challenges of the possibility of a nuclear war, both superpowers have taken some steps to avert this possible catastrophy largely by internal checks. Both powers have instituted, for instance, a reliable technology of "command and control" to prevent an accidental war or a war initiated by unauthorized personnel and the establishment of a direct communications link between Moscow and Washington in order to prevent to the extent possible any misunderstanding or miscalculation of each other's intentions. Both nations, realizing the uncertainties and instabilities of the international system, now have *at least begun* to pay some attention to the further development of new international laws that are, of course, instruments of predictability that both superpowers need in the international system. This realization of the potential of international law is shared with varying degrees by all states, and it is a good sign for international law, because international law has always depended on the values and needs of the states and their bureaucracies to become more "relevant" to its times. Contemporary attitudes in the international society (despite a general reliance on weapons and conflicts) and the values and actions of the leaders are slowly but unmistakably changing to create a more favorable climate for the rule of law.

There are other hopeful signs. The process of international integration, communication, and the need for interdependence has been increasing for some time. In this area Western Europe has set the example for other regions to follow. The net result of these trends is to create a more favorable environment for peace and the role of international law. Also, this trend, in time, is bound to accelerate the transfer of some sovereignty from the nation-states to other international bodies and organizations. Already some of the regional international organizations such as the European Common Market have made an important impact. It is quite possible that before the beginning of the twenty-first century, not only the United Nations but many other international and transnational organizations, regional and worldwide, may come to assume many of the functions now performed entirely by national governments. It is also possible that the individual citizens may broaden their mental horizons to consider these international arrangements worthy of their personal loyalties.

Contemporary international legal system is devoted, among other things, to the management of world conflict. It is based on the recognition of state sovereignty and depends considerably on some of the time-honored legal processes of conflict resolution such as arbitration, judicial settlement, collective conciliation, and United Nations peacekeeping arrangements. These principles of conflict management shall be discussed in detail later in this chapter. But at this point it is important to remember that whatever new legal arrangements may be developed in the field of conflict management in the future, in all likelihood these arrangements will be the extensions and modifications of the present system. Several writers have attempted to isolate areas where modifications of existing norms are needed or the development of entirely new norms is considered feasible.

One of the areas frequently talked about is that of special international conventions designed specifically for the purpose of limiting the actions of states through mutual agreement concerning the use of strategic weapons. The major roadblock in the way of conflict management and international security has been the self-propelling armament race. Any attempt to curtail this race or actually to achieve disarmament will lead to the development of international laws of conflict management. A modest beginning in this area has already been made through the first Strategic Arms Limitation Treaty and several treaties signed prior to that, for example, The Limited Nuclear Ban Treaty and the Non-Proliferation Treaty. These accords are extremely modest; nonetheless, they do represent the emergence of a new consensus in this area.

Here are other areas that can contribute to the development of laws of conflict management. (1) The need to regard certain types of domestic activity as dangerous to the maintenance of international peace and security; thus they do not automatically fall under the so-called "exclusively domestic" jurisdiction. (2) An urgent need to monitor and curtail the international traffic in conventional arms. (3) A need to put some international control on the production and the separation of plutonium in connection with nuclear programs. Conceivably strict international laws could be developed and appropriately enforced against the violators. (4) On the political plane, certain types of civil wars may not be allowed to run their course without any intervention from an international body because the potential widening of the conflict may threaten international peace. (5) Specific laws could be developed against the treatment of minorities by states that are in stark violation of the very basic principles of human rights. For instance, in cases such as South Africa and its apartheid policy the United Nations resolutions and the public opinion have failed to persuade that government to change its policy of discrimination against the majority and as such tougher laws with enforcement action are needed to contain a possible future large-scale violence in that area. (6) Still another broad area is the formal and systematic review of existing norms of international law that are outdated and thus no longer reflect the true nature of modern international society. (7) To this task one can add the important job of law codification and the further development and elaboration of new norms of international law. Clearly, if the challenges of the future international conflicts are to be faced at all, new international consensus reflecting the present makeup of the international society will have to be developed, translated into legal norms, and ratified by national legislatures. Legal concepts such as the following may have to be *redefined* and included into the new laws: (1) legitimate national interests; (2) right of individual and collective self-defense, (3) the limits of one state's intervention into the domestic affairs of another state; (4) the proper role of regional defense organizations, called "security communities," such as the North Atlantic Treaty Organization or the Warsaw Pact, vis à vis the role of such universal international organizations as the United Nations in the management of international conflict; (5) a reinterpretation of relevant U.N. Charter provisions concerning United Nations peacekeeping efforts in the light of past experiences; and (6) a redefinition of the role of international law concerning such current practices as ceasefire and armistice boundaries, etc.

Perhaps the most difficult challenge facing international law in the field of conflict management is the *definition*, perhaps the further *elaboration*, of the basis of law itself. Law can no longer remain subservient to the sovereignty of nation-states for the simple reason that sovereign states have not been able to manage conflict in their international relations and now the very survival of these states themselves and of their inhabitants depend on the proposition that these states limit their sovereignty. This will allow the world society to develop meaningful legal norms based on the welfare of the human race rather than on useless notions of state sovereignty, the so-called state's "inherent right to be unpredictable," and to enforce these norms against international violence. Later, attempts still have to be made on behalf of the new laws of conflict management to inform all members of the international society (e.g., states, international organizations, and individuals) about the new rules and structures of law with the hope of persuading them to observe these rules in their own self-interest. To be sure, the task of communicating and creating a climate of opinion favorable for the observation of law will be made extremely difficult by many factors. Consider, for example, that we have today about 150 states with their own value systems and peculiar national interests as members of the international system. The incredible differences in attitude, political culture, race, political ideology, and economic development will not be easy to overcome, but the task is not impossible because all of mankind shares a desire for survival as well as other aspirations for the future and the present.

One need not to worry too much about the so-called "above the law" behavior that the superpowers exhibit in their support of local and regional conflicts. In the age of destructive weapons it may well be that the strong nations need international law more than the weak ones. Perhaps it is the most valid explanation for the broad consensus that is now emerging between the United States and the Soviet Union on the rejection of force in international affairs. Although enforcement mechanisms are neededd to a certain extent to make international law more effective, the real challenge of law is in identifying the legitimate expectations and demands of clients and providing satisfaction to them so that they will be encouraged to observe the law for their own good. There are hopeful signs of interest articulation, and aggregation of the international community aided by a developing system of international political culture. This system is slowly being articulated by a large body of international prescription that aims to establish certain standard norms against the use of violence. There are, of course, counterforces. But if this trend should continue, this prescription will later be internalized by individuals and supported by internal controls within the personality without the need for external controls such as force and coercion.

International law and present techniques and mechanisms of conflict management

Contemporary international law has affected both the intensity and the extent of armed conflict in the international system in several ways. It has, for instance, discouraged conflict by encouraging the disputants to rely on the various techniques used for the peaceful settlement of disputes, be they of nonjuridical or juridical nature. However, if once the conflict has been initiated, it then offers an elaborate set of legal rules and restrictions concerning, for example, the treatment of prisoners of war, protection of civilian life and property, status of neutral nations during the conflict and, above all, principles concerning the cessation of hostilities and enforcement of cease-fire agreements, etc.[2]

Many legal norms of the international law of conflict management combine the national interests of states and the interests of the international society at large. They satisfy both humanitarian concerns and motives inspired by legitimate national self-interest. This approach of international law has essentially meant, first, limiting the activities of states beyond their national frontiers. Second, it has meant preserving the laws of neutrality that can be invoked by any state in any conflict, which may succeed in limiting the scope of conflict. Of course, if there were an all-out nuclear conflict, it is doubtful just how many, if any, nations will be able to invoke neutrality and not suffer widespread destruction.[3] Apart from the possible universality of a nuclear war, the legal aspect of neutrality is clouded because under the provisions of the United Nations Charter, all member states are required to contribute their armed forces in the service of the United Nations if called upon. In other words, should the Security Council of the United Nations decide to establish a peacekeeping force with enforcement duties in a conflict situation and call on a neutral country to contribute its armed forces to this force, from the point of the United Nations Charter, this country cannot refuse, on the basis of neutrality principles.

Nonetheless, since the United Nations Charter apparently has not forced any country to contribute its armed forces to a United Nations mission against its will, many nations have recently found it useful to invoke the legal principles of neutrality in regional conflicts. Third, the contemporary international law has outlawed the use of certain types of

[2]See Greenspan, *The Modern Law of Land Warfare* (Washington, D.C.: U.S. Government Printing Office), 1957; see also Robert W. Tucker, *The Law of War and Neutrality at Sea* (Washington, D.C.: U.S. Government Printing Office), 1957.

[3]See G. Von Glahn, *Law Among Nations*, pp. 624–635.

weapons of modern warfare. For instance, weapons of radiological and bacteriological nature as well as certain deadly gas weapons have been outlawed.[4] A growing number of scholars led by Professor Richard A. Falk have argued that international law also forbids the use of nuclear weapons.[5]

Contemporary international law is also attempting to create an atmosphere of public opinion against wars in general. There is some evidence of change in the existing norms on this whole question of the legitimacy of war as an appropriate instrument of foreign policy. As far as the United States and to a lesser degree, perhaps, the Soviet Union are concerned, the present costly stalemate in the Indo-China war must have taught some lessons along this line. Declaration of war now is a political liability. In the period since the Second Warld War almost all armed conflicts have taken place without an explicit declaration of war. This, of course, does not mean there has been less conflict; on the contrary, more conflicts have occurred since the War than say during the same amount of time between the two world wars. What is different about the present period is that international law has begun to represent, in this area of no formal declarations of war, a general attitudinal change, throughout the international system, against war.

Returning to the theme of contributions of international law in the encouragement of states to resort to the principles of peaceful settlement of their disputes, we see that these principles are fairly widely practiced today. These are, essentially, final attempts to replace armed conflicts as the ultimate arbiter of international disputes with several peaceful techniques that can be divided into two categories: for example, (1) nonjuridical modes of conflict management and, (2) juridical modes of conflict management. A detailed discussion of both of these modes is considered useful to our understanding of legal techniques and mechanisms of conflict management.

Nonjuridical modes

A number of techniques of conflict management can be discussed under this category, for example, (1) diplomatic negotiations, (2) good offices of third parties and third party mediation, (3) commissions of inquiry

---

[4]Ibid., pp. 587–588.

[5]See Richard A. Falk, "The Shimoda Case: A Legal Appraisal of the Atomic Attacks Upon Hiroshima and Nagasaki," American Journal of International Law, 59 (1965), 559–594.

and commissions of conciliation, and (4) settlements by international organizations.

Diplomatic negotiations. Perhaps the oldest and most widely used method of resolving conflict among nations is through the use of diplomatic negotiations, popularly knownn these days as "international bargaining." There has always been a legal obligation to negotiate before going to war. In recent centuries diplomatic negotiations have been regarded by law as a *prerequisite for the "just" use of force.* Negotiations were conducted even when it was clear to all parties concerned that a compromise was not possible and therefore war was inevitable. The pretense of negotiation was still necessary to satisfy the legal principles. Of course, there was always that remote chance that something could be worked out and a war could be averted. Today, this is still true. Resort to force without diplomatic negotiations or an attack without warning are still condemned. Apart from the questions of morality and justice, the negotiations were regarded highly desirable simply because they were deemed to be a very inexpensive means to achieve a foreign policy objective, "without a shot being fired," as the old saying goes. In the contemporary international system diplomatic negotiations for the purpose of averting a war are fairly extensively used and frequently with good results. To satisfy a need for the understanding of increased diplomatic activities and to predict with some accuracy their outcomes, bargaining theories have been developed by students of international politics and law.[6] The United States alone in the last 25 years, according to a rough estimate, has successfully concluded an average of 150 agreements a year. Not all of them, of course, deal with the management of conflict.

Even with the best of intentions it may not be possible for the disputing parties to arrive at a satisfactory solution to the problem. In the case of the failure of diplomatic negotiations there are several other techniques of peaceful settlement that we will discuss later. However, the point to remember here is that these negotiations have to be tried. For instance, according to some scholars these negotiations are considered prerequisite to arbitration and other forms of binding solutions to the dispute. The Convention for the Pacific Settlement of International Disputes clearly states the need for arbitration in a dispute *only* when diplomatic negotiations have failed to resolve differences.[7] Similarly, one

---

[6]See Ahmed Sheikh, "Analysis of Contemporary International Law Development—A Social-Psychological Perspective," *The International Lawyer,* 4, (4) (July 1970), 785–800.

[7]*Convention for the Pacific Settlement of International Disputes,* Article 41.

finds in the famous "Kellogg" Conciliation and arbitration treaties references to various settlement procedures and techniques, once again, *only* after diplomatic negotiations have failed.[8] Certainly, the same is true of the United Nations Charter that asserts the need for diplomatic negotiations before any procedure for pacific settlement is initiated.[9]

Good offices and mediation. When the parties to a dispute are unable to resolve their differences through diplomatic negotiations, they are encouraged to use the technique of third-party "good offices." This is a form of third-party intervention to which both parties agree in advance. A third party is usually a country or an individual who enjoys the respect and certainly the trust of both disputants. In the literature, quite frequently one observes that the terms "good offices" and "mediation" are discussed together, as is true in this text. The two techniques are very closely related since both call for a third-party intervention. However, there are important differences in the role that the third party plays. "Good offices" simply means that a disinterested (i.e., by not taking sides) party provides a place on a neutral territory for the disputants to meet without giving the appearance of "weakness" by meeting on each other's territory or on a nonneutral territory. An offer of "good offices" does not normally imply an offer to take active part in the negotiations with the purpose of coming up with a proposal or even making compromise recommendations to the disputants.

Mediation, on the other hand, is a rather specialized role played by a third party. It involves a direct participation by the third party with the express purpose of contributing to the settlement of the dispute. There is no legal obligation on any state or a leader to offer their services for mediation. But once the services have been offered, a mediator is expected to come up with one or more concrete proposals that may settle a dispute amicably. In other words, he is more than a go-between. He may wish to meet the disputants jointly or separately, frequently or infrequently, and the disputants have an obligation to facilitate his task by cooperating with him as much as possible. His proposals usually are a little more than advice to the parties, but they do not carry the weight of a binding solution that the disputants must accept. A good, recent, yet unsuccessful example of mediation is the task assigned to Ambassador Gunner Jaring by the United Nations to mediate between the Arabs and Israelis after their 1967 war, which resulted in the capture of large areas of Arab land by the Israelis. Another, not too recent, but equally unsuc-

[8]See the two treaties that the United States signed in the 1920s, with Poland, (the *Treaty of Conciliation*, 1924, USTS 806, Article 1, and *Treaty of Arbitration*, 1928, USTS 805, Article 1.

[9]*United Nations* Charter, Article 33.

cessful example of mediation is the U.N. efforts to mediate between Pakistan and India, concerning the states of Jummu and Kashmir.[10]

Commissions of inquiry. In any international conflict situation there are always two or more sides to a dispute which, of course, is to be expected. However, in a dispute when there are two or more sets of conflicting "facts," a need to establish correct factual information before a judgment could be made is recognized. In realization of such a need the concept of "commissions of inquiry" has been developed. Such a commission is essentially a fact-finding mission. Usually it does not make a decision or an award concerning a dispute. It simply ascertains the facts on the basis of its own independent inquiry and reports them to those responsible for further action. Perhaps the most widely discussed case that used this kind of a commission is the *Dogger Banks Case* of 1908. The disputants were England and Russia. The dispute arose out of an attack by Russian warships on the unarmed British fishing vessels in the North Sea. This was the time when a war between Russia and Japan was in progress. It was a foggy day with poor visibility and according to the Russians they attacked the British vessels in error, mistaking them for Japanese torpedo boats. The British disagreed with this interpretation of the incident. They insisted that the Russians knew what they were doing. Because of the dispute concerning the facts of the incident, the French government suggested a commission of inquiry be used to determine the facts. A high-powered commission was created; it consisted of top ranking naval officers from England, Russia, France, Australia, and the United States. According to the findings of the commission the Russians were blamed for an unprovoked and totally unjustifiable attack on unarmed vessels. It was pointed out that there were no Japanese ships or boats anywhere near the North Sea. The report was accepted by both sides, and the Russians paid £65,000 to the British in damages.[11] Recently there have been several occasions when the United Nations has established and sent its commissions of inquiry to various areas where international disputes existed. The Security Council particularly has used this method of determining facts.

Conciliation. Conciliation is the borderline method of pacific settlement between the nonjuridical and juridical modes of settlement. Under its procedures a third party makes specific recommendations concerning the settlement of a dispute. The recommendations, sometimes also called

[10]See Michael Becher, "Kashmir: A Case Study in the United Nations Mediation," *Pacific Affairs*, 26 (September 1953), 195–207.

[11]Please consult J. B. Scott (ed.), *The Hague Court Reports* (New York: Carnegie Endowment for International Peace), 1916, pp. 403–413.

awards, are not binding on either party. Many old as well as the contemporary agreements and multilateral treaties provide for the establishment of commissions of conciliation in cases of disagreement.[12] A good example of the conciliation technique used in the past is the many recommendations of the International Joint Commission that was set up between Canada and the United States in 1909 as a result of a treaty signed by both states.[13]

Conciliation techniques have not been used as widely as its potential would allow. This is true even though a great many treaties and conventions have been recently agreed upon, and most of them call for the use of conciliation technique if disagreements surface later. It is quite possible that recent treaties are so explicit that disagreements have not surfaced, thus there is no need for conciliation. It is also possible that other procedures have been found to be more desirable by disputants because of the binding nature of their awards, for example, arbitration and adjudication. Nonetheless, several scholars have suggested that the use of conciliation be widened to cover the entire international system.[14]

Peaceful settlement by international organizations. The United Nations Charter and indeed the charters of several other international regional organizations provide several provisions for the peaceful settlement of disputes. In the case of the United Nations, the Security Council can recommend various methods of settlement. It can, of course, also make binding decisions concerning peace settlements and, in cases of noncompliance, it can enforce them if it so chooses by the use of armed forces made available to it by member states under Chapter Seven of the Charter.[15] The General Assembly, under the "Uniting for Peace" resolution, legality of which is disputed by some states and scholars, may also take enforcement action if world peace is clearly threatened and if the Security Council is deadlocked because of the veto of a permanent member.[16]

[12]See *Pacific Settlement of International Disputes,* General Act, Geneva, 1928, 93 L.N.S.T. 343, published in the *American Journal of International Law,* 26 (October 1931), 204.

[13]Consider the *Treaty Between the United States and Great Britain Relating to Boundary Waters Between the United States and Canada,* Washington, D.C., 1909.

[14]A very interesting proposal in this area comes to us from the widely read book of G. Clark and L. B. Sohn, *World Peace Through World Law* (Cambridge, Mass.: Harvard University Press), 1958, pp. 321–330. In their work the authors outline a detailed plan for the revision of the United Nations Charter. They propose to create, as a part of their comprehensive proposal, a World Equity Tribunal and a World Conciliation Board.

[15]See *United Nations Charter,* Articles 33–55.

[16]A copy of this resolution is available in the official documents section of the *American Journal of International Law,* XLV (January 1951), pp. 1–6.

The entire subject of the legal aspects of the United Nations Charter that govern the United Nations' role in the maintenance of international peace and security and the much debated legality of several United Nations peacekeeping operations of the past is *extremely important*. Therefore, this topic will be treated in some detail under a separate topic in the latter part of this chapter. However, with regard to what is generally called "nonforceable" methods of conflict management the Charter lays down several traditional devices that can be employed by the disputants. As a matter of record, the United Nations has frequently encouraged peaceful settlement of disputes by various regional arrangements outside the framework of the United Nations. Beyond that, there are several devices available to the United Nations itself in its own attempts to resolve disputes without the use of force. For instance, the Security Council may investigate a dispute and make recommendations, either at its own initiative or at the request of one of the parties to the dispute.[17] The General Assembly may consider a dispute, but it cannot make a recommendation while the same dispute is being considered by the Security Council.[18]

There are several devices that the United Nations has frequently used to help resolve conflict. Here are some of them. (1) Sending a United Nations commission to a troubled area and, thus, perhaps more than anything else, symbolically creating what some writers have called the "United Nations presence." (2) Offers of its good offices. (3) Employment of familiar techniques of peaceful settlement as listed in the preceeding pages for example, conciliation, mediation, and inquiry commissions, and (4) passing a resolution concerning a dispute and asking the parties involved to comply, or making available an "official" opinion indicating that the World Body is concerned about a dispute.[19] (5) Asking the Secretary-General to intervene in a dispute. He performs the function of "peacemaker" in this area. As a result of his own personality factors, for example, and because of a deadlock in the United Nations, the Secretary-General has been asked again to play this role in the past and will certaily be asked to play it in the future. At the same time he also has constitutional powers of his own to take initiatives in the maintenance of international peace. He may be approached in this connection either by the General Assembly, by the Security Council, or by one or more members of the United Nations.[20]

[17]See *United Nations Charter*, Articles 34 to 38.

[18]*Ibid.*, see Articles 35, 10, 11, 12, and 14.

[19]For details, see D. C. Blaisdell, *International Organization* (New York: Roland Press), 1966, pp. 91–105.

[20]For details see S. S. Goodspeed, *The Nature and Functions of International Organization* (New York: Oxford University Press), 1959, pp. 347–353, *ct. passim*; see also, Ahmed Sheikh, "The Dynamics of the Role of Secretary-General in Divided

Juridical modes

These modes involve the settlement of disputes through a legal process. That is, disputes are submitted to a court that may be permanent or may have been temporarily created for this purpose. A *binding* decision is then handed out. There are two legal modes of settlement of disputes. They are not mutually exclusive.

Arbitration. Arbitration is a time-honored process of conflict resolution by which a third-party settlement of disputes is attained. The parties agree in advance to the *binding nature* of the decision. It is a technique that became popular around the early part of this century.[21] It has been widely used both at the international and domestic levels. The first important characteristic of arbitration is that the selections of arbitrators, be they judges or diplomats, is free and flexible since the tribunal representing them is usually ad hoc. Arbitration is a very flexible technique. It is regarded particularly useful when highly technical disputes arise that necessitate the selection of technically qualified people. The flexibility of this technique is further underlined by the fact that it can rely on any principles, recognized in the agreement that sets up the tribunal initially. This means that a decision can be made on the mutually agreed upon framework rather than necessarily on the existing legal principles. The full potential of arbitration is yet to be recognized in world affairs. One problem in this area seems to be the reluctance of parties to the conflict to submit to a binding decision. There are several examples of the successful use of this technique in the history of international relations. Consider, for instance, the 1910 Newfoundland Fisheries dispute between England and the United States,[22] and United States-Mexican arbitration from 1923 to 1934.[23]

From a procedural point of view an arbitral arrangement ordinarily progresses through the following steps. (1) A fair selection of the arbitrators. This step is not to be found in judicial settlements that are generally made by the judges of *permanently established courts of law.* (2) The treaties of arbitration usually indicate that in the proceedings of arbitration, rules of international law must be upheld or the decision

---

Counsels on U.N. Peace-Keeping" *Political Science Review*, 9 (3 and 4), (July to December 1970), 237–257.

[21]For a detailed discussion of this technique see J. Stone, *Legal Controls of International Conflict* (New York: Rinehart), 1954.

[22]See, Note of the Secretary-General, *Permanent Court of Arbitration*, March 3, 1960, in the *American Journal of International Law*, 54 (1960).

[23]See, A. H. Feller, *The Mexican Claims Commission 1923–1934* (New York: Macmillan), 1935.

must come very close to the existing law, so that the decision could be regarded as a "legal" decision. (3) Disputants to the conflict, explicitly or implicitly, agree to accept the award of the arbitration tribunal and to uphold its provisions. Since many rules of international law are not clear beyond a shadow of a doubt, the disputants frequently stipulate in the prior agreement the *principles* under which the award is to be made. The practice is called *compromis*, which may in certain instances lay down specific rules under which a decision is to be arrived at. Keep in mind that it is not an easy matter to determine what disputes should be submitted to arbitration. The problem generally arises in the determination of whether a dispute is political or legal in nature.

Adjudication. The adjudication process is closely related to arbitration. The major difference between the two, however, is in the court to which a dispute is referred.[24] If the court involved is a permanent court, the term "adjudication" applies. There have been several regional and bilateral tribunals responsible for the application of international law to specific disputes, but perhaps the most important development in the early part of this century was the establishment of the *Permanent Court of International Justice* after the First World War. The other two significant developments were the *Central American Court of Justice* and, of course, the present *International Court of Justice*. Besides these three significant courts, there have been attempts to establish regional specialized international courts. Much of the progress made in this area is restricted to Western Europe, in connection with the development of such international organizations as the European Economic Community and the European Coal and Steel Community.

The first serious attempt to set up an international court of adjudication was made as early as 1899. At this time a draft convention was developed for the establishment of a *Judicial Arbitration Court* and about the same time the *International Prize Court* was also established. Unfortunately, draft convention for the arbitration court never went beyond the stage of mere recommendations, and the prize court failed because enough states never ratified the treaty.[25]

However, soon thereafter the states of Central America got together and under a 10-year agreement established a *Central American Court of Justice*. It considered approximately a dozen cases and then ceased to exist. Its charter was not renewed by the signatories. Certainly, there were several problems that the court faced in the brief history of its

[24]See Wilfred Jenks, *The Prospects for International Adjudication* (Dobbs Ferry, N.Y.: Oceana Publications), 1964.

[25]See detailed comments in M. O. Hudson, *The Permanent Court of International Justice* (New York: Macmillan), 1943, Chapters 4 and 5.

existence. But perhaps the most complex case it dealt with was a dispute between Nicaragua and Costa Rica, which may have contributed to its short life. It involved the legality of a treaty that Nicaragua had signed with the United States. The court declared that the treaty violated the rights of Costa Rica, but the difficulty for Nicaragua arose from the fact that the United States insisted its treaty with Nicaragua must be honored. Since the United States was not a party to the dispute before the Court, it was under no obligation to abide by the ruling of the court and it did not. Neither did Nicaragua. In 1923 fresh attempts were made to establish another Central American Court, but the agreement was never put to practice.

After the First World War, when the League of Nations was established, it was felt there was a great need for the creation of a true permanent international court. Article 14 of the League's Covenant refers to such a body. Therefore, *The Permanent Court of International Justice* was established in 1921. It was the first court with world wide jurisdictions. It decided its first case in 1923, and after considering 57 cases and rendering both judgments and advisory opinions, it ceased to function at the conclusion of the Second World War in 1945.[26]

The present *International Court of Justice* was established under the provisions of the United Nations Charter in the post-World War II period. For all practical purposes it is the successor of the former *Permanent Court of International Justice*. A major difference between the two courts is the fact that the present court is a part of the United Nations system. The old court was far less closely tied to the League of Nations.

There are three major areas of the Court's jurisdiction. (1) Cases that are brought to the attention of the Court by the mutual consent of the disputants, especially the cases that have their legal bases in the United Nations Charter or in conventions and treaties that are still in force. (2) Cases that are brought to the Court by one of the disputants against the other and in the circumstances where both parties have recognized the *jurisdiction* of the Court in the case and have agreed to the *binding nature* of the decision with regard to only that particular case and the specific disputants involved. (3) Cases referred to the Court by various organs or agencies of the United Nations.

Presently, approximately 50 states have accepted the binding nature of the Court's decisions and accepted what is commonly called the "optional clause" on the compulsory jurisdiction of the Court. Some countries' acceptance is contingent on certain reservations. The United States' major reservation in this area is known as the Connally Amendment, which simply excludes the "domestic" disputes from the Court's consid-

[26]*Ibid.*

erations and *binding decisions*. What characterizes a dispute as a "domestic" dispute is, of course, also determined by the American domestic courts themselves.

By virtue of its statute the Court is authorized to apply the following principles of international law in its deliberations:

(a) International conventions, whether general or particular, establishing rules expressly recognized by the contesting states;
(b) International Custom, as evidence of a general practice accepted as follows:
(c) The general principles of law as recognized by civilized nations;
(d) Subject to the provisions of Article 59, judicial decisions and the teachings of the most highly qualified publicists of the various nations, as subsidiary means for the determination of rules of law.[27]

Apart from the above stated legal principles, the Court's jurisdiction and its area of action are further widened by the fact that these legal provisions do not *limit* the Court's activity. It has powers to decide in cases above and beyond the legal principles that are stated in its statute, provided the disputing parties agree to this arrangement prior to the Courts' deliberations.

The role of the United Nations peacekeeping operations in the management of international conflict

A brief overall view of the debate on on the question of United Nations military forces

Even though every significant proposal on world disarmament, along with the prospects of achieving and maintaining international peace and security, has embodied in it as a crucial feature some concept of an international or supranational military force, it is amazing how little serious and systematic treatment has been given to this idea as a whole. There is little doubt that the many varied problems encountered by the United Nations in its experiences with the international military forces in the past in Africa and elsewhere raise some difficult issues of a practical as well as of a theoretical nature; yet quite frequently much of the literature on the subject is limited either to a particular peacekeeping operation or to a particular aspect of peacekeeping operations.

[27]International Court of Justice, *Statute*, Article 38.

Although it is recognized that the contributions of scholars such as Lincoln P. Bloomfield, D. W. Bowett, Andrew Boyd, A. W. Cordier, Ernest Gross, Rosalyn Higgins, Ernest W. Fefever, Julius Stone, John G. Stoessinger, and a few others are significant in their own areas of specialization as these relate to the U.N. forces,[28] no elaborate systematic efforts have been made to integrate coherently this body of ilterature and to analyze its utility for future peacekeeping operations and its potential for theory building.

The above is particularly true in the crucial area of U.N. forces military command, strategy, logistics, and with regard to a host of problems in the area of forces' morale, combat effectiveness, integration of military units, loyalties of the international soldiers, and so on.

On the political side, it is frequently taken for granted that once a system of world law and order has been established, there will of course be an international military force to enforce it. At the same time elaborate and imaginative proposals for the establishment of an international force of a sort are put forward, which more often than not, fail to draw on the actual experiences of the past and, as such, seem to have limited relevance for the immediate or even distantly foreseeable future. The question is rarely asked that given the nature of contemporary politics at the United Nations and elsewhere, what kind of a force would conceivably be acceptable today to much of the United Nations membership and what is the relationship between this membership's aspirations for and expectations of such a force and their general reluctance to establish it.

The need for more debate on the subject of United Nations peacekeeping operations and their *legal basis and further legal implications as a result of various operations* still exists. There seems little doubt that on the basis of the United Nations Charter and in view of contemporary political realities almost all nations have accepted a general need for some kind of peacekeeping operations, but we still do not know a great deal

---

[28]See Lincoln P. Bloomfield, *International Military Forces* (New York: Little, Brown), 1964; D. W. Bowett, *United Nations Forces* (New York: Praeger), 1964; Andrew Boyd, *United Nations: Piety, Myth and Truth* (Harmondsworth, Midd. England: Penguin Special 5214), 1962; A. W. Cordier and W. Foote (eds.), *The Quest for Peace* (New York: Columbia University Press), 1965; Ernest Gross, *The United Nations: Structure for Peace* (New York: Harper), 1962; Rosalyn Higgins, *The Development of International Law through the Political Organs of the United Nations* (New York: Oxford University Press), 1963; Ernest W. Lefever, *Crisis in the Congo: A U.N. Force in Action* (Washington, D.C.: The Brookings Institution), 1965; Julius Stone, *Legal Controls of International Conflict* (New York: Rinehart), 1954; and John G. Stoessinger and Associates, *Financing the United Nations System* (Washington, D.C.: The Brookings Institution), 1964.

about the political, legal, and financial feasibility of continuing to conduct the future peacekeeping operations as we have generally done in the past. Since the inception of the United Nations Emergency Force in the midst of the Suez crisis in 1956, the term "international police force" has acquired remarkably diverse meanings. To some scholars and military experts it has meant, on one extreme, a large military force in possession of nuclear weapons and capable of coercing any nation regardless of how small or large it may be; to others, on the other extreme, it simply means an observation corps of men wearing United Nations insignias and patrolling a cease-fire line. As a consequence, one of the important questions in the discussions of the concept of an international military force has been whether the force should be a military force amounting to a "world army" or whether a more modest force would do the job of establishing and maintaining world peace. Indeed, in much of the discussions on a future disarmed world many scholars have assumed that a large world army would be required to keep the international peace, to symbolize and support the agreed-on international order, and to coerce any nation that might attempt to violate the agreements establishing that order. This assumption is largely and frequently based on the contention that once a general and complete disarmament has taken place an international military force, to be effective, would need to have at its disposal a preponderance of physical force that no power could challenge.[29]

Other scholars have taken issue with this position. They argue that a host of serious problems can be pointed out in regard to the establishment of such a force. First of all, they submit, given the political realities of the contemporary world it is extremely doubtful that various agreements for a general and complete disarmament and for the establishment of such a force would be forthcoming in a foreseeable future. To these scholars the question that some governments simply would not accept a world army is in itself not crucial, for states have been known in the past to change their minds on what is acceptable to them and what is not, and they might do so on this matter as well. The more crucial reason for their refusal to accept such a comprehensive force is their fear of not being able to exert control over it. The prevailing belief seems to be that if a preponderance of physical power without adequate controls were to be given to any international institution, it might soon become unmanage-

[29]For a good statement of this position see Grenville Clark and Louis B. Sohn, *World Peace through World Law* (Cambridge, Mass.: Harvard University Press second edition), 1960; and Arthur I. Waskow, *Keeping the World Disarmed* (Santa Barbara, Calif.: Center for the Study of Democratic Institutions), 1965. Also see *Blueprint for the Peace: Outline of Basic Principles of a Treaty on General and Complete Disarmament in a Peaceful World* (Washington: Government Printing Office), 1962.

able and expand its sphere of influence into areas that it was not originally intended to influence—areas such as purely domestic affairs of sovereign states.[30]

It is further contended that the fear of an international force of such proportions is largely based on the contention that a force of this magnitude could only be financed, supported, and controlled by an effective world government, or that, to put it differently, in order to protect and perpetuate itself this world force may well take upon itself governmental attributes that are clearly undesirable. To pursue the contention further, This development or any other number of developments may conceivably result from the needs of a world force to indulge in myriad political decision making at an extremely significant level with regard to recruitment, training, and movement of huge numbers of individuals, to make arbitrary decisions concerning where, when, and how to use the only truly powerful force of the world. The argument goes on to point out that decisions of such significance can only be "governmental" decisions, simply because of the amount of power to be used or withheld. In view of this contention it can be safely assumed that no member state at this time or in a foreseeable future is willing to voluntarily accept a world government or a world force.

A cursory analysis of much of the literature on the question of U.N. military forces also supports the above position against a comprehensive world army. In fact, there seems to be a consensus of sorts among most scholars in the field that regardless of what benefits a world force may accrue toward maintaining peace and security, the present conflicting interests of member states are unlikely to permit sufficient political consensus on whether either a supranational government or a supranational police force should be built. It is further agreed that presently it is also not possible to create sufficient political consensus to establish institutions large enough to control a force of such power.[31]

Any writer attempting to survey the literature on United Nations peacekeeping activities in the area of international forces soon finds that the

[30]For a good statement of this position see C. B. Marshall, "Character and Mission of a United Nations Peace Force, Under Conditions of General and Complete Disarmament," *American Political Sciences Review*, LIX (2) (June 1962), 350–364; and I. L. Claude, Jr., "United Nations Use of Military Force," *The Journal of Conflict Resolution*, VIII (2) (June 1963), 117–129.

[31]The concept of consensus for the purposes of this study is taken to mean essentially an agreement on a perspective of the future world—How it should be run? What should then be the substance of politics?—or agreement on the nature of political institutions and "rules of game" through which a conflict may be resolved in practice. In the context of establishing large international military forces, it may be added that any kind of consensus would inevitably require some surrender of what is popularly considered today as national sovereignty.

product of United Nations experiences has been not a single kind of international force but rather a variety of combat units, supervisory armies, border patrols, observer groups ranging from small groups of selective officers to contingents carrying thousands of soldiers in several diverse situations. A close glance at the spectrum of international forces, according to Bloomfield,[32] helps visualize six basic types:

(1) At the bottom of the scale are what can be called guard duties—policing the U.N. buildings and meeting rooms, including installations in the field; or bodyguard to the Secretary-General (U.N. Field Service personnel so served in Leopoldville, and a personal guard was killed with Dag Hammarskjold).

(2) Next is the function of observation and patrol. The man with binoculars is a uniquely valuable asset, often worth as much as a platoon of infantry; but he is usable only when conflict has been suspended or stopped by agreement of the parties (or never really broke out). Here is the "eye-balling" task exemplified by the lonely sentries on the postwar border watches in Northern Greece, Palestine, Kashmir, Lebanon; the "presences" so useful for their psychological value, as in Laos, Jordan, Cyprus and, perhaps some day, Berlin.

(3) Next is more militant enforcement of ceasefires and truces, for keeping the armed parties apart (but with far less actual military power than would be needed if they resumed hostilities). Here is the Palestine of 1949, Suez of 1956, and the Yemen effort commencing in June, 1963. Cyprus and Malaysia are good candidates here, too.

(4) Another brand of mission is internal policing and order-keeping, as in the Congo. It is guaranteed to be controversial because of inescapable involvement in internal partisan politics. And it is likely to keep the United Nations in turmoil because of great-power differences that are inevitable . . .

At this point Bloomfield argues that an important threshold is crossed. For the remaining two types of international forces include missions involving combat. This combat may result either from an invasion of a country by another country or countries, or from internal disorder or civil war. It seems thus far that the powers for one reason or other have not wished to get United Nations forces involved in situations such as Laos (in its acute phase) or Vietnam. However, the fifth type will be a standby fighting force and the sixth one can be conceived of as: (a) a great-power contributed force with veto—an extension of what was put in the United

[32]Lincoln P. Bloomfield, *International Military Forces* (New York: Little, Brown), 1964, pp. 8–9.

Nations Charter in 1945 under Article 43; and (b) a force recruited from all sources, with no great-power veto.

It is hard to identify what they have in common except that they are all "forces" of a sort. Holmes conceives the role of force as "an instrument of United Nations, armed or unarmed, [that] interposes rather than enforces, develops the United Nations role neither as a policeman nor an avenging fury but as an objective entity. The United Nations accepts as inevitable the quarrelsomeness of its Members and seeks in this way to get them to agree."[33] It is submitted that the pure objectivity of the force, however, is far from reality. The United Nations often does not pretend to be neutral in international disputes.

If any generalization can be made regarding the various purposes and functions of United Nations forces, it would be that the fuction of these forces is adjusted and adopted to accord with the moral, political, and military strength that the United Nations is able to muster in a particular situation and in the strength of its convictions about the right and wrong of the case. The certainty of its convictions is determined almost always not just by the validity of the respective arguments put forward by the disputing states, but also by the political support these disputants can enlist in the United Nations councils. The power and authority of the United Nations is directly affected by the degree of unanimity that prevails in the United Nations—and particularly among the major powers.

An interesting insight in the functions of United Nations forces as they have actually developed is offered by Claude:

> This [U.N. force] is not a device for defying aggressors and certainly not for coercing great powers determined to expand the sphere of their control—but for assisting the major powers in avoiding the expansion and sharpening of their conflicts and the consequent degeneration of whatever stability they may have been able to achieve in their mutual relationships. The best hope for the United Nations is not that it may be able to develop a military establishment which will enable it to exercise coercive control over great powers, but that it may be able to continue the development of its capability to serve the interest of great powers—and of the rest of the world—by helping them to contain their conflicts, to limit their competition, and to stabilize their relationships. The greatest political contribution of the United Nations in our ime to the management of international power relationships lies not in implementing collective security or instituting world government, but in helping to improve and stabilize the working of the balance of power system, which is, for better or for worse, the operative mechanism of contemporary international politics. The immediate task, in short, is to

---

[33] J. W. Holmes, "The Political and Philosophical Aspects of U.N. Security Forces," *International Journal*, XIX, (3) (Summer 1964), p. 293.

make the world safe to the balance of power system, and the balance of power system safe for the world.[34]

Claude's definition attempts to place United Nations forces in the history of international relations. It might be interesting to look at the accumulated United Nations peacekeeping activities of the past in relation to two concepts: *first*, the persistent anticipation on the part of many of an "international police force" capable of enforcing world law or at least agreed-upon international decisions anywhere in the world; and *second*, the provisions embodied in the United Nations Charter for a force composed of national contingents placed at the disposal of the United Nations and acting on the basis of great-power consensus.

The United Nations is now confronted with a conflict between practical and political realities. It has been conducting military operations that according to experts defy every rule of good soldiering. In the present world political situation another international force could be required at any time, but a direct attack on the military and operational problems has never been made.

Some of the literature indicates that much of the reasoning for a permanent force or at least a substantial military establishment in the U.N. Secretariat, the training of stand-by forces, perhaps even military bases, and intelligence network operated by the United Nations, may be acceptable by a majority of member states. But a further study of the literature makes it quite clear that for international political reasons a standing United Nations force may be out of the question. It seems that there is no consensus that would authorize the United Nations to go, for instance, very far beyond Dag Hammarskjold's recommendation of ad hoc forces established with the help of contributing countries.

Given the current international situation it seems reasonable to argue that any plans for the future international military forces must be based on the recognition of extremely modest resources available, be these personnel, material, or financial. Only if there is a collaboration among the great powers in peacekeeping can the United Nations ever hope to apply effectively its resources to the great issues of today.

If we look at the United Nations Charter, it can be further argued that perhaps the most important and original part of the document are the articles concerning the maintenance of peace and acceptance of the threat of aggression by the United Nations, Chapter VII is particularly relevant because it provides for the military forces to be put at the disposal of the Security Council.[35] These provisions were based on the assumption that

[34]Inis L. Claude, *Power and International Relations* (New York: Random House), 1964, p. 285.

[35]A substantial discussion of the legal aspect of United Nations forces will be presented later in this chapter.

there will be unanimity among the major powers on peacekeeping operations. Radical changes in the nature and instruments of war and in the conditions for political rivalry has since rendered this assumption false.

Note also that the framers of the Charter further assumed that the U.N. would deal with crises connected with interstate relations and that member states will be viable units. The Congo experience has clearly demonstrated to many people the inadequacy of such an assumption. In reality, one of the tasks the United Nations had to take on itself during peacekeeping operations, and may well have to do again, was nation building, that is, attempting to weld the *infra* structures of nations through technical assistance and training in the maintenance of law-and-order programs capable of creating viable political entities in several developing member states.

There is a general agreement in much of the literature that a substantial majority in the United Nations feels the Organization should be strengthened as an instrument for maintaining peace and security, even though important members have expressed strong disapproval of the manner in which the Congo operation was handled. As stated earlier, even in disarmament negotiations the concept of a peacekeeping force under the control of the United Nations has been discussed. This, of course, must not be interpreted to mean that the two major countries are anywhere close to an agreement on the means of attaining this objective; however, it is reasonable to state that they have, in principle, agreed that the progress toward general and complete disarmament must be accompanied by the establishment of effective international apparatus for maintaining peace and security. Perhaps the main stumbling block in the way of achieving this goal is the inability of both sides to work out a mutually acceptable political basis for peacekeeping forces.

Perhaps basic to all political issues involved in peacekeeping operations has been the question of political control. It is no longer sufficient to attempt to resolve this question purely on the basis of the constitutional provisions of the Charter since countless political and military developments have taken place in the world since 1945.

The example of the Congo operation gives sufficient support to the argument that there has been no clear-cut direction for United Nations operations in the past. The area commanders on United Nations field services have continually found their orders ambiguous and contradictory.

From the military standpoint it will be desirable for the international forces to operate under reasonably precise directions emanating either from the Security Council or from the General Assembly, whichever is politically feasible. There are some indications that the political control is perhaps beginning to swing back to the Security Council, but given the makeup of the Council and in the light of political realities, it is difficult to see how it can be sufficinetly effective. Its composition, procedures, and functions may have to be modified and redefined before it can be considered an acceptable agency for political control.

According to some literature there is also a general lack of confidence and goodwill toward the United Nations peacekeeping operations among most national press systems. Urquhart expresses the view:

> In most of these crises there have appeared, almost as a tradition, editorial campaigns in some sections of the press which, starting with a standard pessimism, have worked up to a furious indignation with the United Nations for what it either was or was not doing, and concluded with the, to them, consoling thought that at least the world has learnt never again to ask the United Nations to assist in a critical situation. What is interesting is that both the premises and the conclusions of this process have proved to be wrong time and time again. If anything, the pressure for the United Nations intervention and mediation is too frequent and too unselective. There is certainly no lack of tasks or requests for United Nations intervention, and the dumping of insoluble problems on the shoulders of the Secretary-General has also, at times, threatened to become a dangerous habit.[36]

Much of the literature on the establishment of some sort of a United Nations police force reflects a favorable attitude with certain reservations or qualifications. For instance, Pyman, in an article entitled "The Significance of the United Nations 'Presence' for International Security," argues that the United Nations Executive machinery has in fact achieved impressive success in conflicts such as the Suez crisis in terminatng hostilities and preventing further major outbreaks of violence. Pyman is impressed because these modest advances were made in an area in which the antagonisms of the great powers were a crucial factor. The effectiveness of U.N. executive authority, according to Pyman, has deepened as the Secretary-General has increasingly assumed a directing role in the arrangements to meet any disputed situation. Pyman is in favor of a United Nations stand-by force in the future.[37]

Categories of United Nations peacekeeping operations

Some functions can be classified as *cease-fire, truce, and armistice functions carried out largely by United Nations "Observer Groups."* It has

[36]Brian Urquhart, "Evaluation of the Peace-Keeping Functions of the United Nations," in G. R. Bunting and M. J. Lee (eds.), *The Evaluation of the United Nations* (Great Britain: Pergamon Press), 1964, p. 55.

[37]T. A. Pyman, "The Significance of United Nations 'Presence' for International Security," *Australian Outlook*, XIV (3) (December 1960), 229–245.

been often observed that even after the fighting between two warring countries or between warring factions within a country has stopped, there frequently remains an uneasy truce or a cease-fire that can be called off with the slightest provocation by either side. Here the United Nations force has effectively provided supervisions of truces and patrolling of cease-fire lines, and has at times sufficiently guaranteed the good faith of all contestants concerned that peace and security be maintained. Some examples of the function of U.N. observer groups can be found in Indonesia, Kashmir, Palestine, and most recently in the 1973 Mid-East conflict.

In United Nations operations the distinction between a "cease-fire" and a "truce" is difficult to make. In fact, in the discussions of the Security Council and General Assembly both terms have been interchangeably used. However, according to Bowett:

> . . . a "truce" as opposed to "cease-fire" is normally more than a simple cessation of hostilities and incorporates a complex of mutual undertakings and conditions: it is, however, a temporary state of affairs as opposed to an "armistice. . . .[38]

During United Nations activities in Yemen and West New Guinea the concept of a "disengagement" agreement came into practice. It meant primarily two things: a worked-out agreement to cease fire and a further agreement to withdraw armed forces from the front. This agreement, when fulfilled in West New Guinea, resulted in no forces confronting each other in the territory, and in Yemen it meant a withdrawal of Egyptian troops leaving the Saudi-Arabian and Yemeni forces on their respective sides of the demilitarized zone.

In Indonesia there were easily recognizable front lines; therefore the U.N. observers helped delineate a status quo line and established demilitarized zones on either side of this line. In Kashmir the United Nations observers helped the local commanders from both sides set up a single cease-fire line. In Palestine the observers through an extremely complex formula were able to establish several truce lines with no-man's-lands in between. The Armistice Agreement of 1949 finally fixed a demarcation line that the respective forces were prohibited to cross. The Agreement read in part:

> No element of the land, sea or air military or para-military forces of either party, including non-regular forces, shall commit any warlike or hostile act against the military or para-military forces of the other party, or against civilians in territory under the control of that party; or shall

[38]D. W. Bowett, *United Nations Forces*, pp. 73–74.

advance beyond or pass over for any purpose whatsoever the Armistice Demarcation Line. . . .[39]

The United Nations observers perform several major functions: first, checking all violations of cease-fire lines, truces, and other agreements; second, discouraging and frequently preventing these same violations. Closely linked with these two functions is a third major task of observer groups; they supervise and check the withdrawal of troops agreed to by the contestants. In Indonesia under the Renville Truce Agreement of January 17, 1949 the observers of Consulor Commission supervised the withdrawal of some 35,000 Republican troops from the rear of Dutch forces' positions.[40] In the Armistice Agreement between the Arabs and Israel it was specifically stated that the United Nations would supervise the withdrawal of all troops;[41] the Chief of Staff of United Nations Truce Supervision Organization (UNTSO) was to define the order of priority of withdrawal. The observers attached to United Nations Commission on Korea (UNCOK) were particularly depended on to report the progress of withdrawal of the occupying troops from Korea. The observer group attached to United Nations Temporary Executive Authority (UNTEA) was to check upon the withdrawal of Dutch forces from West New Guinea,[42] and the group in Yemen was entrusted with the task of confirming that the United Arab Republic forces and their equipment were actually moved out of Yemeni territory.[43] The observers of UNOGIL, while not entirely supervising the withdrawal of United States troops in Lebanon, actively facilitated this process. The August 21st Resolution of the Third Emergency Assembly specifically directed the Secretary-General to make practical arrangements that would help "facilitate the early withdrawal of foreign troops"[44] from both Jordan and Lebanon. However, Jordan refused to let United Nations observers in and, consequently, a single U.N. Special Representative became the only United Nations observer there.

Another very important function that can be effectively performed by the United Nations observers is the supervision of exchange of the prisoners of war and handling of the refugees because of a war. Toward

[39]SCOR, 4th yr., Spec. Suppl. No. 3 (Israel/Egyptian Agreement of 24 February 1949) and Suppl. No. 4 (Israel/Lebanon Agreement 23 March 1949).

[40]For details see the Third Interim Report of the Committee of Good Offices to the Security Council (3/848/Add. 1), SCOR, 3rd yr. Suppl., Spec. Suppl., p. 122.

[41]See Israel/Egypt Agreement S/1264/Rev. 1, Arts. III (3), VII and Annex 1.

[42]U.N. Doc. A/5170, Aide Memoire from Acting Secretary-General to Representatives of the Netherlands and Indonesia, Para. 2.

[43]U.N. Doc. S/5298, Para. 4.

[44]U.N. Doc. A/3893/Rev. 1; Resol. 1237 (ES-111) and GAOR 735th Mtg., Para 51.

the conclusion of the Armistice Agreement in Palestine it became possible for the United Nations to supervise exchange of prisoners under Article IX (1) Israeli/Egyptian Agreement. The Security Council also on January 19, 1956 passed a resolution calling on the Chief of Staff to proceed immediately with the exchange of prisoners of war.[45] There are also sufficient examples in the practice of UNTSO to show that its Chief of Staff has performed quasi-judicial functions as Chairman of the Third Armistice Commission. These functions are largely in the area of solving disputes such as harvesting in no-man's-lands, or helping both sides reach a decision on the determination of truce lines, and so on.

The United Nations forces can also usefully perform functions of *controlling the frontier between two hostile countries* and, thus, help reduce border tension between them. Such a force can be established with the consent of both countries, or of one country if it were to patrol solely on one side of the border. Thus, in patroling the border, the force can check on disputes, for example, regarding the illegal infiltration of the frontier and so on. For instance, in the Balkan dispute the military observers were specifically assigned to report on the violations of the Northern Greece frontier. In Korea the military observers working with the United Nations Commission on Korea concentrated their observations of the 38th parallel. In Palestine, it can be argued that although the armistice lines agreed upon were far more important than the international borders, the Security Council insisted that its mediator and his observers consistently check the international borders to report that neither fighting personnel nor war material were brought into Palestine, Egypt, Iraq, Lebanon, Saudi Arabia, Syria, Transjordan, and Yeman in violation of the cease-fire agreement.[46] United Nations Observation Group in Lebanon (UNOGIL) was primarily assigned the task of border control. As the importance of UNOGIL's functions became clear, the utility of fixed-border checkpoints was increased as an addition to mobile patrols and a great deal of reliance was placed on aerial reconnaissance.[47] In Yemen also, the observer group, among other functions, performed duties of border patrol in an effort to make sure that "no forces belonging to any of the parties entered the demilitarized zone of twenty kilometers from either side of the demarked border between Saudi Arabia and Yemen."[48]

From the examples given above it is argued that there can be numerous

[45]See Resol. S/3538. For a detailed account of earlier UNTSO's activities refer to Lt. Gen. E. L. M. Burns, *Between Arab and Israeli*, (New York: Ivan Obolensky), 1963. Chapter 3.

[46]Resol. S/801 of May 20, 1948.

[47]For details see Second Interim Report of UNOGIL, U.N. Doc. S/4052, para. 12.

[48]U.N. Doc. S/5298, para. 4.

situations in international conflict where a truce, armistice, or a cease-fire may not be involved, yet the United Nations force in the form of a border patrol can play a significant role. UNOGIL is a good example. Functions of a U.N. border patrol may also include such activities as controlling the entry points at an international border and inspecting legal travel documents for movements across the border and so on.

The third type of functions that the international military forces can effectively perform are classified under the title of *interpositionary functions* between two hostile nations. Bowett points out "such a Force could be effective only if the vital interests of the two parties did not, in their own eyes, necessitate the continuation of hostilities irrespective of public opinion and diplomatic pressures."[49] Interpositionary functions do not include a large-scale fighting with one or both belligerents; therefore, it is understood that the United Nations force will be fairly small and without heavy military equipment such as envisaged for United Nations forces with enforcement functions. Perhaps the major utility of such a force would be to insulate the front lines and provide a "trip-wire" so that the contact between the belligerents could be eliminated. Conceivably in some situations its mere presence on the spot would be sufficient to deter both sides from engaging in further hostilities.[50] A force with interposition functions could also be used when the fighting is still in progress, but only if it is clearly understood that both sides will refrain from firing on the United Nations force once it has appeared on the scene to enforce a defacto separation of the belligerents and a tentative cease-fire, or immediately after a truce has been agreed on by both sides but with an imminent danger of the resumption of hostilities; here the force can help maintain a status quo.

Thus, an interpositionary force will not only secure a cessation to hostilities but also maintain this cessation. Maintenance of the cessation of hostilities will also include border patrolling. An interpositionary force can also be used in an area where there is a danger that hostilities will break out. Such a force, will be used to prevent breaches of peace rather than to restore the peace. A good example of an interpositionary force is United Nations Emergency Force (UNEF) that took over the functions of patrolling Gaza strip demarcation line from UNTSO.[51]

---

[49]Bowett, *United Nations Forces*, p. 269.

[50]For details on the usefulness of interpositionary activities carried out by international military forces, see A. James, "U.N. Action for Peace," *World Today*, 18 (11) (November–December 1962), 478–486.

[51]Read Report of the Secretary-General on Basic Points for the Presence and Functioning in Egypt of the United Nations Emergency Force, November 20, 1956. See also ANNEX: *Aide-Memoire* on the Basis for Presence and Functioning of UNEF in Egypt.

The fourth type of functions that the international forces can perform effectively can be classified as *defense and policing of areas placed under United Nations control*. A United Nations force defending an area under its control and maintaining law and order there will need both military and police personnel. Conceivably, the need for such a force can arise in several situations. For instance, one of the plans drawn by the General Assembly in 1948 to solve the problem of Palestine was to make Jerusalem an international city. This city was to be controlled and policed by a United Nations police force until responsible Israeli and Arab militias could take over. It was forcefully argued that only in this manner could general anarchy, chaos, and bloodshed be minimized.[52] Such a force can also be used as an Administering Authority in the territories that fall under the United Nations trusteeship or in any place where the United Nations assumes territorial responsibilities. Perhaps the best practical example of the need for such a force is the West Irian dispute between the Netherlands and Indonesia. In 1962 the United Security Force was established in this disputed territory, also called West New Guinea as part of the United Nations Administration entitled, UNTEA.

It is also conceivable that probably there will be situations in the future where disputed territories will be temporarily placed under the supervision of the United Nations, and the example of UNTEA has already provided sufficient proof of the utility of United Nations forces in this area.

Another category of the functions of the United Nations forces is the *maintenance of law and order in a country*. The example of ONUC in the Congo is applicable here. Bowett, for example, talks in some detail about such a function of international military forces. He points out:

> The precedent of the Congo has shown that the United Nations may be willing to establish a force not only to assist in bringing about the withdrawal of foreign forces, but also to aid in the maintenance or restoration of public order in a State, at that State's request, and where the breakdown in law and order has been caused by or resulted in the intervention of foreign forces, and where the situation constitutes a threat to international peace. . . .[53]

However, at no time did the United Nations regard ONUC as a replacement for the Congolese domestic police or militia forces and never declared that ONUC will assume the functions of enforcing Congolese municipal laws. In fact, an analysis of the agreement between the United Nations and the Republic of the Congo concluded on November 27, 1961 clearly states in paragraph 43 (a) that ONUC "shall not apply domestic regulations and procedures, but shall act in accordance with its interpre-

[52]For details on this subject see U.N. Doc. A/AC.21/13, pp. 7 and 10.
[53]Bowett, *United Nations Forces*, p. 271.

There are still others who have argued convincingly that the present stalemate stems from the basic differences among the members in the *interpretation* of the Charter with regard to the legal limits of United Nations activity on behalf of international peace. They further point out that the Soviet Union and France are the chief exponents of a "strict constructionist" view of the Charter. That is, the Charter, being a treaty between sovereign states, should be read simply as conferring only those powers upon the United Nations' various organs that are explicitly written down.

All moves with the slightest appearance of having been designed to extend the powers of any United Nations organ beyond those explicitly given to them by the Charter are regarded as illegal so long as they are not formally approved by all parties. All powers beyond those expressly granted to the United Nations organs are reserved to the member states and can be exercised by the United Nations only if and when an expressed consent of the members has been obtained.[60]

On the other hand, it is argued that there are several countries led by the United States and several other nations that have at times reluctantly supported the General Assembly's right to call for peacekeeping forces in emergencies, and particularly if the Security Council has been incapacitated by the usage of veto. These countries also defend the Assembly's right to apportion expenses of all peacekeeping operations whether initiated by the General Assembly or the Security Council, and to demand payments.[61] Followers of this school are in full agreement on the Council's right to take the initiative in all kinds of peacekeeping activities. In fact, they insist that the Security Council has the primary responsibility in this area, *but* they maintain that they have turned to the Assembly only when the Council was unable to take action in grave crisis situations calling for a peacekeeping force. They also believe that the General Assembly has the right to apportion expenses of such operations on the basis of Article 17, paragraph 2 of the Charter.[62] Despite the advisory opinion of the International Court of Justice, affirmed by a vote of 9 to 5

[60]For a comprehensive discussion of this point, see U.N. Doc. A/AC. 121/WG. A/ PV. 2 (March 22, 1967), 11–13; see also "Issues before the 22nd General Assembly," *International Conciliation*, (564) (September 1967), 28–33; *Financing of United Nations Peace-Keeping Operations: Report of the Working Group on the Examination of the Administrative and Budgetary Procedures of the United Nations* (U.N. Doc. A/5407, March 29, 1963); and, Norman J. Padelford, "Financing Peace-Keeping: Politics and Crisis," in Norman J. Padelford and Leland M. Goodrich (eds), *The United Nations in the Balance: Accomplishments & Prospects* (New York: Praeger), 1965, pp. 82–83.
[61]For further information on the views of countries supporting this school of thought see *U.N. Monthly Chronical*, 1 (5) (October 1964), 50–56.
[62]*Ibid.*

tation of the mission assigned to it by the Security Council."[54] Here perhaps a distinction can be made (with a great deal of difficulty, however) between the Council's mandate to let ONUC assist the Congolese forces in the maintenance of law and order and a mandate to enforce Congolese law: the first mandate refers to "law and order" in a broad sense of internal stability where the efforts of a force are concentrated on protecting life and property from mob violence from any source. These kinds of functions would actually amount to prevention of a civil war by the international military force. On the other hand, the outright enforcement of Congolese law would have reduced the status of ONUC to an arm of the government carrying out its directions.

There can be, however, situations where the United Nations force will take up the functions of local police or militia, such as in the case of UNTEA where the United Nations itself can become the effective or in some cases the only administrative authority in a territory. Envision a situation where some natural disaster has taken place and a national government stands in need of United Nations assistance in enforcing law and order. The experience of the Congo operation also raises the question of whether United Nations force should take over the functions of maintaining internal law and order in situations where there is no evidence of foreign intervention or the likelihood of it in the future.

Returning to the example of the Congo operation again, there is another problem that the United Nations forces may very likely face again; that is, the United Nations may be placed in a position where it will be required to decide whether it should assume the responsibility of maintaining law and order in a state where the internal chaos is neither caused by foreign intervention, nor would be likely to encourage foreign intervention. In such a situation the international organization may be hard put to locate a threat to *international peace*. Despite the example of UNTEA, it is generally accepted that the United Nations may not intervene in such situations with a military force when forms of non-military assistance may be made available to the legal government of that country in the form of expertise and technical advisors in local law enforcement. There seems to be a widespread consensus among the international law experts that it is not within the proper legal scope of the United Nations to offer international forces to support or suppress one particular government in power.[55] Such an action would also violate the state's right of self-determination. However, as pointed out by Lauterpacht, it is not clear whether

[54]For details see the comprehensive agreement relating to the legal status, facilities, privileges, and immunities of ONUC, signed in New York on November 27, 1961 (UNTS Vol. 414). Also see U.N. Docs. A/4986 and S/5004.
[55]For a comprehensive examination of the views of international law experts on this question read, Brownlie, *International Law and the Use of Force by States* (1963), pp. 321–327.

according to international law even a government can legally help another government to suppress an internal rebellion if there is no evidence of outside intervention.[56] This may also be true, as Higgins points out, in situations where the unrest has not yet reached the proportion of a civil war that would entitle the rebels to the right to overthrow their government and bring into practice the rule of nonintervention by the third parties;[57] the reason is that if any government feels that it cannot control the situation and requires foreign assistance, either from its allies or the United Nations, then almost by definition the rebellion has reached civil war proportions and it will be even more contradictory to the principles of the United Nations and tenets of international law to commit the United Nations force in such circumstances or give them the functions of curbing civil wars.

Some functions of an international force may be classified as *plebiscite supervision*. In order to determine the legal status of a territory that is contested by two sovereign states and in order to accord the residents of that territory the right to self-determination, the international Organization may call for a plebiscite in the area to be conducted with the assistance of United Nations personnel. A limited United Nations force may play a significant role here in maintenance order and distributing information and instruction to the residents and helping the civil authorities to see that an impartial plebiscite is carried out in an orderly fashion. Examples of Togoland and Cameroon are appropriate here.

Still other functions could be classified under the title of *assistance and relief for national disasters*. Over the years the United Nations and its specialized agencies have developed a vital concern over the social, economic, and humanitarian problems of its members and is frequently called to provide long-term aid to various development plans and short-time instant relief to the victims of natural disasters such as flood, epidemics, famines, and so on. Although in the past, it is the civilian experts of the United Nations specialized agencies who have been primarily used in response to such needs but conceivably under circumstances of panic and disorder it may be more feasible if a United Nations force were to fulfill these functions. It could distribute medical supplies, food and water, reopen communications, enforce quarantine precautions; in other words, it would perform all the functions that a national armed force is normally required to perform in response to a national emergency.

United Nations forces could also be used in the *prevention of international crimes*. Under the international law there are certain crimes that are universally recognized, and the United Nations force here could

[56]E. Lauterpacht, "Intervention by Invitation," *I.C.L.Q.*, 7 (1958), 99.

[57]R. Higgins, "Legal Limits to the Use of Force by Sovereign States—United Nations Practice," *British Yearbook of International Law*, 37 (1961), 308–331.

in fact act as a police force in the prevention of these generally acknowledged international crimes. Some examples of these crimes are genocide, narcotics, piracy, and slave traffic. The source of international law could be either by a treaty such as in the case of Genocide Convention and the numerous conventions on the control of illicit narcotics trade, or by custom such as piracy, or by a general and common affirmation as resolved by the United Nations.[58] A word of caution is necessary here: an international force can perform police functions in the prevention of international crimes only as an arm to a judicial body such as an international criminal court. In the absence of such a court the functions then can only be effectively performed by an international force if and when the member nations accept the proposition that the United Nations is capable of and should be given "supernational" authority.

Perhaps in a distant future the United Nations force can also take up the functions of supervising disarmament plans and inspecting arms control, after an international treaty has been signed for a complete and general disarmament. With the above understanding of United Nations forces both in past and future we can turn to the legal sources of United Nations authority in the area of peacekeeping activities.

United Nations peacekeeping forces—a reappraisal of relevant charter provisions

There is no lack of agreement among the scholars in the discipline and the delegates to the United Nations on the significance of the legal basis of the United Nations peacekeeping activities. The question of legal limits to the use of force by the world organization has been debated before and no doubt will come up again and again in the international arena and no doubt will come up again and again, for it is directly related to the future effectiveness of the organization in keeping world peace. Several times in the last two decades or so, the United Nations has authorized military forces to deal with a threat to peace. In each instance there were some who have pointed out that the United Nations operation may have averted a third world war. But in each instance there were others who have argued that perhaps the world organization is not equipped, within the constitutional framework of the Charter, to deal with such actual or potential threats to world peace.[59]

[58]See, for instance, the affirmation of United Nations members in the General Assembly Resolution 95 (1) of the Nuremburg Principles, and the Draft Code of Offenses against Peace and Security of Mankind which includes the crime of "terrorism," genocide and so forth, *American Journal of International Law*, Special Supplement 19 (1955), p. 49.

[59]Consider, for example, the repeated urgings by Brazilian delegates that the U.N. Charter must be revised to "provide for a new chapter on peace-keeping operations," U.N. Doc. A/AC 121/PV. 33 (March 29, 1968), 2.

of the judges in July, 1962,[63] that the expenditures authorized by the General Assembly for operations in the Congo and the Middle East were "expenses of the Organization" within the meaning of Article 17, paragraph 2 of the United Nations Charter, and despite the acceptance of this opinion in the General Assembly,[64] and the resolution entitled "General Principles to Serve as Guidelines for the Sharing of the Costs of Future Peace-Keeping Operations Involving Heavy Expenditures," which was adopted by an overwhelming majority of the General Assembly,[65] it must be pointed out that followers of this school have not been able to convince the other side of the legal soundness of their position. Debate between the two camps continues without any signs of compromise. The legal issues today seem more confused than ever.

Starting with the Korean and Suez operations and moving on to United Nations involvement in the Congo and Cyprus, one thing becomes quite clear: there is now an urgent need for a greater understanding and clarity of legal implications of international military actions. Although much of the public attention has been focused mainly on the military and political aspects of United Nations peacekeeping, the past operations, particularly the Congo operation, have given rise to many new legal developments and problems of Charter interpretation that are still far from being resolved.

With the experience of these several United Nations operations one might have thought that by this time the United Nations would have a solid legal foundation on which to establish the most desirable kind of force needed for any future crisis. But for two reasons this has not been possible. First, the existing political climate in the United Nations and elsewhere simply did not permit past forces to be established under ideal or consensual interpretations of the Charter concerning the use of force by the organization; and, second, because these forces were put together in direct response to crisis situations, the legal authority of various U.N. organs responsible for their creation has remained unclear and unsatisfactory up to the present time.

Because of this continued confusion and lack of consensus, which have resulted in persistent stalemates, fresh and determined efforts must be made to liquidate the legacies of the past so-called "illegal" peacekeeping operations. Relevant Charter provisions must be reviewed in the hope

[63]For details read *Certain Expenses of the United Nations* (Article 17, paragraph 2, of the U.N. Charter), Advisory Opinion of July 20, 1962; I.C.J. *Reports* (1962), 151–308.

[64]General Assembly Resolution 1854 (XVII) (December 19, 1962), which was adopted by a vote of 76 to 17, with 8 abstentions.

[65]General Assembly Resolution 1854 (S-IV) (June 27, 1963), which was adopted by a vote of 92 in favor, 11 opposed, with 3 abstentions.

that the future will bring a meeting of minds between the various factions of U.N. membership on the question of legal competence of various U.N. organs in the area of peacekeeping activities.

A concluding remark

On the desirability of a United Nations intervention and the extent of it, the legal problems associated with the United Nations interventions in an international crises may be regarded as secondary to the problems of political consensus among the conflicting member states. One can go a step further and state that even most legal problems have in the final analysis political foundations. But it would be folly not to realize that once such a consesus has withered after the initial establishment of a peace-keeping operation (or if it never existed, as has been true in most instances), the disillusioned states never fail to raise constitutional objections to the authority of the Secretary-General, the mandate of the force under consideration, and most important, the legal competence of the United Nations organ responsible for initiating the establishment of the force.

chapter 5
international law and economic development

Because of the vast disparities in the living standards of poor and rich nations and because modern communication has now made it possible for the inhabitants of poor countries to be keenly aware of their plight, economic development, modernization, and industrialization remain among the most powerful goals for most nations. It is a goal to which international law has responded in several positive ways, and there is still room for further development in this area.[1]

First, international law is deeply concerned with the important need of developing societies to share world resources and the material benefits from such exploitation. Several legal questions of jurisdiction and criteria of allocation are involved here. The problem is particularly complex when applied to the natural resources of such a new and potentially rich area as the seabed. Consider, for instance, the growing disutility of the doctrine of the continental shelf; by defining the area of national jurisdiction on the shelf, this doctrine has encouraged exploitation of the resources on the shelf *beyond* the limits of national jurisdiction by the few technologically advanced nations that can most afford to indulge in this enterprise because of their technology, and yet least need to because of their already very high standards of living as compared with the rest of the world, which is essentially poor. Exactly what laws apply to the control of these potentially rich resources under water? Do the advanced nations have an a priori right to exploit these resources for their own economic benefit just because they have the technology and the expertise to do so? Most important, what about the oldest and one of the most cherished international laws of the sea that says the "sea is the heritage of all mankind"? This law clearly implies that the sea's resources belong to all nations regardless of who does the exploitation? There have been several long and

[1]Consider the International Covenant on Economic, Social and Cultural Rights, developed in 1966. In part, it reads "rights of everyone. . . . to enjoy the benefits of scientific progress and its applications."

heated debates between the industrial and nonindustrial nations in the United Nations in this area. No definite conclusions have yet resulted. Legal questions of jurisdiction are not yet settled. The shelf doctrine has had the reverse effect of what it was intended for. It has encouraged a new era of land grabbing, or as someone has put it, "colonialism all over again," this time underwater by the rich and more powerful states who have already developed the technology to exploit these resources for their own benefits. This subject will be further discussed later in this chapter. Clearly all the pertinent legal questions are not settled, although the subject remains very much alive in international discussions in the United Nations and elsewhere, and some new legal norms have begun to emerge in this area.

With regard to the resources on the land, international law has always been concerned with the use of international rivers and waterways that travel through the territory of either one nation (but have been used by others as well according to usage and old custom) or cross the territories of several nations. It has in the past offered legal norms of, for example, navigation and custom, and now new principles are emerging to broaden the scope of law to include the regulation of flood control efforts, irrigation, recreation, and power generation activities by the states in relation to these waterways. With the growth of law in this area of economic development, interstate commerce will be better managed. The latest in the series of international concerns is the problem of pollution control and, to be sure, new legal norms are being developed to curb pollution among states that share a common river or waterway.[2]

Second, major concern of international law in the economic development of nations is to make available nuclear energy for peaceful purposes. For some time many developing and other countries have hoped to acquire the skills to harness nuclear energy for developmental purposes. They consider this energy vital for the rapid economic development of their countries. Specific areas of interest are the use of nuclear explosions to excavate large areas of land for purposes such as the construction of artificial lakes for water storage in irrigation, the control of weather patterns for agricultural growth, the construction of canals and harbors for navigation and trade purposes, and for gaining access to the underground to tap more efficiently their oil, gas, and other mineral resources.

For two main reasons nuclear energy has not been made available to these countries. Development of relevant international legal norms has

[2]See International Law Association, *Final Report of the Committee on the Uses of the Waters of International Rivers* (London), 1966. See also, U.S. Department of State, *Memorandum on Legal Aspects of the Use of Systems of International Waters* (Washington, D.C.), 1958.

helped and can further help to eliminate at least one of these two reasons. The other reason is not an insurmountable problem because it is technical in nature. First, the use of nuclear energy for excavation is still very dangerous for fear of uncontrollable fallout. Second, present nuclear countries (who also possess weapons of mass destruction) have no real desire to let proliferate the development or distribution of nuclear weapons through this rather "harmless" method of nuclear energy sharing. To distribute this energy without proper laws and controls means to alter the status quo in which these countries reap whatever political benefits might be associated with being a member of the so-called exclusive "nuclear club." However, along with some benefits there are also grave political liabilities associated with this membership. It should be noted that the nuclear technology involved and the amount of plutonium needed for large-size excavation purposes are roughly the same as needed for constructing a medium-size nuclear bomb.

The first reason for the reluctance to share nuclear energy is a purely technical one and is being resolved at that level. The second reason involves important questions of national security and the maintenance of international peace and security that probably will be jeopardized if there was a proliferation of nuclear weapons. It is here that international law has made its contribution. The need for the use of nuclear energy for peaceful purposes was one of the major factors that led to the conclusion of two very important treaties designed to curtail the spread of nuclear weapons, provide assurances for security and stability, and thus free the use of nuclear energy for peaceful purposes from the fear of its misuse for belligerent purposes. These treaties have undoubtedly contributed to the growth of international law in general and of specific international laws that provide necessary assurances against violations. One of these treaties is Non-Proliferation of Nuclear Weapons Treaty. This treaty limits the spread of nuclear weapons to areas where they already existed when the treaty was signed. On the other hand, it encourages cooperation among all states in the peaceful uses of atomic energy. One of its important features is that the nations who possess nuclear weapons for developmental projects will provide other states with what is termed by some scholars a "nuclear explosive service" *at cost*. The treaty was signed in 1968, and during this year many developing societies got organized and demanded, under the provisions of the treaty, that all relevant information concerning the nonmilitary uses of this energy be turned over to the International Atomic Energy Agency (IAEA). They further demanded that a special fund be set up from the contributions of "have" nations under the supervision of IAEA for the purposes of partly financing the special nuclear explosives service, which they further demanded be set up right away.

They have, to this writing, achieved some modest success in their demands.[3]

The second treaty referred to here is the Treaty for the Prohibition of Nuclear Weapons in Latin America, signed in 1967. This treaty, which establishes a "nuclear free zone" in this region, eliminates the chances of the development of nuclear weapons by the states of this region. The legal norms developed out of this agreement have opened up the way for the use of atomic energy for development of these national economies. This treaty specifically permits the signatories to cooperate with each other for the purpose of employing nuclear energy for excavation under the safeguards developed by IAEA.

Similarly, new international laws have also emerged concerning fishing in the high seas. Here the law provides access to all states, although unlike the treaty governing atomic energy and its uses, it does not obligate the rich nations to help the poor states develop their fishing techniques in order to be able to take the equal advantage of the law. In contrast to the practice in the high seas, the treaty concerning the uses of outer space, signed in 1967, specifically states that the exploration and the uses of outer space will be carried out for the benefit of *all countries of the world*. Yet this philosophy that "all nations share" is not to be found in legal norms concerning the exploitation of the continental shelf, just as is true with fishing in the high seas. While the Convention on the Continental Shelf, signed in 1958, at least temporarily resolved the problem of jurisdiction by giving states sovereignty over a specific portion of the shelf for purposes of exploration and exploitation of its resources, thus halting the onslaught of industrially developed countries, *it created no obligation* for the rich to help the poor in their attempt to explore and exploit the resources of the shelf. No significant cooperative legal doctrines have been developed in this area yet.

The third major concern of international law in the field of economic development deals with the monetary problems of the world: for instance, with the perennial foreign exchange problem most acutely faced by many poor countries. This problem is the relation of *foreign exchange* earned by a poor nation in return for the *sale of its raw material* (or several primary agricultural crop commodities). Many developing societies at present are heavily dependent on the foreign exchange they accumulate (in "hard" currencies) through these sales. They need the foreign exchange to purchase heavy machinery and other capital goods badly needed for the success of their modest developmental efforts. Barring all natural catastrophies (which international law cannot regulate and which

---

[3]For a stimulating discussion of this topic, see L. Scheinman, "Nuclear Safeguards, the Peaceful Atom and the IAEA," *International Conciliation*, (573) (March 1969).

can and often does destroy marketable products) if the prices of these products were *also* to fall in the international market, a poor country can very quickly have its foreign exchange reserves wiped out. This would result in a total upset of the balance of payments, thus halting various developmental projects that depended on the government's ability to earn foreign exchange.

In order to resolve the above dilemma and many more related problems, international law has attempted, in the above case for instance, to stabilize the prices of various commodities that are bought and sold in the international market place. International commodity commissions have been established for the specific purpose of relating world output to world needs, establishing the minimum and maximum prices of commodities and setting up national quotas. Paradoxically, given the present complexities and contradictions of international economics, there are conflicting goals involved in the fields of law and economic development. For instance, the economic goal of greater food production to feed the millions of hungry people in these countries makes it extremely difficult for international law to regulate and maintain high prices for these products, thus resulting in shortages of foreign exchange for developmental projects.[4]

The fourth major concern of international law in the field of economic development deals with the technological advances that have been made in the last two decades. Let us consider, for instance, the development of satellites and their remote sensing devices such as multispectral photography. According to the experts in this field,[5] this development promises a great deal for the economic development of regions that need it the most. The device takes pictures of the earth from outer space, detects undiscovered earth resources, such as minerals and gases and monitors their present status by detecting radiation emission across the wavelength spectrum. The use of this device can also indicate climatic changes, approaching storms, and tidal waves (these two tasks are already being performed by weather satellites), the movement of wildlife, conditions of crops, and conditions in this sea. Most of this information can be used to develop meaningful international laws for the purpose of establishing a worldwide system of efficient utilization of untapped or presently wasted

[4]In fact, this has already happened in several areas. For instance, in 1967, The International Grains Agreement was signed to stabilize wheat prices in the world market. The whole agreement suddenly collapsed two years later, when in the summer of 1969 the wheat producing countries were able to harvest a bumper crop. Under the pressure of "surplus" wheat in the world market, it was not possible to maintain a minimum price.

[5]See the publications of the National Academy of Sciences—National Research Council, Division of Engineering, *Useful Application of Earth-Oriented Satellites-Systems for Remote Sensing Information and Distribution*, (Washington, D.C.), 1969.

global resources. This can be done without having to ask the rich nations to give up their resources already in use to help the poor. In other words, new international law could deal essentially with the economic potential of this globe, which at the present time is either being wasted because of inefficiencies or not being used at all. Within such a context it should not be too difficult to develop laws that threaten no one and promise to help all by bringing the new technological breakthroughs within the province of international law. Several scholars in the social sciences and in law have suggested that the first step toward the development of international legislation in this area should be the creation of a worldwide resources data-retrieval system, perhaps under the auspices of the United Nations; this system would be similar to the informational system that is already in service in connection with communications satellites.

Fifth, and a relatively new area of concern for international law, is the population explosion in the poor countries of the world that are already heavily populated and are the least prepared, both psychologically and physically, to control it. There is a need for international legislation in this area. Such a legislation could be coupled with the availability of necessary information and assistance for effective birth control programs. In addition, legal norms may provide various material incentives to the people who help control the population growth and impose sanctions against those who continue to contribute to the already aggravated problem by their irresponsible behavior. Birth control, especially involuntary birth control, is an extremely sensitive area because of the religious and other values involved. But this sensitivity must be measured against other values of human dignity that a continuing population explosion violates; for example, by any conservative estimate there must be millions of children with problems of poor health and malnutrition and with a generally bleak future in this world, many of them barely managing to keep body and soul together from day to day. The plight of grown-ups in some parts of the world is even worse. Most of them are ignorant about how to improve their lives and are stifled in their attempts to change by the straightjacket of their religious taboos. Is it not reasonable to suggest that any contribution that international law can make to slow down the rate of population growth is bound to help the goal of economic development at a global level? By slowing down this rate, law can slow down the rate of consumption of world resources and, moreover, in a more concrete sense it can provide an opportunity to the poor countries to raise their standard of living.

A sixth area of concern for international law in economic development is the concept of full employment as a possible goal for law to support. In recent decades there has been an increase in economic interdependence and this has also affected the content of international law. There is a general acceptance, among most nations today, that full employment represents the most far-reaching change in economic thinking that has occurred since the eighteenth century.[6] During the first 10 years after the Second World War, this thinking resulted in the general acceptance of the responsibility of pursuing the goal of full employment and this acceptance has since led to an increasing concern in international law. The United Nations Charter recognizes this responsibility of the world community and so does the constitution of the International Labor Organization. An analysis of the Articles of Agreement of the International Monetary Fund also indicate this concern, as does the Charter of the International Bank for Reconstruction and Development. Even the General Agreement on Tariffs and Trade supports this responsibility. There are also supportive provisions in the legal documents that are regionally applicable, for example, the Convention on European Economic Cooperation to which 17 European nations subscribe, and the Charter of the organization of the American states that is signed by 21 states.

In other words, most nation-states, by their consent to one or more legal documents have recognized the need for full employment and accepted this responsibility. For instance, the United Nations Charter embodies a pledge according to which states are "to take joint and separate action in cooperation with the Organization for the achievement of . . . higher standards of living, full employment, and conditions of economic and social progress and development." This pledge marked the beginning of state responsibility in this area and thus a concern by international law.

A seventh area of concern for international law in the field of economic development deals more particularly with the needs of developing societies. It can be titled "concerns of law for general international welfare." International law has been slowly expanding in this area to include the interstate cooperation for purposes of international welfare. This expansion has led to the new term, "international welfare law." To a certain extent this law of welfare corresponds to the term used by W. Friedman, "cooperative international law." It is essentially a law concerned with the creation of circumstances conducive, for example, to the well-being of states, promotion of higher standards of living, full employment, and various forms of social and economic progress.

At the present time, much of this relatively new, but constantly developing body of law, is more truly regional than universal in scope and nature. Much of it is based upon articulate lawmaking techniques such as conventions, declarations, and treaties rather than custom or judicial

[6]In support of this point see G. Myrdal, *An International Economy—Problems and Prospects* (New York: Harper & Brothers), 1956.

interpretation. However, in certain areas of human welfare there is a universal interest and consensus, for example, on effective international cooperation and mutual assistance in cultural, educational, as well as medical matters.

A concluding remark

With each passing year the revolution of sinking expectations in the world is spreading rapidly, thanks to our systems of modern communication. Along with the spread of this revolution, the gap between the rich and the poor countries, in terms of differences in the standards of living, is increasing. The entire field of international economic development poses two pressing major problems for the world community to resolve. (1) At a certain minimal acceptable level, somehow a more just allocation of resources of the world must be achieved. Rich nations have a choice here; they can either share their existing resources more justly with the poor nations and, at the same time, really help the poor nations develop their own resources rapidly, or further contribute to this revolution. It appears that contemporary international law favors the first alternative. (2) If the first alternative is acceptable, then some kind of universal mutual technical assistance program must be initiated. It must be free as possible from the dictates of political considerations and narrow self-interests. Such a program would allow the poor countries to exploit their own resources for economic development. In both problem areas, the international community *has* begun to organize and mobilize itself. Some international legal norms in this area are already here, waiting to be further articulated by the political will of the international community.

A note of reemphasis is appropriate at this point. In the evolution of a more peaceful and lawful world we should not underestimate the significance of international economic development in the poor countries. National leaders of developing societies who are struggling with the problems of mass poverty, disease, and hunger are more concerned with the construction of laws supporting economic development than, for instance, with laws of conflict resolution, because in their order of priorities they rate economic development higher than the avoidance of violence. To most of them avoidance of a possible nuclear war is too far removed from their everyday concerns of survival to be rated extremely high among national objectives. To argue that prevention of a general war or management of conflict is *all* we require from international law is to sell law short. This view may be an overriding and a sufficient aim for a handful of rich and well-armed states oriented toward the status quo. But, surely, it is a view that leaves much of the countries in the rest of the world stuck in their daily miseries and poverty (which their colonial past contributed to) and stuck with the "comforting" thought: now that the international law has made war impossible, they can continue to exist as always. It is the kind of view that frequently ensures the condemnation of international law as nothing more than "Western" law or the law of the "rich."

The entire field of international law and economic development points out one of the serious problems in our study of international law. It appears that neither the law experts and lawyers nor the scholars who have restricted their enquiry to the classical methods and norms of international law are equipped to handle such dynamic and relatively new subjects under the domain of international law without the cooperation of the social scientists. International law is becoming extremely complex. This complexity alone is a genuine proof of its relevance to international politics, which has become complex.

chapter 6
international law: an agent of international communication, socialization, and integration and a catalyst for the development of an international political culture

Contemporary international law and the multiple institutional arrangements (such as the United Nations, International Court of Justice, and a host of special purpose international organizations) created to facilitate its role in the international system, work to communicate a climate of opinion more conducive to the establishment of a lawful society.[1] They also work to socialize the members of the international society (e.g., states, international organizations, private groups and corporations, and individuals) to the norms of international law and the advantages in following them in their international relations. Moreover, international law and its supportive institutions perform some important integrative functions in the international area, thus nudging its members, slowly but surely, toward the development of a greater and wider consensus on the nature of the international system and the place of international law in it.

International law, in its role of communicating and developing a climate of opinion about the nature of international system, as Professor W. D. Coplin has so aptly and convincingly put it, is not very much different from municipal law that plays the same role in democractic

[1]For an interesting discussion on this point see William D. Coplin, "International Law and Assumptions About the State System,: *World Politics, 17* (1965), 615–635.

societies where it attempts to develop a consensus on the nature of civil society.[2] However, the task of communication in the international system is made complicated because of the presence of conflicting ideologies that make the attainment of international consensus difficult, because of seemingly incompatible national interests, and because of the existence of disparate value systems made further complicated by the perception of differences in all of these areas.

The task of international socialization and integration is also hampered because the international law and its supporting institutions are the only agents of socialization that attempt to express and inform the members of the international society about the legal norms and structures of this society. There is no significant number of public or private institutions in the domestic system that could help international law and organizations in their job of socialization. There do not seem to be any parental concerns in the family with regard to the socialization of the young concerning international norms, values, or political culture. There is not a great deal of educational activity even in the most "international" national systems that is directly related to international understanding, the building of legal norms, and the process of international consensus development.

With almost 150 independent and sovereign states vigorously pursuing their own interests in the international system today, contemporary international law, in order to be successful in this three fold task, must overcome an infinite number of socioeconomic, political, and cultural differences further underlined by differences of habits, thoughts, and priorities. Moreover, in the minds of most individuals, and in the international system and its legal norms, rewards and sanctions are decidedly secondary to the concerns and jurisdictions of the domestic system. Then, there are the technical problems of communication, and the difficulty posed by the multiplicity of languages, as well as the nonavailability of the masses for specialization to the norms of international law.

Even with all the above stated difficulties and roadblocks, international law has done modestly well. Despite its limited resources and spokesmen for its cause, *it has succeeded* in initiating the process of communication for the development of a more favorable atmosphere for its own rules and in the initial growth of an international political culture that can only emerge after some success has been achieved in the socialization of the international community to its legal norms and in the integration of the value systems of its membership.

Let us begin our analysis of the success of international law in this

[2]W. D. Coplin, *The Functions of International Law: An Introduction to the Role of International Law in the Contemporary World* (Chicago: Rand McNally), 1966, Chapter 5.

area by first noting that international law is spelled out in the language of a logically interrelated set of rules and expectations. Therefore, it does provide a common set of mostly commonsense-oriented norms, deeply influenced by "reasonableness" and "fair-play" types of philosophy. This common set of norms performs the important function of communication across the international system. It orients the policymakers and all other members of the system to the "rules of the game." Most states generally use these rules to communicate with each other. According to Professors W. L. Gould and M. Barkun, there is a great deal of similarity between the language that nations use to communicate with each other and the language of contemporary international law.[3] Consider, for instance, the important communicative role that diplomatic channels play in international relations. This traditional mode of communication uses international law as a language. Although the techniques of international communication have been recently modified because of the impact of science and technology and other radical changes in the system, international law remains one of the most effective languages of communication.

The very fact that despite the concurrent revolutions in the nature of international politics, international law remains the standard language for communication and the standard method (e.g., in diplomatic procedures) of communication, clearly suggests it is succeeding, slowly but surely, in socializing its subjects toward a commonality of beliefs, attitudes, and behavior. This "international law socialization" is not a very complicated concept at all. It simply means that in their relationships the members of international society must learn, accept, and abide by international legal norms. Compared with socialization in the domestic system, it is a much slower process of feeling the need, coming to rely upon, and conscienciously learning to live with the norms of international law. It is the process that has in the past, and still today affects the way individual states view international relations. Western societies have for the most part already gone through this process and now are learning to accept the changes in the content of law that are being initiated under pressure from the other two camps, the socialist and the Third World camp. Socialization to the norms of international law is admittedly a more painful process for the Third World countries because law is mixed up with the legacy of past colonial exploitations and because of the apparent reluctance of the West to accept into the body of the law reforms initiated by the Third World, reforms that will close the last chapter of a seemingly priviledged position of the West under the law.

[3]For details see W. L. Gould and M. Barkun, *International Law and the Social Sciences* (Princeton, N.J.: Princeton University Press), 1970, pp. 136–151.

International law, although far less developed and far less assisted in its mission than is domestic law, has succeeded in socializing the states to the acceptance of its norms if only in their own national self-interest. It has persuaded and has prevailed to a remarkable extent in an international society torn by an impressive variety of conflict being waged by its membership with varying degrees of intensity. For example, at the superpower level, it has played a significant role in socializing the United States to its recently acquired role of world leadership (since the Second World War). With the beginning of the Presidency of Teddy Roosevelt, the United States entered into the international arena, overcame its abhorrence of the web of diplomatic tangles and moods of isolationism and has continued to play a role in world politics with increasing significance. Today, the world leadership status of the United States is shared by the Soviet Union. The United States has, however, made some terrible errors of judgment in international relations, and it is still at times tempted to revert to an era of the comforting seclusion called "isolationism"; nonetheless, it has long accepted the role of international law in the making and execution of its foreign policy. We do not suggest that the United States always acts legally in world affairs, but simply observe that in everyday decision making, the United States usually follows legal norms even though there is little more than a simple self-enforcing mechanism for law observance. With due respect to those observers who insist that the only task international lawyers and other legal advisors to the U.S. State Department perform is to make a "legal case" for foreign policy decisions based on purely political grounds, it can be *equally* observed that these people do in reality also advise the policymakers of the legal constraints applicable to an issue.

International law has partially succeeded in socializing to its norms even the Soviet Union and the People's Republic of China. The Soviet Union, after becoming a "have" nation and acquiring a superpower status, is now apparently replacing its revolutionary impulses with more conservative, stable, predictable, and status-quo–oriented behavior in the international arena. There is some truth to the Chinese characterization of the Soviet Union as being a "revisionist," "soft on capitalism," and socialist state. The recent handling of several international crises by China, its role in the United Nations and its successful attempt to break through its recent isolationist past are indications that international law will probably make a greater impact on the People's Republic of China in the decades to come.

In our attempt to analyze the relationship between international law and international politics we are now becoming more sensitive to the role of international law as an agent of communication, socialization, and integration because of three important recent developments in the study of international law. First, a general recognition by the social scientists that the United Nations is more than what its charter says; indeed this recognition also applies to dozens of other regional, functional, and international organizations to a lesser degree. The United Nations is an effective agency of international communication, socialization, and integration. Despite its shortcomings in the area of conflict resolution, it remains an effective arm of international law in the realization of these tasks. Some one hundred and thirty-five nations belong to this organization, and membership is constantly enlarging. East and West Germany have just been admitted to its membership. They may be followed perhaps by North and South Korea. Because all of its members are required to maintain permanent missions at its headquarters in New York, serve on its various committees and councils, take part in its deliberations, and vote on a wide variety of international issues, the United Nations assists in the role of international law. To a lesser extent the same functions are also performed by other international organizations (lesser because their membership and functions are restricted).[4] Second, articulation of the notion by international relations and law experts that the concept of "socialization" need not apply only to individuals in a domestic political system. For functional purposes it can be applied to states as members of the international political system.[5] Third, a broad probing of international law by contemporary social scientists and a utilization of their tools to determine the role of law in politics empirically. For instance, some scholars have argued that fairly well-developed theories of communication, socialization, and integration can be fruitfully used in conjunction with legal theory to develop important insights in the complex question of *why states observe or violate international law?* Dictates of national interests is a simplistic answer at best. It does not tell us much. Is it not reasonable to suggest that the behavior of a state in this area is partly determined by the degree of information, communication, and socialization that exist between inhabitants of this state and international law and therefore between this state and other states because of law?

What is being suggested above is that the concept of "a world of law and order" is similar to the concept of "international law as an agent of communication, socialization, and integration." As law becomes a more successful agent of these tasks, more of the law will be observed; consequently more law and order will exist and, thus, more legal rules will tell us about a state's predisposition to observe law. Conceivably, a combi-

---

[4]On this topic see C. F. Alger, "United Nations' Participation as a Learning Experience," *Public Opinion Quarterly*, 27 (1963), pp. 411–426.

[5]Social psychologists and political sociologists have helped us realize this notion. A good work in this area is H. C. Kelman (ed.) *International Behavior: A Social Psychological Analysis* (New York: Holt, Rinehart, and Winston), 1966.

nation of the above stated concepts can help us understand the existence of this process in international society's acceptance of international law as such an agent. This degree of law acceptance then can be used to measure actual observable state behavior and develop from this observation an index of law "effectiveness" or an index of distance between the present practices of states vis à vis a "world of law and order." In any event this law and order—the communication, socialization, and integration relationship—offers us a concept of international legal order grounded in empirically observable phenomena. These phenomena can help us measure the degree of law observance without any reference to the notions of force and sanctions that are reasons for observing the law. Note that international law as an agent for social communication, socialization, and integration can help states to put a high priority on its observance without the fear of sanctions.

It is extremely important that at least for the present a student of law must view international law as a multipurpose phenomenon performing many functions along with, of course, the important traditional function of imposing restraints on uninhibited interstate behavior. The task of integration of the world society is closely related to communication-socialization functions of law. In fact we can view integration as the final product of many other functions of law. In this respect the study of international law can be regarded as study of international integration. One can view, for instance, the integration of Western Europe, partly because of the impact of international law in that region. In many other regions of the world there seems to be a growing emphasis on social, economic, and political integration. It is reasonable to suggest here that international law can promote integration in these regions because it serves to express and communicate common values and provides the basis for cooperation. After all, these two objectives are not inconsistent with the "general principles of international law" referred to in Article 38 of the Statute of the International Court of Justice.

Finally, it must be emphasized that as communication, socialization, and integration in the world society increase, not only the state responsiveness toward international law will increase, but also further development of international political culture will eventually take place. International law and its supportive institutions thus can also contribute to a still vaguely felt feeling by decision makers that international political culture provides a suitable framework for international politics.

There are forces in the international arena that tend to work against the further development of an international political culture. For instance, there is the ever-present reminder by national institutions that "states have just too little in common," "there is too much conflict among states," "states are here to stay," etc. to allow sharing a common set of beliefs or development of an international political culture. Second, there is another prevalent attitude. Here are some examples: "Sure we need an international political culture, but its too early" and "there is some basis for sharing common attitudes toward the international system but it's insufficient." International law has attempted to curtail these attitudes because these attitudes usually stem from unpredictability and suspicion of "other" states' intentions that law through its norms of behavior attempts to combat. Professor Coplin has called these types of attitude zero-sum thinking, because states perceive their international relations with each other as gains or losses that are essentially made at the direct expense of others or at their own expense.[6] For instance, international conflict in any region or the East-West conflict on the global scale is viewed from the perspective of "pure conflict" situation. In such a situation, cooperation, communications, and bargaining are minimized, and certainly there is little possibility of developing common sets of attitudes. However, in reality, much of international politics is a nonzero-sum game or, as the game theorists have indicated, a positive-sum game. This implies nations do not always make their gains in foreign affairs at the direct expense of other states and that it is possible out of an international bargaining situation for all sides to be somewhat if not totally satisfied. Moreover, a state's gains are derived generally from its coalition-formation ability with other states, its knowledge of its opponents value scales, and on the quality of its communications and bargaining skills. There are other forces that tend to inhibit the maturation process of an international political culture. International law and its supportive institutions provide means to inhibit somewhat the effects of these forces and, thus, through its functions discussed in the preceeding pages attempts to develop an international political culture.

[6]Coplin, *The Functions of International Law*, p. 192.

chapter 7

international law as
a procedure for
the transaction
of interstate commerce

Contemporary international law today offers a variety of rules and principles for the governance of international commercial transactions. In this respect, in the field of international commerce, trade, and monetary transactions it is commonly known as "international commercial law." Given the problems of legal jurisdictions on commercial transactions, concepts such as "international public law," "international private law," and the applicability of the principles of "conflict of laws," it is not easy to define clearly the role of *international commercial law* in international transactions.

First, while international commercial transactions, trade and aid programs have been in operation for hundreds of years, until recently agreements resulting out of this activity were not treated under the rules of international (public) law. Up to now business transactions were generally regarded as the concern, for example, of private groups, organizations, and merchants who actually conducted them. Consequently, these transactions were governed by well-established business practices out of which later emerged the "private" international law, thus creating the need to call the "regular" international law as "public" international law for purposes of distinction. In the past there were occasions, as is indeed true now, when it was not clear whether a particular transaction was under the jurisdiction of public or private international law; as such a determination was made under the rules of conflict of laws, which is in fact international private law, particularly in cases where one party to the transaction was a government and the other a private foreign corporation.

Since the Second World War and particularly in the past two decades the nature of international business transactions have changed significantly. An ever-increasing proportion of commercial activity is being conducted either by governments themselves or under strict, at times complex, governmental regulations and controls. Because of this increasing interjection of governments in matters of trade and other financial transactions, it was inevitable that many agreements and treaties to cover this activity had to come under the jurisdictions of contemporary international law, better known as international commercial law. It is possible to establish a set of circumstances under which we can view present-day international commercial transactions as being facilitated by the norms of contemporary international law.

Circumstance 1. If a business transaction is completed between two states, or between a state and an international organization, or between two international organizations having a legal personality, this transaction can be covered by the norms of contemporary international law. One of the major reasons why governments have increasingly become involved in international business and monetary transactions is the nature of present economic interdependence in the international arena. This interdependence has resulted in a tremendous increase in the sheer volume of transactions with an increasing complexity and variety. In an age of supremacy of international politics over international economics in many instances, and the simple fact that more and more international rules and regulations are required to keep the international transactions within a mutually acceptable and predictable political framework, the increasing role of states and thus of international commercial law is understandable.

There are several other important reasons for such wide governmental involvement in business affairs. A fair amount of international trade in arms and other strategic materials deals directly with the question of national security or military preparedness to start a war. No government is willing to leave such international transactions entirely to its private groups. Another important area is the so-called welfare, or economic assistance area. This includes situations where a government receives aid or "buys" foreign products in its own "soft" currency from a government of another country. On either side the necessity of receiving and giving economic assistance inevitably involves governmental participation. Two examples will illuminate what is being suggested here. The sale of French military equipment by a French corporation to the Egyptian government could not now take place without the consent of the French government, or the sale of American surplus wheat to India in Indian rupees could not occur even between two private organizations, without some involvement of American and Indian governments.

Apart from important security or welfare needs as a motivating factor in governments becoming involved in business transactions, there are important considerations of "balance of trade" and the shortages of (for developing societies, particularly) foreign exchanges badly needed for imports. Such considerations have always invited governmental controls and other related involvements. These could take place between states or between a state and an international organization. Another major reason why governments have increasingly become directly involved in international trade is, of course, the growing complexity, sensitivity, and the great volume of commercial transactions today.

There are many types of international financial transactions that have always been handled by governments exclusively and as such are subject to regulations of international commercial law. Some of these transactions are, interstate currency agreements, financial loans to other states, economic and technical assistance programs, and exchange rates agreements.[1] Many industrial states have fairly well-developed domestic laws to guide their business conduct in international transactions. However, it is politically desirable that their activities in this area should be also governed by international rules of commerce. It is true contemporary international commercial law does not have a well-developed body of codified, formally agreed upon legal rules. In the absence of specific rules, states generally follow the well-established principles of private international law. This is true for loans, service contracts, or sales. The sources of these principles can be traced to the general principles of law as practiced by civilized nations. These principles can be discovered by systematic comparative studies of legal norms practiced by major governments in the world.[2]

A great deal of governmental commercial activity at the present time is the activities of semiautonomous business enterprises in which governments have controlling shares, such as government-controlled airlines, shipping corporations, and oil and steel companies. These business enterprises have a dual nature. They usually tend to be *public* in their sales and services abroad and have governmental controls in their operations and administrations, but they are *private* in their motive of making profits and in their everyday operations. To what extent international transactions between such private-public corporations can be treated under the norms of international commercial law is subject to speculation. However, since the conduct of these enterprises is governed by the commercial instead of political motives, international commercial law should be applicable here.

---

[1]Consider the significance of barter agreements made under the provisions of international commercial law. These agreements are very important in the commercial transactions between Communist bloc states and the other states, because in the face of vast shortages of foreign exchanges, the ability of these Communist states (by virtue of their government controlled economics) to purchase large quantities of stable commodities is affected.

[2]For details see W. Friedman, *The Changing Structure of International Law*, p. 171.

Circumstance 2. If the commercial and financial transactions are carried out by international monetary organizations or other large public international financial agencies that have sprung up since the Second World War, their activities are subject to the rules of contemporary international commercial law. Several good examples here are the activities of the International Bank for Reconstruction and Development and its two recently acquired affiliates, the International Development Association and the International Finance Corporation; the European Investment Bank of the European Common Market; or the Inter-American Development Bank; all of these agencies negotiate financial agreements for loans with various states and private corporations that are financially backed by their governments. It is generally agreed by most scholars that transactions by such organizations fall within the jurisdiction of international commercial law.

Circumstance 3. This area of international transactions is one of the newest and most controversial from the perspective of law application. It deals with commercial agreements signed between a state and a private business corporation of another state. Such transactions are rapidly increasing. In the past centuries they were not considered to fall within the jurisdiction of classical international law, simply because at the time international law was narrowly defined to recognize the activities of nation-states *alone* as worthy of application of law. However, today, in the light of the expanding role of international law and the changes in the international system, it is possible to consider some of these transactions under the norms of contemporary international commercial law.

First, the present international system gives a high priority to general economic development in the world, and particularly in the backward regions of the world. At a time when poor nations, who constitute a very large number of the subjects of international law, are trying to modernize and, in the process, are signing commercial treaties with huge corporations of industrial states for various developmental projects, the suggestion that these agreements involving millions of dollars with payments conveniently spread over the years have no legal basis under the norms of international law, sounds unreasonable and unfair. Second, large business corporations with substantial investments in other countries, in part, do play the role of diplomats, advise, and influence the foreign policy of their country concerning the states in which they have investments. For their own governments they perform quasi-diplomatic tasks. Their transactions, in other words, are of mixed political-economic nature. Some times they are even "financed" by their governments for their *extra*-commercial duties abroad by way of "tax breaks." Because of the nature of their transaction, certainly the agreements signed by them and the governments of these foreign countries, can be considered to be under the jurisdiction of international commercial law.

Yet there are scholars that continue to insist that these agreements have no place under the international commercial law, because in their opinion international law deals strictly with the transactions conducted by two or more governments. In the light of the above stated significance of these transactions it seems illogical to persist in this insistence and thus hamper the growth of international commercial law. One must not forget, however fragmentary and ill-defined the present system of law may be in this area, that it is constantly evolving in the light of new demands that are made upon it by a dynamic system of international commercial transactions. A more charitable view of law at this time will go a long way to develop the domain of law in international business.

In the contemporary industrial world the dynamics of postindustrial revolution are responsible for the rapid internationalization of industry, commerce, and trade in the advanced countries. These areas of essentially private activity in the Western democracies are forcing the big corporations to spread out in the world by offering their services to other countries. In a contemporary nonindustrial world of poor countries they are most welcome. The outcome of this phenomenon of international law is an ever-increasing pressure to broaden its norms to include these activities under its jurisdiction. The outcome of this phenomenon for the nation-state is the first important signal that it can no longer continue to enjoy the legal and political monopoly of international law. This internationalization of industry, commerce, and trade in advanced countries has indeed contributed to what are being called "transnational" movements and to the development of a transantional law. This phenomenon is briefly discussed below.

Nature of transnational movements

One of the many attributes of international law is that it works as an instrument for the authoritative allocation of fundamental values in the world, for the important purpose of attaining an optimum maximization of the interests and objectives of the membership of the world community. This membership includes not only states, but also many transnational pressure groups, private associations, political parties, business organizations, and huge multinational business corporations. All of these groupings, particularly these corporations, have begun to play a significant role in the broader transnational movement. The present international legal system that has taken note of some of these movements is now expanding to provide an appropriate framework within which the relationships and interactions of all the participants in these movements could be assimilated.

For analytical purposes it is useful to discuss, first, the nature of transnational movements and the interaction of some of its participants within the broader framework of world socioeconomic processes. Only then, as a second task, can attention be focused on their relationship to the international law.

Most transnational movements today are controlled partially by states through domestic rules and regulations on the one hand, and through interstate agreements and treaties on the other. A large amount of nongovernmental transnational activity at the present continues to take place within the traditional, state-controlled framework of international relations. However, much of this is now changing. Many private organizations and associations in their interstate relationships are exerting a greater degree of autonomy, freedom of decision, and coupled with this, *a new sense of international responsibility and welfarism*, not known to exist in the past. In recognition of this development the notion of "transnational law" has been developed by some scholars, to identify the international legal norms that regulate transnational relations of these organizations and associations.[3]

Transnational activities now cover many aspects of international life and represent what has been called the "new cooperation" in the international society, especially in the areas where common concerns exist among the participants, for example, in the fields of international transportation and travel, international communications, health and welfare of mankind, conservation of fisheries and wildlife, and weather reporting and meteorological standards. Most transnational activities are carried out by semipublic and private concerns that deal directly with each other. The governments usually participate with varying degrees of involvement through their *regulatory* power. Apart from the important role of business corporations and their economic activities, these movements also include cultural, religious, scientific, and ideological cooperations on a transnational basis. For instance, organizations such as The International Red Cross, World Council of Churches, International Chamber of Commerce, International Air Transportation Association and many international labor organizations, along with literally hundreds of multistate business corporations, can be considered subscribing to transnational activities.

In an interesting article Professor G. A. Sumeda divides the transnational movements in five categories: (1) parties representing ideological affinity and political movements such as the Communist, Socialist, and

[3]See the works of M. S. McDougal, "International Law, Power and Policy: A Contemporary Conception," *Recueil des Cours*, 82 (1953), pp. 105–179; W. Friedman, *The Changing Structure of International Law* (New York: Columbia University Press), 1964, pp. 37–39; P. Jessup *Transnational Law* (New Haven: Yale University Press), 1956; C. W. Jenks, *The Common Law of Mankind* (New York: F. A. Praeger), 1958; and G. A. Sumida, "Transnational Movements and Economic Structures," in C. E. Black and R. A. Falk (eds.) *The Future of International Legal Order: The Structure of International Environment* (Princeton, N.J.: Princeton University Press), 1972, pp. 524–568.

Christian Democratic movements in the world; (2) international movements dealing with social and welfare programs, particularly in the area of labor movements, humanitarian concerns, and antislavery activity; (3) all kinds of international peace movements; (4) movements for independence, self-determination, and creation of new states based on religious, moral, and linguistic distinctions; and (5) religious movements, for example, drives for the spread of Islam in Africa or Roman Catholicism in many parts of the globe or the Christian ecumenical movement. Despite their differences in purpose, style, and scope, each of these movements is transnational in its character and activity. All of them continue to have important impact on the world social and legal order.

Most of the transnational movements have some degree of organization. They are involved in what can be broadly described as large-scale continuing collective social action that transcends national boundaries and seeks to modify the existing world order or to bring about a new order in areas where none previously existed. While there are several good studies on transnational movement, most of them tend to be case studies of a specific movement. This practice has resulted in a general neglect of their comparative and theory-building potential. Concerning their relationship with international legal norms, much remains to be done, especially in the field of legal scholarship.

The multinational business corporations are a relatively new phenomenon in the world. It has become prominent in interstate relations in the last two decades. The activity of these corporations has attracted the attention of international lawmakers primarily because of their growing influence in world affairs. In many instances their influence is directly related to their impact on world economics that is the function of their size and wealth. Many of these corporations' annual gross sales are larger than the Gross National Product of many countries. For instance, in 1967, the combined worldwide sale of less than 100 such multinational corporations, having their parent companies in the United States or the Soviet Union was greater than the GNP of any state in the world except the two superpowers.[4] General Motors Corporation now has production facilities in around 25 countries. In 1967 it had a total sales of over 20 billion dollars. This amount is greater than the GNP of all but 14 of the 124 nations in the United Nations and all but 17 nations in the world.[5]

Even though at the present time there are few international legal norms that regulate the affairs of transnational business corporations, some order does prevail. Much of the basis of this present order is in the national laws of various states. The International Chamber of Commerce is probably

[4]See Business International Research Report, *The United Nations and the Business World* (New York), 1967.

the most effective organization in creating the foundations for emerging transnational law in this area. It has also been responsible for establishing many uniform worldwide standards for business intercourse. Through its encouragement since its inception in 1920, uniform commercial legislation has been passed concerning business laws. It works closely with many other economic and business organizations. It has its national committees in over 40 countries, organizations, and associations in nearly another 40 countries. Part of its success in the improvement of transnational economic relations and in the development of transnational law can be attributed to its Court of Arbitration and to the work of its International Council on Advertising Practices.

Development of transnational law

The transnational movements, their structures, and their areas of competence have influenced the development of transnational law in several ways. First, they have added to existing national and international laws specific and new norms in areas where none existed. Also, they have been instrumental in changing and adjusting the old norms to the new conditions of transnational activities. Second, they have attempted to alter the wider social and economic order of the contemporary world through the authoritative allocation of new values, new sets of conduct, and expectations that all concerned can recognize and follow confidently in the knowledge that others are expected to do the same. In the process of influencing the international legal system, the transnational movements have also been influenced by it. They have also influenced the course of international relations and have been influenced by it too. The emergence of transnational economic structures reveal the growing economic and social interdependence among countries of the world. The trend is that this interdependence will intensify in the future. The need for economic development and the realization that it must be, in certain aspects supported by and coordinated with the economic growth patterns of other states, is important because it suggests that future development in this area will be more concerned with the human economic welfare. Certainly the managers of these large multinational corporations are aware of this eventuality. In recognition of these developments, George W. Ball suggested a few years ago that there is a need to develop an effective "international companies law."[6] It will be a law that will help stifle unnecessary restrictions imposed by state governments.

---

[5]G. A. Sumida, "Transnational Movements and Economic Structures," p. 553.
[6]See G. Ball, "The Promise of the Multinational Corporation," *Fortune*, 80 (June 1, 1967).

chapter 8
international law as a protector of human rights

One of the more positive outcomes of the Second World War was a new and vigorous emphasis on the protection of individual human rights. The commonplace horrors of the degradation of life during the war were certainly a strong reason behind this emphasis. Today, over a quarter of a century later, such an emphasis seems even more important because the present is marked by the existence of so many totalitarian and other non-democratic nation-states.

Protection of human rights under the contemporary international law starts from the premise (which is, incidentally, a democratic premise) that all human beings, regardless of their color, cast, language, religion, and nationality are entitled to certain basic human rights that no government can legally violate. Furthermore, the contemporary international law has increasingly come to recognize that individual human beings are the ultimate benefactor and recipient of law, because they are the ultimate members of the international society. Such a premise is not entirely new. It has been with us as a part of international law (although perhaps not very well articulated) ever since the emergence of secular nation-states in Europe.[1]

Even those scholars who continue to doubt the status of individuals as the direct subject of international law (in the sense that individuals possessing a legal personality as states do under the law) *also* continue to devote much of their time and energy elaborating and underlining the legal norms that are designed to protect the individual from the arbitrary actions of the state.

From a historical perspective, international law has been most con-

---

[1]For an interesting discussion on this subject see A. Cowels, "The Impact of International Law on the Individual," *Proceedings of the American Society of International Law* (1952), pp. 71–85.

cerned about human rights in the following four main contexts. *First,* a complete abolition of any kind of slavery and the elimination of slave trade. In this specific area there is an impressive history of the development of antislavery laws and their enforcement by the international society. The period of vigorous activity in this field begins with the Congress of Vienna and ends with the adoption of the famous 1958 Supplementary Anti-Slavery Convention. *Second,* protection of backward people living in various parts of the world. Several international measures have been taken over the years resulting in law development in this area. Two acts are particularly noteworthy here: the Berlin Act of 1885 and the Brussels Act of 1890. Recently a number of mandates and trusteeship agreements have been signed that fix the responsibility of protection of these people living in specific areas of specific states. *Third,* protection of various ethnic, religious, linguistic, and other types of minorities living in the present modern nation-state system. There have been several so-called "minorities treaties" and other declarations signed in the early part of this century and administered by the League of Nations. The main thrust of international legal norms that has developed out of these arrangements has been to assure complete protection of life and liberty to minorities living in various states. It is only fair to admit that international law has not done too well in this area. In times of internal crises, minorities, if involved, have paid dearly, and frequently with their lives. *Fourth,* the protection of aliens. In this area international law has developed rapidly and vigorously, as a part of the laws of state responsibility, to offer an internationally uniform set of conduct in relation with the treatment of aliens. As a result of this uniformity, aliens today are not only better protected under domestic law but also it can be predicted what kind of treatment they shall be accorded under what circumstances. However, despite the development of law in these and many other areas, the violations of basic human rights during the first half of this century have been rather frequent when you consider the two world wars, the Communist takeover in China in 1948, and the widespread communal riots from 1947 to 1948 in India, immediately after the partition of the subcontinent, followed by many civil-war type of situations in several countries in which minorities were involved.

The major breakthrough in the period after the Second World War came when the Universal Declaration of Human Rights was passed by the United Nations.[2] It was a legal expression of the conscience of mankind. There have been other legal developments since then, such as the development and entry into force of the celebrated European Conven-

---

[2]For details see H. Lauterpacht, "The Universal Declaration of Human Rights," *The British Yearbook of International Law,* 25 (1948), pp. 354–381.

tion for the Protection of Human Rights and Fundamental Freedoms. Norms concerning the protection of human rights have been embodied in several other international agreements and treaties, notably in international labor conventions.

The scope of the term "human rights" itself has been broadened in the past two decades. For instance, today it includes all aspects of civil rights practiced in Western democracies, a number of extremely significant social, political and economic rights, along with what is commonly called "collective rights" (meaning, for example, freedom of assembly and association). It is fair to complain that in some instances international laws of human rights, as they stand today, do not accomplish much more than simply proclaim the law in the midst of some of its most flagrant violations. But it is equally correct to point out that in many instances they create specific and definite obligations for the states to uphold the law and provide procedures for redress to the individual even against his own state.

In most democracies, many principles of international law concerning fundamental human rights have been long in practice. These principles also provide the necessary protections to aliens and various minorities living in democratic states. Such is the case, for instance, with the guarantees provided in the United States Constitution and its amendments. It guarantees fundamental rights to its citizens, such as the right to life, liberty, and the pursuit of happiness, the rights to security, freedom from arbitrary arrest and detention, the rights to a fair trial, and the benefit of the presumption of innocence until proven guilty. The American Constitution also guarantees freedom of thought, conscience, religion, and expression, freedom to assemble peacefully and associate with each other, the right to effective means of redress against governmental officials, and the right to equal protection of the law. This particular philosophy concerning the applicability of human rights in the domestic political system to all nationals including minorities and aliens, has already been accepted and is practiced by many European countries who are signatories to the European Convention for the Protection of Human Rights and Fundamental Freedoms. The present trend indicates that we are rapidly moving in the direction of evolving a *common law of mankind* in this particular area. It is conceived as a law that embodies certain guarantees of individual fundamental rights that are enforceable simultaneously by both national and international procedures.

Although we should recognize the broad progress made in the area of human rights, we should also be equally aware of the continuing shortcomings of the present arrangements concerning procedures for their enforcement. For instance, most individuals lack the ability for numerous reasons to assert their rights before an international tribunal. In the absence of such ability it is then left up to the national governments and their courts not only to provide means and specific procedures for redress but also to dispense justice. This system works reasonably well in several democracies and either breaks down in other systems (especially with regard to impartiality and justice) or is simply nonexistent. Unfortunately, most human beings in the world today do not live under democratic political systems. This amounts to admitting that the sovereign state generally remains the major subject of international laws and that the way to a closer relationship between the law and the individual continues to be blocked. A democratic state in this instance as in many instances becomes an effective arena of implementing international law in the protection of individual human rights. A nondemocratic state is merely a hinderance, an obstacle, or at worse an enemy of both the individuals and the international law in this area. We can either move toward the establishment of more democratic political systems by giving whatever encouragement we can to the suppressed people of the world, or we can encourage cooperation between the democratic and nondemocratic states, on the already developed principles of international law concerning human rights, so that compliance to the law by governments of nondemocratic states in this area will be carried out for international if not domestic reasons. We could move on both fronts simultaneously.

chapter 9
international law and the protection of international environment from pollution

A new subfield of contemporary international law, called *international ecological law*, is developing rapidly. Its norms are designed to protect, under the force of the law, further deterioration of world environment. As a result of the concern of fast-growing governments and private groups in this area, the United Nations and many other international agencies have become involved. Many general conferences on ecology have already taken place, the latest of which were a conference in Czechoslovakia in 1971 and one in Sweden in 1972. The Sweden conference has now resulted in a successful vote in the United Nations General Assembly that sets up a general ecology project based in Nairobi. This is by far the most ambitious international program yet for protecting the world environment. One of its many important features establishes an "Earth-Watch" system for actively and systematically monitoring the quality of the soil, the atmosphere, and the oceans through the establishment of a worldwide network of 110 stations. Several treaties have been signed in the last decade and a half that either partly or entirely deal with the environment protection safeguards, and various international courts' decisions have been handed down on cases dealing with man versus the environment. The present international ecological law is made up of principles, doctrines, and norms that recognize the causes and cures of environmental pollution and other disruptions of ecology. Recently the greatest impact of international law has been felt in the following areas. (1) Environmental pollution caused by the disposal of fuels and various kinds of industrial waste; the industrially advanced nations are clearly most responsible in this area. (2) Environmental disruptions and dislocations as a direct result of what can be safely called large-scale technological projects, generally known to be carried out by the United States and the

Soviet Union, either for themselves or for their client nations. (3) Environmental alterations, climatic changes, etc., caused by scientific experiments, particularly in nuclear energy, conducted by major powers. (4) Environmental pollution as a direct result of the population explosion.[1]

Environmental pollution caused by disposal of fuels and individual waste

For several reasons the problem of environmental pollution caused by deliberate disposal of fuels and industrial wastes remains one of the hardest problems for international law to tackle. There are several reasons for it. For instance, in a world of "no self admitted guilty; all innocent" states, it is extremely difficult to assign overall responsibility for this pollution beyond the observation just made, that industrial states are clearly more guilty of causing pollution than nonindustrial states. There are problems even in this simple dicotomy. Yet another difficulty for law is the task of establishing fair liabilities for violations and, finally, the hardest task is of enforcing the "payment" of whatever damages might be awarded. At the bottom of all these difficulties lies one simple fact concerning the complex and mixed makeup of the actual and potential pollutors involved. By mixed makeup we simply mean that some of these pollutors are individuals, large and small, private and semigovernmental corporations or industries, and others are states themselves, or any combination of all of them.

This problem is further complicated by the difficulty of scientifically establishing the exact nature of the threat to the environment in each case, whether the threat is temporary, permanent, immediate, or long in materializing. While the public concern and debate in the United States and other countries has created an urgency in the minds of most decision makers concerning the need to protect ecology, it has also created some problems. In the midst of heated arguments between the environmentalists and their opponents (generally the people who have a vested interest in the status quo that the environmentalists wish to alter) and the onslaught of polemics and counterpolemics, it has become difficult even for the scientists, charged with the responsibility of establishing the nature of

[1]For an interesting and most informative treatment of these four areas of concern for international law, see D. Livingston, "Science, Technology and International Law: Present Trends and Future Developments," in C. E. Black and R. A. Falk (eds.), *The Future of International Law—The Structure of International Environment*, (Princeton, N.J.: Princeton University Press), 1972, pp. 96–110.

environmental damage, not to get involved emotionally in the pros and cons of the entire subject.

All polemics apart, one thing is quite clear: global pollution is continuing at an alarming rate. Even with the present rapid rate of law development in this area we might loose the "war," unless states are willing to cooperate at an unprecedented level to curb pollution effectively. The task of the development of new legislation and its enforcement is also hindered by the fact that even at a domestic level, not all states are equally concerned about the problem. Part of the difficulty here is that not all clearly understand the long-term ramifications of pollution. Then there is the familiar problem, in the absence of any self-proclaimed guilty parties, of tracing the exact source of the pollution. As a result of these difficulties, it is not surprising that some national and international laws have been enacted "after the fact," that is, after the damage has already been done, often permanently.[2]

Development of international ecological law on the problems of pollution can be classified into three general categories: (a) a concern with technical and political issues; (b) a concern with the punishment of pollutors after they have been identified, along with the political impact of these sanctions on the international system; and (c) a concern with the establishment of effective institutional frameworks that will assist the task of pollution control by laying down the rules, identifying the pollutors, fixing the sanctions and enforcing them, with of course, appropriate procedures for appeals by the alleged pollutors, built into the framework. We shall discuss briefly all of these three areas.

(a) A concern with technical and political issues involves the job of universally defining the precise levels of acceptable pollution, beyond which damage to the environment will require investigation and punishment of the defaulters, and the corrective measures must be taken by the appropriate agency. Given the nature of problems involved, these jobs are not simple matters. Past investigation of various international rivers (which cut across the territories of several states) has indicated the difficulties involved in determining the cause and sources of pollution.[3] The introduction of political factors such as the sovereignty of the state, its

---

[2]For a more serious work on environmental issues in general, see Max Michelson, *The Environmental Revolution* (New York: Harper and Row), 1970; U.S. Congress, House Committee on Science and Astronautics, *Environmental Quality and Managing the Environment* (Washington, D.C.), 1968.

[3]In 1969 there was a fish kill in the Rhine river. The investigative authorities from the European states involved in contributing to the pollution of the river had a difficult time in establishing whether the cause of the kill was agricultural, industrial, or commercial ship sewage. It was also found to be equally difficult to establish the place or places where the waste originated.

prestige, its need to retain the polluting industry, and yet its inability to develop sophisticated pollution control devices (in the case of an under-developed country striving to industrialize) help only to complicate the situation for international law.

In this particular area where technical-political issues are involved, international law thus far has made the most progress only in defining an unacceptable level of pollution in the high seas, especially concerning oil pollution. Some laws now specify the amount of oil or oily wastes that can be let loose by vessels in specific areas of the seas.[4] Many recent treaties usually contain procedures for the detection of pollution and the determination of "substantial damages." This is particularly true of treaties forbidding the pollution of fresh water sources, such as rivers that border or pass through more than one country or lakes shared by more than one nation. For instance, the treaties are now in force applicable to pollution by civil nuclear reactors. The International Commission on Radiological Protection monitors the activity of these reactors and determines acceptable radiation levels for the disposal of radioactive waste.

In the last few years several specialized agencies such as the World Health Organization and the International Civil Aviation Organization have teamed up to help develop international norms that will force the states to curtail international noise and air pollution. In their efforts they have been joined by the Council of Europe. In these two specific areas the United States has already passed some domestic legislation; more, however, is needed.

(b) A concern with the punishment of varied pollutors and its political consequences has led international ecological law to articulate further the concept of "state responsibility." The thrust of the law is to assess the degree of state responsibility in the case of various violations and then to determine the nature and extent of the liability to be assessed against the state or states involved. A quick survey of various existing treaties and recent courts' decisions confirms this thrust.[5] Even though the actual pollutor was an industry privately owned, the prevailing rationale has been that as long as it operates from within the national jurisdiction of a specific state, the state is responsible. However, whenever a private corpo-

---

[4]For details concerning treaties and other agreements in this area see U.S. Congress, House Committee on Merchant Marine and Fisheries, Report on the International Control of Oil Pollution (Washington, D.C.) 1967; see also V. P. Nanda, "The Torrey Canyon Disaster: Some Legal Aspects," *Denver Law Journal*, 44 (Summer 1967), pp. 400–425, and "Oil Pollution of the Sea," *Harvard International Law Journal*, 10 (Spring 1969), pp. 316–359.

[5]For a good example of a case of "state responsibility" on water pollution, see "Lake Lanoux Arbitration" in the *American Journal of International Law*, (January 1959), pp. 156–171.

ration or an industry is involved in violating the environmental laws in areas not under national jurisdictions (usually under international jurisdictions, such as in international waters or the air space above them) the international law deals with it directly, provided the corporation is registered with, or is located on the territory, of a country that has signed the formal agreements creating legal obligations. For example, if a merchant marine ship registered in Pakistan has been caught dumping oil in international waters and if Pakistan is a signatory to antipollution treaties that have created legal norms, these norms can be applied directly to the shipping company involved and thus a punishment can be meted out to the company. In such cases international law has already perfected its detailed system of sanctions and liabilities to be levied against the defaulter and offers an appropriate set of procedures to be followed by the company if it wishes to appeal. Moreover, it offers to all concerned forums for legitimate disagreement, an encouragement for buying appropriate insurances, and an insistence that each state as soon as possible incorporate appropriate sections of its norms into domestic legal rules.

(c) A concern with the establishment of appropriate institutions to carry out the task of law application and enforcement in the area of environment pollution has led nations to initiate discussions for this purpose. At the present we do not have institutional structures effective enough to enforce the laws that already exist. Of course, in many areas the problem of law enforcement does not arise because of voluntary cooperation of the states. This cooperation has arisen because of a conviction, moral, political, or otherwise, that it is in their interest to uphold the law. This was the case in the abolition of the use of certain dangerous agricultural pesticides (quite damaging to the environment) by several industrial nations. In other areas, several treaties negotiated and signed without coercion have created an atmosphere of compliance with the law without the threat of sanctions. In such circumstances one of the best self-enforcement mechanisms is the general fear that if "we violate the norms of a treaty that we have signed, it will allow the others to do the same, resulting in an intolerable situation." A good example of this attitude is the several arms control and disarmament treaties that have been recently signed and that depend in part on a self-enforcement mechanism. Clearly, a fear of a rearmament race in the areas where these treaties have slowed the race down is among the more effective incentives not to violate the norms of the treaties and of subsequent international law.

But this still leaves the field of environmental pollution control with insufficient enforcement mechanisms. Some progress has been made in this context at regional levels. For example, in Europe the Organization for Economic Cooperation and Development is currently working on a single set of what it calls Environmental Control Standards that the member states plan to adopt on a regional basis. This modest plan can be enlarged later to include countries in other regions of the world. Perhaps the best approach at this time is regional rather than universal. Regional organiaztions in this decade can be set up if only to disseminate information concerning environmental pollution controls, investigate violations and weigh their seriousness, fix responsibility, levy fines, and hand down corrective measures to be carried out by the polluters involved. The problems of enforcement and appeals can be left to some other more universal agency.

Environmental disruption caused by large-scale technological projects

The second major functional problem area for international ecological law is the protection of world environment from large-scale technological projects carried out by major industrial powers. Most of these projects, which are certainly beneficial to the nation conducting them, are detrimental to world ecology. Man has now acquired the scientific knowledge and technological capacity to make the entire planet his experimental lab and to alter its ecology for better or worse, permanently in some cases. Is it not possible, for instance, that the continuing large-scale underground explosions of nuclear devices conducted by the United States and the Soviet Union may eventually contaminate the ground water with radioactivity? These explosions may cause earthquakes or change the ecological balance in other ways.

In this major problem area much of the pressure for restraint, selectivity, and control has come from private groups and individuals within the states involved. This is particularly true in cases of the United States and the Western European Nations. Governments of these states in this area have shown some environmental responsibility, but not nearly enough. In the case of the Soviet Union, one generally does not expect public protest or criticism of governmental decisions concerning ecology. For instance, it is not known if there was any public concern exhibited by the Soviet people concerning the decision of their government to construct huge pipelines and reservoirs to transfer fresh water from Russian Siberia to population centers in other parts of the Soviet Union. On the other hand, it is known to all that in the United States there were public protests and many concerns exhibited in regard to the construction of oil pipelines through Alaska. The debate is not yet over, although the government has now decided to go ahead with the project and the Congressional approval has been given in the light of present energy crisis.

The damage to ecology as a result of the projects will, of course, have to be balanced with the other benefits these projects bring. On a balance sheet it is difficult to decide. For instance, how badly does the United States need Alaskan oil? Is there no other way to transfer this oil, perhaps a more expensive but a much safer way for ecology? In the United States, well-informed and well-coordinated public opinion has made some difference here by obliging the government to act more responsibly.[6]

Environmental alterations and climatic changes caused by explosions of atomic energy

Major powers for some time now have been conducting nuclear energy explosions either underground or in the air. It might be of some interest if not comfort to know that France and the People's Republic of China have not yet signed the Limited Nuclear Ban Treaty; therefore they are free to explode, and they have exploded nuclear devices in the air. To the extent these experiments are related to the so-called "national security needs"(a concept that apparently gives the green light to almost anything that the government wishes to do for practically whatever cost) in the United States at least, public opinion has not been very successful to persuade the government to change its mind for reasons of ecological protection. A recent example of this is the nuclear explosion on the Amchitca Island for national security purposes by the United States. The government's decision in this instance was vigorously protested by the American public or a portion of it and by some citizens of Canada.

There are other examples of the United States activity in this area. In most of these cases it has been extremely difficult to determine long-term and permanent damages to the environment. This difficulty in itself has been primarily responsible for the continuing activity of governments in this area. A few years ago the United States conducted an experiment entitled Project Starfish that entailed the detonation of a large nuclear device in the atmosphere around 200 miles above the Pacific Ocean in 1962. The explosion caused widespread damage to several satellites and the interruption of Van Allen belts. Then there was another project that the United States carried out. It was entitled Project West Ford. This

---

[6]Thus the U.S. Department of Interior, under pressure from the public, has finally established proper regulations, to make sure, for instance in the case of oil pipelines from the Arctic North Slopes coming down south to Valez and Alaska, that the laying of these lines must take place within the framework of very careful investigation (a standard procedure now) and constant inspection of these lines with regard to their environmental consequences.

entailed the orbiting of a thin band of copper dipoles for the purpose of finding out if it were possible to develop a prototype, interference-free communications system. Both projects encountered protests in and outside the United States and within and outside the American scientific community concerning the actual and potential tampering with the environment, particularly in the case of Starfish Project. Both projects led to new controls for the future. Project West Ford was also reviewed after the fact by the International Council of Scientific Union and the International Astronomical Union. In the area of large-scale nuclear explosions the Limited Nuclear Ban Treaty has forbidden the explosion above ground. The United States and the Soviet Union have thus far lived up to this agreement.

Population explosion and environmental pollution

We have talked about the problem of overpopulation briefly in a different context; here the concern is its impact on the international ecology. International ecological law for the first time has been extended to cover this very old problem that acquires a more dire emphasis with each new generation. Any international norms developed to control the high rate of population growth will be regarded as a big breakthrough for international law not only in the area of the protection of international ecology but also in the field of protection of human rights. This is so because a continuing population explosion threatens the environment as well as the achievement and maintenance of human rights. In the past two decades several resolutions and declarations have appeared on the international scene. All of them stress the need for legal norms in this area. Suggestions have been made that these norms could be included in the existing norms on human rights. Sociologists have stressed the need to develop a comprehensive family-planning program to go with appropriate laws. The ideal goal for international law (which is conceived to become more deeply involved in this area as the time passes) is to achieve first an international consensus for a zero population growth and then set guidelines for the state to follow.

International law must attempt to bridge the gap between religious taboos, ignorance, unavailability of information concerning birth control, and related physical facilities on the one hand, and an *absolute need* to have a global birth control program on the other. International legislation can be developed to stress the *qualitative aspect* of life in the developing societies where the problem of overpopulation is at its worst. Conceivably, with proper communication, it is possible to convince the poor that a relationship exists between higher standards of living and maintaining a small family.[7]

A concluding remark

Present direction that the contemporary international law is taking in the broad field of world ecology will result in the promotion of two very important goals: first, it will mean, finally, an extension of traditional legal norms, usually most concerned about *state* behavior, to cover the environment-related behavior of the state. This simply means that the state will remair. the most important subject of international law, according to some writers, but it will be held responsible for violations of environmental pollution control law. This is being done under the concept of "state responsibility," which after all means that *states are simply not free to do whatever they please to the world ecology.* Second, it will also mean the establishment of a new important human right, that is, the fundamental right of every human being to breathe clean air and drink clean water and to continue to live on this globe in freedom from the harmful, perhaps deadly, effects of environmental pollution or drastic alternations. This second goal has already been partly included into legal norms through codification as a general principle in the International Covenant on Economic, Social and Cultural Rights, established in 1966. This principle obligates the signatories to the Covenants to do all they can to improve the environmental hygiene to safeguard the legal right of all human beings to enjoy the highest attainable standards of physical and mental health.

A covenant should also be drawn concerning the self-enforcement aspect of these norms. It is gratifying that already the international society has developed some shared expectations concerning a common responsibility for a common stake. Nonetheless, we have a long way to go in this field. Traditional international laws can be stretched only so far to manage the present crisis in the man-environment relationship. The society of nations may have to go *all out* to develop a new international legal order to protect the planet. After all it is the only planet we have to live on.

[7]For a stimulating discussion of this problem see R. A. Falk, "World Population and International Law," *American Journal of International Law*, 63 (July 1969), pp. 514–520; see also, R. N. Gardner, "Toward a World Population Program," *International Organization*, 22 (Winter 1968), pp. 332–361.

chapter 10
international law, foreign policy and state behavior— two case studies

International law as a tool of foreign policy

Guide for state actions

International law provides a convenient framework for state actions if the state chooses to use it. It sets the standards of conduct that states use when they wish to act reasonably and, of course, legally. A state can present its claims, express its position, and fight its case entirely in legal terms. In this respect, international law serves to stabilize international relations and introduces an element of predictability. It encourages the states to take the law seriously and commit themselves to its relevant rules if they expect their opponents also to follow the basic conduct norms of international law. At a time when international communications seems imperative in order for states of various motives and capabilities to pursue their objectives, international law provides a *common language* and a *common code of legitimacy* for those who choose to listen to its urgings. Moreover, its rules give states an opportunity to perpetuate an era of "business as usual" and enjoy the psychological gratifications that are obtained from such an era, at a time when we seem to be living in an international system that moves from crisis to crisis. This period of "normalcy" can be used to bring about a host of reforms that are badly needed in the system.

Legal norms as criteria for state guidelines also help to draw a clearer line between what can be regarded as responsible, acceptable, and reasonable behavior under law and what cannot be. Therefore, a state can be expected to act reasonably under the law and in return can expect other states to act reasonably, thus avoiding confrontations and provocations among each other. Rules of guidance can be altered with mutual agreements, thereby keeping the criteria of guidance relevant to the requirements of the international system.

Helps to protect and enhance a state's position in the international arena

Through the establishment of a network of rights and privileges international law provides a state an opportunity to resort to legal arguments for the protection or enhancement of its own position. A few examples will clarify this advantage of international law. West Berlin uses international law to support its existence as an independent political unit when it feels the status quo is threatened by East Germany. President Nasser's nationalization of the Suez Canal was helped by his appeal to contemporary international law. President Sukarno's invocation of the law of self-determination was a factor in his designs against Malaysia. Both the United States and the Soviet Union have used international law in this regard. Consider the American use of law to support its quarantine during the Cuban Missile crisis, and the Russian use of legal arguments in the United Nations in support of their refusal to pay for the United Nations peacekeeping expenses incurred in the Congo and Mideast.

In numerous instances such as cited above, foreign policy decision makers use international law to put pressure on the adversary. This is done by invoking certain principles of international law that suits a country's position on a particular issue, which then makes the adversary appear unreasonable in the eyes of the rest of the world, for disagreeing with this lawful position. This sometimes results in a general mobilization of international support for the country on the side of the law. States are also known to use international legal arguments in support of a position that they had wished to take for purely political reasons, but were afraid to take for fear of antagonizing another power. Law makes it easier to take this position because to do that is simply to act in accordance with the law. In this context any leader who fails to take full advantage of international law leaves this field of "advancement of national interest through legal manipulation" to its opponent to use. International law as a *tool* of foreign policy provides an arena where states can try out their legal wits and win or loose the contest.

A *technique for political mobilization through reciprocity and solemnity of a commitment*

Through the technique of reciprocity and solemnity of a legal commitment international law helps to create a political atmosphere more suitable for law observance. First consider reciprocity. In interstate relations appeals to reciprocity always carry an implicit but usually clearly understood threat to the "other" side that if "you will not agree to or give in to my invocation of legal rules against your position and thus if you insist on violating international law at my expense, someday I shall do the same to you." Since reciprocity "cuts both ways," both sides have a vested interest in observing international law because *in the long run it benefits them both*. At the same time reciprocity discourages the misuse of international law. The argument can be viewed as follows: "If I stretch legal arguments once too often to make a 'case' for my position against him, he may get wise and resort to a similar legal arguments against me in a different situation; thus I shall be obliged to give in to him."

Therefore, during the Cuban crisis the American logic maintained that Soviet missiles in Cuba were offensive missiles and American missiles in Turkey were defensive missiles. This was an effort to build its case and use the OAS Charter to provide a legal basis for its blockade. The American position established a dangerous precedent from the point of view of international reciprocity. Might not the Soviet Union someday use the Warsaw Pact to provide the same legal argument against the United States? In another example the United States was deterred from pushing too hard the legal arguments against the Soviet Union under Article 19 of the United Nations Charter. This article was invoked in the General Assembly a few years ago to force the Soviet Union and others either to pay the expenses of the Congo and the Middle East peacekeeping operations or loose their right to vote in the Assembly. The United States realized that someday there might conceivably be a United Nations peacekeeping operation against its wishes and thus, it might not want to pay for it. Under the circumstances it might not be a good idea to push the legal arguments against the Soviet Union too much.

International law tries to inculcate among its followers the *solemnity of a legal commitment*. In other words, a treaty or a charter signed with all the publicity and fanfare marks the occasion as an *important* event in international affairs. When a party to an agreement decides to break the norms of that agreement or to violate international law in general with regard to an issue, international law gives a warning signal to others parties to the agreement. These parties then have a choice: either uphold the treaty, follow the law all the way at all cost and possibly escalate the conflict, or, play down the "legal issue" involved and resolve the conflict politically.

In foreign affairs, for very good political reasons, states sometimes drop their legal claims and counterclaims to arrive at political solutions.

The loopholes and other ambiguities in international law allow for multiple interpretations of some of its norms and thus provide an opportunity for its subjects in crisis situations, sometimes to act as if law did not exist or to support two apparently conflicting positions with the help of some legal norms. On other occasions legal rationalizations are religiously used as if pursuit of the law in foreign policy was an important objective in itself.

A counterproductive force in international politics

If states frequently resort to the norms of international law in crisis situations, this may be detrimental to the future of international law and thus to the future of world order. There is a marked tendency among all states to appear to "act legally" in international disputes. Sometimes they go to great lengths to justify their actions as consistent with the dictates of international law; moreover, in many instances the law is stretched to its limits, misused, and abused to make a "legal" case for a clearly illegal act. Under such practice, law is the first victim; it suffers a further downgrading by contributing to a "credibility gap" at its own expense.

A frequent use by the United States of highly debatable legal arguments to support its intervention in the Dominican Republic and Vietnam are examples of what is being suggested here. Such practices, which are by no means unique to the United States, simply demean international law, retard its growth, diminish its respect, and undermine the very pretense that states use (that they are contributing to world order by invoking international law in their disputes) by trying to justify their unilateral acts under law.

International law can also be regarded as contributing to the powers of the states. Both its use and misuse by states give them an extra "something," that may be called "influence," "power," or "a moral support." In other words, a state that chooses to invoke international law as compared with a state that does not adds some extra strength to its case *by internationalizing an otherwise national issue*. Because law adds strength to the position of a state, many countries do not hesitate to misuse international law by attempting to justify what clearly appears to be an illegal behavior. The logic that appears to emerge out of these circumstances is simply this: a poor legal case for an otherwise clearly illegal act in world affairs is better than no legal case at all. Attempts to enforce international law vigorously in those political situations where conflict is rampant and deep tend to backfire. This is the lesson that we have apparently learned in the United Nations, for instance, on the issue of legally trying to force "defaulters" to pay for the United Nations peacekeeping expenses or loose their right to vote in the General Assembly.

All of the above stated considerations should be fully understood if we are to realize the *multiple role* that law plays in the hands of the makers of foreign policy. These considerations *do not* tell us, as many students of law and politics seem to believe, that international law is a farce, a hoax, or a joke. What they really tell us is that in the law-politics relationship, international politics seems to have the upper hand, but the supremacy of politics over law is not a frozen situation. Law too, perhaps less frequently, does have the upper hand.[1] The following two case studies are provided to acquire some behavioral insights in the law-politics relationship in a couple of frontier areas of international law.

indepth study 1

Doctrine of the Continental Shelf, the Resources of the Sea and Poor Countries

Within our framework of law-politics analysis, we can begin our study of the continental shelf by making some generalizations on the changes in the doctrine of the "law of the sea" and particularly in the time-honored principle of the "freedom of the seas." Incidentally, the principle of freedom of the sea has been a part of customary international law for so long that it could not be easily subjected to the current turmoil on the present and future use of resources of the ocean floor and the seabed, particularly the so-called continental shelf. But it is difficult to escape the fact that exploitation of the resources of the sea is an issue with far-reaching economic, political, and legal consequences for the international system. It is apparently the most vigorous onslaught yet on the traditional doctrine of "freedom of the seas." Thus the doctrine of the shelf, as presently formulated, and the associated powerful questions of the resources of the sea permits us a unique opportunity not only to analyze present states' attitudes and behavior with regard to present laws of the sea but also to assess future prospects for an orderly development of new laws of the sea based on international consensus. The issue in question

[1]For a brief but interesting outline of some of the above stated functions of international law, see Stanley Hoffmann, "Introduction" in L. Scheinman and D. Wilkinson, *International Law and Political Crisis: An Analytical Casebook* (Boston: Little, Brown), 1968, pp. xi–xix.

acquires a crucial focus when viewed in the context of the use of the underwater resources for the economic development of Third World countries and the general issues of peace and security. With the ability of sophisticated civil and military technology today the vast mineral resources of the sea are no longer inaccessible to human exploitation. In the decades ahead the resources and the space of the ocean floor and seabed will provide unprecedented opportunities both for economic development and military expansion.

At the present (even when one includes the treaty forbidding the placing of weapons of mass destruction on the ocean floor) there is no significant body of international law and regulations to control state activities beyond the continental shelf. Unless the community of nations acts wisely and promptly to develop new laws, it is quite likely that the seabed and the ocean floor will increasingly become subject to economic exploitation, competitive appropriations, and military use under a wide variety of circumstances by the few countries that now possess the technical facilities and are actively seeking military superiority in the world. Indeed, as we shall point out, the process has already begun.[2]

For clarity and comprehension the analysis in this study will proceed as follows: (1) a brief survey of realms of national jurisdiction beyond the continental land mass in order to understand current trends in states' attitudes and behavior with regard to future of the seas; (2) an analysis of the present state of the doctrine of the continental shelf to assess its role in creating confusion and problems in the orderly development of future laws of the sea; (3) a detailed analysis of recent United Nations debates and activities, for example, on the question of the seabed and the ocean floor that indicates states' attitudes, behaviors, and intentions with regard to future uses of this area and the kinds of laws of the sea they would like to see develop in the 1970s.

Realms of national jurisdiction beyond the continental land mass—a survey

One of the prime components of the doctrine of "state sovereignty" is the inalienable right, that is, duty, of the state to protect the societal order existing within its territorial borders and to provide its inhabitants with some measure of security from unwarranted outside intervention of any

[2]See the Secretary-General's report, On Resources of the Sea Beyond the Continental Shelf. U.N. Doc. E/4449/Add. 1 (February 19, 1968); see also John L. Mero, *The Mineral Resources of the Sea* (New York: Elsevier Co.) 1965; and another report by the Secretary-General on Marine Science and Technology, U.N. Doc. E/4487 (April 24, 1968) that was prepared in response to General Assmbly Resolution No. 2171 (XXI) (December 6, 1966).

kind.[3] In the seventeenth century under this doctrine as the interstate contact increased, so did the subsequent concern for national strategic naval superiority. As a result the nation-state was accorded the right to establish a perimeter or zone of safety beyond the territorial confines of its landmass into its surrounding waters. According to some of the earliest scholars of international law, the zone known as the "territorial sea" was to extend to a distance equal to the range of the furthest shot fired from a cannon which, incidentally, at that time was roughly three miles.

Paralleling the later development at a time of increased European competition for overseas markets was the enunciation and elucidation of the doctrine of the "freedom of the seas," which reserved the right of all legally recognized entities known as states to unrestricted use of the sea for navigational and all other purposes.[4] The widespread acceptance of this doctrine against the notion of "closed sea"[5] became clear by the time of Hugo Grotius. In fact, even the earliest concepts of "free seas" stressed granting the widest possible freedom to the "inclusive" interests of the international community and the narrowest possible freedom to the "exclusive interests of the sovereign states participating in that same community."[6] The states that controlled the formulation, execution, and adjudication of international law of the sea at that time had a vested interest in keeping the seas free.[7]

However, since these early times, and more particularly since World War II, states have developed several new, overlapping, and often con-

---

[3]For an interesting discussion of the psychology of state sovereignty see Charles De Vesscher, *Theory and Reality in Public International Law* (Princeton: Princeton University Press), 1957, Chapter 4.

[4]Major concerns of most states at this time seem to have been trade and navigation. Later on with the growth of technology, freedom to lay submarine cables, for example, was also included.

[5]One of the better formulated statements on the doctrine of the "closed sea" can be found in the Treaty of Tordisillos of 1443.

[6]The terms "inclusive" and "exclusive" have been used by such scholars as Myers S. McDougal and William T. Burke. An area of "inclusive" interest in this context simply means that the interests of the international community prevail in toto. Diametrically opposed is the area of "exclusive" interest, where the interests of the sovereign state predominate. For details see M. S. McDougal and W. T. Burke, "Crisis in the Law of the Sea: Community Perspectives Versus National Egoism," *The Yale Law Journal*, 67 (February 1958), 544–546.

[7]Thus, W. L. Griffin, speaking of the state interests at that time comments that ". . . the more absolute the coastal states' authority, the greater is the interest of other states in a narrow width of such authority. Conversely, the wider the area of the coastal states' sovereign authority, the greater is the interest of other states in reducing the content of the coastal states' authority therein." See W. L. Griffin, "Development of Law for Ocean Space Activities" *Transactions of the Second Annual Marine Technology Society and Exhibit* (June 27–29, 1966), p. 351.

flicting interests in the sea. For instance, with growing national populations and the often projected rapid depletion of land-based resources, states have increasingly become aware of the potential of the sea in providing for the domestic needs of their national economies, as well as for additional export products. The renewed interest in the sea, or more precisely in the resources of the sea, has led states to make demands aimed at expanding the realms of national jurisdiction beyond the traditional territorial waters. As a result concepts such as "fishing conservation zones," "contiguous areas," and "continental shelf" have emerged.

While economics has been a decisive factor in the rising challenges to the doctrine of "freedom of the seas," the age-old demands for national security have also become inextricably intertwined in the process. As the situation stands now, on the one hand the desire for a strong national economy self-sufficient in providing the material resources necessary to conduct a large-scale conflict; this has led states to frame doctrines appropriating such resources for national interest.[8] On the other hand, the military establishments of the superpowers have become increasingly conscious of the importance of a national defense strategy fairly heavily reliant on missile-laden submarines cruising at great depths under the high seas.[9] At least one author has carried the logic so far as to suggest that states are shifting to marine-based defense strategies in order to minimize the necessity of attacks during a war on land-based installations with nuclear weapons, thus making war, that is, nuclear war, a less destructive alternative in future policy considerations.[10] Similarly, the more technologically advanced states have, and not without protests by other states, made demands for zones of temporary national jurisdiction to conduct nuclear weapons and missile tests.[11]

Both of these trends, the economic and the strategic-political, have inevitably meant the expansion of zones of national jurisdiction to varying distances from the national borders. The doctrines that have emerged from the national interests in the sea are summarized in Table 1. These doctrines are expressed in the form of a continuum from zones of "exclusive" to zones of "inclusive" use of the sea.

---

[8]For details see J. W. Robertson, "Security Interests and Regimes of the Sea" *Proceedings of the Second Annual Conference of the Law of the Sea* (June 27, 1967) pp. 47–51. See also K. R. Stuggard, "Implications for the Future Distribution of the Seas' Resources if Present Regimes Continue in Force," *Ibid.*, pp. 63–69, and relevant parts of Robert A. Craemer "Title to the Deep Seabed: Prospects for the Future," *Harvard International Law Journal*, (2) (Spring 1968), 205–231.

[9]J. W. Robertson, "Security Interests and Regimes of the Sea," pp. 47–51.

[10]R. A. Craemer, "Title to the Deep Seabed: . . ." p. 217.

[11]M. S. McDougal and Schler, "The Hydrogen Bomb Tests in Perspective—Lawful Measures for Security," *Yale Law Journal*, 64 (1955), 648.

Table 1. Realms of national jurisdiction, expressed in doctrines, from zones of "exclusive" to zones of "inclusive" use

Doctrine	Zone of "exclusive" use	Zone of "inclusive" use
(High)		(Low)
Internal waters	Complete national regulation	None
Territorial waters	National ownership of land, water, and air	Innocent passage
Contiguous zones	Exceptional fishing rights due to contiguity	Unlimited access to fishery resources, unless agreement to the contrary
Continental shelf	Sovereignty over resource exploitation to 200 meter depth of water column; or beyond that, to point where subsurface admits of exploitability	Unlimited national access beyond 200 meters or where depth does not admit of exploitability
Nuclear weapons and missile testing zones	Temporary regulation of vehicular traffic through zone	Of temporary effect and duration
High seas	None	Free navigation, travel and cable laying
(Low)		(High)

In each case, except for the two extremes—"internal waters" and the "high seas"—the rights and responsibilities of both the state and the international community are poorly defined. In fact, a mixture of rights and obligations on the part of both is evident. In some cases, such as "innocent passage," the counterpart to the "exclusive" right, has taken the form of a concrete doctrine. A few additional observations can also be made. For instance, in the zones lying closest to the state borders and in the internal and territorial waters, the state sovereignty tends to be absolute with only very precise and well-defined exceptions. As one moves beyond these zones, state sovereignty becomes far from absolute; yet very precise (although limited) rights are still accorded to states. The contiguous zones, for example, apply solely to the exploitation of fishery resources; no sovereignty is claimed over the water column itself. In the case of the continental shelf, as another example, sovereignty of a state applies only to the exploitation of mineral, nonsedentary resources on or below the seabed. Again, sovereignty is not allotted over the land itself or the water column.[12]

At the present time it is in the contiguous zones and the continental shelf that the states are concentrating their activity, because it is within these zones that states expect to derive substantial economic benefits. They have found it profitable, for instance, to expand the scope of their fishing operations by claiming broader zones of "exclusive" interests. The famous decision of the Anglo-Norwegian Fishery case confirms this trend. As a result of this decision several states have been encouraged, particularly in South America, to establish their own fishing zones extending up to 200 miles into the sea.[13] A recent survey conducted by W. Neblet[14] summarizes this trend, as in Table 2.

The above trend toward increasing national jurisdictions can be further demonstrated by comparing a list of territorial water claims compiled in 1950 by the U.S. Department of State with a list compiled in 1966 by Lewis Alexander for the Law of the Sea Institute at the University of Rhode Island.[15] The results are summarized in Table 3.

Since 1958, 24 states have expanded the limits of their territorial waters to 12 miles, and in some cases to encompass exclusive rights to fishery

[12]The whole question of state sovereignty in these areas is further confused by the insistence by several states that this distinction between "precise and limited" rights on the one hand, and "sovereignty" on the other is merely a matter of semantics. Supporting this contention, a number of scholars of international law have advanced the argument that sovereignty in these areas must be regarded as in existence, because control of a zone by one state even for specific activities only generally pre-empts activities of another state in that zone, although the activities might be of a different nature. See Gilbert Gidel, "The Continental Shelf," *University of Western Australia Annual Law Review*, III (1) (December 1954), 101; Richard Young, "The Geneva Convention on the Continental Shelf: A First Impression," *American Journal of International Law* 52 (4) (October 1958), 733–739.

[13]In an extreme case a Peruvian Air Force plane once attacked fishing vessels owned by A. S. Onassis at a point 350 miles from the nearest coastal state. More recently the Peruvian government has repeatedly captured American fishing vessels in what the United States considers international waters, and forced them to pay fines for violating Peruvian "territorial" waters. For an interesting article related to the subject see J. L. Kunz, "Continental Shelf and International Law: Confusion and Abuse," *American Journal of Interational Law*, 50 (4) (October 1956), 837.

[14]William P. Neblet, "The 1958 Conference on the Law of the Sea: What Was Accomplished" *Proceedings of the First Annual Conference of the Law of the Sea* (1966), 42.

[15]Lewis M. Alexander, "Offshore Claims of the World," *Ibid.*, p. 78.

Table 2. Distribution of states on the basis of contiguous zones claimed

	Conservatives	Moderates	Radicals
1. States holding territorial sea, including fishing zones (3–10 miles).	19		
2. States adhering to 12-mile territorial sea, including fishing zones.		26	
3. States adhering to the territorial sea of 3–10 miles, but, fishing zone 12 miles.		29	
4. States claiming areas beyond 12 miles and up to 200 miles.			12
Totals:	19	55	12

Table 3. Distribution of states on the basis of extent of the territorial sea

	3 miles	6 miles	12 miles	50 kilo-meters	130 miles	200 miles	Total
			(between 3 and 12)				
1. 1950 list compiled by Dr. Boggs, State Department.	40	18	3				61
2. 1966 list compiled by Dr. L. Alexander Law of the Sea Institute.	32	16	26	1	1	6	85

exploitation.[16] While the Geneva Convention of 1960 demonstrated that we were far from a unanimous agreement among states on the exact limit of state jurisdiction, a tentative consensus seems to be emerging at setting 12 miles as the "normal" outermost extent of the contiguous zone.

Doctrine of the continental shelf and beyond: confusion and problems

What is of concern here is not the state activity on the continental shelf per se, or the legality of shelf doctrine itself; the main problem is the confusion that exists today in the interpretation of this doctrine and its negative consequences on the development of future laws of the sea. Multiple interpretations by various states have been instrumental in compounding the difficulties inherent in the debate on the legal distribution of the resources of the sea. The dispute centers on the *extent* of national jurisdiction on the continental shelf. In an attempt to compromise the disparate and often conflicting interests of various states, the matter was referred to the International Law Commission (ILC), a United Nations-sponsored group charged with the task of clarifying legal ambiguities. The Commission sought to employ a compromise definition for the continental shelf and after some indecision succeeded in adopting the following as embodied in Article 1 of the Continental Shelf Convention:

> For the purpose of these Articles, the Continental shelf is based as referring (a) to the seabed and subsoil of the submarine areas adjacent to the coast but outside the area of the territorial sea, to a depth of 200 meters or, beyond that limit to where the depth of the superjacent waters admit to the exploitation of the natural resources of the said areas; (b) to the seabed and the subsoil of the similar submarine areas adjacent to the coasts of islands.

In practice, the ILC avoided a firm decision that would have created the parameters necessary as a prelude for the development of a badly needed consensus on the outermost extension of national jurisdictions. The identification of parameters, physically measurable in miles, for example, would have placed *some limits* (however tenuous and subject to unique local or regional situations) on the widest extent of *legitimate* state demands, and this was desirable. This desirability can be discerned from state attitudes toward the limits of territorial waters and contiguous zones. For instance, although there are exceptions to state acceptance of

16W. P. Neblett, "The 1958 Conference on the Law of the Sea: . . ." p. 46. A 12-mile territorial water limit was proposed by the United States and Canada in the 1960 Geneva Convention, but the proposal fell short of adoption by one vote.

the 12-mile territorial water zone, the general consensus appears to be that the 12 miles is the most "logical" point to which state jurisdiction can be legitimately extended.

In the face of this general consensus, the interstate rivalry and the subsequent patterns of state behavior tend to take more definite forms and, at the same time occur within the framework of a perceived need for more regularity. Thus, while the territorial waters and fishing zones rivalries have led to conflict, they have also generally led to cooperation, for example, a series of agreements between the United States and Soviet Union on fishing off the North Atlantic coast of the United States and in the Bering sea, United States-Japanese agreements in the North Pacific and, more recently, attempts at creating an arbitration commission to handle fishing disputes between the United States and some of its South American neighbors. We are suggesting simply that by being able to define the parameters of the area of conflict in specific terms (e.g., in miles or meters) the incentive to bargain generally assumed to be present in most interstate disputes today can be more effectively brought to bear on the whole process of arriving at consensus through various compromises.

Because of the apparent failure of the ILC to set physical parameters on the continental shelf by defining the area of national jurisdiction and its outermost limit such as the shelf edge by specific mileage, states have been unable to focus their attention on specific demands. A bargaining process cannot be meaningful unless specific demands are made and unless it takes place within a previously recognized framework to accommodate divergent interests. However, this should not be taken to mean that no attempt has been made to arrive at a measurable definition of the continental shelf. Recently, several renowned international law experts and some states have attempted to do just that; unfortunately, the confusion and lack of consensus persisted.

K. O. Emery, for instance, argued the "continental shelves are characterized by structure and stratigraphy that are similar to, or are natural continuations of, the structure and stratigraphy of the adjacent land.[17] William C. Tubman asserts that "geographically, the continental shelf commences at the low-water mark and is a gently sloping plane which underlies the sea adjacent to most land masses, extending seaward from shore to the point at which there is a marked increase of the gradient of the decline and where the continental slope leads to the true ocean bottom.[18] Another scholar, A. Mouton, in an unsuccessful attempt to

[17]K. O. Emery, "Geological Aspects of Sea Floor Sovereignty," The Law of the Sea (Proceedings of the First Annual Conference of the Law of the Sea Institute), 1966, p. 148.

[18]William C. Tubman, "The Legal Status of Minerals Located on or Beneath the Sea Floor Beyond the Continental Shelf," Transactions of the Second Annual Marine Technology Society and Exhibit (June 27–29, 1966), p. 379.

develop a firm yardstick, reflects on the problem by commenting, "To define the seaward limit of the continental shelf satisfactorily from the geographic and oceanographical standpoint the depth-line of the rim should be used; but that varies quite considerably."[19] As an alternative, Mouton further suggests that "The definition of the continental shelf should express the geographical-geological conception of this formulation. Although, the end of the shelf . . . generally appears to coincide with the 200 meters isobath, this naturally is not an exact figure."[20]

However, two means of measurement have resulted from persistent attempts to derive a quantitatively measurable length and depth for the outermost limits of national jurisdictions: (1) water depth and (2) linear distance from the shore (a baseline). Again, concerning linear distance and water depth, confusion prevails, as highlighted by the comments of these same scholars. Emery states, "differentiation by depth alone is impractical because the shelf edge ranges from 20 to 550 meters and averages 133 meters deep."[21] Tubman adds to the debate by suggesting, "undersea platforms vary from less than 3 miles to 250 miles."[22] And finally, Mouton states that ". . . the average depth at which the greatest change in slope occurs is 72 fathoms (131·688 meters)."[23] In other words, the distance from the coast or the baseline, at which the geological unity of the continent with the subsurface ends, varies considerably in both water depth and linear distance from the shore.[24] Incidentally, the shelf is somewhat narrow along the west side of both North and South America, but on the opposite side of the Pacific along the Asian coast, it is wider than any other point in the world, reaching from 750 to 800 miles in the Yellow Sea and in the Gulf of Siam.[25] There is then no uniform measure for the shelf as is true for the territorial sea or a contiguous zone. Since the problem concerns both depth and width, the confusion and imprecision remain not only in terms of fathoms and miles, but also because of geological differences. The scholars who have suggested adopting a strictly geological measurement based solely on a geological configuration relative to the nearby landmass have simply neglected several potential problems that will arise if this approach is to be used. For instance, consider that the continental slope is approximately the real limit of a

---

[19]A. Mouton, *The Continental Shelf* (The Hague: Nijhoff), 1952, p. 13.

[20]*Ibid.*, p. 14.

[21]Emery, "Geological Aspects of Sea Floor Sovereignty," p. 149.

[22]Tubman, "Minerals Located on or Beneath the Sea Floor," p. 329.

[23]Mouton, *The Continental Shelf*, pp. 13–14.

[24]For linear presentations see the maps of the United States coasts in: T. W. Nelson and C. A. Bark, "Petroleum Resources of the Continental Margins of the United States," *Transactions of the Second Annual Marine Technology Society Conference and Exhibit* (June 27–29, 1966), p. 239.

[25]For details see Mouton, *The Continental Shelf*, p. 22.

continent, or the general boundary between the rocks of a continent and the denser rocks of the seabed. Thus assuming, as most of these authors have, that the geological unity of the land under water to the continental mass is the basis of their legal relationship, one must then contend with whether such a relationship ends at the shelf edge or at the edge of the slope.

Thus far we have considered the realms of national jurisdiction beyond the landmass, the extension of these jurisdictions in the light of diverse and often conflicting state interests in the ocean and its resources, and how these events are related to the ambiguities of the doctrine of the continental shelf that is marred by a lack of precise definition. It must be stressed that the orderly development of international law concerning the seabed and the ocean floor is contingent on a resolution of these ambiguities in the shelf doctrine. Unless these ambiguities are understood, particularly in the light of apparent conflict over underlying values and interests of states, the issue of the seabed and the ocean floor will not lend itself to the management of conflicting and divergent interests and to the development of viable laws.

With the above analysis in mind we can now turn to one of the most vexing problems in this area that has emerged in the international arena and continues to stifle the formation of a necessary consensus leading to the development of international law. This problem is the failure to define the shelf edge in clearly measurable terms, which has resulted in *states expanding their jurisdiction to areas not normally associated with a geographical configuration.* Thus the concern here is to what extent have states claimed jurisdiction beyond a geographical shelf edge or beyond the so-called "200-meter" depth?

Factual data on this matter is scarcely available because it is only during the last decade that states have begun to think about these subjects. Business corporations in the United States, the United Kingdom, the Soviet Union, Australia, and Japan are now starting to conduct research on the recovery of manganese nodules and calculate probable economic returns on such investments.[26] The potentiality of cheap exploitation of natural resources has led companies to obtain leases from national governments to explore undersea zones. Thirty lots between Wolves Bay in the north and the Oliphants River to the south have been leased by South African government for diamond exploration. A newly created American company now holds 55,000 acres of undersea land off Alaska in Norton

[26]See David B. Brooks, "Deep Sea Maganese Nodules: From Scientific Phenomenon to World Resources," *Proceedings of th Second Annual Conference of the Law of the Sea* (June 26–29, 1967), 32–42. See also John L. Mero, "Alternatives for Mineral Exploitation," *Ibid.*, pp. 94–97.

Sound. The same company also controls 10,000 square miles of underseas property in the Bais Strait area off Tasmania and Australia.[27]

Perhaps more publicly known than these leases are the rights granted by the United States Government to the American oil companies, off the coast of California, Oregon, and Washington.[28] A recent oil leak from one of the wells owned by the Union Oil Company off the coast of California near Santa Barbara for the first time shifted public opinion to curtail the granting of rights until adequate measures have been instituted to protect the public interest.

In most cases, however, the leasing has thus far been permitted within the framework of the provisions of the Geneva Continental Shelf Convention in 1958, which the United States has ratified. Generally, it has conformed to the so-called provisions of 200 meters in depth or to the geological extent of the continental shelf. But the process is now changing. The states are devising various kinds of "legal technicalities" to expand areas of their national jurisdiction. For example, as early as May 5, 1961, a memorandum was sent to the Director of the U.S. Bureau of Land Management from the Associate Solicitor, Division of Public Lands, U.S. Department of Interior,[29] which expresses this trend in legal technicalities:

> . . . phosphate deposits [are] located some 40 miles off the coast of California. . . . The area lies in the open sea and between this area and the mainland lies a deep channel in which soundings are at least 600 fathoms and soundings in designated areas range between 43 and 670 fathoms, the greater part of the area being at a depth or more than 100 fathoms.
>
> The sea floor, between the mainland shoreline and the continental shelf off California is much more complex than the typical continental shelf of most other areas of the world. For this reason, it was named the continental border land . . . to distinguish it from ordinary continental shelves. The continental border land is an arrangement of high and low areas having a general elongation. . . . Some of the topographic highs extend above sea level constituting banks, most of which are flat-topped. Still other highs are deeply submerged. Between the high seas are slopes that lead down into adjacent deep areas formed by 13 closed basins and several open but flat troughs. Flat basin and trough floors comprise about 17% of the total of 30,370 square statute mile area of the continental border land. 70% of the area consists of slopes, bank tops, and shelves similar to underwater mountains.

[27]William Bascon, "Mining in the Sea," *Proceedings of the First Annual Conference of the Law of the Sea* (1966), 161–163.

[28]N. E. Montgomery, "Drilling in the Sea from Floating Platforms," *Transactions of Second Annual Marine Technology Society and Exhibit*, (June 27–29, 1966), 238.

[29]Cited in Tubman, "Minerals Located on a Beneath the Sea Floor," pp. 387–388.

The author of the memorandum justifies national jurisdiction on the grounds that the geological configuration is *not typical*. If this experience is any indication, nation-states will find the means to extend their jurisdiction to areas in which they develop an interest. A similar process has occurred in the North Sea area where the United Kingdom, Norway, Denmark, West Germany, the Netherlands, Belgium, and France have competed for national claims to natural gas resources beneath the sea.[30] Similar to the American case, here too legal technicalities were devised to bypass rigidities inherent in a geographic definition of the continental shelf.[31]

This, then, has been roughly the extent of national experiences and involvement in submarine areas on and beyond the continental shelf. Indeed it is a meager basis to project future developments or even construct comprehensive conceptual schemes for analysis. However, noting the limitations on effective analysis, it is now our purpose to analyze critically some of the recent United Nations debates and proposals on the general subjects of need for regulating state activity on the seabed and the ocean floor and on the peaceful uses of the same area. It is hoped that a critical analysis of the United Nations record will assist to determine states' present attitudes, beliefs, and intentions with regard to the kinds of laws of the sea they would like to see develop in the present decade.

An analysis of recent United Nations debates and activities as indicative of states' attitudes and intentions

Realizing that the present situation will result in ever-increasing competition, conflict, and exploitation of the resources of the ocean floor and the seabed eventually endangering world peace, the United Nations at the initiative of Malta decided to discuss the entire issue in 1967.[32] During the Twenty-second General Assembly Session, the United Nations created the first formal ad hoc committee to study the scope and important aspects of the problem and to provide "an indication regarding practical means promoting international cooperation in the exploration, conserva-

---

[30]Richard Young, "Offshore Claims and Problems in the North Sea," *American Journal of International Law*, 59 (1965), 505–522.

[31]The main problem here was the Norwegian Trench. Also unique was the fact that national jurisdictions were applicable across a fairly small area relative to the distance, for instance, among nations separated by Atlantic and Pacific Oceans. For details see map by Francis T. Christy and Henry Heijindahl in 'A Hypothetical Division of the Sea Floor," prepared for the Law of the Sea Institute, University of Rhode Island, December 1967.

[32]See U.N. Document A/C. 1/Pv. 1515 (November 1, 1967), 60.

tion, and uses of the seabed."[33] Much of the work of this committee was done in 1968.

On the basis of the recommendation of the above ad hoc committee and as a result of rapidly expanding interest in the resources of the sea among much of the membership, the United Nations took further action. In its Twenty-third Session in December 1968 it passed four resolutions, thus fully committing the international organization to this area. Under the first resolution the General Assembly created a permanent 42-member committee on the peaceful uses of the seabed and the ocean floor. Under the second resolution it requested a study by the Secretary-General on the danger of marine pollution. Under the third resolution it requested another study by the Secretary-General on the establishment of the international machinery to exploit the resources of the area, and under the fourth resolution it approved a request to declare the 1970s to be a decade of oceanographic exploration.

On the basis of recommendations received as a result of the above stated four resolutions, the United Nations in its Twenty-fourth Session of the General Assembly, on December 15, 1969 adopted four more resolutions under the general title of "Examination of the Question of the Reservation Exclusively for Peaceful Purposes of the Seabed and the Ocean Floor, and the Sub-Soil thereof, Underlying the High Seas Beyond the Limits of Present National Jurisdiction, and the Uses of Their Resources in the Interest of Mankind." Under the first resolution, the Assembly requested the Secretary-General to ascertain the views of member states on the desirability of convening a conference on the law of the sea with a view to arriving at a definition of the seabed beyond the national jurisdiction. Under the second resolution it requested the 42-member committee to consider further the questions entrusted to it a year earlier. It further emphasized that the committee should arrive at comprehensive and balanced statements of principles and present it to the Assembly in the form of a draft resolution during its Twenty-fifth Session in December 1970. Under the third resolution, the Assembly requested the Secretary-General to prepare a further study on various types of international machinery. Under the fourth resolution, it declared that, pending the establishment of an international regime in the area, states and persons, whether physical or juridical, are required to refrain from all exploitation of the resources of the area and that no claims to any part of that area or its resources shall be recognized.

[33]Consult General Assembly Resolution 2340 (XXII) December 18, 1967; also see the Secretary-General's very interesting report on the Living Resources of the Sea. U.N. Doc. E/4449/Add. 2 (February 7, 1968).

The ad hoc committee, which was established during the Twenty-second Session in December 1967, represented nations of all sorts reflecting worldwide interests. It started its work by establishing its own two working groups of the whole, one on legal and other on economic and technical matters.[34] The obviously complicated political aspects of the problem were reserved for the consideration of the whole committee after two working groups had submitted their final reports.

In its deliberations the working group on economic and technical matters emphasized the great need for research and exploration beyond the continental shelf, mainly for the purpose of improving man's existing knowledge. On the important question of exploiting the resources of the sea for the benefit of the mankind as a whole the group, numerically dominated by poor nations, unanimously agreed that intensive and expanded cooperation among states must be established for the benefit of the *entire human race*. It was further agreed, although not without protest by the more technologically advanced and economically well-off nations, that "the benefit for the entire human race" should not refer only to the immediate profits gained by leasing claims or granting licenses, but should be interpreted to include "the larger value of international output, in particular the increase in value at stages subsequent to the primary production including the distribution and consumption phases."[35] The problem, of course, with this type of profit-sharing agreement, if it is ever formalized and legalized, is always the built-in mechanism for disenchantment for the nations that would invest their resources for the exploration and exploitation of the sea only to find that profits will have to be shared with all because the *sea is the heritage of all mankind*. They shall always be tempted not to uphold strictly whatever international laws may subsequently develop from such agreements.

The working group on legal problems discussed several legal issues. There was a general agreement among the group members that the area beyond the limits of the present national jurisdiction cannot be subject to national sovereignty. But what constitutes the present national jurisdiction has never been settled in clearly measurable terms. And the group

[34]For the provisional reports of the two working groups see U.N. Doc. A/AC. 135/L. 1 (July 16, 1968) Annexes I & II, respectively. The present exploitation techniques, which can be considered as "economical" by American standards, are still restricted to depths no greater than a few hundred meters. Since the costs of marine mineral development are considered much higher than those analogous land-based operations, the incentives necessary for further progress by the commercial organizations will have to be created, probably by governmental agencies. Even in shallow areas of the continental shelf, daily average operational costs are four times higher than those of comparable land operations.

[35]See Annex 1, p. 17.

obviously felt inadequate to handle this challenging task. While the group's discussions frequently overlapped with the debates of the group on economic and technical matters, however, several additional issues of legal significance were discussed. Issues such as the legal status of the sea in broad terms, reservation of the seabed exclusively for peaceful purposes, use of sea resources in the interest of mankind, freedom of scientific research and exploration, questions concerning the consideration of other states in their exercise of freedom of the high seas, and questions of sea pollution and other hazards were tossed around and some consensus was arrived on these principles in general.

This concept of sea as the "legacy of all mankind," clearly visible behind the discussions of both groups, raises some complicated legal problems that are simply not dealt with in this aspect of international law. For instance, the 1958 Geneva Convention on the Continental Shelf (which incidentally sought to establish guidelines for the exploration of the continental shelf and the "workable" seabed). According to this particular convention, states' sovereign rights may be exercised over the continental shelf defined as "the seabed . . . adjacent to the coast but outside the area of territorial sea, to a depth of 200 meters or . . . *to where the depth of the superjacent waters admits of exploitation of the natural resources.*"[36] Since the facilities available in most technologically advanced countries will soon enable these countries to exploit the ocean floor resources *beyond* a depth of 200 meters, reputable observers have argued that the Convention actually had the effect of encouraging exploitation of the sea resources solely for *national* purposes.[37]

Neither the Geneva Convention nor any other international agreement made at the time these groups were meeting forbid the use of the seabed for military purposes. There was, however, a possibility that a treaty forbidding the use of this area for military purposes may emerge out of concurrent discussions in the Geneva Disarmament Committee.[38] The

---

[36] For details see *United Nations Conference of the Sea,* U.N. Publication Sales No. 58, Vol. II, p. 142. Emphasis on "Where the depth of . . ." is added by the present author.

[37] See, for instance, Louis Henkin, *Law for the Sea's Mineral Resources,* ISHA Monograph No. 1 (New York: Columbia University Press), 1968. See also W. L. Griffen, "The Emerging Law of Ocean Space" *The International Lawyer,* (July 1967), 548–587.

[38] In late 1968 both the Soviet Union and the United States submitted draft resolutions asking the disarmament committee in Geneva to take up this question. Since that time there is every indication that negotiations have gone well and a treaty might be forthcoming. See U.N. Documents A/AC 135/20 (June 20, 1968), and A/AC 135/24 (June 28, 1968) respectively. Note that the United States has submitted another draft resolution containing a "statement of principles concerning the deep ocean floor," which, incidentally, also sums up the views expressed by the two working

group however, was not able to make any progress on this sensitive issue beyond an expression of concern. It was suggested by some members of the group that the disarmament committee in Geneva may use the Antarctic and Outer Space Treaties as guidelines for the development of a new treaty forbidding weapons of destruction in this area.

Following the initial deliberations of the working groups the ad hoc committee as a whole took up the issue of the uses of the seabed and the ocean floor for further discussions, with the intentions to make comprehensive recommendations to the General Assembly through its permanent Political and Security Committee. In its discussions the ad hoc committee found a near unanimous support of such broad concepts as "peaceful uses of the seabed and the ocean floor" (with landlocked countries going so far as to say *all areas* outside territorial waters should also be included in this concept), a "decade of ocean exploration," and "conservation of marine environment."

There was a near unanimous agreement that the General Assembly should be asked to create a new standing committee with more time at its disposal and a broader mandate than the present ad hoc committee. The purpose of the new committee was to provide direction and purpose to all activities related to the seabed without duplicating or replacing the work of the existing specialized agencies of the United Nations already in operation. It was further suggested that the committee could also serve as a *focal* point of study on all the various present and future aspects of the item. Several members submitted proposals containing guidelines for regulating the exploitation and use of these areas and their resources. It was widely desired that the General Assembly should be provided with a minimum position of the committee on which a wide area of agreement existed, in the hope that such an indication of consensus could provide a practical means for decisive actions by the Assembly at a later date. Unfortunately, despite all the efforts to arrive at a common formulation up to the last day of the committee's session, a final agreement simply could not be reached. Consequently, more than one set of recommendations were included in the body of the report made to the Political and Security Committee of General Assembly on October 28, 1968.

The Political and Security Committee held its session on December 19 and 20, 1968, and simply endorsed much of what had transpired in the sessions of the ad hoc committee, with a reemphasis on certain aspects

---

groups on the questions of disarmament in this area. See U.N. Doc. A/AC 135/25 (June 28, 1968). India has also issued a statement of principles in this area. See U.N. Doc. A/AC 135/25 (June 28, 1968). A treaty in this area has since then emerged.

of the issue. For instance, the need for intensive and expanded international cooperation in the field of marine mineral development was frequently emphasized. Several delegates pointed out that most countries for technical, financial, and other reasons are not in a position to participate in the exploitation of these resources and will in reality be "left out," while the rich and the advanced nations will grab up the most promising areas. This will inevitably increase the already existing economic imbalance between the "haves" and "have nots." Some delegates argued that to ensure benefits of the sea resources for all of mankind, some kind of international machinery must be established. A few suggested the establishment by agreement of international jurisdiction and control over the seabed; others argued for the establishment of an authority under the aegis of the United Nations.

On the legal aspects of the issue delegates generally agreed that there was a need for a precise and more widely accepted definition of the area and limits of the continental shelf, but found themselves unable to make any headway on this problem, beyond a mere suggestion that another conference on the law of the sea be called. There was some heated discussion on the "freezing" of national claims over the seabed and the ocean floor beyond the vague limits of present national jurisdiction, pending a clarification of these definitions, but no agreement was reached. Various views were expressed on the kind of regime of legal principles that should apply to the activities of all states in these areas, and exploitation of its resources. Several speakers referred to the concepts of *res nullius* and *res communis* in connection with the sea. While some considered the concept of *res communis* as applicable, others held that neither concept was helpful in this context. It was pointed out that the areas under discussion had special legal status as the common heritage of mankind, but no one was willing to define this "special" legal status in precise terms. Several representatives declared that states and individuals should conduct their activities according to whatever principles of international law and the United Nations Charter they consider applicable to the issue. Others emphasized the rights of states to have access to freedom of the seas. A number of speakers stated that the exploitation and use of the ocean floor should be carried out in accordance with rules and regulations concerning the prevention of pollution, radioactive contamination, and conservation of the living resources of the sea.

With regard to military aspects of the issue, several delegates stressed that in the interest of all nations urgent attention must be given to trends and possibilities regarding the potential use of the area for military purposes, and that immediate efforts should be made to reverse those trends before they are completely out of hand. It was widely recognized that the area should be used exclusively for peaceful purposes. Much of the debate on this particular subject can be summarized by two distinctly different views expressed: One "peaceful use" view *completely excluded all military use*; the other view suggested that a "positive approach" required the affirmation and the acceptance of the principle that the area be used exclusively for peaceful purposes, and that military activities in pursuit of "peaceful aims" or in fulfillment of "peaceful intents," consistent with the United Nations Charter and the obligations of international law, *should not be banned*. In support of the position that military use of the continental shelf should *also be* banned, it was held Articles 2, 3, 4, and 5 of the Geneva Convention on the Continental Shelf limited the coastal states' rights *only* to exploration and exploitation of the natural resources of the shelf and did not give the coastal states unlimited jurisdiction over it. The underlying assumption behind this view concerning the continental shelf was that the military use of the seabed under the high seas, beyond territorial waters, in the area of the continental shelf, would inevitably affect the peaceful exploration and uses of the seabed. It was further pointed out that the greater the area of demilitarization the better it would be for the peaceful uses of the sea. Repeated attention was drawn to the fact that the term "territorial waters" itself means a claim ranging anywhere from 3 to 200 miles beyond the landmass, depending on the state.

The broad and frequently vague recommendations of the Political and Security Committee were eventually presented to the Twenty-third General Assembly on December 21, 1968. The Assembly, as stated earlier, adopted four resolutions. The first resolution established a permanent 42-member committee on the peaceful uses of the seabed and the ocean floor. The second requested a study by the Secretary-General on the dangers of marine pollution. The third requested another study by the Secretary-General on the establishment of international machinery to exploit the resources of the area. The fourth welcomed an International Decade of Oceanographic Exploration.

The members of the 42-member permanent committee were selected on the basis of an equitable geographical distribution, a fair balance between technically developed and developing countries, a further balance between coastal countries and landlocked countries. It was also agreed that the composition of the committee will be subject to rotation in order to provide greater participation.[39] Representatives of the International

---

[39]The (1969–1970) membership was composed of the following states: Argentina, Australia, Austria, Belgium, Brazil, Bulgaria, Cameroon, Canada, Ceylon, Chile, Czechoslovakia, El Salvador, France, Ireland, India, Italy, Japan, Kenya, Kuwait, Liberia, Libya, Madagascar, Malaysia, Malta, Mauritania, Mexico, Nigeria, Norway, Pakistan, Peru, Poland, Romania, Sierra Leone, Sudan, Thailand, Trinidad and Togoland, U.S.S.R., U.A.R., England, Tanzania, U.S.A., and Yugoslavia.

Atomic Energy Agency, the International Labor Organization, the Food and Agriculture Organization of the United Nations, UNESCO and Its Inter-Governmental Oceanographic Commission and the Inter-Governmental Maritime Consultative Organization attended the Committee's sessions. Several countries not represented in the Committee requested and received permission to send observers.[40] The Committee held three sessions consisting of numerous meetings in February, March, and August 1969. During its first session this committee also established two sub-committees, one on legal matters and the other on economic and technical matters. During its third session on August 29, 1969, the Committee finally approved the reports of both the Economic and Technical Sub-committee and the Legal Sub-committee.[41]

The reports of the two subcommittees, among other things, made it clear that the issues involved were extremely complicated and would require much more time than the Assembly resolution originally provided to the main committee. In spite of lengthy discussions and arguments, the subcommittees simply did not reach the level of agreement from which they could make some meaningful recommendations. Realizing its apparent failure, the Committee decided to ask the General Assembly to allow it to continue its discussions in 1970.

An analysis of the proceedings of the legal subcommittee of the above committee, for instance, clearly indicates the inability of member states of the United Nations to arrive at an agreement on the substantive issues involved in the area. There is clearly a strong predisposition on the part of many countries not to go beyond a vague consensus on the broader principles involved.

The Legal Sub-committee convened 11 times during March 1969. Eighteen additional meetings were held during August 1969. Its mission was to study the following areas, and elaborate and recommend legal principles relating to these areas: (1) legal status; (2) applicability of international law, including the United Nations Charter; (3) reservation exclusively for peaceful purposes; (4) uses of the resources for the benefit of mankind as a whole, irrespective of the geographical location of states, taking into account the special interests and needs of developing countries; (5) freedom of scientific research and exploration; (6) reasonable regard to the interests of other states in their exercise of the freedom of the high seas; (7) questions of pollution and other hazards, and obligations and liability of states involved in the exploration, use, and exploitation.

[40]Countries with observer status were Barbados, Burma, Denmark, Gugana, Jamaica, the Netherlands, New Zeland, Nicaragua, Philippines, Portugal, South Africa, Spain, Sweden, Turkey, Ukranian S.S.R., and Venezuela.

[41]See United Nations Documents A/AC 138/17 and A/AC 138/18 (August 1969).

On the question of legal status of the area many delegates once again felt both the concepts of *res nullius* and *res communis* were of no practical value in determining the legal status of the ocean floor beyond the present national jurisdictions. Some also argued that the occupation and national lake theories were legally questionable and certainly politically unacceptable. The notion of the sea being the "common heritage of mankind" was again argued as the starting point for providing the basis for specific principles concerning the area. Here are some of the principles developed out of this notion: principle of trust and trustees; indivisibility of the heritage; the regulation of the use of that heritage by the international community; the most appropriate equitable application of the benefits obtained from the exploration; use and exploitation of this area to the developing countries; freedom of access and use by all states; and the principle of peaceful use. Supporters of the principle of "common heritage" further argued that an international machinery for the regulation and management of the area be set up, preferably under the auspices of the United Nations. On the other hand, some delegates argued that the concept of "common heritage of mankind" was contrary to existing norms and principles of international law that it was devoid of legal content and, from a practical point of view, tended to be dysfunctional. This argument was combined with the statement that before their adoption all legal concepts are devoid of legal content and, thus, the argument was irrevalant.

Some delegations expressed the view that a practical solution based on international law could be provided if the provisions of the Convention on the High Seas were used. This convention declares that high seas are open to all nations on equal terms and are not subject to national sovereignity. Some argued that pending the establishment of an international regime the exploration and exploitation of its resources should not be allowed to continue without appropriate compensation to the international community, particularly to the developing countries. The only consensus that could be achieved on the legal status of the area was that it is not subject to national appropriation except as may be provided in a future regime.

On the question of applicability of contemporary international law and the United Nations Charter to the seabed and the ocean floor some delegates argued that both are applicable, if broadly interpreted. References were made to some general international legal principles as examples, such as international responsibility of states and respect for territorial integrity. It was impossible even to suggest from the discussion of these delegates that a legal vacuum existed and that international law was only partly applicable to the area. The people who supported the "common heritage of mankind" concept argued that much of existing international law was customary or contained only very broad legal principles, if any, to regulate state behavior in the area. In their estimation the existing international law could not be applicable here and, it is useless to invoke analogies from a different environment. At best, it was further argued, one can only draw certain guidelines from the existing international law and the United Nations Charter, but these guidelines certainly do not constitute norms. Some delegates accepted the above argument with some reservations; that is, they felt specific principles of international law may be suitable to the area, which require clarification. On the other hand, in some cases application of other principles of existing international law may well result in grave and inequitable consequences for many states; the 1958 Geneva Convention was a case in point.

On the question of exclusive reservation of the area for peaceful purposes, it was expressed frequently that unless the international community took immediate steps to prevent the militarization of the area, the arms race will be extended to this area, thus prohibiting its use for peaceful purposes. Several delegations stressed the urgency of banning from the area nuclear and other weapons as well as military bases and other fortifications. Frequent references were made to the desirability of successful negotiations on this topic in the Committee on Disarmament at Geneva, which was then in progress. The initiative of the U.S.S.R. in submitting a draft treaty to the Committee on Disarmament on March 18, 1969 was applauded by some delegates. A view was expressed that any military activity on the seabed is incompatible with the use of the area for peaceful purposes, and it was further contended the United Nations in the past had always invariably understood the use of a given environment for exclusively peaceful purposes to mean its complete demilitarization; that is, there were to be no military activities of any kind and for any purpose. It was argued there should be no departure from this principle in the case of the seabed. Other delegates simply asserted that the expression "exclusively for peaceful uses" in no way precluded military activities that are *consistent* with the United Nations Charter and international law. Others, while supporting the principle of excluding military activities from the largest possible area of the seabed, suggested it might be difficult to achieve this goal because of the difficulty in distinguishing between scientific and military activities and the uncertainties surrounding a possible inspection system to verify with present technology that certain military activities did not in fact take place on or under the seabed. It was also pointed out that the sovereign rights granted to coastal states under the Continental Shelf Convention were limited to the exploration and exploitation of the area for natural resources and thus could not be interpreted to mean the right to military use. It was also emphasized that the principle of the peaceful uses of the area meant setting up physical limits of the area to which this principle could be applied. Others felt this was beyond the scope of the Committee's mandate.

On the use of the resources for the benefit of all of mankind irrespective of the geographical location of states, taking into account the special interests and needs of the developing countries, some delegates thought that the committee's mandate to study the establishment of an international legal regime for the area implied in itself the use and the exploitation of the area by all without discrimination. Furthermore many delegates specifically emphasized that the special interests and needs of the developing countries must figure significantly in any international regime that may be established in this area. This should not be taken to mean that equality of opportunity is sufficient and thus that there is no need to provide for actual equitable sharing of the derived benefits. The upshot of the whole argument on the question of *special needs of the developing countries* was that the Committee avoid erecting situations that would be detrimental to the less developed countries in any way possible. It was widely accepted that the landlocked countries have the same rights to the sea and its resources as the coastal states. A view was also expressed that the uses of the sea should not endanger the legitimate interests of coastal states, particularly the poor states who do not have the means to protect these interests themselves.

On the question of freedom of scientific research and exploration it was pointed out that the principle of freedom of scientific research does not in itself give the exclusive right of economic exploitation of the resources of the area or provide the basis for freedom of economic exploration and exploitation. This particular freedom should entail the obligation to make results of scientific activities available to other states. On the question of pollution and other hazards and obligations and the liability of states in the exploration, use, and exploitation, the provisions of the Convention for the Prevention of Pollution of the Sea by Oil of 1954 were considered inadequate. It was pointed out the convention did not deal with all existing sources of pollution and lacked effective means of acting against new sources of pollution. Many delegates argued that new international instruments must be adopted that should include enforcement measures in national laws to provide firm obligation of states. Some emphasized the need for international regulations on liability for violations. Still others insisted that to make any set of principles more balanced and coherent it should include the principle of liability for damages caused by exploration, use, and exploitation of the area. On the question of legal status of the ocean floor beyond the present national jurisdictions a common denominator reached was that these areas should not be allowed to become subject to national appropriations and that no state shall exercise or even claim national sovereignty over any part of these areas. The overall concept of the sea being the common heritage of mankind was widely supported, but there were some who disagreed. On the question of applicability of existing international law and the United Nations Charter, the only consensus reached was that there are principles and norms of international law that are applicable to the area. There was no agreement on which specific laws or rules were applicable and to what extent. Or, whether any existing rules of international law apply to the economic exploitation and exploration that is presently in progress. On the question of reservation of the area exclusively for peaceful purposes all members agreed to this in principle. No agreement, however, could be reached on the geographic limits of application of this agreement or, more importantly, on the scope of the prohitition of military activities.

On the question of the use of resources for the benefit of mankind as a whole irrespective of the geographical location of states and taking into account the special interests and needs of the developing countries, an agreement appeared to have emerged on the need for the establishment of an international regime consistent with this philosophy. The qualifications of that regime were not agreed upon nor was the scope of its applicability. Regardless how the regime is characterized (e.g., legal, international, or agreed upon) there was an agreement that the regime should be legally binding. Nothing was decided on the important question of whether the regime shall apply to *the area* or only to *the resources*. On the question of freedom of scientific research, the principle was found to be acceptable in general, and so was the notion of the promotion of international co-operation in the conduct of scientific research. However, it was emphasized that research be carried out with the intention of open publication because it would be necessary to be able to distinguish scientific research in progress from exploration for commercial purposes. There were some strong differences that remained unresolved, on the relationship between freedom of scientific research and possible obligations regarding prior communication of programmes and subsequent communications of results, as well as differences on whether the notions of *accessibility* or *availability* on the one hand or dissemination on the other should be employed. Also, no agreement was reached on the question of whether such research should or should not be the basis for claims for rights to exploitation.

There was unanimous agreement that the question of reasonable regard for the interests of states in the exercise of the freedom of the high seas should be upheld. On the question of pollution, other hazards and obligations, and the liability of states involved in exploration, use, and exploitation, there was again unanimous agreement that appropriate safeguards against the dangers of pollution must be adopted. Similar consensus prevailed with regard to safeguards to protect the living resources of the marine environment and the safety measures concerning the activities in the area. On the rights of the coastal states to conduct activities, including scientific research and exploration undertaken in the area, there was no agreement. The question of liability for damages caused by activities in the area was also undecided at the time.

Since the time of the above-stated debate concerning the member states in the meetings of the special United Nations Committee concerning the seabed, several important events have happened that have a positive effect on the development of a comprehensive body of the law of the sea. First, the important Seabed Disarmament Treaty has been signed and ratified by many nations.[42] This treaty bans the emplacement of nuclear weapons on the seabed and the ocean floor. Sixty-two nations signed the treaty at Washington on February 11, 1971. This was the time when the United States and the Soviet Union also signed it. Second, the subsequent proceedings of the Seabed Committee have resulted in the adoption of important principles governing seabed exploration by the United Nations. The United Nations also declared that 1973 will be the year to convene a comprehensive Law-of-the-Sea Conference. These principles, approved by the General Assembly in 1970, were meant to serve as broad guidelines for future exploitation in the sea, and were as a basis for a future treaty. Admittedly some principles were vague but others were explicit, generally reflecting the attitudes of nation states as previously outlined. For the first time, the resources of the seabed were explicitly recognized as "common heritage of mankind."

With regard to the forthcoming conference on the law of the sea, the United States has already submitted a proposal for the conference to consider. It is in the form of a draft United Nations Convention on the International Seabed Area. An analysis of the draft convention reflects the common interest of the international community, even though not every member of this society may be fully satisfied with this draft. Some of the major principles of the American draft convention are as follows:

1. Preservation of the broadest possible precisely defined area of the seabed as the common heritage of mankind, open to use by mankind, open to use by all, with equitable sharing of benefits by all, particularly developing countries.

2. Preservation of the area exclusively for peaceful purposes.

3. Creation of new and uniform rules of law.

4. Establishment of a new international organization with regulatory powers

42The Department of State, "Treaty Banning Emplacement of Nuclear Weapons on the Seabed Signed by 62 Nations at Washington," *Bulletin*, LXIV (1654) (March 8, 1971), 288–290.

that permit it to adapt rules to changing situations and to insure that rights and obligations are respected.

5. Protection of human life and safety and of the marine environment.

6. Creation for the first time in history, of an independent, substantial source of international revenues to be used for international community purposes, particularly to promote economic development of developing countries.[43]

Initial reaction to the American draft convention has been a positive one among the developing countries for obvious reasons. It remains to be seen how this proposal will eventually affect the outcome of the forthcoming conference.

A concluding remark

A great deal remains to be done before we can have an effective and comprehensive body of the law of the sea. All the indications are that an era of the exploratory work in this field is ending and that the world community is getting ready to develop new laws. Negotiations for a multilateral treaty have already begun. We shall indeed learn a great deal about the new laws of the sea just as soon as a treaty in this area has been concluded, hopefully during the forthcoming conference on the law of the sea.

indepth study 2
Legal Order and Political Problems in Outer Space

It was not until Sputnik was sent into orbit on October 4, 1957 that interest in political and legal problems associated with space exploration began. Since it has now been 15 years since the Russians inaugurated the space age, it seems appropriate to review the past trends in the legal regulation of outer space activities and outline some of the major problems that will require legal controls in the future. In reviewing the past trends, we shall briefly retrace the developmental steps in outer space law mostly through the United Nations, and also appraise the 1966 Treaty on Principles Governing the Activities of States in the Exploration and

---

[43]The Department of State, "U.N. Adopts Principles Governing Seabed Exploitation and Decides to Convene Comprehensive Law-of-the-Sea Conference in 1973," *Bulletin*, LXIV (1649) (February 1, 1971), 150–158.

Use of Outer Space, Including the Moon and Other Celestial Bodies, better known as the Space Law Treaty, which was actually signed in 1967.

Legal problems associated with space can be best studied when it is assumed that the evolution of a public order in outer space will continue to be in large measure affected by political developments in the international arena. When one looks at the development of space law over the last 15 years, it does not appear impressive especially when compared to other areas of international lawmaking, or with mature legal systems surrounding the statutes, judicial decisions, formal agreements, and semilegal customs, or with the early expectations of many countries and individuals. However, if one considers the dynamics of the international arena in which the legal regime for outer space had to be built, the lack of knowledge about space, the rapid technological changes, the military implications for the use of space, and the present structures of international decision making, one concludes the progress achieved thus far has been impressive.

Development of space law

Legal problems of outer space were first discussed at the United Nations in 1958 where, in recognition of the potential legal and political problems that might arise as space is explored, the General Assembly established an Ad Hoc Committee on the Peaceful Uses of Outer Space. Although five members of the committee did not participate in the discussions of the committee (U.S.S.R., Czechoslovakia, Poland, India, and the U.A.R.) the committee nonetheless produced a report in 1959 that was adopted by the General Assembly through a resolution.

This resolution is important in the history of space law since the committee not only surveyed the potential activities that could be exercised in space but also considered the possibilities for international cooperation, and made recommendations concerning priority treatment for several problems that it identified. The resolution also "expressed the 'common interest of mankind in outer space,' urged 'international cooperation in the study and utilization of outer space,' called for the 'fullest exploration and exploitation of outer space for the benefit of mankind,' and pointedly emphasized the 'sovereign equality' of all member states of the United Nations."[44] Through this resolution a permanent committee on the *Peaceful Uses of Outer Space* was established and, with full participation of members this time, it started giving annual reports in 1962 that have been the basis for further General Assembly resolutions concerning problems of outer space. These resolutions have stressed two principles: (1)

[44]C. Wilfred Jenks, *Space Law* (New York: Praeger) 1965, p. 320.

outer space should be used only for peaceful purposes, and (2) the desirability of maximizing international cooperation in developing these peaceful uses.

Two important resolutions emerged as a result of the work of this committee, and they state general agreement on the specific application of legal principles to the legal and political problems in outer space—Resolution 1721 (XVI) and 1962 (XVIII). General Resolution 1721 (XVI), entitled *International Co-operation in the Peaceful Uses of Outer Space*, has added three general principles to what already existed: (1) international law, including the United Nations Charter, applies to outer space and to all celestial bodies; (2) outer space and celestial bodies are not subject to national appropriation; and (3) outer space and celestial bodies are free to be explored and used by all nation-states in conformity with international law.[45] Sensing the potential problems in space, the resolution further declared that the application of international law, including the Charter of the United Nations, extends also to outer space. In addition, it called upon member states launching vehicles into space, to furnish information concerning the object launched to the Secretary General, who would keep a public registry of launchings. The registry commenced functioning in March 1962, when first reports were filed, and has since recorded hundreds of launchings.

With more practical experience being gathered, the inevitability of more nation-states entering the satellite-launching phase of space exploration, and the rapid advancements in space technology and activities, it was increasingly felt desirable and necessary to state in another resolution certain basic principles that should guide states in their usage of the new international arena. So the second principal statement of agreement on the legal principles applicable to the space environment was unanimously adopted on December 13, 1963. Resolution 1962 (XVIII), the *Declaration of Legal Principles Governing Activities of States in the Exploration and Use of Outer Space*, was undoubtedly a landmark achievement in the continuing process of the regulation of space activities. Besides reaffirming the essential freedoms of outer space, already asserted in Resolution 1721, the Declaration prescribed that activities in outer space are to be conducted so as to stimulate international cooperation and maintain international peace and security; that nation-states are internationally responsible for national activities in outer space; that any private activity in space must be carried out with the authorization and regulation of the nation-state; that when international organizations sponsor any type of space activity, both the organization and the member nation-states will bear the responsibility; that both nation-states launching an object in space

[45]*Ibid.*, p. 321.

and nation-states from whose territory the object is launched are internationally responsible and liable for damages resulting from accidents on the earth, in airspace, and in outer space; that the launching nation-state retains jurisdiction and control over objects of its registry, and such objects should be returned to the launching nation-state when a return is requested; that ownership of spacecraft is not affected by their passage through outer space, or their landing beyond the boundaries of the state of registry; that astronauts should be regarded as envoys of mankind, should be rendered all possible assistance when it is required, and should be returned promptly to the nation-state of registration of their space vehicle; that nation-states should consult with each other when they intend to conduct some space activity that might cause harm to another nation-state or interfere with some other space experiments; and that any use or exploration of outer space must be carried on within the framework of international law, including the United Nations Charter.[46]

The committee stated this declaration was only an initial step, a statement of those principles on which there was unanimous agreement, and not a codification of all legal principles that might be applicable to outer space.[47] Apart from condemning the use of propaganda in outer space for provoking or encouraging threats to peace or acts of aggression, the Declaration contained nothing dealing with activities in outer space that would threaten international public order. It was not until August 1963 that the first concrete step in the prevention of the militarization of outer space was taken. This was the signing of the (Moscow) Treaty Banning Nuclear Weapon Tests in the Atmosphere, in Outer Space, and Under Water. This treaty ended any testing at high altitudes of nuclear devices that were causing considerable fallout and contamination of the earth's environment.[48]

The next step in the process of keeping outer space outside the military activities came in the General Assembly Resolution 1884 (XVIII), which called upon all states "to refrain from placing in orbit around the earth any objects carrying nuclear weapons or any other kinds of weapons of mass destruction, installing such weapons on celestial bodies, or stationing such weapons in outer space in any other manner."[49] Even though this Resolution may not have been intended to create legal obligations, the incorpora-

---

[46]Ibid., pp. 317–319.

[47]The legal character of any resolution passed by a unanimous vote in the General Assembly is far from settled.

[48]The virtually universal acceptance of the Moscow Treaty, except for France and the People's Republic of China, and the proven harmful effects of nuclear testing in all states should soon give it the character of international custom, thereby making conduct contrary to its prohibitions a violation of international law.

[49]Jenks, Space Law, p. 327.

tion of its body in the Space Treaty makes it an important landmark in the field of arms control.

Probably the most remarkable feature of the short history of space law, and one that could have far-reaching consequences extending beyond the immediate issues of outer space, was the emergence of the United Nations General Assembly as the principal world community organ for setting standards of conduct for space activities. Soon after the advent of the space age, it became apparent that the overwhelming majority of members thought the United Nations to be the place to formulate the basic rules of behavior in this frontier. They felt that the absence of any community-guided policies would only lead to conflict and encourage the growth of vested interests, both a potential threat to the immediate goals of exploration and the eventual establishment of an effective legal order in this frontier. Through its quasi-legislative intervention in the early stages of space exploration, the General Assembly may be said to have laid the foundations of space law and thus created conditions contributing to peaceful utilization of the new international arena.

The main provisions of the earlier declaration of the General Assembly and the provisions drawn from the Antarctic Treaty along with the provisions from Assembly's own resolution of October 18, 1963 (against stationing weapons of mass destruction in space) were embodied in a general treaty on space law. The space treaty entitled: Treaty on Principles Governing the Activities of States in the Exploration and Use of Outer Space, Including the Moon and Other Celestial Bodies, entered into force on October 10, 1967. The treaty formally states the rule of freedom of space and the applicability of international law and the law of the United Nations Charter in space. The treaty also forbids the setting up of military bases, testing of weapons, or any kind of military maneuvers on celestial bodies. It creates certain obligations for assistance to astronauts in distress and for their prompt and safe return to their country by the state that rescues them. It establishes rules for international liability for damage caused by space vehicles and also contains provisions on jurisdiction and ownership of vehicles. It details obligations on the avoidance of harmful interference and contamination in conducting space activities. The treaty also contains provisions on exchange of information and access to installations on various celestial bodies.

A cursory look at the above stated provisions and their implications tends to confirm the view that the international society has already initiated a fair amount of international space law. Space is an area where man's technology and his ability to explore the unknown is equally matched by his ability to devise law to deal with the avenues opened up to him by his technological ingenuity. The scientific and legal developments have taken place with almost the same speed. In fact, the law has become applicable to some situations that have not yet become a reality. For instance, the law's applicability to "other celestial bodies" is an indication of man's attempt to harness his technology by anticipating its future stages of development.

The 1967 Treaty should not be regarded as an end to space lawmaking; rather it is a beginning. Various space scholars and experts have already enumerated over 20 distinct problem areas concerning space needing regulations. The present space law does not deal with all of them. More than anything else this caution against rushing to enact a law is a reflection not of a general lack of desire to cooperate with each other on the part of states; instead it is an attempt to guard against the temptation to make too many laws on the basis of too little knowledge or experience in space.

The 1967 Treaty has invoked some criticism in the literature. Much of it suggests that it did not go far enough to include several new areas in this field that need legislation. Some scholars have argued that it did not add too much to what already existed in terms of "rules" applicable to space exploration through United Nations resolution and declarations. J. E. F. Fawcett concludes that the Treaty only adds four areas that were not already in the Declaration: (1) a provision concerning the prevention of contamination of both celestial bodies and the Earth; (2) provisions governing specific aspects of exploration and exploitation; (3) a provision prohibiting the establishment of military bases of various kinds, weapons testing, and military maneuvers on celestial bodies; and (4) a provision for inspecting on a reciprocal basis, space stations. installations, equipment, and space vehicles on celestial bodies.[50] But even these new provisions "are so loosely drafted as to suggest that the authors did not expect them to be put to a real test of interpretation, but thought that as long as the instrument looked reasonably like a treaty, the main purpose was served," and that purpose, according to the author, was political expediency.[51] In many instances the only difference between the two documents is that where the Declaration speaks of outer space, the Treaty adds, "the Moon and Other Celestial Bodies." Fawcett states that this Treaty was a step in "retrograde" and that now even the most solemn outer space resolution of the General Assembly is merely a nonbinding expression of intent.[52] Some of the problem areas not covered include communication satellites and systems, establishment of the airspace–outer space boundary, reconnaissance and espionage, weather satellites and weather control, metalaw, and flight rules and interference.

[50]J. E. S. Fawcett, *International Law and the Uses of Outer Space*, (U.S.A.: Oceana Publications), 1968, pp. 86–91.

[51]*Ibid.*, p. 15.

[52]*Ibid.*, p. 16.

Problems of sovereignty and jurisdiction

Claims concerning rights and activities in outer space involve economic and security interests and are closely related to claims in territorial airspace; this relationship is not surprising since airspace and outer space are a physical continuum.[53] For example, if spacecraft are to be used as a means of commercial transportation, rules concerning access to territorial airspace will have to be adopted, and the location of the airspace–outer space boundary will then become a practical problem. Commonsense suggests that "just as airspace has come to be understood in terms of the functions of aircraft, so outer space is where they do their essential work, that is in orbit or beyond."[54] However, the conclusion that satellites are in outer space when orbiting the earth implies not that the lower limit of outer space is where satellites can have the lowest effective orbit, but that it is not higher.

Although nations have not protested overflights by satellites engaged in the peaceful exploration of space, they may very well protest overflights by spacecraft at less than orbiting altitudes and by spacecraft engaged in other than peaceful exploration. And common carrier spacecraft might well operate at suborbital altitudes, particularly when entering and leaving territorially small, noncoastal nation-states. Successful use of spacecraft systems for transporting cargo, mail, and passengers will, therefore, be possible only if satisfactory policies concerning delimitation of territorial airspace and access between territorial airspace and outer spaces are adopted.

The problem of sovereignty and jurisdiction can be approached from two firm positions: (1) that outer space is for common use and is incapable of being appropriated at least down to the lowest effective orbiting level; and (2) that although the celestial bodies are physically capable of being appropriated, they are open to all nation-states.

Demarcation is the major problem of sovereignty and jurisdiction; and it has two limiting factors: *geometrical limitations* and *boundaries*. Since the earth is continually rotating about its axis and orbiting the sun, geometrically it can be seen that no particular volume of space can be attached, in the sense of ownership, to any particular area of the surface of the earth, since they are in constant relative movement; space is therefore incapable of appropriation.

The description of the rights of a nation-state above its territory is "cast in terms of imperium over person, things and activities there, rather

---

[53]Myres S. McDougal, Harold D. Lasswell, and Ivan A. Vlasic, *Law and Public Order in Space* (New Haven: Yale University Press), 1963, p. 244.

[54]Fawcett, *International Law and the Use of Outer Space*, p. 17.

than dominion over a volume of space."[55] Thus the exclusive jurisdiction above its territory, the sovereignty of a state, is simply a matter of terminology. The expression "above the territory" can geometrically be defined as an object that can be "hit" with a straight line drawn from the center of the earth to the object, if the line passes through the nation-state or its territorial waters. This line can extend to the upper limits of the nation-state's airspace.

The boundary problem, in its most general form, is the issue of an upper limit to the exclusive jurisdiction and control of a nation-state in the space above its territory. The question arises: Is there already a limit in existence? Some scholars have said that because of the absence of protest by nation-states against the overflight of their territories by spacecraft, a customary rule has already been established, setting earth satellites beyond their jurisdiction and control. But still, the lower limit or boundary of outer space remains in law clearly undetermined. The only accurate statement that can be made is that although the upper limit of jurisdiction and control may be set lower, it cannot now be regarded as higher than the *effective* orbiting altitude of earth satellites.

One major concept of airspace–outer space boundary has been the Von Karman line. It seems wise for the lawyer to obtain help from the physicist to determine where airspace ends. As A. Haley said, "no lawyer should indulge in abstract speculation on the subject without first familiarizing himself with the scientific background and outlook. . . ."[56] Because the scientific explanation of the Von Karman line would be detailed, for our purpose a simple brief statement defining the line can be given: it represents the line of demarcation between the aeronautic and astronautic regions. It is at approximately 275,000 feet above the earth's surface, which may well change as physicists and lawyers clarify where an aeronautical vehicle may no longer perform and where molecular oxygen dissociates and airspace no longer exists. Some factors included are aerodynamic lift, physical constitution of the air, and the biological and physiological viability. The major problem confronting the Von Karman line theory is in the use of the X-15 or rocket plane. Because of this, one scholar states that, "a definition of space which permits sovereignty to extend to the extreme limits of the atmosphere will be largely meaningless."[57]

As briefly stated earlier, the problem of access and passage is related to the problems of sovereignty and demarcation. On this basis, then,

[55]*Ibid.*, p. 70.

[56]Andrew Haley, *Space Law and Government* (New York: Appleton-Century-Crofts), 1963, p. 97.

[57]*Ibid.*, p. 102.

national decision makers perceive that interest in outer space is similar to that perceived on the high seas or in the airspace above the high seas. Recognition of the inclusive interest in the right of access and usage came almost with the orbiting of the first satellite. Since the Space Law Treaty has been signed by some 89 nation-states, including the major space explorers, freedom of access into and the use of outer space appears to be universally applicable as general principles of international law. In addition, there seems to be in practice a widely accepted right of passage; however, since the boundary question has not been resolved, any right of passage is bound to be ambiguous.

Problem of the military usage of space

It is no exaggeration to suggest that the success or failure of a legal regime in outer space will depend on the degree of militarization of this new international arena. The realm of outer space from the beginning of the space age has been regarded by the space powers as an extension of the traditional theaters of military operations, and in this light, it is easy to see that the inspiration for space activities has been thus far predominantly military. The all-pervasive fear of a militarily significant technological breakthrough, which might upset the balance-of-power, has often been cited in justification of the continuing interest of the defense establishment in outer space, even though no such breakthrough has occurred. The threats of force from space have been regarded as much more frightening than comparable threats from adjacent land, air, and sea areas. The Space Law Treaty does deal with several of these threats: orbiting nuclear weapons and other weapons of man's destruction, placement of such weapons in outer space and on celestial bodies, establishing military facilities on celestial bodies, and conducting military maneuvers on celestial bodies are forbidden. There are also provisions for on-site inspections of "all stations, installations, equipment, and space vehicles on the moon and other celestial bodies . . ." on the basis of reciprocity.[58] Although the treaty emphasizes peace and cooperation, there are several areas under this emphasis that are undefined, unresolved, or simply ignored for the present.

The preamble of the Declaration of Legal Principles and the space treaty stress the interest of mankind in the exploration of and use for peaceful purposes of outer space, but the difficulty lies in the terms "peaceful" and "purpose." "Peaceful" could mean "nonaggressive" and, therefore, allow any type of "defense" activity, or it may mean strictly nonmilitary. "Purpose" may mean only immediate use or it can be ex-

---

[58]Fawcett, International Law and the Uses of Outer Space, p. 89.

tended to cover any long-range capability of a device or operation. Included in the difficulties are the convertibility of many peaceful devices into a military realm; that is, any spacecraft or a station being used for peaceful exploration could be converted into a launch pad for missiles, antimissile missiles, or inspection satellites, reconnaissance satellites, or a communications point in a weapon or command system.

Reconnaissance has been the earliest application of the military uses of space technology. Observational satellites today provide comprehensive and continuous surveillance over wide areas of the world, which are inaccessible by other means. Some satellites are equipped with infrared sensors to detect ballistic missile launches. "Ferret" satellites collect electronic intelligence by monitoring radio traffic and obtaining the operating frequencies of military radar over a potential enemy's territory. Navigational satellites provide precise positioning data for submarines and other naval vessels that require accurate position fixing. The recent production of Russia's ABM system and the United States' MIRV system add further problems to outer space. Since antiballistic missiles are designed to destroy hostile missiles by high altitude explosions, they may require further operational testing involving the use of nuclear warheads in outer space. Although this is prohibited by the Moscow Test Ban Treaty, a member may withdraw from it "if it decides that extraordinary events . . . have jeopardized the supreme interests of its country."[59] It is conceivable that to penetrate effectively the ABM defense, a permanently stationed nuclear-armed offensive system could be developed for outer space. The American development of an antisatellite weapon; the Russian experimentation on the Fractional Orbit Bombardment System (FOBS); the Project West Ford, a project to "blackout" enemy satellite communications; the United States Manned Orbiting Laboratory (MOL) project; and various projected uses of space—orbital weapons programs, global surveillance platforms, and aerospace planes—all illustrate several points: the wide scope of anticipated military activities in outer space; the assumption that there will be, in the future, hostile weapons deployed in space that will have to be destroyed; and the lack of concern about the effect of these measures on the legal regime of space. As one author has said: "Although the military implications of technological advances have to be assessed, it does not follow that the full range of conceivable military applications will be pursued."[60] Thus it is appropriate to discuss the demilitarization of outer space.

---

[59]Jenks, *Space Law*, p. 330.

[60]Maxwell Cohen (ed.), *Law and Politics in Space* (Montreal: McGill University Press), 1964, p. 71.

Nonmilitarization of the moon and other celestial bodies is provided in the Space Treaty. The Treaty states that these areas will be used for peaceful purposes, and that the establishment of military bases or weapons there is forbidden. The relevant article gives the impression that a limited demilitarization of the moon was intended, and that its use for peaceful purposes does not exclude measures of defense.[61] The control of non-militarization of celestial bodies and of placing weapons of mass destruction is dealt with in Article 10 of the Space Treaty. The article lays down three conditions: first, requests for observation will be received equally and considered fairly; second, the observation will be determined by agreement; and third, the opportunity to observe the flight of space objects must be given. This article lays the basis for setting up a tracking system. As it has been shown above, the Space Treaty deals with many areas of military uses of outer space; unfortunately, these areas are not adequately dealt with. Two things are needed to make sure the Treaty is not broken: first, a strict definition of terms such as "peaceful," "purposes," and "self-defense" and, second, an effective inspections system, preferably before the space vehicles leave the ground.

Problem of harmful space activities

The second biggest threat to the welfare of the earth may be brought about by the indiscriminate application of the new technology and from uncontrolled scientific experiments in space, both upsetting the balance of nature. (The first threat, of course, is thermonuclear warfare.) Advances in space technology have created the opportunity for new experiments that may increase the risk of danger to the earth. There are three activities at this time that may be hazardous to both the earth and the space environment: (1) the uses of nuclear energy in outer space, (2) interplanetary travel that may lead to the biological contamination of the earth or other planets, and (3) large-scale weather modifications.

Some source of energy is needed both in the propulsion of a vehicle to reach required velocities and aboard the spacecraft for the operation of the scientific instruments, for the execution of guidance and control commands, and for the transmission of radio signals—energy. The present voyages of short duration with light payloads can aptly be carried by chemical propellants and electric batteries; however, for long journeys deeper into space carrying heavier payloads in large vehicles, new types of more efficient and reliable energy will be needed, and nuclear energy has been considered. For example, the anticipated energy requirements for

[61]Fawcett, *International Law and the Uses of Outer Space*, pp. 34–35.

manned exploration of even the nearest planets to earth—Venus and Mars —are regarded as extensive enough to require nuclear energy.[62]

Even immediate interests of an improved cost-efficiency ratio for future moon missions can be realized with upper-stage nuclear energy. The application of nuclear power plants are being designed for future orbiting laboratories and in spaceships. The use of nuclear energy in space was foreseen early in the space program and a considerable amount of work has been done on harnessing nuclear energy for space use. Spacecraft carrying nuclear devices of course present a serious danger, because of the highly toxic substances and because of radioactive pollution to the environment in which they operate—the area where the launching site is located, the atmosphere, the void of outer space, and the celestial bodies. The anticipated increase in the number of space powers and the widening range of space missions will inevitably augment the risk of radioactive contamination.

Another type of contamination that will present a second hazard to the earth in the coming years is interplanetary, biological contamination. A possibility exists that astronauts returning to earth from journeys to celestial bodies may bring back microorganisms that could cause contamination of catastrophic proportions to the earth. Such a contamination is explained in the following excerpt:

> Even if extraterrestrial organisms have a different chemistry, they may do incalculable damage on earth by multiplying wildly in competition with native plants. A more subtle danger is that they may upset the delicate chemical balance on which earthly life depends. An exotic organism living humbly in the soil might starve native plants by turning some vital nutrient, such as nitrogen, into a form they cannot use. If the Earth's plants die of starvation, its animals, including man, will die too. Since the nature of extraterrestrial life is not known, the most farsighted scientists cannot imagine at present all the ways that it might affect earthly life.[63]

The immediacy of this threat is exemplified by the fact that one of the primary missions of the voyage to the moon was to bring back samples of lunar material, in which there is a remote possibility of a dormant life form. An illustration of the somewhat casual attitude toward unknown biological risks was the relaxed quarantine measures announced by NASA just before the first moon landing.

An additional aspect of interplanetary contamination is that of infecting

[62]Glen Seaborg, "The Nuclear Path to Deep Space: A Report on Progress," *Air Force and Space Digest*, XLIX (April 1966), 69.

[63]*Time*, (June 4, 1965), 52.

celestial bodies with germs of earthly origin. A panel of experts related this problem to landings on Mars:

> Contamination of the Martian surface with terrestrial microbes could irrevocably destroy a truly unique opportunity for mankind to pursue a study of extraterrestrial life. Thus, while we are eager to press Martian exploration as expeditously as the technology and other factors permit, we insist that our recommendation to proceed is subject to one rigorous qualification: that no viable terrestrial microorganisms reach the Martian surface until we can make a confident assessment of the consequences.[64]

Hence, without appropriate safeguards on the interplanetary probes, incalculable damage to the scientific exploration of outer space will result. To prevent this, measures must be taken not only to "sterilize the terrestrial objects but to protect against impacts which could result in the dissemination of bacteria-size particles over large areas of the moon."[65] Possible preventative measures would include: (1) both prelaunch and inflight sterilization of the rocket exteriors; (2) provide for internal sterilization to avoid contamination from the breakup of the rocket or payload on impact; (3) limit areas of landing to localize any possibility of contamination; and (4) prohibit explosion of nuclear devices.[66] Another area of contamination, besides preventative measures, is compensative measures. It was stated by John A. Johnson that in projects such as the West Ford Project, when nuclear explosions occur in upper atmosphere and in outer space, causing contamination and pollution, that the responsible country compensate for any country that is harmed.[67]

The third hazard to mankind from space activities, potentially one of the greatest, is the experiments to alter weather patterns. Various proposals include orbiting satellites doing the primary work because of their unique position outside the earth's atmosphere. Such schemes include artificially induced rainmaking over limited areas, changing the course or intensity of large storms, increasing the amount of solar radiation in certain areas by the use of orbital reflector satellites, and major alterations of climate over wide regions of the globe. Of course, the major danger in this area is initiating climatic alterations that have irreversible effects. The possibility of causing, through tampering with the natural force in one place, undesirable, even catastrophic, weather alterations in another, compouds this danger: "To destroy a typhoon threatening

---

[64]Report by a panel on space research of the U.S. National Academy of Sciences. *New York Times* (April 27, 1965), 24.

[65]Haley, *Space Law and Government*, p. 281.

[66]*Ibid.*, p. 285.

[67]Cohen, *Law and Politics in Space*, pp. 37–51.

Kyushu, for example, might deprive a drought-ridden corner of India of needed rain or even parch Eastern Europe."[68]

The three hazards illustrate the range and magnitude of the problems and risks that may face mankind as a result of the future application of space and related technologies. In this area, as in the above problems, the Space Law Treaty has made a modest beginning in writing provisions dealing with these matters, but we have a long way to go. Recognizing that nation-states may experiment with activities potentially detrimental to other states, the treaty creates an obligation on the signatories to conduct their experiments in outer space so as to avoid its "harmful contamination and also adverse changes in the environment of the Earth resulting from the introduction of extraterrestrial matter"; and it provides in general terms for international consultation before any potentially harmful activity is undertaken.[69] Although the principle of international consultation is established, the Treaty neither prescribes the procedure for such consultation nor designates the agency to which states may turn for an authoritative evaluation of proposed experiments.

Concern with possible space resources

Although this is a smaller and more positive area of concern compared to military uses of space or contamination, it deserves a brief mention as to what states may expect if bases are put on celestial bodies. *Accessibility* and *location* are among the measures of the value of any resource. At the present time, there is no element on the periodic table that can be brought in economically from outer space; however, those natural resources that are reasonably accessible to men in space and that can be used by men in space can be valuable assets in the exploration of outer space. If moon bases are to be built, it obviously will be to the advantage of the builder to find satisfactory building material on the moon instead of transporting them from earth. It will also be a great advantage if sources of fuel are found in outer space. Thus the expensive transportation of these essential materials from earth would be eliminated. Past volcanic activity of planets suggest there might be sources of water and sulfur for building materials.

The Space Law Treaty provides in Article I that space exploration shall benefit all countries, and numerous provisions of the Treaty provide for the regulation and use of outer space. The basic claims made concerning the resources in outer space, then, provide that outer space shall benefit all

[68]"Forecast: A Weatherman in the Sky," *Reader's Digest,* LXXXIX (October 1966), 124.

[69]Fawcett, *International Law and the Uses of Outer Space,* pp. 88–89.

mankind and that the use of space will be open equally to all states, so that the claims made concerning resources are essentially conservation claims similar to claims made in the adjacent sea and shelf areas except that the primary claims are those beneficial to world community interests instead of to state interests. As can be seen from this, problems might arise if the resources on the moon or any celestial body are concentrated and if difficulties concerning joint usage of these concentrated resources arise.

Problems of liability, nationality, registration, and safety

The last problem discussed here is composed of a group of interrelated functional problems: liability, nationality, registration, and safety. Although these are functional in nature, in any environment the solutions to these problems are necessary and useful to peaceful and routine state interaction. There are two fundamental reasons for insisting that carriers such as spaceships and airplanes have a nationality or be registered: first, to assign responsibilities and, second, to afford protection. Claims concerning liability, registration, and safety are obviously interrelated, and since there is no real enforcement agency, assigning responsibility to nation-states is likely to be the most effective means of enforcing what are essentially the protective rules concerning liability and safety.

The General Assembly Resolution 1721 (XVI) calls upon "States launching objects into orbit or beyond to furnish information promptly to the . . . Secretary-General, for the registration of launchings."[70] The United States and the Soviet Union "have sent dozens of vehicles out to the unpaved, unrestricted highways of outer space, and . . . a system of lawless anarchy is developing."[71] The Space Law Treaty refers to the registration and responsibility of the registory nation-state, and also to the international responsibility of nation-states for national activities conducted in outer space.

Although no liability rules have been worked out, the United States submitted a proposal in 1962 on the liability for space vehicles and personnel for space accidents; liability for personal injury and loss of life or property caused by space vehicles was assigned to the launching nation-state, with proof of fault not required. No mention was made of injuries, damages, and losses by private exploiters, the assumption apparently being that *nation-states* will be internationally responsible. One view of liability for the damage that a fallen vehicle may cause was expressed by I. U. Levett: "the flight of a space vehicle is like that of a meteor, in that no

[70]Cohen, *Law and Politics in Space*, p. 134.
[71]Haley, *Space Law and Government*, p. 137.

human controls can be exerted upon it, assuming it's an unmanned craft. Since the vehicle is not subject to human control . . . the launching nation should be free from liability for re-entry damage."[72] Since the craft will be free from liability, apparently it will become the property of the state into which it falls.

Another question under liability deals with spacecraft that are lent from one nation-state to another. Although the Space Treaty states that the lender can be held responsible, the consensus seem to be on the splitting of the responsibility, with the larger share going to the state that is actually operating the spacecraft. As mentioned earlier, liability should be irrespective of fault; however, there are two factors that have to be considered in assessing fault. First, in determining the reparation due to the claimant, any failures by the claimant to show reasonable care should be considered; obviously, if an airplane sustains damages while flying on an announced launch site, the extent of liability is narrowed. Second, there is a distinction between injury, loss of life, or damage occurring on the ground or at sea, and injury, loss of life, or damage occurring in outer space. Persons in the first case cannot be presumed to have accepted the risks of outer space; persons and property in space, however, share in the risks of activities in space, and the principle of strict liability is therefore inapplicable to them. The final brief area of liability pertains to an accident in which more than one state has some measure of responsibility as a launching state, to a state that procures the launching, or to a state from whose territory or facility the object is launched or in which an international organization is involved.

For safety, there are very detailed rules and regulations concerning the construction, manning, and operation of both ships and aircraft, and safety is the main concern of astronauts too. Currently there is a concern for surface injuries that might result from spacecraft, but there will no doubt be an increasing concern for personnel safety, a point underscored by the tragedies suffered by both the United States and the Soviet Union in the loss of life of astronauts. Control over spacecraft is a primary concern in connection with surface damages; for example, the uses of destructive devices gives the launching nation-states a degree of control over the hazards associated with launching a spacecraft. Another type of control is associated with both safety and interference, the ability to recover or destroy spacecraft that have completed their missions. Too many crafts are floating in space today—six years ago there were over 1000 orbiting manmade objects and less than 300 of the objects, mostly satellites, are still transmitting a flood of data.[73]

---

[72]*Ibid.*, p. 265.
[73]"The Jam in Orbit," *Newsweek* (October 17, 1966), 73.

A concluding remark

Outer space is an exciting new frontier and offers many problems and challenges to the decision makers, leaders of international communities, scientists, and international lawyers. Although the United Nations and numerous private associations and organizations have dealt with outer space's legal and political problems, many of the kinds of problems that have traditionally been within the scope of interest of political scientists have not been dealt with at all. Questions of sovereignty, boundaries, resource allocation and use, access and passage, nationality, registration, liability, safety regulations, and military uses have either not been dealt with in great detail since the Declaration of Legal Principles Governing the Activities of States in the Exploration and Use of Outer Space in 1963; or have been superficially treated in the Space Law Treaty of 1966; or have been left for future discussion because its relevance to international space law has not yet been fully recognized. Other areas that can also be included in the present discussion are space medical jurisprudence; functions of intergovernmental organizations in space activities; nongovernmental organizations in space activities; metalaw (the law governing possible other worlds with intelligent life); space communications; rescue and return of astronauts; meteorological, observational, and navigational satellites; orbiting space stations; and crimes in space and on planets. All of the above areas are the new challenges in establishing and maintaining effective legal regime in space.

International lawmaking processes always have been essentially political processes; this has increasingly become clear to all concerned including the international lawyers who in the past have dealt with "static" law and have now begun to focus on the dynamics of law-in-action. Laws of outer space and an outer space legal regime are slowly developing, and the United Nations has played a major role. The Space Law Treaty is the current authoritative statement of the extent of agreements that exist among member nation-states on the applicability of selected legal principles to outer space. But the Space Law Treaty is obviously less than comprehensive, for several potential problems are either given cursory attention, or not dealt with at all.

Major research efforts are required if the data base for national decision making is to be available to those responsible for making such decisions, for example, where or whether to locate airspace-outer space boundaries, what reasonable restraints to impose on activities in outer space; what limits to set on the jurisdiction of the subjacent nation-state; how to provide for the peaceful joint usage of any resources that might be found in outer space; and how to set up effective international cooperation in such areas as liability agreement, demilitarization of space, and peaceful, beneficial future activities in outer space.

section IV
International Law and Patterns of Compliance and Noncompliance

chapter 11
shaping of national attitudes and practices with regard to international law in the nonwestern world

For a long time now Western scholarship has been comparing and contrasting the attitudes and behavior of Western states toward the observance of international law with those of the Communist states and the developing societies. Much of this comparison has been made on the degree of compliance of the laws of treaties. It is frequently implied in the literature that somehow the international legal norms in the West are taken more seriously and are observed more religiously than is true in the Communist or the Third World countries. Several scholars, however, have exaggerated this difference. According to them the Soviet Union, China, and other socialist as well as Third World countries were frequently breaking international law while the United States and other Western societies were almost always upholding it.

Specific causes of international observance and violations are discussed in Chapters 12 and 13. In this chapter we evaluate the attitudes and behavior of the following countries concerning international law in order to eliminate some of the misgivings of the past, and more importantly, to get a deeper understanding of the aspirations, expectations, and some of the fears that the people and policymakers of these states have toward international law.

In the remaining part of this chapter we shall analyze the attitudes and behavior of (1) The Soviet Union, (2) The People's Republic of China, and (3) the countries of the Third World.

Soviet Union and the international law

Most students of international law agree that historically it is difficult to find anything in the political socialization of Bolshevik revolutionaries who came to power in the Russia of 1917 that might have motivated them to uphold the existing norms of international law. On the contrary, it can be argued that theoretically a true Marxist will look on much of the international law of that time with a great deal of suspicion, certainly with some resentment. He would be inclined to dismiss it as an "establishment tool," an instrument of the capitalist ruling class that developed it for its own use. However, this is not the current position of the Soviet Union concerning international law, or the position of many other states that officially subscribe to the Marxist-Leninist philosophy. As a matter of history, even in the early years of the rapidly developing Soviet Republics, the new rulers of Russia were aware of the need to uphold certain norms of existing international law for *pragmatic reasons*. They clearly realized that they could not openly challenge Western internationl law, so they decided to use it when they found it to their own advantage, a *practice that continues up to the present time.* For instance, apparently without a great deal of ideological agony, they signed several treaties for trade and national security.[1] They used international law in other ways, for example, as a means of protection from foreign intrusion in what they considered their "domestic" affairs. They never failed to invoke it against the hostile acts of Western nations while criticizing it at the same time as an unacceptable tool of the West.

After the Second World War interest in international law, or more accurately, interest in a distinct Soviet view of international law developed quickly in the Soviet Union. Within a year after the war the Central Committee of the All-Union Communist Party, which reflected the official view, instructed all concerned that from now on increased attention must be paid to the study of international law.[2] Since then international law, as understood by the Soviet political hierarchy and Soviet scholarship, has continued to gain significance in the Soviet Union. The steady stream of publications on law that started in 1946 received a further boost after the death of Stalin, an event that resulted in several important changes in the Soviet attitude both in domestic and foreign affairs in 1957. This was, incidentally, also the year of the creation of the Soviet Association

---

[1]Consider the famous German-Soviet treaty of 1921, signed only three years after the Revolution. Interestingly enough it referred to the existing international law as a vehicle for improved relations between the two countries in certain areas. Quoted in Ministerstuo Inostrannykh Del SSR, *Dokumentry Vneshnei Politiki*, 3 (1959), 99. Please refer particularly to Articles 8, 10, and 13 of the Agreement.

[2]Kul tura i Zhizu (Nov. 20, 1946).

of International Law. This association subsequently joined the worldwide International Law Association. Now it also publishes the Soviet Yearbook of International Law which, interestingly enough, carries the English summaries of major articles published in it. The official textbook of international law that was published by the Soviet Academy of Sciences in 1957 has now been translated in several major languages in the world and widely distributed within the U.S.S.R. and other countries.[3] Recently the Soviet Union has also allowed the translation and publication of several Western works on international law in the Soviet Union. Today, it will be fair to say that the Soviet government takes an active interest in various international conferences convened to codify existing international law and to create new laws. Soviet participation in the Sixth Committee (Legal Committee) of the United Nations, for instance, has generally been recognized as casting a positive influence on the creation of new laws. Soviet position on the interpretation of law, as gathered from Soviet statements in various international conferences and disputes, particularly involving United Nations peacekeeping operations, is that of the strict constructionist.

Development of Soviet attitude toward international law

As suggested above, the Soviet Union's attitude toward international law developed soon after the 1917 Revolution. Marxist legal philosophers have never found the Western-developed international law an acceptable standard of international relations between the Socialist and Western states, certainly not among the Socialist states. However, this lack of acceptance has never meant that the Soviet Union would not use existing international law to serve its foreign policy objectives. To this day one finds this kind of pragmatism in Soviet attitudes toward international law, even though Soviet jurists and scholars continue to talk about their differences pertaining to law.[4] Perhaps an appropriate generalization regarding Soviet attitude toward law is as Professor Oliver J. Lissitzyn once aptly put it, "All doctrines, formulations, and applications of international laws are appraised [by the Soviets] in terms of their usefulness to the Communist cause."[5] An impressive amount of literature published in the Soviet Union supports Professor Lissitzyn's contention

---

[3]Academy of Sciences of the U.S.S.R., Institute of State and Law, *International Law* (Moscow: Foreign Languages Publishing House), 1961.

[4]See, for instance, the work of B. A. Ramundo, *The (Soviet) Socialist Theory of International Law*, (Washington: George Washington University, Institute for Sino-Soviet Studies) Series No. 1, January 1964.

[5]O. J. Lissitzyn, *International Law Today and Tomorrow* (New York: Oceana Publications, Inc.), 1965, p. 48.

concerning Soviet attitude toward international law. As early as 1924 leading Soviet scholars were arguing that during the period of transition of the Soviet Union toward a classless society, it could benefit from certain existing legal norms in its relations with the capitalist states.[6] A decade later Soviet legal scholarship was advising the Soviet decision makers in no uncertain terms that if they desired they could use the Western-oriented international law to the advantage of world socialism.[7] Still later, at the height of the Stalinist era, a prominent Soviet writer summed up the prevailing Soviet attitude toward international law as follows: "Those institutions in international law which can facilitate the execution of the stated tasks of the U.S.S.R. are recognized and adopted by the U.S.S.R., and those institutions which conflict in any manner with those purposes are rejected by the U.S.S.R."[8]

At least before 1964, the Soviet attitude toward international law can be viewed according to its emphasis on such words as "cooperation" and "struggle" in their definition of international law. The notion that international law can be used in the struggle between the states appears to be valid, because in the past and even more so today states do use this notion to enhance their own policy objectives.[9] However, the emphasis on the word "struggle" in the *Soviet* language of law has a somewhat different meaning. It is unmistakably consistent with their philosophy of history and class struggle. In this context an important definition of international law according to the Soviets was once expressed by A. Y. Vishinsky who stated that international law is "the sum total of the norms regulating relations between states in the process of their struggle and cooperation expressing the will of the ruling classes of these states and secured by coercion exercised by states individually and collectively."[10]

While the end of the Stalinist era brought many changes in the Soviet attitude on politics in general that resulted in changes of substance in their domestic and foreign policies, the above definition of international law that was expressed in 1948 survived. Thus, when one examines the Soviet literature on international law published in the late fifties, the only change that one notices in the definition is the additional reference to

[6]E. A. Korovin, *Mezhdunarodnoie Pravo Perekhodnogo Vremeine* (Moscow: Gosizdat), 1924, 2nd edition.

[7]E. B. Pashukanis, *Ocherki po Mezhdunarodnomu Pravu* (Moscow: Sovetskoie Zakonodatel'stvo), 1934.

[8]*Sovetskoie Gasudarstvo i Mezhdunarodnoie Provo*, by F. K. Kozhevnikov. An English translation of this work is to be found in J. N. Hazard, *Law and Social Change in the U.S.S.R.*, (Toronto: Carswell), 1953, p. 275.

[9]More will be said on this subject later in this chapter.

[10]See A. Y. Vishinski, "Mezhdunaradnoie Pravo i Mezhdunarodnaia Organizatsiia," *Sovetskoie Gasudarstvo i Pravo*, No. 1/1948, p. 22.

this new concept of "peaceful-coexistence," reflecting the new emphasis of the post-Stalin era.[11] A detailed discussion of this concept is forthcoming in next chapter. As the Soviet Union acquired a more prominent place in world affairs, further modifications of the Soviet definition of international law have appeared in the Soviet literature. For instance, G. I. Tunkin, the official legal advisor to the Soviet government and the head of the department that deals with international legal affairs in the Soviet Ministry of Foreign Affairs, came up with the notion that the most important source for the development of international law is the formal consensus among states. This is tantamount to implying that a state can unilaterally free itself from the obligation of upholding a particular international law by simply not giving or withdrawing its consent to that law. This comment also clearly deemphasizes the role of force that an international body so empowered, such as the United Nations, may bring to bear on a state to make sure that its laws are observed. Along with this, the Twenty-second Congress of the Communist Party also ruled that the Soviet Union is no longer governed by a class but by the citizenry at large.

Approaching the contemporary Soviet scene one notices that the recent Soviet textbooks on international law as well as the publications of the Soviet Institute of International Relations reveal some further changes in their definition of international law. For instance, overt references to concepts such as "struggle" and "cooperation" among nations have been formally dropped. The current definition is as follows:

> Contemporary international law has as its principal content the generally recognized principles and norms designed to regulate the most varied relations of sovereign wills between the subjects of international community on the basis and for the purpose of effectively securing international peace, and above all peaceful co-existence in some cases and socialist internationalism in others.
>
> The degree and forms of such securing are determined by the very character of the given international legal order. Under the conditions of peaceful coexistence, the element of coercion is greatly limited but not excluded. In the world system of socialism all legal principles and norms, being based on socialist internationalism and therefore having a fundamentally different content, are invariably observed, and their securing is subordinated on this content.[12]

---

[11]For details see, Academy of Sciences of the U.S.S.R., Institute of State and Law, *International Law*, p. 7.

[12]F. I. Kozhevnikov (ed.), *Mezhunarodnoie Pravo* (Moscow: Izdatel'stvo Instituta "Mezhdunarodyne Otnosheviia"), 1964, p. 32. Also quoted in O. J. Lissitzyn, *International Law Today and Tomorrow*, p. 50.

This apparently major development in the Soviet view of international law is the by-product of an increased need felt by the Soviet Union to use international law in its relations with other socialist states and more importantly with the new states of the Third World. The contemporary era, as the Soviets view it, remains one of struggle between the socialist and the capitalist political systems.[13] Despite selective cooperation with the West, it is the Soviet emphasis on antagonism that remains the focal point of the relations between the socialist and capitalist systems that considerably downgrades the role of existing legal norms in international affairs. On the other hand, portions of international law having considerable flexibility and emphasis on states' sovereign equality, for instance, have resulted in a wider appeal for countries of various political ideologies and systems. These portions have served the aims of Soviet foreign policy rather well. Here, the sometimes uncertain and confusing substance of law has provided the Soviet Union with ideological fireworks to use against the Western interests in the Third World countries. Some of the most frequently used norms of international law by the Soviet Union are, for instance, equality of states, territorial integrity, nonintervention, and sovereignty. They have not, however, made any particular effort to apply these principles in their relations with other socialist countries, especially those of Eastern Europe. Among the legal norms that have been developed more recently the Soviets have frequently invoked such principles as self determination to condemn colonialism and therefore to champion the cause of independence all over the world, except of course in Eastern Europe.

Whether old, new, and regardless of origin, all the legal principles available to the Soviet Union have been used either in defense of a position that it took or to condemn a position taken by the "other" side. In support of its foreign policy objectives these principles have been used to back up their slogans, to make their propaganda more effective, and to champion popular causes in Third World countries. For instance, the principle of self-determination has been further used to diminish the influence of colonial power in their former colonies and other capitalist states, particularly the United States, in their spheres of influence. Soon after the Bolshevik Revolution one of the first acts of the Soviet Union was to give up extraterritorial claims and privileges that Imperial Russia either had obtained or wanted from the Asian nations. To this day, over half a century later, Soviet leadership continues to denounce colonialism; in fact, it stresses that modern international law is anticolonial.

---

[13]*Ibid.*, pp. 30, 68–80.

Peaceful coexistence as interpreted by the Soviet Union

Legal implications of the Soviet Union's recent and perhaps most dynamic concept in their international relations, namely "peaceful coexistence," must also be assessed. The initial official view of the Soviet Communist Party is translated from the Soviet document by Professor J. F. Triska. It reads: —

> Peaceful coexistence implies renunciation of war as a means of settling international disputes, and their solution by negotiation, equality, mutual understanding and trust between countries; considerations for each other's interests; non-interference in internal affairs; recognition of the right of every people to solve all the problems of their country by themselves; strict respect for the sovereignty and territorial integrity of all countries; promotion of economic and cultural cooperation on the basis of complete equality and mutual benefit.[14]

The Soviets view international law as made up of two different principles, which Bernard Ramundo describes as "peaceful coexistence" and "socialist internationalism." The first principle regulates relations between the Socialist and non-Socialist states while the latter regulates relations among the Socialist states.[15] Socialist internationalism is considered to be a more developed form of international law than the law of peaceful coexistence, simply because it does not represent struggle or competition between different ideological systems. On the contrary, it supposedly represents a class partnership and unity of purpose among all the socialist countries of the world. However, the Soviets rationalize the seeming disparity between these two codes of international law by stating:

> The basic principles of contemporary international law are binding and states cannot establish in their bilateral or regional multilateral relationships norms which would conflict with basic principles. Nevertheless, states can create principles and norms binding upon a limited number of states, if these principles and norms do not conflict with the mentioned basic principles, especially if they go further than these principles of general international law in furthering friendly relations and securing the peace. Such are the international legal principles of socialist internationalism.[16]

[14]Translation of official U.S.S.R. documents by J. F. Triska (ed.), *Soviet Communism: Programs and Rules* (San Francisco: Chandler), 1962, pp. 65–68.

[15]Bernard Ramundo, *Peaceful Coexistence*, (Baltimore: The Johns Hopkins University Press), 1967, p. 20.

[16]V. I. Tunkin, *Problems of the Theory of International Law* (1962), p. 14. Cited by Ramundo, *Peaceful Coexistence*, p. 21.

The above definition of peaceful coexistence shows rather well the somewhat hazy image that the Soviets themselves have concerning their relationship with the capitalist countries. There is no spelling out of definite concrete principles; moreover, the door is left open for future principles to be included. *This "open-ended" definition has created some questions as to what is exactly meant by "peaceful coexistence."* Obviously, something more than the basic definition of the term is meant to be embraced. From the time man first settled into community life, there has been some form of peaceful coexistence—when war was not being waged. Therefore, we must attempt to arrive at a somewhat clearer understanding of what exactly is meant by this term.

It is generally agreed that the Soviet basis for peaceful coexistence originally was based on the Pancha Shila (the five principles in the Sino-Indian Agreement of 1954 concerning Tibet). They are (1) mutual respect for territorial integrity and sovereignty, (2) nonaggression, (3) noninterference in internal affairs, (4) equality and mutual benefit, and (5) peaceful coexistence.[17]

As can be observed, the principle of peaceful coexistence is listed as number five. Apparently this is the single general principle of a peaceful world order. Leon Lipson discusses the evolution in Soviet thinking in the following passage:

> In the Bandung Conference of 1955, the list (principles of peaceful coexistence) has swollen to ten. The first four principles of the Sino-Indian Pact survived in altered or lengthened form. Several new ones including (among others) respect for fundamental human rights and for the purposes and principles of the Charter of the United Nations, respect for the right of each nation to defend itself singly or collectively in conformity with the Charter of the United Nations, abstention from the use of arrangements of collective defense to serve the particular interests of any of the big powers, abstention by any country from exerting pressure on other countries, and respect for justice and international obligations. Peaceful coexistence was lifted from the list of enumerated principles to the caption of the list.[18]

Again in 1962, Tunkin listed four more principles to be added to the growing list. These were "peaceful settlements of disputes, self-determination of nations, disarmament, and prohibition of propaganda for war.[19] It

[17]Ivo Lapenna, "The Legal Aspects and Political Significance of the Soviet Concept of Coexistence," *International and Comparative Law Quarterly* (1963), 762–765.

[18]Leon Lipson, "Peaceful Coexistence," *The Soviet Impact on International Law* (Dobbs Ferry, N. Y.: Oceana Publications), 1965, p. 29.

[19]V. I. Tunkin, *Problems of the Theory of International Law* (1962), pp. 26–65. Cited by Ramundo, *Peaceful Coexistence*, p. 30.

seems that the Soviets add more "principles" every time they make a statement concerning peaceful coexistence.

Perhaps the most coherent (evolved) view of what the Soviets see as peaceful coexistence emerged in the 50th Conference of the International Law Association at Brussels, which the Soviet representatives attended. They categorically stated:

The Soviet Branch draft proclaims the following principles of peaceful coexistence: (1) the principles of peaceful coexistence is a fundamental principle of modern international law. No distinction in the social and state structure shall hinder the exercise and development of relations and cooperation between states, since every nation has the right to establish such a social system, and to choose such a form of government as it considers expedient and necessary for the purposes of ensuring the economic and cultural prosperity of its country.

(2) All states shall practice tolerance and live together in peace with one another as good neighbors, without recourse to the threat or use of force against the territorial integrity or political independence of any nation, and shall settle all their international disputes by peaceful means. All states shall, in accordance with the United Nations Charter, take individual or collective measures to prevent or suppress acts of aggression, and to maintain international peace and security, and shall prevent and suppress propaganda of a new world war, and acts constituting a threat to international peace and security, as well as the fomenting of enmity among nations. All states shall do their utmost to promote the prompt implementation of general and complete disarmament, which is the most effective means to secure international peace.

(3) All states shall develop and strengthen international cooperation in the economic, social and political fields, as well as in the field of science and culture, on the basis of free will, equality, and mutual benefit, without any discrimination for economic, political, ideological, or other reasons.

(4) Relations between all states shall be developed on the basis of respect for the sovereignty and territorial integrity of states, for the right of peoples and nations to self-determination. The right of peoples and nations to self-determination, i.e., the right to freely determine their political, economic, social, and cultural status, also includes inalienable sovereignity over their natural wealth and resources. Peoples may in no case be deprived of means of subsistence belonging to them by any title whatsoever claimed by any other state; colonialism in all its forms and manifestations must be done away with.

(5) No state has the right to interfere in the internal affairs of any other state. The recognition of the right of every people to settle all questions concerning its own country by itself is an immutable law of international relations.

(6) All states, regardless of size, and political and economic might,

are, to one and the same degree, equal participants in international intercourse. No state may be prevented from participating in the settlement of international problems affecting its interests. States shall be represented in international organizations with consideration for the fact of the existence at present of three large political groupings.

(7) All states shall fulfill in good faith their international obligations arising from treaties and other sources of international law.[20]

These seven principles put forth by the Soviet Union at Brussels are the closest thing to codification of the concept of peaceful coexistence yet advanced. From a somewhat nebulous birth in the five principles of 1954, the concept of peaceful coexistence has started to emerge into a more concrete form. The seven points of the Soviet declaration rest heavily on the concept of sovereignty. This is easily apparent if one looks closely at these principles. For example, the Soviets call for disputes to be settled by peaceful means, and the right of a state to settle all domestic questions by itself. The Soviet Union at least in these principles does not consider the possibility of third-party determination, such as the International Court of Justice. Also, in the sixth principle the implication is clear that all international organizations are to be based on the "Troika" principle. This may be carrying sovereignity too far.

The Western nations, meanwhile, have been calling for a program of peaceful cooperation in international affairs. This cooperation would be built less on the concept of sovereignty, and more on a basis of international unity, in order to govern the world through the application of international law. This idea is based on the premise that the nuclear stalemate and the breaking up of the bipolar world has created a situation where, even after considering the ideological and other differences, sovereign nations may work together to create an international order free from war and also free from vast economic inequalities and various forms of oppressions. This idea of peaceful cooperation, as pursued by the Western capitalist nations, is an attempt to introduce into the realm of international law the concept of functionalism in place of (or at least to be emphasized more than) the concept of sovereignty. By creating and using international organizations for the betterment of man (mainly by economic means) and by the use of third-party arbitration (such as the International Court of Justice) international law has the best opportunity of satisfying the needs of the world.

Needless to say, the concept of peaceful coexistence, as put forth by the Soviet Union, has a fundamentally different emphasis when compared with the Western concept of peaceful cooperation. For all practical

[20]Quoted in John Hazard, "Coexistence Codification Reconsidered," *American Journal of International Law* (January 1963), 92–93.

purposes the theme of the Soviet concept is to keep nations peacefully apart, generally through the notions of nonintervention and mutual respect. The theme of the Western concept is to bring the nations actively together in peace and cooperation for mutual benefits. In the Soviet thinking, whether or not it is currently exhibited in these foreign policy objectives, norms of the "true" international law cannot be fully realized until the so-called Marxist World Revolution has taken place, at which time the concept of socialist internationalism is supposed to come into universal usage, thus marking the beginning of a newer and more improved international cooperation than the present system of international law affords.

The Soviet concept of peaceful coexistence does not conflict with existing international law, since it motivates the Soviet Union to act within the framework of existing international laws of, for example, noninterference, respect for sovereignty, and peaceful solutions of international disputes. However, the problem surfaces when one considers the Soviet ideological commitment to world revolution and thus the establishment of socialist internationalism and the "true" international law. It is difficult to see how this commitment can be fulfilled without violent disregard of the present system of international law and of the norms of their own philosophy of peaceful coexistence. One scholar sums up Soviet peaceful coexistence as follows:

> Soviet policy of peaceful coexistence is extended to achieve simultaneously several purposes which can be concisely summed up in these three points: (1) popularity because of the strong appeal of the idea of peace; (2) attaining political maxima in foreign policy without being involved in a world war; and (3) further internal development of the Soviet Union for which a long period of peace is an essential condition.[21]

One thing is quite clear: over the years the Soviet Union has used this principle of coexistence to enhance its own interests, some of which clearly do not necessarily lead to *peaceful coexistence* among states. It has further used this principle to protest both real and imagined discrimination levied against itself and other socialist states in international trade and other programs. However, Western scholarship appears to have concluded that the real reason behind this concept is the Soviet desire to influence the development of international law not only to suit their own political philosophy but to cast Western nations and their view of international law in a negative role in the eyes of the rest of the world.

[21]Ivo Lapenna, "The Legal Aspects and Political Significance of the Soviet Concept of Coexistence," p. 774.

Certainly, the thinking of some leading Soviet scholars has supported this conclusion.[22]

Nonetheless, peaceful coexistence as put forth by the Soviet Union after 1955 is a dynamic attempt to promote Soviet foreign policy objectives. It is an attempt to seek peacefully these goals by using and molding the present system of international law. It remains to be seen, if their notion of peaceful coexistence will, if at all, be the guiding force toward a superior order as conceived under the concept of socialist internationalism. This latter concept has suffered from two recent trends: (1) The Sino-Soviet rift and (2) the trend toward nationalism prevalent in many of the Third World countries today. The continuing Sino-Soviet rift and the emerging differences among other socialist countries have cast serious doubts on the future emergence of socialist internationalism. The two great socialist powers in the world today are at each other's throat. The second factor that casts doubt on the goal of world revolution is nationalism. New, emerging nations are not overanxious to unite under a world socialist movement even if there was one. Although many of these countries espouse some kind of socialist ideology, mostly for symbolic reasons because of economic injustices in their social systems, they try to be extremely pragmatic in their international dealings, and frequently join one "camp" or the other for reasons of economic and military assistance instead of for ideological identification. At the same time, mindful that they have recently achieved their independence, they exhibit reluctance in joining either camp totally and permanently.

Present attitude toward international law

Currently, the attitude of the Soviet Union attaches great importance to international law.[23] Soviet scholars and jurists affirm the presence of a

---

[22]Consider, for instance, Tunkin's comments: "peaceful coexistence serves as a basis for the peaceful competition between socialism and capitalism on an international scale and constitutes a specific form of class struggle between them." He goes on to suggest that "in upholding the international law principles of peaceful coexistence and using them to support their foreign policy, the socialist states are striving for the constant strengthening of the position of the world socialist system in its competition with capitalism." Tunkin, "XXII Seza KPSS. . . .", *Problems of the Theory of International Law*, p. 12.

[23]Consider, for instance, the statement that former Soviet Premier Khrushchev made first before his trip to the United States for his Camp David conference with President Eisenhower: "We are deeply conscious that without the observance of the norms of international law, without the fulfillment of the undertakings assumed in relations between states, there can be no trust, there can be no peaceful coexistence." Quoted in O. J. Lissitzyn, *International Law Today and Tomorrow*; p. 55.

general international law that they consider binding on all nations. Over the years they have also referred to the so-called "socialist" legal norms that operate only between the "socialist" states. These norms are regarded as supplementary to the existing international law rather than a substitute. Nonetheless, in reality these norms have tended to limit the significance and applicability of general international law. Several of these norms are embodied primarily in treaties that the Soviets have signed with other socialist countries.[24] Despite the acceptance of general international law by the Soviets, its scope apparently falls somewhat short of the generally recognized scope by the Western countries. The problem is that the Soviets have consistently argued that they have *the right to accept the existing norms selectively*. They have advanced what they label as the "New Doctrine of Agreement," meaning that general international law is mutually binding on the states of "two existing systems" (socialist and capitalist) as long as it is composed of legal norms that are agreed upon by both sides. Agreement may be expressed in several ways, for example, through custom and treaties.[25] The Soviet literature indicates that Soviet jurists, while not necessarily rejecting custom as a source of international law, have always insisted on treaties as the most important source of law. It is quite clear that the Soviet Union is interested in rejecting parts of customary international law that they find unacceptable and that were mostly developed before the 1917 Revolution. For similar reasons, the Soviets also reject the proposition, generally accepted in the Western world, that certain legal norms practiced in domestic systems of law may be applied by analogy in international law as "general principles of law." This attitude of the Soviet Union toward international law, it must be admitted, does not destroy the claims of universality by international law, but it does narrow its scope somewhat. It is difficult to find a clear statement in the Soviet literature indicating specifically what legal principles are not acceptable to them. Soviet scholarship tends to refrain from a clear exposition, thus leaving the Soviet government a great deal of freedom of action not enjoyed by the Western governments.

In the past and even now the Soviet Union simply prefers to deny that certain traditional legal norms practiced in the Western world ever achieved such general acceptance that they could be included in general international law. In other instances, it prefers to reinterpret the traditional norms rather than reject them outright. Consider the Soviet atti-

[24]See J. N. Hazard, "Soviet Socialism as a Public Order System," *Proceedings of the American Society of International Law* (1959), 30.

[25]In support of this statement see V. I. Tunkin, "Remarks on the Judicial Nature of Customary Norms of International Law," *California Law Review*, 49 (3) (August 1961), 419.

tude toward current international law development. The Soviet Union is, of course, not alone in emphasizing the creation of new principles of international law. However, it does insist that a new general international law is being developed under its own direction. It refers even to "general and complete disarmament" as being part of this development. Depending on the state and to varying degrees, Western nations, partly out of their own narrow views and partly because of the fear of Socialist nations, have been reluctant to accept as legally significant such concepts as "anti-colonialism," "peaceful coexistence," "self-determination," and "general and complete disarmament."

The limited attitude of the Soviet Union toward international law in general has been quite noticeable in several areas, particularly in the field of adjudication and arbitration as a means of resolving political conflict. The Soviet Union has generally dismissed the role of the International Court of Justice as ineffective. The same attitude is exhibited toward international arbitration. They have generally opposed attempts to broaden the compulsory jurisdictional powers of the world court by relying mainly on the "optional clause" of Article 36 of the Court's Statute. However, even the United States is not very eager to submit to the jurisdiction of the Court. In fact the Connally Amendment makes it very difficult for the United States to do so. Similarly, many other Western powers have shied away from making the Court a truly effective body. On the other hand, the Soviets have not completely rejected the concept of international adjudication. They have frequently signed multilateral treaties such as the Constitution of the International Labor Organization, which provides for the submission of disputes connected with the organization to the International Court of Justice. In the spring of 1962, the Soviet Union strongly supported a Cuban proposal in the Security Council that the International Court of Justice be approached for an advisory opinion on the legality of the exclusion of the Cuban government from the Organization of American States (OAS). The United States and its allies defeated this proposal.[26] Despite this flexibility, the broader picture still conveys the strong impression that much of the Soviet weight has been exerted against the improvement and extension of the international judicial system. This is one of the several manifestations of the strong influ-

---

[26]There are historically other examples of Soviet flexibility in this area, for example, in 1947 it gave in (by its abstention) to a recommendation by the U.N. Security Council that Albania and Britain should take their dispute arising out of incidents in the Corfu Channel to the International Court of Justice. Even previously on several occasions the Soviet Union, without any success, suggested that its disputes with the British be decided by arbitration or by third-party decision, etc. For details see J. Degras (ed.), *Soviet Documents on Foreign Policy* (London: Oxford University Press), 1951, Vol. 1.

ence of Marxist-Leninist ideology on the Soviet attitude toward the role of international law in world politics.[27] The Soviet attitude here seems to be that as long as the world is still hostile toward Communism and there are conflicting ideologies, it will always be difficult to find impartial judges. It considers itself and other Communist nations still a minority in the world and therefore finds itself unable to entrust its interests to the decision of all those international legal bodies where the role of unanimity does not apply. Indeed, if one considers the impact of ideological differences in an already divided world on a broader area than strict international law, if one examines the unshakable belief of the socialist societies that eventually their camp will be victorious in the present struggle, one can easily understand why international relations, to which international law is only a part, cannot be carried out on genuine faith, trust and cooperation among the Communist and non-Communist nations. This belief is of course self-complimentary for the Soviets. Apart from the obvious question as to how realistic it is, given the current trends of international relations, it has succeeded in creating mistrust and hostility in the non-Communist countries, thereby confirming the Communist image of implacable antagonism. In such circumstances it becomes difficult to extend the role of law in the world. Moreover, in an international system of constant, rapid, and *dire* change, it becomes even more difficult to emphasize the long-term advantages of stability and faith on which any law must rest.

Although in the Western societies self-interest remains the fundamental motive for the observance of international law, it is often reinforced by a sense of moral obligation, since its observance is regarded as a symbol of rectitude. For the Communist nations, however, the moral obligation to observe the law is not regarded as a legitimate concern. Despite the changing Soviet-American relations and a growing pragmatism in Soviet foreign policy in the post-Korean War era, there is still no great body of evidence that the Soviet leaders have given up the Marxist-Leninist concept that emphasizes that the supreme criterion of Communist morality remains in the struggle for Communism.[28] Another factor, which is important in the shaping of Soviet attitudes toward international law and is also related to the Communist ideology, is the nature of the

[27]For a detailed study of influences of ideology on the Soviet Foreign Policy see Z. K. Brzezinski, *Ideology and Power in the Soviet Politics* (New York: Praeger), 1962, pp. 102–113; A Dallise, *The Soviet Union at the United Nations* (New York: Praeger), 1962, pp. 3–12, 182, 189.

[28]See A. Shishkin, *Osnovy Kommunisticheskoi Morali* (Moscow: Gosudorstvennaie Izdatel'stvo Politicheskoi Literatury), 1955, p. 955. This book has also been translated in English by Robert C. Tucker, *Philosophy and Myth in Karl Marx* (Cambridge: University Press), 1961, pp. 13–14.

Soviet system of public order. Two features of this system are of concern here: the direct state control of virtually all economic activity in the Soviet Union, and the totalitarian nature of Soviet control over its population. The development of international law in the Western societies has partly resulted from the ever-increasing requirements of private persons and groups indulging in economic activities beyond their national borders. These frequently find expression in the form of pressures applied upon the government through various lobbies and special interest groups, and have frequently served to strengthen the role of international law in their governmental policies. This has also meant acquiring the services of professional men such as international lawyers who have an occupational interest in the maintenance and broadeing of the domain of international law. Their influence strengthens the "law habits" of the decision makers, which reinforces other variables responsible for the sustained observance of international law. Moreover, in relatively democratic societies public opinion can sometimes be mobilized to criticize the government if too many violations of international law occur.

In the Soviet Union and other Communist states, private economic interests are limited or nonexistent and, thus, have had little impact on the development and observance of international law. Lawyers have little influence on governmental policies and hardly ever rise to the top levels of the party or administrative hierarchy. The Soviet Union has simply not yet developed what is generally regarded in the Western societies as "law habit." The absence of private enterprises and the special interest groups traditionally associated with it has also affected the Soviet attitude on several other important aspects of international law. Consider, for instance, the Soviet official attitude concerning private property. The Soviet economy, which is essentially state owned and operated, was developed on the fundamental principle of wholesale expropriation of private property, including foreign property. The Soviet Union continues to believe that a state has the legal right to confiscate private property without compensation whether it belongs to its own citizens or foreign nationals.[29] This is obviously in complete contrast to the view and interest of the Western countries, who have a well-developed free enterprise system and respect for private property.

Soviet practices and international law

Most textbooks on international law generally do not deal significantly with Soviet practice in relation to international law. Whenever an occasional reference is made, it tends to be negative. Thus the prevailing

---

[29]For example, consider the remarks of the Soviet delegate to the United Nations as representative of their attitude. U.N. Doc. A/C 2/SR 834 (November 15, 1962), 16.

impression among the public as well as most students of international law in the West is that the Soviet Union cannot be trusted to uphold international law, that it violates laws at will, and that it has no hesitation whatsoever in violating international treaties if that suits its national interest. The conclusion generally arrived at is that it is inherent in the nature of totalitarian states to be lawless in the international arena. By contrast Western nations are assumed to be law-abiding. Frequently, depending on the temperament of the author, a stark contrast is drawn between the so-called "law-abiding" nations of the West and the "lawlessness" of the Soviet Union.

In Western countries governmental lawyers have worked full time in developing exhaustive lists of alleged violations of various treaties by the Soviet Union.[30] However, the reality concerning Soviet practices is far more complex than generally understood when Soviet behavior is contrasted with Western behavior. It should be clearly understood that all nations violate international law under given circumstances, some more frequently than others. Also there is nothing new about mutual charges of violations of treaties and other legal norms among states.[31] Given the very nature of legal norms it is very difficult to determine and compare with any accuracy the frequency with which various states in the past have violated international law. At this time many legal norms, regardless of their source lend themselves to multiple interpretation, depending on the ingenuity and imagination of the individual doing the interpretation. Because of the controversial nature of these norms, the major problem arises when one attempts to determine a nation's violations of international law and compares them to the violations committed by other nations. Consider, for example, the researcher's problem when he finds that the legal norms associated with a particular treaty are still in the middle of a controversy. This is true of the doctrine of *rebus sic stantibus*. Even the most respected judges, including justices of the International Court of Justice, frequently disagree with each other in their interpretation of the laws. The problem is further complicated when one attempts to assess the relative significance of various treaty violations.[32]

---

[30]In the United States, for instance, see a Department of State document entitled: "Soviet Violations of Treaties and Agreements," U.S. *Department of State Bulletin*, 23, (574) (July 3, 1950). See also U.S. Senate Committee on the Judiciary, *Soviet Political Agreements and Results*, 84th Congress, 2nd Session, Senate Do. 125 (1956). *Congressional Record*, Vol. 109, Part 13, p. 17827 (Sept. 24, 1963) can also be referred.

[31]Richard A. Falk, "The Adequacy of Contemporary Theories of International Law: Gaps in the Legal Thinking," *Virginia Law Review*, 50 (2) (March 1964), 250.

[32]A frequent question also, for instance, is: Can a breach of a relatively minor provision of a treaty containing many provisions be given the same weight as the outright and well-publicized repudiation of a major political treaty. Also, reputable

Yet, at the same time, stretching legal norms does result in the breaking of law, and here even a very cautious and impartial observer is most likely to subscribe to the view that the Soviet Union is not above treaty violations whenever it feels the treaty is against its important national interests. Moreover, the same is true of international law in general, particularly in important political matters. The impression that one gets from the Soviet practices is that the principles most frequently proclaimed by the Soviets are precisely the ones most frequently violated by them; principles such as sovereignty, territorial integrity, nonaggression, nonintervention, and self-determination, in relations with other states such as the Baltic Republics, Poland, Hungary, Czechoslovakia, and Finland.

The Soviet Union has frequently pledged in its many treaties and agreements signed with other nations that it will not support subversive activities in their territories, yet these pledges have been quite unreliable.[33] Soviet twisting and manipulation of international legal norms to facilitate implementation of Soviet policy and to justify it to the world has been rather frequent. It tends to be so obvious that it has created a great deal of cynicism in the West and an impression that the Soviets lack good faith.

However, it must be reemphasized that concerning the routine observance of international law the Soviet record is good. Despite some minor violations, which incidentally one can find in the West also, diplomatic immunities have been generally observed, most agreements kept, and procedural laws upheld. Western bloc and Soviet-led Eastern bloc's ships sail the seas in mutual trust and respect of each others rights, so that freedom of the seas is preserved and maintained. The Soviet claim of a 12-mile zone of territorial waters is certainly not unique today. It has not in any way prevented the further development of a legal order at the sea. As indicated earlier, the Soviet Union has generally lived up to its international commitments made under various treaties. Their record is, of course, good, even better in fact, on commitments concerning technical, economic, and other functional matters. The Soviet record of law observance in many areas of international concern need not surprise anyone. It simply, once again, reminds us of the important and necessary role international law plays in many aspects of international life, even among the antagonistic states. Obviously relations among states simply cannot be maintained without a *modus operendi* of mutually accepted and observed norms. A lack of observance here would certainly result, for example, in a

---

scholars have refrained from passing definitive judgment on the frequency of treaty violation by the Soviet Union. See J. L. Triska and R. M. Slusser, *The Theory, Law & Policy of Soviet Treaties* (Stanford: Stanford University Press), 1969, pp. 395–395.
[33]*Ibid.*, pp. 394–395.

breakdown in communications and a neglect of mutually desired goals, an alternative not acceptable to anyone.

If nothing else, considerations of reciprocity alone have frequently forced the Soviet Union to bring its practices closer to those of the Western world.[34] At a behavioral level, the Soviet Union does not usually persist indefinitely in maintaining an uncompromising position toward international law. This is clearly shown by changing government behavior toward the consequences of reservations to multilateral treaties. Triska and Slusser point out, for instance that in the General Assembly debates that took place in the early fifties and during the same time in the proceedings before the International Court of Justice with regard to reservations to the Genocide Convention, the Soviet Union clearly argued that any country could become a signatory to a general multilateral treaty with any reservation it desired, regardless of the consent of other signatories. This position later became so difficult to support that during the late fifties the Soviet Union modified its behavior by introducing a rather important qualification; that is, other signatories objecting to such a reservation are also free not to consider themselves bound by the treaty with respect to the state with the initial reservation.

People's Republic of China and the international law

Almost a quarter of a century has passed since the "agrarian reformers" led by Mao Tse-tung began sweeping away the old culture of China, a nation with a history of nearly 4,000 years. For 20 years the Bamboo Curtain has been drawn around the People's Republic of China. One-

---

[34]Good examples are the changes made in the Soviet protocol system in 1956 concerning diplomatic immunities. Before 1956, under an earlier regulation, enacted in 1927, full immunities were extended only to foreign personnel with at least the rank of a diplomatic officer and denied to other subordinate administrative personnel. Several other countries such as France and Switzerland made similar distinctions. However, in the United States, England, and many other countries, administrative and other service personnel with certain exceptions enjoy diplomatic immunities. To correct this imbalance, in 1955 the British government passed a new act giving it powers to withdraw certain immunities from other nations' diplomatic personnel who had denied these immunities to British personnel. This power was then used to restrict the immunities of Soviet personnel in London. These personnel had subordinate administrative status. Several months thereafter the Soviets came up with a decree providing diplomatic immunities to "technical and service" personnel of other nations' diplomatic missions in Moscow on the basis of reciprocity. As a result, of course, the British restored the immunities of Soviet personnel in London.

fourth of the world's population, more than seven hundred million people, has been sealed off by their leadership. Now ping-pong players have reopened the lines of communication, the Chinese have taken seats in the United Nations, and an American President has visited mainland China. It is a paradox of our times that the new China remains as remote and mysterious to many of us in the West as the old China was to the Romans, who knew of the Chinese only as "the silk people." Thus, at least in the United States, the shock of recent political developments has been great. A United States president who as a senator gained fame as an arch-enemy of Communism, visited Peking; the overwhelming vote in the United Nations to oust the Nationalist Chinese government of Taiwan and seat the mainland Chinese as an influential world power after 20 years of almost self-imposed isolation. But, can anyone deny that with the largest population in the world, estimated at more than seven hundred million—roughly one-fourth of mankind—and with the third greatest land area, by sheer size alone China must inevitably play a leading role.

Despite the emergence of the People's Republic of China as a nuclear power, and its already growing influence in world affairs, very little thus far has been written on China's attitude toward international law.[35] Systematic attempts have yet to be made to probe the pathology of Chinese contemporary behavior concerning international law observation. We know very little thus far about China's present and future motivations or lack of them to play the role of a law-abiding country. The significance of Chinese legal studies on American campuses at the present cannot be overstated. Lack of scholarship concerning China and international law unfortunately has allowed the students to form opinions on this subject based on values instead of knowledge and on journalistic reports instead of a dispassionate enquiry. The result has been obvious. A generally negative and suspicious view of China's activities in the international arena is carried over in the field of law and, the conclusion is usually drawn that China could not possibly have any respect for international law. One frequently hears oversimplified statements such as "since Chinese have fought the United Nations peacekeeping forces in Korea and mistreated the American prisoners of war, they cannot be trusted to

[35]However, one does find occasional articles on the subject in American political science and international law journals. Examples of good articles are: Hungdah Chui, "Communist China's Attitudes Toward International Law," *American Journal of International Law*, 60 (2) (April 1966), 245–267; Carl Q. Christal, "Communist China and International Law—Strategy and Tactics," *The Western Political Quarterly*, XXI (3) (September 1968), 456–467. Both of these articles are referred to in the next few pages. Students are also encouraged to examine the works of several Chinese Communist scholars on the subject that are frequently translated in English by the United States Joint Publication Research Service.

uphold international law." Another frequent argument that has been advanced is that "since China is a socialist country that has borrowed much of its institutions and practices from the Soviet Union, it cannot possibly have a view of international law that is independent of the Soviet Union." Similar statements continue to be made. China's own frequent statements—often made on political grounds—suggesting that much of traditional international law, even the Western world's recent attempt to make individuals and international organizations subjects of international law, are nothing more than a bourgeois scheme designed to continue the exploitation of the working classes of the world, have not helped matters any.[36] These statements and the process of accusations and counteraccusations have unfortunately succeeded in preempting any meaningful and sustained debate on Chinese attitudes, current practices, and motivations concerning international law violations and observances. It is not suggested that these statements are totally inaccurate, but they are starkly inadequate and therefore misleading. This brief exposition is a small step in the direction of gaining some fundamental knowledge of China's views on international law and setting the record straight concerning China's actual behavior in some instances with regard to law.

Development of the Chinese attitude toward international law

Undoubtedly, the Chinese have always recognized the existence of international law. Recently, they have embodied some of its principles in several international treaties of mutual friendship that they have signed with countries such as Afghanistan and Hungary.[37] They have frequently used international law whenever they felt it was to their advantage and have ignored it when it appeared to them as detrimental to their national interest.[38] They teach international law at their institutions of higher

[36]Consider, for instance, the comments of Ying T'ao: "In the Western Capitalist world, suppression of the weak by the strong and eating of small fish by big fish are not only tacitly condoned by bourgeois international law but also are cloaked with a mantle of 'legality,' " in an article entitled "Recognize the True Face of Bourgeois International Law from a Few Basic Concepts," *Studies in International Problems*, 1 (1960), 42. Also cited by H. Chui, "Communist China's Attitude Toward International Law," p. 250.

[37]The Sino-Afghanistan Treaty of Friendship and Non-Aggression was signed on August 26, 1960. Interestingly enough, the treaty cites the United Nations Charter in its preamble as follows: ". . . conclude the present treaty in accordance with the fundamental principles of the United Nations Charter. . . ."*Peking Review*, 3 (51, 18) (1960). Quotation cited by H. Chui, "Communist China's Attitude Toward International Law," p. 246. The Sino-Hungarian Treaty of Friendship and Cooperation, signed on May 6, 1956, in Article I also refers to international law.

[38]A good example of Chinese use of international law in order to make a point for their position is the harsh statement made by the Chinese Embassy in Jakartha on

learning and write about it. However, an acknowledgment of the existence of international law, its teaching and even its invocation to serve specific foreign policy goals does not necessarily imply acceptance to the Western view of international law or even that of the Soviet Union. A strong case can be made that major differences exist between the Chinese and Western views, and at least some significant differences have now appeared between the Chinese and Russian views of law as well.

In general, in most Western societies law is frequently considered an objective body of rules that have the understanding and uncoerced support of the people. These rules are generally regarded as the outcome of a successful political process in which the people have had some say. Once the rules have been established in a statutory form, their application, at least ideally, is divorced from political considerations. In the People's Republic such a view of law simply does not exist. In fact in the late 1950s, during the "Rectification Campaign," this Western view of law was ruthlessly criticized by Chinese scholars.[39] On the other hand, in the Soviet Union for instance, law is viewed primarily as an instrument of state policies. Law is subservient to the dictates of the state. It is accepted as a body of rules established by the state specifically to promote the Marxist social order. It seems difficult to ignore that the state's powers are also further enhanced and consolidated in this setting.

Although the Chinese accept several principles of international law proclaimed by the Soviet Union and applied by Soviet jurists, they have also engaged in frequent criticism of the Soviet views that they feel are becoming increasingly antirevolutionary. They blame the revisionist attitude of the Soviet Union concerning international law on the Soviet desire to support the status quo in international politics that benefits the Russians and the Americans because of their privileged positions as superpowers. The following remarks made by Wu Te-Feng a rather well-known Chinese law professor, highlights Chinese sentiments:

Imperialism is the basic source of war, and American imperialism, moreover, is the most ferocious and ambitious aggressor ever to exist in the history of mankind, and it is the most flagrant violater of the principles of modern international law. Naturally, democratic legal workers in vari-

---

the forcible house arrest of the Chinese Counsul by the Indonesian security forces on May 13, 1960. The statement in part reads: "[The] forcible house arrest of the Chinese Counsul Chiang Yen, the crude encroachment upon the functions and rights, the personal safety and freedom of the Counsul . . . have violated the universally acknowledged international norms. . . ." *Peking Review* 3, (20), (1960), 34–35, quoted by H. Chui, *Ibid.*, p. 246.

[39]Several articles appeared on this subject in the *Fa Shues* (Science of International Law) (5 and 6) (1957) in China.

ous countries should engage in the thorough exposure of, and determined struggle against it. However, modern revisionists (meaning the Soviet Union) make great efforts to propagandize the carrying out of "peaceful coexistence" with imperialism without being subject to any principles, disseminating the view that contemporary international law is the "law of peaceful coexistence," and to propagandize the carrying out of "full cooperation" with American imperialism.[40]

Before Chinese present attitudes, their practices and motivations concerning international law are examined, it will be fruitful to examine briefly the major characteristics of their classical internal legal system. Much of it is now history, but it has left some marks on Chinese thinking. In an interesting article Jerome A. Cohen identifies four significant characteristics of this system. First, it was obviously a very old system, taking the Chinese society almost 2000 years to develop it, expand it, and bring it to maturity. Second, despite the length of the tradition, Cohen argues, the influence of law on the interpersonal relations of a man in the street remained relatively mild. There were several reasons that minimized the role of government and law in the everyday life of an average citizen. Among them were certainly the vastness of the country itself and the poorly developed, often nonexistent channels of communication between the elite and masses; the inability of the political system to institute effective internal and external controls; and the prevailing value system and the heritage of Confucianism. The people recognized the prevalent standards and rules of law, but apparently several factors worked to minimize their desire to become involved in legal proceedings. One factor was their strong tradition that emphasized the virtues of informal, friendly persuasion instead of the mandatory decisions that courts made as a third party in disputes. Another was a high value placed on privacy, coupled with the perennial fear of loss of face in the community. Cohen points out, "It was considered almost disreputable even for an innocent party to go to court to get help. These attitudes still appear to persist in large measure in China."[41] Third, during an approximate period of 125 years of the dynastic rule that spread over parts of the eighteenth and nineteenth centuries this traditional legal system became thoroughly cor-

---

[40]Professor Wu is the president of the China Political Science and Law Association. This quotation, provided by H. Chui, "Communist China's Attitude Toward International Law," p. 245, comes from a report delivered by the President on October 8, 1964 to the general meeting of the Association. It was reported in *Cheng-Fa Yen-Chia* (Studies in Political Science and Law), No. 4, p. 28.

[41]J. A. Cohen, "The Chinese Legal System," *Chicago Today*, 3 (Spring 1966), 13. See also some of the relevant literature: "The People's Republic of China and International Law—Observations," *Proceedings of the American Society of International Law*, 61 (1967), 108.

rupted because of favoritism and long delays in handling the cases and also because of newly acquired elements of harshness that are readily available in a regimented society. It finally crumbled. Fourth, viewed from the Western perspective, the Chinese traditional system had some grave deficiencies. For instance, it never adequately provided a client with the right to a lawyer, even for purposes of defense, to say nothing of advocacy, or even simply to ascertain the crucial facts in a case and cite the applicable legal doctrines. Chinese tradition, again emphasizing the need to preserve "face" under all circumstances, enabled the courts to use mediational or adbitrational techniques in resolving disputes far more freely and more often than practiced in the West.[42]

Some of the marks left by the traditional legal system that still persist in Chinese thinking today are an attitude of aloofness from the law perpetuated by a sense of its irrelevance in everyday life and, at the same time, a fear that officials who invoke and implement law are corruptible. For example, to submit to law is to submit to the mercy of officials without an appropriate "adversary" system. The Chinese view of the role of international law, at least in part, continues to be influenced by this sort of thinking.

With the eventual acceptance of Marxist-Leninist-Maoist political ideology a new set of values was introduced in the Chinese legal system and, as the "cultural revolution" picked up momentum, almost all classical and Confucian values were set aside, if not totally destroyed. Today the People's Republic is an ardent supporter of a socialist philosophy in its political, economic, and social activities. Its internal structure with certain exceptions is essentially totalitarian. Acceptance of Soviet prolitarian institutional innovations had also meant almost full acceptance of Soviet political and legal doctrines. However, with the continuing ideological and political conflict between the Soviet Union and China, the two countries are moving in opposite directions from their earlier somewhat limited commonality of attitudes concerning international law. Chui, among several other scholars, points out that "law in Communist China is considered to be an instrument of the state, undergoing successive adaptations to make it conform to Communist-party dictated policies."[43] In

---

[42]Cohen points out that whenever a litigant found himself involved in a court proceedings he was "expected to rely completely on the tender mercies of officialdom," *Ibid.*, pp. 10–11. For a similar commentary see also F. Michael, "The Role of Law in Traditional, Nationalist and Communist China," *China Quarterly* (January-March 1962), 126–127.

[43]H. Chui, "Communist China's Attitude Toward International Law," p. 245. In support of his position the author directs attention to an article, recently published in China, entitled: "Some Questions on the People's Democratic Legal System in Our Country." The article states: "Since the policy of the party is the soul of the legal

much of the Communist world the party of course remains the most powerful force. In China there is a uniqueness to the party's foreign policy, which may well be in part responsible for China's own typical view of international law. Most importantly, since the emergence of the People's Republic, the party's foreign policy has been consistently directed to eradicate China's past humiliations incurred during its rather brief history of subservience to the Western powers and to become the new strong center of the emerging prolitarian world. History tells us that traditionally the Chinese have been lovers of culture, propounders of great ethical systems, and bound by an elaborate etiquette designed to smooth human relationships (which puzzled and seemed hypocritical to Westerners). Yet the Chinese were capable of outbursts of anarchy and cruelty. Although brilliant inventors in the past, the Chinese never developed science because they did not wish to master nature but to live in harmony with it. Very proud of their long history, self-sufficient as an agricultural people, static and satisfied, and convinced of their great society, they simply wished to be left alone. This was China on the brink of invasion by an alien culture armed with technology. Unlike previous invasicns from "barbarians" this one was to be by sea. Its impact on the Flowery Kingdom, the Central Nation, and the Celestial Empire could not have been more profound had it come from another planet.

Two factors combined to humble proud China—her refusal to treat Western nations as sovereign equals and opium. China's attempts to eliminate the growing trade in the one product the Chinese were eager to buy brought her into armed conflict with the British in 1839. The Anglo-Chinese war, the so-called "Opium War," quickly revealed the superiority of Western military technology and the astonishing impotence of the Manchu government. Under the porvisions of the Treaty of Nanking in 1842, four ports besides Canton were opened for the West to trade with China, extraterritoriality—the jurisdiction of foreign powers over their own nationals—was recognized, and a "most-favored-nation" clause, requiring that any concession granted to one nation was automatically granted to all, was imposed. China attempted to ignore the treaty, and in 1856 Britain and France used this as a pretext to launch another war. A series of treaties after this war in 1858 opened still more ports, levied more indemnities, brought to Europeans their long-sought diplomatic recognition, the protection for missionaries who followed the soldiers, and the right to travel freely in China. Still China was not reconciled to the political realities of her times. In 1860, after the Europeans sacked Peking and burned the

---

system, legal work is merely the implementation and execution of party policy . . . the new law of our country is a changing law, adopted to the perpetual revolution." *Cheng-Fa Yen-Chiu* (Studies in Political Science and Law) (2) (1959), p. 3.

Summer Palace, China agreed to a new convention widening the provisions of all the others she had been brought by the scruff of the neck to sign. In 1858, Russia had wrested Manchuria from the Chinese totaling 185,000 square miles. Two years later, for using his "influence" with the allies, the czar received an additional 133,000 square miles, including the port of Vladivostok. In the mid-nineteenth century, not only the Western powers but chronic floods and successive famines and a phenomenon known as the Taiking Rebellion ravaged China. It took Manchu rulers almost a decade and a half to put it down and, when it was all over, it had claimed 20 million lives.

Of all the humiliations the Celestial Empire suffered in the nineteenth century, the worst was defeat by the "dwarfs from beyond the Eastern Sea." In 1894, newly industralized Japan launched a major war. In a relatively short period of time Japan showed herself as the most brutal of all the invaders to enter China. This, of course, set off a new scramble for trade concessions and "spheres of influence." Fearful of commercial consequences if China were carved up into colonies, the United States in 1900 enunciated the principle of the "open door." Although essentially an extension of the most-favored-nation clause that guaranteed equal rights of exploitation to all powers, it had the effect of preserving China as a territorial and political entity. For this China was grateful. By this time, it was quite clear to many Chinese that their country was doomed unless it rapidly modernized, and so the process of modernization started in the middle of many political upheavals, including the Communist takeover, and it continues today.

The net effect of China's past history of humiliations on the present Chinese regime has been to overcome its own sense of inadequacy and to hide a lack of self-confidence in international relations. This has frequently meant talking tough, picking fights, providing foreign aid to friendly countries, and encouraging Communist revolutions. Some of this international activity has gotten them into trouble in some countries, particularly in Africa where they tried to encourage counterrevolutions in the 1960s.

The question that needs to be posed here is does the Chinese government, as in the case of the Soviet Union, regard international law as a convenient tool of a state's foreign policy to be used whenever desirable, or is there more to its attitude? An answer to this question will hopefully clarify the differences not only between the Chinese and Western views of international law but also between the Chinese and Russian views.

A response to this question should be sought at several levels. (1) At the *level of attitude* that China has toward international law. This can be determined from several things, for example, official statements of public policy that may have some relevance to law, espousal of ideological preferences concerning law, and national expressions of expectations and hopes concerning the future role of international law in world affairs. (2) At the *behavioral level*, that is, an analysis of actual practices of the People's Republic as viewed from the perspective of international law. What is the Chinese record toward international law? (3) At the *level of national motivations*, particularly the motivations of national decision makers concerning law observance or violation in the future.

Present attitude and ideological position

There is sufficient evidence to suggest that at least verbally the Chinese have respect for international law. A determined probing of what the Chinese have been saying for some time about Western and Soviet attitudes toward international law reveals this. There appears to be three important positions China has adopted at the attitudinal level.[44] First, along with the Soviet Union, the Chinese have recently decided to assign overwhelming significance to the concept of peaceful coexistence, although their interpretation of the concept is somewhat different than the Russians'. Nonetheless, it is a concept generally consistent with the principle of contemporary international law. Second, following the initial lead of the Soviet Union, but later traveling an independent path more suitable to their own circumstances, the Chinese have attempted to develop some unique theories of international law. These are based on their own preferred understanding of socialist ideology. In general, they have argued that there are several systems of international law, for example, Socialist, Western and, what appears to them a mixture of these two, one that is followed by the Soviet Union. Relying quite heavily on their understanding of socialism and their own brand of "peaceful coexistence," they have been able to generate some formidable challenges to the popular view that there is a general or universal international law. In this challenge they have been able to muster frequent support from some Third World countries. Third, while recognizing multiple systems of international law, they have however never attempted to hide their hopes and sometimes faltering confidence that their own view of international law will eventually be accepted universally and thus eliminate the necessity of multiple legal systems. Chinese scholars as indicated earlier have never hesitated to criticize Western international law as an imperialistic device designed for the exploitation of the working classes of the world. The Soviet view of international law is regarded as purely revisionist, designed to appease the West—a betrayal of Marxism-Leninism.

[44]These three positions have also been recognized by C. Q. Christal, "Communist China and International Law—Strategy & Tactics," *The Western Political Quarterly,* *XXI* (3) (September 1968), 458.

The Chinese are apparently convinced that the present ideological struggle between socialism and capitalism will conclude in their favor, at least in the sense that many of the Third World countries, out of economic necessity and temperament, will end up accepting a socialist philosophy. Therefore, they feel they have a great deal of support to gain by extending this struggle to the field of international law. They say they have now formulated a "Chinese" socialist view of international law which, of course, is the logical outcome of their own newly acquired ideological independence from the Soviet Union. This view is strongly influenced by their own concept of "peaceful coexistence" that can be found in the broad theoretical discussions and official policy pronouncements, for example.

A more sustained examination of China's present attitude toward existing international law reveals some inconsistencies that can be attributed to two important factors that have not been given sufficient attention in the past literature. (1) The significance of the present China's period of transition from a relatively poor, weak, and internationally ineffective nation to a strong, well-developed, and powerful nation in world affairs. (2) China's own persecution complex, a sense of being deprived, that it acquired during the period of humiliation by the Western powers. There have been times, since the establishment of the People's Republic, when the Chinese were not sure of themselves and felt that they could live with the present general international law, provided the Western powers clearly renounce their earlier outmoded definition of law that suggested international law regulates the relations of only the "civilized" nations. The Chinese feel that a truly universal international law should govern the relations of all nations, civilized or uncivilized. Besides, they argue, in the light of history the "older" nations' expressed right to be called "civilized" is suspect. Apparently, no formal renunciation that could satisfy the Chinese has ever been attempted by the West. Apart from semantics and historical judgments, the Chinese are evidently afraid that if the current definition of international law is not challenged, it may be used at some future time to deny the People's Republic, along with other countries of the Third World equal protection under the law. Knowing the impact on our thinking of nineteenth century evolutionary social theory—the notions of the "white man's burden," the eloquence of Kipling's thought, and passions of Teddy Roosevelt—and realizing that most nation states still possess strong propensities to make invidious distinctions, one can sympathize with China's concern.

The Chinese, for the time being at least, regardless of their claims of multiple systems of international law, would like to continue to use the existing international norms, both contemporary and classical, to their benefit; for example, they would still like to invoke them in support of their own foreign policy objectives and against those who disregard these norms to the detriment of Chinese interests.

On the question of multiple sources of international law, the Chinese feel the most important source remains the international treaties of consensus. Although they have respected custom as a source of international law in procedural and noncontroversial areas, they have generally rejected this source in more substantive areas, particularly in contemporary political disputes. However, since the requirements for the establishment of international law through custom are multiple, complex, and demand valid precedents, the Chinese have shied away from passing a definite negative judgment on this source.

On other traditional sources of international law China's attitude has also not been very clear and consistent. At times it has criticized famous judicial decisions and ridiculed the writings of renowned law professors, yet on other occasions it has praised the decisions of international tribunals, including the International Court of Justice. Recently it has cheered various resolutions of the General Assembly of the United Nations as having implications for contemporary international law, including the one that admitted its delegate as the rightful representative of China to the United Nations. Part of the thrust of contemporary international law has been to consider individual human beings as direct subjects of international law, both to afford them the protection of the law and to require from them their responsibilities and obligations under the law. Some considerations in law are also given to international organizations as bodies having jurisdictions. Both of these developments have tended to undermine the traditional concept of state sovereignty, the state's right to be unpredictable, and the state's claim of being the most important and perhaps the only subject of international law. The Chinese have a negative attitude toward these developments. Their view, consistent with their philosophy of the role of the state, is that nation-states are the only proper subject of international law. Most socialist countries have the same position, at least until the state "withers away" according to Marxist philosophy. Certainly the Soviets still subscribe to this view.[45]

At the attitudinal level, one can conclude that the Chinese position concerning international law is in a period of transition. This is the result of their rapidly changing status in world affairs. At best their thinking is

---

[45]The Soviet position can be understood from the writings of scholars such as Y. A. Korobin among others. For instance, he argues: "International law can be defined as the aggregate of rules governing relations between states in the process of their conflict and cooperation, designed to safeguard their peaceful coexistence expressing the will of the ruling classes of these states and defended in case of need by coercion applied by states, individually or collectively." In F. Y. Kozhernikou (ed.), *International Law* (1957), 7.

inconsistent. For instance, some Chinese scholars and statesmen have recently argued that international law is universal; at the same time they have asserted the existence of their own special view of law that does not coincide with the views of much of the rest of the world. Concerning the universality of law, their attitude is pragmatic. It is conditioned by their desires to use international law in the service of their foreign policy and by their fears that an all-too vehement rejection of law may result in the denial of its ability to protect them. Assertion of the existence of their own "socialist" view of international law is an expression of their ambitions and hopes that someday international political circumstances will make possible its acceptance by other nations, particularly the countries of the "Third World." This view is based upon their own somewhat unique understanding of Marxist-Leninist-Maoist philosophy, prolitarian internationalism and, most importantly, their own principles of peaceful coexistence.

Chinese practices and international law

For fairly routine and procedural international law China's record of law observance is good and certainly no worse than any other country, including Western countries. The presence of mutual interests among states coupled with an ever-increasing requirement of interdependence in world affairs has obliged China like all other states to conform readily to every basic principle of international law and to come to expect and demand compliance from other states. However, at the same time, what Christal has called "another level of discourse" (meaning where crucial national interests are involved) the Chinese record is inconsistent. They have clearly disregarded some of the most cherished principles of international law, while observing others to the letter of the law.

At the procedural level, even though most laws tend to be traditional in the sense of having deep roots in Western heritage, the Chinese have been one of the most law-abiding nations. For instance, they have exchanged diplomatic representatives with many countries, insisting on proper protocol, and protesting bitterly whenever they felt their representatives were denied rights under international law. Now that the Chinese have formally signed the United Nations Charter and have established diplomatic relations with many Western countries, they will be probably drawn even more closely into the community of nations. As a result, their record of observance to procedural law is likely to improve further.

International treaties developed and ratified through international consensus remain the most important source of international law for the Chinese. Since their emergence to power in October 1949, the Chinese have signed several treaties of mutual friendship and respect. In fact, as early as October 1, 1949, Chinese leaders declared: "Our government is the sole legal government representing the entire people of the Chinese People's Rpublic. Any foreign government which is willing to observe the principles of equality, mutual benefit and mutual respect for territorial sovereignty, is welcome to enter into diplomatic relations with our government."[46] The People's regime, with what appears to be some minor reservations, has also upheld many important conventions of this century; for example, the 1925 Geneva Protocol Prohibiting the Use in War of asphyxiating, poisonous, or other gases, and bacteriological methods of warfare; the 1949 four most important Geneva Conventions pertaining to the use of warfare in general; the 1930 Load Line Convention in London; and another London convention concerning prevention of collisions at sea, signed 1948.[47] In their bilateral treaties they have consistently attempted to incorporate their five principles of peaceful coexistence. It seems clear these principles are important to them, and they would like to see them accepted by most if not all nations as one of the enlightened sources of international law. Their incorporation in treaties is a step in that direction.

On the other hand, Chinese reliability in upholding some of their legal commitments has been widely questioned. There are several Chinese violations that have not escaped criticism. For instance, in 1953 the Chinese clearly disregarded their commitment undertaken during the Korean Armistice and refused to implement their promise made in 1955 that they will facilitate the return of American citizens held in Chinese prisons. On the question of treaty obligations and Chinese practices, Christal has this to say "Apparently the Chinese do not subscribe so much to the sanctity of treaties although this would seem to be desirable in order not to lose face in the world community—but rather are inclined to examine the power relationships of the signatories in determining if the agreements should be kept."[48] Writing on the question of respect for treaties in the socialist countries in general, another scholar put it this way: "all treaties and agreements concluded between capitalist and socialist countries are reached only after a fierce struggle between the two parties resulting in a compromise which reflects not common values but the realities of the power balance between them."[49] Chui's comment is tantamount to saying that the only thread that unites the capitalist and socialist states on a

[46]Cited by J. Chester Cheng, "The Chinese Communist View of International Law," mimeo, private circulation (January 28, 1961), 2. Cheng was cited by Christal, "Communist China and International Law—Strategy and Tactics," p. 463.

[47]For a complete list of treaties signed by the People's Republic and ratification of other existing legal documents consult the Chinese official publication entitled: International Treaty Series, 10 volumes.

[48]C. Q. Christol, "Communist China and International Law—Strategy and Tactics," p. 463.

[49]H. Chui, "Communist China's Attitude Toward International Law," p. 253.

common set of contemporary treaty international laws is not the commonality of attitudes and beliefs; instead, a community of pragmatic interests forged together on specific issues. Presumably, if this community of interests withers away the temptation to violate relevant laws would become irresistible. Indeed, this is a shaky basis for future law development. There are several old treaties that the Chinese have now dismissed as simply "unequal treaties," presumably consented to under unfavorable circumstances and therefore not worthy of support. Yet other treaties signed during the same periods of Chinese history are honored. The real difference seems to be the continued interest of China in a particular treaty instead of the circumstances of its original acceptance—an observation that supports Chui's fears. However, the expedient position of the Chinese concerning the binding nature of some treaties signed essentially before the emergence of the People's Republic is no different than the position taken by many developing countries today concerning their legal obligations undertaken during colonial days.[50] Also there are no known significant violations of treaties that the People's Republic has signed in recent years. Even during the early days of the People's Republic, in September 1949, it was stated by the Communist regime: "Concerning the various treaties and agreements signed between the nationalist and foreign governments the Central People's Government of China's People's Republic shall examine them, and shall, according to the contents and separately, grant their recognition, abrogation, revision of renewal."[51]

There are specific areas of international law where Chinese practices can be judged. For instance, on the question of laws of territorial asylum, the Chinese have a good record: on several occasions they have provided political asylum to individuals of various nationalities. Article 99 of their national constitution adopted in September 1954 clearly states the responsibility of the state to provide political asylum to individuals. It reads: "The Chinese People's Republic shall confer the right of residence upon any alien who received persecution on account of his support of a righteous cause, his participation in a peace movement or his pursuance in a scientific work." On the question of "territorial waters," it should be recalled that during the important 1958 Geneva conference on the Laws of the Sea when delegates were unable to agree on a common limit and there were demands for the recognition of from three miles to 250 miles, the

---

[50]Many developing countries have illegally nationalized foreign investments and properties in their territories after independence. Consider, for instance, the nationalization of the Suez Canal by the late President Nasser of Egypt and the nationalization of the oil industry in Iran by the late Premier Mussaddag in the midfifties.

[51]Quoted by J. C. Cheng, as reproduced by C. Q. Christal, "Communist China and International Law—Strategy and Tactics," p. 464.

People's Republic argued that the classical notion that the "sea is the heritage of all mankind" must be respected. It unilaterally declared on September 4, 1958: "The breadth of the territorial sea of the Chinese People's Government is 12 nautical miles. This regulation is applied to all territories of the Chinese People's Republic, including the Chinese mainland and its coastal islands by the high seas, such as Taiwan, and its surrounding islets, the Pescadore Islands, the Tung-Shau Islands, the Hsi-Sha Islands, the Chung-sha and Nan-sha Islands, and the other islands belonging to China."[52] Still another area is the protection of rights of Chinese nationals living abroad. In this area China has observed international legal norms. She has signed several treaties consistent with international law and invoking the law when she felt the rights of these individuals were violated.[53]

In balance, the People's Republic's record of law observance is perhaps no better and no worse than many other states. China, not too unlike other countries that are active in the international politics, has extensively used diplomatic techniques and procedures that carry the weight of law, in order to brand others as violators of legal norms. On the other hand, China has occasionally used international law to justify otherwise generally unpopular courses of action. Thus, she made a legal case in the justification of her recourse to the use of force in her border dispute with India in 1962. The Chinese argued convincingly that the 1914 Simla Convention that laid down the McMahan line dividing the Chinese and Indian territories was never ratified by China and, therefore, no legally valid boundary between the two countries existed. Interestingly enough in this claim they were supported by the Nationalist Chinese government in Formosa. In those situations where Chinese national interests were at stake they have transgressed international law as if it never existed.

---

[52] J. C. Cheng, "The Chinese Communist View of International Law," p. 4. Note in this context that on several occasions Chinese authorities have declared that the Chinese people will never allow aggression by United States Armed Forces on Chinese territories, meaning various islands. At times this has meant to "fight to the finish" American attempts to neutralize the Taiwan Straits by force. At other times this is supposed to mean to "continue" to hold to the task of liberating the islands of Taiwan and the Pescadores, etc.

[53] Consider, for instance, China's treaty of April 22, 1955 with Indonesia. This treaty permitted persons of Chinese extraction to decide, within two years of the date of ratification, whether they wished to apply for Chinese citizenship or become Indonesians. The treaty further specified that after the expiration of the two-year period an individual will be considered the citizen of either his father's or mother's country of citizenship. This provision can be cited as an example of China's preference for the international role of *jus sanguinis* in determining the nationality of people. Incidentally, as a result of this treaty most of the Chinese in Indonesia either retained Chinese nationality or became nationals of mainland China.

National motivation for the future

There are several domestic and international variables that continue to influence the Chinese attitude toward international relations in general. There seems little doubt that constant internal convulsions, power struggles, and a general lack of self-confidence in their ability to pursue a successful foreign policy have contributed to a sense of insecurity. The Soviet military threat coupled with the past policy of the United States' efforts to keep China isolated from the rest of the world has resulted in suspicion. These developments have important bearing on Chinese motivations to uphold or violate international law in the future. Clearly there is not much motivation to abide by the principles of customary international law that the Chinese consider discriminatory. Any nation with a history of Western exploitation, however brief it may be, can hardly be expected to exhibit a high degree of motivation to uphold a philosophy, legal or otherwise, that was regarded as one of the basic evils of the past. Chinese hostility toward some of the customary norms and a lack of motivation concerning classical, nonprocedural law observance is starkly reflected in the writings of contemporary Chinese scholars and jurists. For instance, Professor Kung-meng, writing in the early 1960s, warned the world in no uncertain terms that the Western—particularly American—efforts to include individuals and international organizations as appropriate subjects of international law is a poorly disguised unholy trick to provide a "legal basis for imperialist intervention in the internal affairs of other countries or to facilitate the establishment of the world hegemony of the United States."[54] Another mainland scholar of high reputation, Chiang Yang, has interpreted the writings on international law in the United States, particularly writings on such well-known topics as "world government through world law," as another effort to initiate a new imperialistic order. To this scholar, the concept of "universalism" and its objective: ". . . is to destroy state sovereignty so as to facilitate the establishment of a world government under the domination of American imperialism."[55] It can be concluded from these writings of Chinese scholars that, first, they believe in what they write and, second, what they write is accepted uncritically by many of the people who read it; this provides psychological support to the writers that they are not alone in their assessment of American intentions concerning the role of law in future world affairs. Thus, the process continues in the form of thought control, typical of totalitarian societies. The outcome is a great deal of

[54]Kung-meng, "A Criticism of the Theories of Bourgeois International Law and the Recognition of States," KEWTYC 2 (1960), 46–49. Quotation is provided by Chui, pp. 250–51.

[55]Chiang Yang, "The Reactionary Thought of 'Universalism' in American Jurisprudence," People's Daily (December 17, 1963).

suspicion of any new concepts, regardless of how earnestly and hopefully inspired, such as "a world without war," "world government through world law," and "international law of an organized world." These ideas are simply regarded as capitalist schemes.

It is difficult to know with great accuracy the psychological configuration of an average, educated citizen on the mainland—that is someone who has a position on foreign affairs—concerning his views on observing international law. However, from the continued writings of Chinese scholars and from the history of Chinese foreign policy, one could tentatively conclude that for the time being at least the Chinese government and its men of scholarship do not possess a high motivation for respect and support of international law.

There are some bright spots on the picture, however. Many doors to China's entry in world affairs as an important influence are now opening. There has been some warming up of Chinese-American relations. China is now a member of the United Nations. All of these factors will undoubtedly work toward alleviating some of the Chinese fears of Western or American "designs" to use law to harm China and other socialist states. They will also provide a sense of security and a certain measure of confidence in their foreign policy decision making. Although it is too early to tell, it appears that the "Chou En-lai faction," which is known for a relatively conciliatory attitude toward Western powers, seems to have won an important struggle against the militants. These developments are positive and will enhance the Chinese motivation to respect international law.

It is clear from the preceeding remarks that, first, significant differences can be found between the view toward international law that the People's Republic of China holds and the one that the Soviet Union holds. The Chinese tend to be more dogmatic in applying Marxist-Leninist philosophy to international law. They are far less responsive to the recent developments of international law both in and outside of the Western community. Many Chinese scholars continue to argue that the basis for a separate Chinese philosophy of international law has been formulated, and it is only a matter of time when it will be recognized by others. This is contrary to the Soviet view that insists that the socialist system of international law is still in the process of development. Concerning the role of "peaceful coexistence" in this area, the Chinese view is different than the Soviet view. The differences can be best explained by their different foreign policy objectives. The Soviet Union, being a "have nation" and having attained a very privileged position in the contemporary international arena, exhibits many signs of being status-quo oriented—a status quo that can be preserved only by drawing closer to West. This the Soviets are doing. Its effect on international law has been a Soviet Union more responsive to the Western philosophy of law in order to develop essentially a common system of law with binding qualities with the West that it needs and the West wants. The Chinese, on the other hand, like the Soviets of a previous time, are still engaging in intense denunciation of "American imperialism." To be sure, like the Russians, they will not continue it. Second, China's past experiences are a strong factor in the present Chinese attitude toward international law (particularly the notion that international law is a law among "civilized" nations) and is certainly a reaction to humiliations of the past. Third, the formulation of the Chinese socialist philosophy of international law, despite claims to the contrary, remains in a very primitive state of development. Much of the incentive for its development has come from anti-American or anti-Western attitudes, instead of from genuine desire to develop a new theory of law based on original research. Thus, roughly half of Chinese scholarly effort in this field is spent on "exposing" Western intentions for world domination and the other half of the energy is taken up by simply compiling or editing old documents.

Third World countries and international law

Few men of knowledge would disagree that as we move closer to the last quarter of the twentieth century we find the world caught up in a very rapid process of deep-rooted changes, the full impact of which is yet to be felt in international politics. In this context one is usually accustomed to think of technological miracles, the nuclear age, and the space age. Certainly these are spectacular developments, but not only these have occurred in the last quarter century. There are other events, perhaps not quite as dramatic, but just as instrumental in affecting the history of our times. The emergence of such industrial giants as Japan and Germany, the rise of nationalism, a rapidly developing Soviet-American detente, the dwindling of colonial empires, the awakening of China, and the birth of many new states, claiming full sovereignty under international law are only a few examples of these "other" changes. Still fewer men would disagree that fundamental changes in one aspect of human endeavor eventually affect other areas too. International law has not stood alone in a splendid isolation from these developments. On its body of rules it not only reflects the scars inflicted by the dynamics of the twentieth century, but it is also caught up in the state of transition imposed on it by the ever-changing circumstances of this dynamic world. Its present state of health and future well-being has become a growing concern of the people who care. One of the questions that has been prompted by this concern is: How closely will the established rules of international law be adhered to by the developing nations of the world? It is, of course, not a new question in the history of jurisprudence. The history of international relations indicates that the number of independent states under international law has always changed. States in the past have ceased to exist, thus losing their legal personality, while new states have emerged as new subjects of international law. However, there is something unique about the relationship of these new states —occurring in such a short period of time in such great numbers—to international law. This uniqueness has raised some problems directly related to the substance of international law. These problems are both qualitative and quantitative in nature. We must first understand the relationship of international law and the development of attitudes of these countries in a historical perspective.

Development of the Third World countries' attitudes toward international law

Despite the fact that several non-Western nations such as Japan and Turkey were admitted into the Western international legal system fairly early, the world's legal institutions retained their Western character, juristic logic, and legal diplomatic processes. Even the appearance of the Soviet Union on the scene did not alter this fact significantly. In fact, prior to World War II Russia was generally not regarded as a significant exception to the rule. But with the influx of so many new states, having not only a tradition of their own but an attitude of suspicion and hostility toward the colonial West, the challenges to international law have been fundamental and unique. Initially it was assumed that all states that were not Communist or under Communist domination were therefore free to join the "Western community" and accept "Western International law."[56] Yet within a very few years many developing countries exhibited their strong anticolonial sentiment in international politics. International law was not immune to this criticism. It could not have been. After all, before the most important principle of self-determination became a political reality and forced its way into the realm of international law, the rules of international law had not only failed to condemn the open and clandestine forms of colonial domination but had clearly supported it. The so-called traditional international law in fact evolved from the many practices of the colonial powers and thus was always available at the service of their interests. It effectively recognized right of colonization, just as it authorized the right to initiate wars. From a historical perspective, since international law evolved among the so-called "civilized" nations, it was

[56]The United States, for instance, apparently working under this assumption, frequently criticized "neutral" or "nonaligned" states during the Eisenhower Administration.

designed primarily to protect their interests and therefore, the rules of international law were simply not applicable to the subjected people, who were already reduced to colonial status by this very community. Some non-Western scholarship makes a strong point that at least portions of modern international law, at the height of the colonial era, were consciously developed to help the colonial powers to maintain their rights and privileges over the colonies and other territories.[57] This makes it somewhat easier to understand why so many newly independent countries were opposed from the beginning to certain rules of international law that were responsible for sanctioning colonial oppression, rules in the formulation of which they had obviously taken no part. An Indian scholar puts it rather frankly:

". . . . present international law [referring to the traditional international law] was developed during the last four centuries and specially consolidated and systematized during the last part of the nineteenth and beginning of the present century. Asian and African countries had very little to do with it because they were conquered and colonized and made to serve merely the interests of the metropolitan states and their masters."[58]

The author goes on to suggest that "it is not therefore surprising to find that states that were victims of such an unequal position, and were passive objects of these rules of international law, often give the impression that they rebel against their application."[59] Rather eloquently, the author points out, "these states which have recently achieved independence have generally begun their existence in the position of a debtor under the traditional legal order. It means their authority or territory or both are burdened with debts, concessions, commercial engagements of various kinds or other obligations continuing from earlier colonial regimes."[60] The writings of many non-Western scholars also clearly indicate that according

---

[57] In this context see an interesting article published in East Germany, written by Dieter Schrader, "Das Verhaltnis der Asiatischen, Afrikanischen und Ihren Recht," *Loccumer Protokoll*, 12/1966, particularly, page 60.

[58] R. P. Anand, "Role of the 'New' Asian Countries in the Present International Order," *The American Journal of International Law*, 56, (1962), pp. 384–385.

[59] *Ibid.*, p. 387. Similar position is also taken by many scholars across the world. See, for instance, the works of Castaneda, "The Underdeveloped Nations and the Development of International Law," *International Organizations*, 15 (1961), p. 40; S. Prakash Sinha, "Perspective of the Newly Independent States on the Binding Quality of International Law," *International and Comparative Law Quarterly 1*, (1965) 130; Padilla Nervo, *Yearbook of the International Law Commission 1*, (1957) 165; and the comments of Judge Redhabinod Pal, *Ibid.*, p. 168.

[60] *Ibid.*, p. 400.

to the attitude of many underdeveloped countries, the contemporary "science" of international law has erred in failing to draw unequivocal conclusions from the statutory recognition of the right of self-determination because it has failed to emphasize the necessity of revising the rules of international law to harmonize them with new developments in the international system, wherein sovereignty has been accorded to some of the weakest nations. The critics further argue that if the substance of international law were to express the true universal interests of all states of the world, the position of the developing countries in the realm of international law would pose no serious problems for law, nor would the theoretical considerations in the field of law present themselves in a situation radically different from the past. Interestingly enough at the present, much of the change in international law and the development of new rules of law are not decisively determined by the opposition of former colonial nations to the revision of traditional international norms but, more importantly, by the developing countries' deep interest and active participation in the international lawmaking process. Thus, as early as 1957, it was admitted by the International Law Commission that ". . . the countries on which international law had formally been imposed in order to facilitate their exploitation were now called upon to partake in its formulation."[61]

A mild plea for caution

Before systematically examining the attitudes, practices and motivations of these new states toward international law, it must be remembered that because of social, cultural, economic, political, and geographical differences these nations have different national interests. This diversity of interests obliges them to view international law somewhat narrowly from their own vantage point. It is not reasonable to expect that just because they all are "developing countries," they will necessarily have similar views on all points of international laws. This diversity therefore should not be ignored in any attempt to understand the psychological configuration of their attitudes toward international law.[62] Broad generalizations are possible if an examination of their international politics discerns several common inclinations and attitudes toward international law, because of their similar experiences under colonial rules and a not too uncommon struggle for independence. Some of the Western scholarship has obviously erred in

[61]*Yearbook of the International Law Commission* I, (1957), 165.

[62]In support of this statement see O. J. Lissitzyn, "International Law in a Divided World," *International Conciliation*, (542) (March 1967), 37; R. P. Anand, "Role of the 'New' Asian-African States in the Present International Legal Order," p. 395.

concluding too hastily that because of their different religious, cultural, social, ethical, and legal background, these new states are unable to understand and appreciate the principles of international law that are the product of interaction among Christian states of Western Europe. This conclusion has been advanced as one of the major reasons for the stubborn attitude of noncooperation with the present system of international law.[63] Some scholars have suggested that the attitudes and foreign policy of these states are determined by their religious and cultural traditions and that this explains their lack of interest in settling their disputes judicially.[64] This conclusion, drawn by such distinguished writers as Quincy Wright, is not based on any empirical research on the comparative principles of philosophy, religion, and culture among different systems and their impact on international law observance behavior of the systems; rather it is based on what appears to him a "reasonable" explanation. In the absence of any exhaustive research, the obvious problem with such a conclusion is, as Professor Lissitzyn has aptly pointed out, that it not only tends to "overlook the diversity of approaches to law that exist both in the Western as well as non-Western part of the world" but ignores the obvious point that even "the Western cultural tradition is no guarantee of adherence to the 'rule of law' in either domestic or international affairs."[65] Is it not equally "reasonable" to suggest that perhaps the most violent disregard of traditional principles of international law and the concomitant principles of Christian morality in this century has been shown by Western nations during the past two world wars? The problem with these kinds of "reasonable" statements is that they are misleading, to say the least, because they tend to ignore that regardless of cultural and religious differences all nations observe international law in a multitude of international relationships out of habit, necessity, and for their own advantages. More will be said on this in other contexts.

Most of these developing states are at odds with some of the norms of international law, particularly customary international law. This situation brings them into conflict with the Western states in specific instances

[63]Thus, only 15 years ago Professor Gerbandy, a former Prime Minister from the Netherlands, seriously questioned if a Moslem or a Hindu could understand the meaning of aggression, and concluded that this could only be possible for states with a Christian background. Quoted in B. V. A. Rolling, *International Law in An Expanded World* (Amsterdam: Djambatan), 1960, pp. 21–22.

[64]See the writings of Quincy Wright: "The Strengthening of International Law," *Recueil des Cours* 98 (1959-III), 74–80; "The Influence of New Nations of Asia and Africa Upon International Law," *Foreign Affairs Reports*, (7) (1958), 38; "Asian Experience in International Law" *International Studies*, (1) (1959–1960), 84–86; see also, F. S. C. Northrop, *Taming of the Nations* (New York), 1952 Chapter 7; *Philosophical Anthropology and Practical Politics* (1960), pp. 160–168.

[65]Lissitzyn, *International Law Today and Tomorrow*, pp. 59–60.

(e.g., nationalization of Western property in their countries) but this is more appropriately the result of prevailing national interests rather than cultural and religious differences. After all, even in the West the law-observance behavior of states is at least partially determined by the consideration of how well the law will serve a national interest.[66] Thus, for example, Professor Anand remarks: ". . . at the two conferences of the law of the sea, no agreement could be reached about the breadth of the territorial waters, not because of different cultural traditions of Asian-African countries, but due to the conflicting interests of the maritime powers and the weak and underdeveloped states, not only of Asia and Africa, but of Latin America and Europe as well."[67] There are several *Western* scholars also who have supported the proposition that the national interest rather than religious or cultural values is the determining factor for traditional law observance or violations. Professor Wolfgang Friedmann, for instance, has noted:

> To confuse policies born of changing positions of interest with religious, cultural, or other values inherent in the national character of the culture pattern of a people, can only lead to a grave distortion of the real problems of contemporary international politics and law. Just as in the Western world, the relative positions of Britain, France, the United States, and other countries have changed, with the change in their political and economic status, so the positions of the presently underdeveloped countries will be affected by their development.[68]

Development of international law, as generally accepted in the Western world, is a by-product of almost 400 years of interaction among the Western European states. Some Western scholars, in their zeal to emphasize the Western heritage of law and its unmistakable influence on legal developments, may have ignored the earlier principles of interstate relations outside the Western world. This seems to be the first bone of contention between non-Western states and Western states. The attitude of Western

---

[66]For an interesting article in this general area see S. D. Metzer, "Nations and the Rules of International Law—A Commentary," *Howard Law Journal*, 8 (1962), 124 in particular.

[67]R. P. Anand, "Attitude of the Asian-African States Toward Certain Problems of International Law," *International and Comparative Law Quarterly*, 15 (January 1966), 72.

[68]W. Friedmann, "The Position of Underdeveloped Countries and the Universality of International Law," *International Law Bulletin*, (2) (1963), 9–10, published by the Columbia Society of International Law, (Spring 1963); see also, Friedmann's other article entitled: "The Changing Dimensions of International Law," *Columbia Law Review*, 62 (1962), 1151. In this position Friedmann is supported also by J. Stone, another well-known Western scholar; see his article entitled: "A Common Law For Mankind?" *International Studies*, (1) (1959–1960), p. 430.

scholarship is amply reflected by the comments of J. H. W. Verzijl: "Now there is no one truth that is not open to denial or even to doubt, namely that the actual body of international law, as it stands today, is not only the product of the conscious activity of the European mind, but has also drawn its vital essence from a common source of European beliefs, and in both of these aspects it is mainly of Western European origin."[69] Most non-Western scholars have disagreed with this conclusion and have pointed out that there were many well-established legal norms of interstate conduct in the old countries of the East such as India, China, and Egypt.[70] These countries no doubt had quite advanced forms of obligations. No one will dispute that even a cursory reading of literature on aspects of these old countries' international law indicates that there are some similarities between their rules and the rules of modern international law. But historical accuracy demands admission that no connection exists between those ancient principles of law and the present international law.

Many of these so-called "new states" are not really new. Contrary to a general belief among students of international law, these states played a significant role in the earlier stages of international politics. For instance, in Asia, if not in America and Africa, when the colonial power initially appeared on the scene they discovered that there was a fairly well-established international society. They were obliged to enter into treaties and establish diplomatic relations on the basis of reciprocal acceptance of sovereignty. Therefore, most international laws that applied in the relations between East and West were laws of reciprocity that were respected until the nineteenth century. It is historical record that classical scholars in the field of international law have testified to the existence of these laws.[71] Not only that, in a recent case concerning the *Right of Passage*

[69]J. H. W. Verzijl, "Western European Influence on the Foundations of International Law," *International Relations*, 1 (1955), 137; similar sentiments are also emphasized by B. V. A. Rolling, *International Law in an Expanding World*, (Amsterdam, Djambaten), 1960, p. 10; J. L. Kunz, "Pluralism of Legal and Value Systems and International Law," *American Journal of International Law*, 49 (1955), 371.

[70]See, for instance, the works of P. Bandgopadhyay, *International Law and Custom in Ancient India* (1920), p. 6; M. Hamidullah, *The Muslim Conduct of State* (1945), p. xiii; see several other scholars cited by C. W. Jenks in his book entitled: *The Common Law of Mankind* (London), 1958, p. 74; S. V. Viswanatha, *International Law and Custom in Ancient India* (1925); K. A. Nilakantha Sastri, "International Law and Relations in Ancient India," *Indian Yearbook of International Affairs*, 1 (1952), 97.

[71]See, for instance, the works of Bynkershock, Grotius, Pufendorf, Vattel, Wolff and many others. More specifically, see the following works of Professor C. H. Alexandrowicz, "Grotius and India," *Indian Yearbook of International Affairs*, (3) (1954), 362–367; "The Discriminating Clause in South East Asian Treaties in the Seventeenth and Eighteenth Centuries," *Ibid.*, (6) (1957), 126; "Treaty and Diplomatic Relations Between European and South Asian Powers in the Seventeenth and

Over Indian Territory, the International Court of Justice recognized a treaty signed by the government of Portugal and the empire of Marath in 1779 as a "valid transaction in the law of nations."[72] During the crucial nineteenth century, as the colonial countries consolidated their hold over the colonies, it was only a matter of time before the legal personality of the Asian states was denied. As early as the Congress of Vienna in 1815, the European powers decided to appoint themselves as members of the "civilized nations" under the Concept of Europe and therefore directors of not only European affairs but of world affairs. As Anand points out: "They assumed the authority to admit new member states or to readmit old members who did not participate in the foundations of this closed club. They claimed to issue, or deny a certificate of birth to states or governments irrespective of their existence."[73] The result was obvious, as Professor Alexandrowicz explains:[74]

> Asian States, who for centuries had been considered members of the family of nations, found themselves in an *ad hoc* created legal vacuum which reduced them from the status of international personality to the status of candidates competing for such personality.

Furthermore, civilization was formally defined as "European." Even though the seeds of civilization were sown in the East, the Eastern nations were branded as "barbarous" and "uncivilized." It was a deliberate attempt to have the states of Asia declared as *terrae nullius*, as was most of Africa and America. Thus, international law became applicable generally only to Christian people of Europe and those of European origins.[75] Divided by strong rivalries, preoccupied with intrigue and jealousies among themselves, the Asian states succumbed to the powers of Europe and not only lost their international status, but also their self-respect, even to the point of not questioning or disputing the obscure claims of the European states. Thus, colonization became valid and *legal*. After losing their international

---

Eighteenth Centuries," *Recueil des Cours*, (100) (1960-II), 207; and "Mogul Sovereignty and the Law of Nations," *Indian Yearbook of International Law*, (4) (1955), 317.

[72]Quoted by R. P. Anand, "Attitude of the Asian-African States Toward Certain Problems of International Law," p. 58.

[73]*Ibid.*, p. 58.

[74]Alexandrowicz, "Mogul Sovereignty and the Law of Nations," p. 318.

[75]See P. C. Jessup, *The Use of International Law* (Thomas M. Cooley Lectures at the University of Michigan Law School) (Ann Arbor), 1959, p. 20; Wheaton, *Elements of International Law* (London), 1866, 8th edition, pp. 17–18. See also Lord Phillmore, I., *Commentaries Upon International Law* (London), 1879, 3rd edition, pp. 23–24.

personality, these Asian states played no significant role in the development of international law *during its most creative period*, that is, at the closing of the nineteenth and beginning of the twentieth centuries. Admittedly five Asian states participated in the Hague Peace Conferences, and during the League of Nations this number increased to 12, but in international affairs, none of these nations, with the exception of Japan, had any effective voice. Since one of the chief criteria of "civilization" (and thus a right to make law) was *power*, the Japanese were accepted. Japan had already shown its muscle against China and Russia by this time. The Japanese at the time had been quoted by Rolling to say: "we show ourselves at least your equals in scientific butchery, and at once we are admitted to your council tables as civilized men."[76] After World War II, and especially after 1955, there came the tremendous upsurge for independence and under the principle of self-determination (aided by the unusual conditions of the "cold war" years) most of these countries became full-fledged members of the international community. More importantly, because of their superiority in numbers, and because of several other factors, they have come to play an important role in the international society. Nevertheless, that meaning of "civilization" as synonymous with the "Christian nations of the West" has been abandoned. Even the term "civilized," meaning commercial, industrialized, and modernized nations, has been rejected. Although the terms "civilized nations" and "civilization" are still used in Articles 6 and 38 (1) (c) of the Statute of World Court and in Article 8 of the Statute of the International Law Commission, they certainly do not conform to the so-called "historical meaning." "Peace-loving nations" is the current phrase in the United Nations. This concept has been defined in the context of qualifications for United Nation membership. "Ability and willingness" to carry out Charter obligations is sufficient. Thus, while the democratization of international society is almost complete, we now must turn to the current attitudes and practices of these developing countries toward international law.

Present attitudes and practices toward international law

Caught up in a revolution of rising aspirations, yet still forced to live a life of dire poverty and frustrations, unable or unwilling to completely erase the bitter memories of alleged past exploitations by the colonial West, yet desirous of Westernization, in the sense of modernization, that will allow them to "catch up" with the new world of industrial miracles, developing countries seek to bring about a new order in the world. The

[76]Quoted in Rolling, *International Law in an Expanded World*, p. 27.

hope is that this order may yet provide them with glimpses of the "good life" that the West has so long taken for granted. All of this has resulted in the adoption of a thoroughly revolutionary attitude in world affairs. International law obviously is not immune from this attitude.[77] There is no doubt that they have challenged some of the rules of traditional international law as inconsistent with the requirements of this new world order, which they feel must reflect a wider international consensus and sharing of values, including their own. However, much of their criticism has been levied generally against the rules that they feel were essentially a product of the colonial era, particularly rules that reflected European imperial attitudes toward the people of the colonies.

However, new states do *accept* much of the present system of international law and its binding nature. In fact, they are great champions of a new international legal system based on the principles of the United Nations Charter and those drawn from the international treaties of consensus freely agreed upon by them. They constantly refer to international law in their international disputes. They invoke its protection when threatened and frequently fall back on it during debates in international organizations. Their contributions are well recognized in the work of the Sixth (Legal) Committee of the United Nation General Assembly. In many other international conferences, particularly those concerned with the codification of existing law, their participation has been very active if not always conciliatory. Their active participation has also been recognized in the proceedings of the International Law Commission.[78] They have ratified numerous international treaties, thus broadening the horizons of international law and adding to its respect. Their discontent with some rules of traditional international law has arisen from a genuine feeling that these rules are harmful to their national interests, but this unhappiness has at no time resulted in a general rejection of international law. Rather, their conviction is, as expressed by one scholar, that "the progressive development of international law would bring about a greater degree of universality through the contributions and active participation of the many new nations which have emerged on the international scene."[79]

[77]These sentiments of developing societies are recognized by many scholars all over the world see for example, K. S. Carlston, "Universality of International Law Today: Challenge and Response," *Howard Law Journal*, 8 (1962), 79–80; see also, G. M. Abi-Saab, "The Newly Independent States and the Scope of Domestic Jurisdiction," *Proceedings of the American Society of International Law*, 54 (1960), 84 and 90.

[78]A good example of developing societies' participation in the projects of the International Law Commission are their contributions to the Commission's discussion on the Law of State Responsibility.

[79]R. Pal, "Future Role of International Law Commission in the Changing World," *United Nations Review*, 9 (September 1962), 31.

The attitude of almost all Third World states at the present time is generally one of international acceptance and observance. However, there are a few exceptions to this broad generality. For instance, most of these states feel they have just as much, perhaps more, right than the Western and Communist powers to choose periodically among laws and observe particularly those which are supportive of their national interests and neglect those which they perceive to be harmful. Their present practices should be viewed in the context of their history which has been briefly discussed, and the sociological impact of this history on their present thinking. What do these nations think and how do they act on, for instance, the following points of law: (1) customary international law, (2) international law of treaties, (3) general principles of international law, (4) questions related to territories and colonial claims, and (5) concept of self-determination.

Toward customary law. One generally finds an attitude ranging from a passive acceptance to negativism, cynicism, and outright hostility toward some norms of international law based on custom. Of course, there are some customary international laws that the developing countries cherish, religiously accept, and insist be observed, such as laws pertaining to diplomatic relations or sovereignty and territorial integrity. Their reluctance in supporting the customary laws of the past was established during a period of their involuntary inactivity in world affairs. Another reason for their reluctance is a more contemporary one. Many feel that their states are going through the pains of development. A rapid transition from orthodoxy to modernity, a desire to develop a more equitable international system, a popular demand for immediate satisfaction of these needs, and many other similar factors tend to undermine their commitment to all law observance, especially those based on custom, for example, the rights of foreign property, the right of innocent passage through their territories, and all those customary laws that they feel are oriented to the maintenance of an unequal world order that they wish to change. Certainly, they accept custom as a valid source of international law development in the future. After all, even today not all international law development is deliberate and, therefore, custom as a source will in all probability continue to play an important role in the future, with the help of developing countries of today.

Just to give a few examples of their distrust of past customary laws, consider the sometimes heated debates in the two United Nation conferences in Geneva concerning the three-mile limit of the territorial sea in 1958 and 1960. Comments made by the delegates of most developing countries clearly reflected their distrust of past customs as a source of law. On another occasion in a United Nations conference when the Declaration of the

Granting of Independence to Colonial Countries and Peoples was being discussed, their hostility toward the customary international law concerning the governance of protectorates and colonies was not even thinly veiled. There are many more instances where one can empirically observe and quantitatively measure this hostility through the use of the quantitative content analysis method.

Toward treaty law. Third World countries generally favor the growth of contemporary international law through lawmaking treaties, provided, of course, they are the result of international (including their own) consensus and are negotiated on the basis of sovereign equality of all signatories. Many of these countries, through their participation in consensus formation process and acceptance of emergent treaties, have helped to broaden the influence of international law both horizontally and vertically. Participation is an opportunity they have never had before. Treaties of consensus therefore are further taken to mean that these countries will not be bound by the provisions of a treaty unless they ratify it first. To most of the new states treaties appear to be an expedient way to get international recognition of their newly acquired prestige and status. Professor C. T. Oliver argues that treaties can be regarded as an effective instrument "to develop not only new norms directly by common agreement, but new power arrangements out of which the norms of a law we do not yet have will come."[80] When one looks at the binding quality of international treaties adopted as a result of general legislation prior to the attainment of independence of these states, one finds a generally negative, although somewhat selective, attitude comparable to the attitudes exhibited toward customary international law. For instance, treaties of reciprocity are acceptable. Other treaties, which at least reflect universally accepted values, including their own, are also acceptable.[81] Treaties that they are unwilling to accept include those concluded by the so-called great powers, particularly prior to the establishment of the League of Nations, some even prior to the establishment of the United Nations.[82] For instance, many new states reject the following treaties as unacceptable, simply because their continued acceptance may mean admission of inequality, even in an historical context. The treaties are:

---

[80]C. T. Oliver, "Historical Development of International Law: Contemporary Problems of Treaty Law," Quoted in S. P. Sinha, "Perspective of the Newly Independent States on the Binding Quality of International Law," *International and Comparative Law Quarterly,* 14 (January 1965), 123.

[81]G. M. Abi-Saab, "The Newly Independent States and the Rules of International Law: An Outline," *Howard Law Journal,* 8 (1962), 95 and 107.

[82]C. W. Jenks, *Common Law of Mankind* (1958) p. 66.

1). Constantinople Agreement of 1888 recognizing freedom of passage through the Suez Canal.

2). Various conventions concerning regime of straits.

3). The famous Vienna Treaty of 1815 eliminating the slave trade.

4). The Aix-laChapelle Treaty of 1818 classifying diplomats.

5). The Paris Treaty of 1856, outlawing privateering.

6). The London Treaty of 1871 against unilateral renunciation of obligations.

7). The Berlin Treaty of 1890 formalizing the Congo Basin arrangements in Africa, etc.

Apart from admission of inequality their rejection in some cases may also be interpreted to mean that they fear recognition of major powers as the sole lawgivers. Thus, to many of these newly independent states the distinction between "equal" meaning "freely agreed to," and "unequal" meaning imposed by duress," has become most important[83] and, accodingly, they insist upon the inalienable right of every state to terminate by denunciation the treaties in which it was forced to enter.[84] Many new states frequently invoke the doctrine *rebus sic stantibus* in order to terminate obligations inherited from an inglorious past. This termination, they feel, serves the cause of justice and, at the same time, recognizes the new much more favorable realities of international politics.

Toward General Principles of Law. Concerning the general principles of international laws, their attitude is positive. In fact, their position in this area is a little like the position of the spokesmen of new doctrines of natural law who see some justification in the general principles of international law.[85] If general principles of international law are developed from the so-called *common legal consciousness of the people*, the developing states fervently hope to play a significant role in law development. They appear to be convinced that their own legal and value systems have a contribution to make here. The significance of this source of law cannot be overstated.

It is deeply imbedded in the context of international politics, which will certainly include all the new forms of international organizations as

[83]O. J. Lissitzyn, "International Law in a Divided World," *International Conciliation*, (542) (1963), 37 and 56.

[84]See the comments made by many Afro-Asian delegates in *Conference des Juristes Afro-Asiatiques, Daneas (November 7–10, 1957)* edité par loudue des Auocats de Dumas (1957).

[85]See G. I. Tunkin, "Co-existence and International Law," *Recueil des Coeus*, (95) (1958), 5 and 23.

well as the transnational arrangements in the contemporary international system.[86] Any attempt to derive general principles of international law for the present and conceivably in the future would mean reliance on the legal systems of all the nations. This will enable the new states, as it apparently already has in various contexts, to play a continuing role in law development. The participation of their delegates as members of the International Law Commission and their judges on the bench of the International Court of Justice already has had an impact on contemporary international law development and, therefore, in the future one can probably expect law compliance from these states in a much wider variety of situations than was possible before.

Toward Sovereignty. Their attitude toward the concept of state sovereignty is fundamental and somewhat dogmatic. Because of their newly achieved independence they continue to cherish sovereignty as one of their most worthwhile achievements. This attitude provides them with psychological gratification because they are "masters" of their own fate; at the same time they feel they need this legal and political shield to ward off any would-be foreign intruders with greater success. However, this concept of sovereignty is basically associated with a certain territory, as was true in the past. They are generally quite pragmatic and willing to mortgage this "right to be unpredictable" as Hans Morgenthau says, in return for services provided to them by other countries or the international functional agencies, both of the United Nations and others. Territory remains the legal shield of their sovereignty and, hence, they deny the servitudes and rights of way created in their countries by the colonial West.[87] On the question of colonial titles based on the customary rules of law that gave the colonial West an inherent right of acquisition of non-Christian territory by discovery and occupation, the attitude of new states is clearly predictable. Therefore, the theory of *"territorium nullius"* under which the Pope could grant territories not under the rules of Christian Princes to the faithful is simply not acceptable to these countries. To most of them, geography, history (meaning precolonial and postcolonial history) local custom, culture, and public opinion are more important in establishing legal title to a territory than the norms of traditional international law. On the question of whether a territory is ready to move from a status of non–self-governing to that of self-governing, these countries reject the notion that under the concept of "domestic

---

[86]Consider the following works, P. C. Jessup, *Transnational Law*, pp. 9, 29–34 and W. Friedman, "Some Impacts of Social Organization on International Law," *American Journal of International Law*, 50 (1956), 475–476.

[87]Q. Wright, "The Goa Incident," *American Journal of International Law*, 56 (1962), 617.

jurisdiction" administrating powers have the right to decide. Hence, by their interpretation, these countries appear to be in contradiction of Article 2, paragraph 7 of the United Nations Charter.

Toward Law of Self Determination. The notion of self-determination, as embodied in the contemporary international law, meets an attitude of enthusiastic acceptance from these new states, regardless of the political and other capabilities of the people involved. More importantly, this concept has been used by newly independent states as a handy tool for political pressure to receive independence. This attitude was reflected in an historical General Assembly resolution passed by the United Nations. In part this read, "all peoples have the right to self-determination."[88] However, most of these states are not at all in favor of the right of self-determination for culturally, linguistically, and ethnically different regions within their own territories. So according to Indonesians, Papuans of West Irian have no right of self-determination; according to the Congolese, Katanga did not have this right; according to Nigeria, the Biafrans never existed; according to Pakistan, Bangladesh is not acceptable; and according to India, there is no need for the right of self-determination for Kashmir. At the same time most of these countries have quickly granted recognition to insurgents fighting a "liberation" war, even at times when the insurgents were far from having acquired control of much of the territory. Attitudes of these states are not based on any legal principle of the past but on political expediency. If politically it suits a country to recognize a liberation front, it is done. This attitude is acquired in part in a colonial context from a sympathy because of common background.

Toward Law of State Responsibility. Their attitude on the concept of state responsibility is not easy to describe. Nevertheless, this concept is fundamental to the observance of the contemporary international law by states, not only in political disputes, territorial jurisdictions, but also in international economic dealings.[89] The binding nature of "state responsibility" under property law is not acceptable to the poor countries.[90] For instance, they have argued, not without reason of self-interest, that rules of state responsibility for injury to aliens simply are not part of universal international law and therefore not acceptable.[91] They take issue with

[88]General Assembly Resolution 1514 (XV) (December 14, 1960).

[89]G. I. Tunkin, "General Debate State Responsibility," *Yearbook of International Law Commission* (1957), 165.

[90]R. Pal, "General Debate, State Responsibility," *Yearbook of International Law Commission* (1957), 157.

[91]For details see S. N. G. Roy, "Is the Responsibility of States for Injuries to Aliens a Part of Universal International Law?" *American Journal of International Law,* 55 (1961), 863.

the Western notion of an "international stand of justice" that underlies the laws of state responsibility.[92] To them, as pointed out by Professor Castaneda, "the doctrine of responsibility of states was merely the legal garb that served to cloak and protect the imperialistic interests of the international oligarchy during the nineteenth century and the first part of the 20th century."[93] The national self-interest behind such an attitude of the poor countries is fairly apparent. These nations are going through a revolutionary process of changing economic and societal development. This inevitably means the elimination of (in violation of the existing laws of state responsibility) foreign economic interests that were acquired frequently on the basis of special privileges, exploitation and inequality. These countries are not willing to continue to tolerate foreign incursions into their territories that are detrimental to their economic well-being just because some antiquated rules of state responsibility so insist. Thus the judges from the developing countries in the International Court of Justice were able to conclude in the *Norwegian Loans Case* that the Court's Jurisdictions were lacking, since these cases fell within domestic jurisdiction.[94] Perhaps the most obvious disregard of existing rules of state responsibility is exhibited between states that expropriate foreign property. The above is usually designed not only to eradicate the "last vestiges" of foreign presence, but also to obtain badly needed capital for developmental purposes. Their conviction seems to avoid international law until they can freely assume obligations under agreements of mutual interest. Professor Sinha offers the following remarks:

> The nature of such [foreign property] expropriations can be truly appreciated in their fuller politico-economic environment with due regard to the nature of origin and consolidation of their interests. Settlement of difficulties in this field has rarely been on purely legal principles. The problem is not so much one of law as of equity.[95]

On the question of settlement of their disputes in the international arena most of these countries propose methods of mediation, conciliation, negotiation and inquiry. They do not generally exhibit a strong preference for adjudication by the application of existing laws. Their preference has usually been for methods that have a nonbinding character. However, the

[92]*Ibid.*

[93]J. Castaneda, "The Underdeveloped Nations and the Development of International Law," *International Organization*, (1961), 38.

[94]Quoted in S. P. Sinha, "Perspective of Newly Independent States," p. 128. This attitude on state responsibility held by new states does not mean they are trying to get away from their obligations freely acquired since independence. On the contrary, their record of state obligation since independence is pretty good.

[95]*Ibid.*

primary means of settlement in the past 20 years have been through non-judicial arrangements.

What appears to be most interesting in the actual practices of new states *vis à vis* the requirements of international law is the simultaneous usage of both legalistic and nonlegalistic approaches. To those scholars who have already concluded that these countries have an aversion to rule of law in international affairs, it may come as a surprise that their record of law violations is selective and limited mostly to the traditional rules of law that they regard as unfair and unjust.

A concluding remark

A few words of caution are necessary. First, no nation has a perfect record of either law observance or law violations.[96] Many charges and counter-charges by states concerning the lawless behavior of the "other" side in the international system can be better explained on the basis of antagon-istic relationships that may exist among states rather than on the realities of law violations. Even among states with similar ideology, political cul-ture, and racial background, but different, perhaps conflictive national interests, mutual accusations of law violations, bad faith, and breaking of treaties are not entirely nonexistent. It should be admitted that compara-tive studies of the frequency of law violations, be it customary law or even treaty law, have never been seriously undertaken by the international lawyers to indicate authoritatively the record of various states. If at-tempted, even with the help of social scientists, it will not be an easy task. The major difficulty is not the empirical observation and quantification of law violations by a state or states; instead the main stumbling block is the difficulty in interpreting disputed treaty provisions or other norms of the customary international law invoked by contending states in support of their own positions. The scholar will have to play the role of judge without partic-ularly enjoying the privileges or the responsibilities of the formal office or the advantage of the "adversary system"—legal proceedings in which his interpretation is contrasted with perhaps equally reasonable or more con-vincing arguments in support of a different interpretation. Besides, it is doubtful if too many social scientists are willing to play the role of judge.

[96]Consider the following remarks of a British scholar, Sir Henry Johnston, quoted from his book entitled: *Common Sense in Foreign Policy*, published in 1913, p. 89. He says: "Treaties in fact, bind the policy of the United States as long as they are convenient. They are not, really, worth the labor their negotiations entail or the paper they are written on. It is as well that his position should be realized, as it may save a great deal of fuss and disappointment in the future." These remarks (except for the somewhat unique English politeness sound as if they were uttered by a scholar from a country that was an antagonist of the United States, perhaps at the time of the cold war.

We should realize that a great deal of international law is conducive to multiple interpretations and the accommodation of more than one point of view *but* always within certain limits. This aspect of legal norms has at times provided irresistible temptation to the decision makers to stretch the law (with the professional help of his legal advisors) to fit the pursuit of specific policy objectives within the framework of the law.[97]

There have been some instances in the West, particularly in the United States, where international law has been used as a symbol of rectitude instead of as a guide to international behavior. Its norms are converted into marketable slogans for consumption at home or abroad to the gratification of both the leader and the people. The need for such an activity is certainly greater in a democratic society than in a nondemocracy, simply because of the democracy's traditional affinity to democratic norms (the place of law in it) and to much of contemporary international law, which is the brainchild of the West. On a comparative basis, because of the nature of socialization, the public in a Western democracy has a relatively greater need to believe that the foreign policy conduct of its government is *not* in violation of the accepted norms of international law than is true of the public in the communist states or in the countries of the Third World. Certainly, this proposition appears to be true if scholarly debates and occasional public indignation in the United States are any guide whenever the American Government allegedly violates an international legal norm. Apart from this, all states with varying degrees use international law as a propaganda technique by advertising themselves as "law-abiding" nations in contrast to their opponents whom they characterize as a law violator. This practice is quite noticeable during acute international crises.

Nonetheless, norms of international law cannot be stretched indefinitely without giving a clear signal of being broken. It is also possible, in most cases, to arrive at what appears to be a reasonable single interpretation of law from which a violation of law can be judged. Above all, given the somewhat nonaccumulative, certainly nonscientific data that we have, the descriptive historical knowledge that exists and finally appears reasonable in the light of evidence, it is *possible* to develop a sort of legal profile of several non-Western countries concerning international law observance or lack of it.

[97]On the important question of multiple interpretations of international law, the following remarks of Professor Dunn highlight the problem. He was talking on the subject of the Mexican-American relations concerning diplomatic protection of citizens. He observes: "One is constantly impressed with the fact that whenever there is a definite clash of material interests, each side is quite able to derive from established legal rules and principles an answer that accords neatly with its own material interests." Quoted in Leo Gross (ed.) *International Law in the Twentieth Century* (New York: Appleton-Century-Crofts), 1969, in the article of O. J. Lissitzyn, "Western and Soviet Perspectives," p. 131.

chapter 12
why nations observe
international law

We begin this chapter on the observance of international law by accepting a broad premise put forward a few years ago, by Professor Richard A. Falk, in his eloquent plea for an *intermediate view* of the law-politics relationship.[1] This view falls between the two extreme views frequently used to characterize the role of law in politics; one view makes a "too much" claim for law and the other, a "too little." He observes:

> The inability of international law to generate an altogether peaceful world does not imply its inviability to promote a more peaceful world, or to deal adequately with the many aspects of international life having nothing directly to do with war and peace. Part of the difficulty of accepting international law as a beneficial, albeit imperfect, source of order in world affairs, arises from the fear of a destructive violation of international law culminating in a general nuclear war. Such an awesome prospect cripples the imagination and inclines observers to conclude that a system of order that cannot offer assurance against such an occurrence is virtually worthless.

Obviously the role of international law in an age of nuclear weapons and other revolutionary transformations that threaten the stability of the international system is related significantly to making the system less prone to war, and to assisting its transition to a new, more secure international order. The emergence of several arms control agreements and the subsequent development of law in this area is an example of this legitimate concern. However, it is possible to overstate the need of law in the management of large-scale conflict. Such an overstatement can and has hurt the cause of law by contributing to a disillusionment with its role in world affairs. Although recognizing the role of law in conflict management,

[1]Richard A. Falk, "The Relevance of Political Context to the Nature and Functioning of International Law: An International View," in K. W. Deutsch and Stanley Hoffmann (eds.), *The Relevance of Intermediate Law* (Cambridge, Mass.: Schenkman), 1968, pp. 143–144.

a student has an obligation to look at the wider and more moderate, but nonetheless, important contributions of international law to the everyday life of the international society. At this level and even at the level of conflict management, international law is neither superfluous nor worthless. A student should be careful to resist the temptation to treat international law as a body of norms whose success can be judged only when they are actually observed. Such a treatment equates law violations with its failures, thus neglecting an important fact that international law, like any other law, also operates covertly and any attempt to correlate its successes with its observance and its failures with its violations, overlooks this important level of operation.

The so-called commonly held belief by many students that nations *frequently* violate international law is simply without foundation. They do not. Even the observation, however casual, that at the first opportunity nations rush to violate international law when it does not serve them is also inadequate and therefore misleading. Still another frequently heard argument is that international law is no "law" at all because there is no centrally developed and operationally effective enforcement agency to deter its violations; therefore, nations will always avail themselves of the opportunity to disregard it, because it does after all restrain their ability to wheel and deal. Such an argument is too simple an explanation for law violations. It ignores the fact that even in the best of domestic political systems law is not observed primarily because of readily available sanctions. Thus, the absence of effective sanctions does not automatically mean that states will violate the law. There are many other powerful forces in a domestic society that encourage law observance. The same is true, perhaps to a lesser degree, in international society.[2]

Contrary to such popularly held views on the frequency of law violations, the evidence suggest that usually *states indeed observe international law for a number of reasons*. Thus, law observance takes place not only in the absence of negative sanctions but also in the presence of many minor temptations to violate the law.

Advantages of lawful behavior

Observance of international law for most nations is generally thought to be more advantageous than law violations. In the case of a law violation,

[2]For two interesting commentaries on this point see L. Henkin, "Enforcement of Arms Control: Some Basic Considerations," *Journal of Arms Control*, 1 (1963), 184–185; and R. Fisher, "Internal Enforcement of International Rules," in S. Melman (ed.), *Disarmament: Its Policies and Economics* (Boston: American Academy of Arts and Sciences), 1962.

it takes an unusual and strong expectation of important, well-articulated advantages to tempt a state to violate an international norm. In the absence of such temptation, for most states there is clearly a strong case for law observance.

A great deal of international law is observed out of *necessity*. The requirements of everyday intercourse among states, the need for *predictability and stable expectations*, force every nation on the globe to observe certain international norms. Much of law is also observed as a *matter of habit or course*, without any particular awareness of it on the part of government officials. More importantly, international law is also observed because it is a *valuable instrument of foreign policy*, as stated elsewhere. Apart from these reasons, nations frequently find it *advantageous* to observe law. In this respect, the rewards of law observance may far exceed the possible advantages of indifference to law, or probable rewards of law violation, to say nothing of the cost of law violation that may sometimes be quite substantial. It is not easy to develop successfully a cost-reward index of law observances or violations for a state, simply because there are too many "ifs" and "buts." For instance, the index will vary from state to state, at different times, with different cases, and with different laws.

First the cost-reward explanation concerning a state's behavior with regard to international law is applicable only to those situations where the formulation of foreign policy was deliberate and due consideration was given to all the relevant significant factors. Second, on occasions a policymaker may not be thinking of cost-rewards at all. Instead, he may be motivated to act on the basis of "other" considerations such as personal vengeance, prejudice, caprice, or he may simply act irrationally. Third, there is always a possibility of an error made by a decision maker in deciding what course of action his nation should follow. Based on faulty information or a miscalculation of the other side's intentions, a country may decide to ignore international law as the most advantageous course for it to follow, but this decision may turn out to be extremely costly. A good example of this kind of miscalculation is President Nasser's decision, prior to the 1967 Arab-Isreali War, to ask the United Nations to recall its troops from duty in Sheram-el Sheikh area and then replace them with Egyptian soldiers. There does not seem to be anything illegal about it. But President Nasser's further decision to bar the Isreali shipping from the Gulf of Agaba can be regarded a violation of customary international law, which precipitated the 1967 armed conflict, costing Egypt enormously in terms of power, prestige, money, and territory. The long-term psychological cost of Arab defeat by a handful of Isreali troops is yet to be assessed on the Arab mind.

A systematic analysis of a state's foreign policy in a variety of situations is undoubtedly one of the best methods to develop a state's profile concerning its predisposition to, or not to, observe international law. We can indeed learn a great deal about this predisposition by making detailed notes on how a state in the past has treated international law and how it deals presently with its international obligations, treaties, or other existing norms. Such an effort need not start from the scratch. It can proceed on the assumption that much of international law is interwoven into the very fabric of the international society and, thus, to a certain extent all states observe the law because they have developed a common interest in the maintenance of the international system because it benefits them all. At this rather significant level states are sometimes obliged to observe international law in certain areas where they would rather not. But they observe it primarily for a *greater* interest, for example to preserve law and order in the international society by not providing others with an opportunity to violate international law by using their example.

Every state in the international system strives to develop some credibility in the eyes of other states. Such a credibility is important in the success of a state's foreign policy. A state's reputation for upholding its part of a bargain in international economic affairs and for honoring its political agreements and treaties is a great asset in its ability to improve its situation in the world. International law observance generally help's a state in these goals. Normally, all states desire to be treated with honor, dignity, and respect. They work for and sometimes demand legal recognition of their governments by the international society in general, by the United Nations, or by individual countries. Law also helps them in this area. No government likes to be called a "lawless" government, to be accused of law violations, or to be criticized. For this reason alone law violations are avoided and, also, because governments are usually aware that law violations will be challenged and "justifications" will have to be provided. In some cases, the states are also aware that the victims may bring law violations before the United Nations, before one of the many other international regional organizations, or even before an international tribunal. This *awareness* also discourages law violations. International law may be observed because states prefer to be *friendly* with each other, and even in those situations where animosity exists, they generally prefer not to *aggrevate* the situation.

International law is also observed because of an expectation of great rewards in particular international conflict situations. Some case studies of various international conflicts where the United Nations presence, for instance, was either demanded or actually existed on behalf of international law, will show how states may decide to cooperate with the United Nations peacekeeping efforts in expectations of rewards. Since not all states took part in the historical development of international law and since some states today are caught up in their own social, economic, and political revolutions, out of necessity instead of from a conscious choice, it is reasonable to assume that not all states have the same commitment to observe international law. After all, international law, like any other law, however dynamic, always assumes a conservative position in time. Even today, it appears to be a conservative force to many nations. It tends to support the status quo in many aspects of international life and, therefore, these states that *are* (such as Western societies) or are *becoming* status-quo oriented (such as the Soviet Union), find it easier to defend its norms. In the emerging Soviet-American détente we see support for this proposition because there is a realization on the part of the Soviet leadership that they have a high stake in the present international order and that the logical way to preserve this order is to draw closer to the United States in those areas where mutual interests are now well articulated and away from those international issues that threaten this order. International law observance can be expected to improve in such a circumstance because law provides for cooperation and stable expectations. In the remaining part of the chapter we shall examine case studies of the United Nations' peacekeeping operations in various international crisis situations and the reaction of states involved in them. These cases are studies of what was done by the United Nations as a *representative of the forces of law and order* and what was the behavior of the states involved toward opportunities during the crises *to observe or not to observe international law*. Among other things, these studies clearly indicate that the satisfaction of issues of important national interest was an important factor in states' behavior. The decision to restrict the case studies to United Nations peacekeeping operations was made for the following two reasons: (1) The United Nations is committed to uphold international law; therefore its activities, including most peacekeeping operations, are regarded to be generally consistent with the dictates of the United Nations Charter and other norms of international law. Its preamble states: "to establish conditions under which justice and respect for the obligations arising from treaties and other sources of international law can be maintained." Its General Assembly is also required to "initiate studies to make recommendations for the purpose of . . . encouraging the progressive development of international law and its radification." United Nations peacekeeping operations mean expressions of a majority of states to support the forces of law and order. (2) For purposes of consistent comparison between the operations where the parties involved in the conflict were unable to reach accord and thus preferred to trust the Secretary-General, the United Nations, and the dictates of international law for the satisfaction of their national interests, and the operations where the dictates of national interests demanded that the Secretary-General, the United

Nations, and the sources of international law be ignored or outright violated. This second category of cases is discussed in the following chapter on law violations.

Case study no. 1 supports the proposition that the international law will be observed and United Nations intervention accepted by a state in a conflict situation where forces of law and order are *consistent with the* state's national interest. Study no. 2 makes the same point by suggesting that when such a consistency does not exist, a state will probably be tempted to violate the law. Case studies 3 and 4 also make the same point, but the conclusion is somewhat different. They support the proposition that in those conflict situations where interested parties are unable to reach a political accord and thus show a definite preference for the dictates of law and its spokesman (in these studies the United Nations Secretary-General). More specifically, these two case studies indicate that during international crises where the states concerned are unable to work out a clear-cut mandate for United Nations intervention and a deadlock appears certain, a way to resolve the conflict will normally be found by adopting broad, somewhat vague, compromise resolutions *based on the relevant principles of international law*, leaving much of the burden of interpretation and therefore discretion on the shoulders of the Secretary-General. The purpose behind such a move is normally an expectation that the interpretation of the mandate and the relevant law will support one's national interest because that *law and (in such resolutions) the United Nations mandate for a peacekeeping operation are almost always subject to multiple interpretations.*

This extraordinary reliance on the Secretary-General in the interpretation of peacekeeping mandates is predicted on the premise that most states accept him as the chief representative of an international organization that plays an even more independent role in world affairs. They also believe that ideally he aspires toward a position of impartiality in the conduct of his office and that he strives to uphold international law. Closely related to the advantages of his structural position in the system are the substantial informal powers of the Chief Executive. States also recognize that he is the man responsible for the direction, coordination, and liaison of all activities related to the role of the United Nations in the maintenance of world peace. He is responsible for the execution of policy decisions and the implementation of law, and controls the actual personnel and material resources involved in peacekeeping operations. But, *most importantly*, states know only too well that should he fail to interprete a United Nations mandate for a peacekeeping operation or the relevant norms of international law consistent with their national interests, they can always withdraw their support of the operation and blame him for *all* the "stortcomings" of the operation as they perceive them. The same is true should the operation proceed in a manner harmful to their national interests during any period of its existence.

case study 1

The United Nations and the Congo Crisis: An Analysis of United States Interests and Behavior in Law Observance

The role played by the United States in the Congo crisis—its strong support of the United Nations mission there—also provides evidence in support of our proposition. Of all the major powers the United States was the chief beneficiary of the United Nations mission in the Congo from 1960 to 1964. The net effect of the operation was to support a moderate Congolese Government capable of sustaining mutually beneficial relationships with the West. Furthermore, since this meant a high degree of concurrence between the interests of the United States and the actions of the Security Council, the mission had the wholehearted approval and active support of the United States throughout its successive periods of operation. Strong and persistent American support was the result of a belief that in the circumstances, the American interests would be best served by a United Nations intervention and, consequently, by virtue of its tremendous power and resources, the American involvement left a brand of its own on the Congo operation, unmatched by any other state. To be more explicit, one can argue today with some measure of confidence that the American approval of United Nations intervention in the Congo was an important factor in the creation and operation of the United Nations Force in the Congo (ONUC), and it was continued American diplomatic and material support of the mission that sustained the operation during the next four years.

In general, the major American aspirations in the Congo were, as they have been elsewhere in Africa since newly independent states began to emerge there, to see the Congolese Republic as a unified nation under the rule of a more or less representative, but a viable and politically moderate, preferably pro-American, government, which would ensure a continued access to its considerable economic resources for the United States and its Western allies. The United States also aspired to seek internal stability in the Congo. From a still somewhat narrower perspective, the Americans felt it extremely important, as they have in other parts of the world, that the Communist bloc and its influence be kept out of the Congo and Central Africa, preferably without inviting a direct major-power confrontation. Before we can analyze the performance of the ONUC in relation to American aspirations, we shall specifically enumerate these aspirations.

American aspirations and the Congo

Americans aspired and consciously worked toward achieving certain goals in the Congo. They are listed below.

1. Unification of the Congolese Republic under a government in Leopoldville sympathetic to the United States' point of view, and capable of representing various factions in the country and maintaining law and order.

To satisfy this aspiration, the United States Government did several things in addition to supporting the ONUC. For instance, it tried to provide bilateral assistance to the Congo—particularly military aid to the Government with the intention of strengthening the Congolese national army (ANC). Remember that one of the major factors contributing to the crisis in the Congo was the weakness of ANC. Once it became clear that the undisciplined and rebellious ANC soldiers were themselves partly responsible for the massacres of civilian population on several occasions, and had at other times engaged in fighting against the ONUC, Washington gave up the idea of providing them with arms. In fact, the emphasis of the American policy now was to help the ONUC disarm them.[3] At the same time, the Americans did not abandon hope that ANC had the potential to help the Government to maintain law and order in the country. As late as November 1961, Adlai Stevenson argued without success in the Council debate that preceded the November 24, 1961 resolution that the draft should be amended to encourage the ONUC to reorganize and train the ANC as an effective arm of the Congolese Government, and the United Nations should consider providing the Congo with a modest national air force.[4]

The origin, character, and the ultimate failure of the Green Plan also provide evidence that the United States was determined to provide aid to the Congolese Government in an effort to attain stability in that country and to save the national government in Leopoldville that was sympathetic to the American point of view.[5] This plan, as developed originally, was to

[3]For details on the American proposal to disarm the Congolese troops see "The American Plan" as developed in February 1960 and discussed elsewhere in this study.

[4]For details see U.N., SCOR, S/PV975 (November 16, 1961), 10.

[5]See, U.N., SCOR, Eighteenth Year, *Official Records*, Supplement for January, February, March, 1963, S/5240 (February 4, 1963), 101.

provide a series of bilateral aid programs to the Congo, supposedly in cooperation with United Nations efforts. After considerable discussion the negotiations with the Leopoldville Government, and consultations with United Nations officials, the United States Government sought to enlist the support of Belgium, Canada, Italy, Israel, and Norway in providing aid. Note that all of these countries at the time were distinctly sympathetic to the American point of view as opposed to the Soviet point of view. Each of these countries agreed to participate. After considerable debate the Plan was abandoned in April 1963, primarily because of the hostility of the militant African group who were suspicious of American motives in the Congo.[6] As a result of the failure of this Plan, Belgium, Italy, and Israel made conventional bilateral military aid agreements with the Leopoldville Government anyway. Also even long before the failure of this plan, the United States had already started its own bilateral aid program as early as October 1962 and formally concluded an aid agreement with the Adoula Government (which was incidentally considered as moderate in the East-West context and had the American blessings) in the middle of 1963. At this time the United States also established a military aid mission in the Congo.[7]

With the emphasis on Congo unity, the United States took a consistent position against the secessionist movements led by Tshombe and Gizenga. The summary of the American position on this count can be found in a statement made by George W. Ball, Under Secretary of State. He insisted that the Leopoldville Government would not be expected to cope with the diversionary activities of Antoine Gizenga and others until the Katangan secession problem was solved.[8] The United States' desire to back up ONUC's efforts to end both the Gizenga and Tshombe movements was also made clear by its decision to place several United States transport planes under the direct command of ONUC for airlift purposes *inside* the Congo.[9] Two months later in the Security Council debate that led to the November 24, 1961 resolution *"deploring* all armed action in opposition to the authority of the Government of the Republic of the Congo, specifically secessionist activities and armed action now being carried on by the Provincial Administration of Katanga with the aid of external resources and foreign mercenaries, and completely rejecting the claim that Katanga is a 'sovereign independent nation,' " the United

---

[6]See, *Annual Report of the Secretary-General on the Work of the Organization* U.N. Doc. A/5501 (June 16, 1962 to June 15, 1963), 14–15.

[7]See Defense Department Announcement quoted by *Washington Post and Times Herald* (July 6, 1963).

[8]For details see George W. Ball, *The Elements in Our Congo Policy* (U.S. Department of State Publication No. 7326), December 1961, p. 19.

[9]See New York *Times* (September 22, 1961), 1.

States argued in favor of this resolution and voted for its adoption.[10] American policy of opposition to the secessionist movements in the Congo was also aired by G. Mennen Williams, Assistant Secretary of State for African Affairs, on November 9, 1962. Williams contended that unless the United States and the United Nations take a harder and more vigorous attitude in eliminating Katangan secession, the moderate government of Adoula will fall and thereby open the way for a left-wing regime.[11]

2. Keeping the Congo free from the domination or even the influence of Communist nations, preferably, without inviting a superpower confrontation.

American emphasis on stability in the Congo was also related to its fear of Communist intervention in that country. It is contended that this emphasis on stability in the underdeveloped countries is largely predicated on a long, outstanding premise of American foreign policy that chaos and confusion in these nations such as in the Congo would be exploited by the Communists. Consider, for instance, United States' repeated warning in the Security Council debates and elsewhere that introduction of any foreign forces (presumably Belgium's forces were excluded from the category of "foreign") in the Congo by any member states, not under the direct Command of the United Nations would be "in defiance of the United Nations, and would "seriously jeopardize any effort to bring stability and order to the Congo."[12] These warnings generally reflected a considerable American fear of Soviet and other Communist nations' penetration in the Congo. At least one scholar has suggested that in an effort to show to the United Nations membership and in particular to the Soviet Union, that if the Communists and others stay out of the Congo, the United States herself will refrain from intervening unilaterally; in fact, the United States Government informed Prime Minister Lumumba during his visit to Washington D.C. on July 27, 1960 that all American aid to his country will be channeled through the United Nations. It will be remembered that Lumumba had asked for a bilateral technical and financial aid.[13] It is very much subject to debate whether this refusal to aid directly was inspired by a genuine desire on the part of Washington to keep "hands off" in the Congo, or whether it was a result of an increasing American apprehension about Lumumba's capacity to take a sympathetic attitude toward the American point of view. On the other hand, there is evidence that the United States, despite its public stand against a unilateral intervention by

[10]For details see, U.N. Doc. S/5002 (November 24, 1961).

[11]U.S. Department of State Press Release, No. 670 (November 9, 1962).

[12]See, U.N., SCOR, S/PV877 (July 20, 1960), pp. 38–39.

[13]See New York Times (July 28, 1960), 1.

any nation (including itself) in the Congo, did in fact help to overthrow Prime Minister Lumumba who was, at the time of his disposal, not the American ideal of a friend, and to install Colonel Joseph Mobuto as the number one man. Mobuto did receive American support almost immediately.[14] A careful analysis of *The Second Report of Secretary-General's Special Representative in the Congo* also implies an American role in the overthrow of Lumumba. Note Rajeshwar Dayal, the Special Representative, and consequently, the United Nations Secretariat, for some time after the overthrow of Lumumba continued to recognize him as the legal Prime Minister even though they did not deal with him. This state of affairs, along with other factors, temporarily strained the American relations with the United Nations Secretariat, because the United States had almost immediately given its solid support to Mobuto's regime.[15]

3. A broad commitment to the decolonization of Africa and an increasing desire not to alienate the leaders of emerging African nations. At the same time, a strong desire not to offend its European allies who happened to be also the colonists—Belgium, in the case of the Congo.

For at least 15 years now, the United States had been involved in a tug-of-war between the newly developing nations and the old European allies of America. There was obviously a commitment on the part of Americans to decolonize the world and to give help to the developing nations. At the same time, the United States Government had shown a strong and consistent desire not to alienate its European colonial allies. Furthermore in dealing with the newly independent states, particularly in Africa, the United States had until recently often paid a great deal of attention to the judgments and initiatives of the former European colonists. This was generally true in the Congo. Consider, for instance, a speech made by the United States delegate in the Security Council debate that preceded the first resolution on the Congo. Here Henry Cabot Lodge worked hard to keep Belgium from being branded as an aggressor. In fact, he argued that the Belgian troops should not be withdrawn from the Congo until the ONUC was able to restore law and order in the country.[16] It was not really until the death of Lumumba that the United States somewhat reluctantly

[14]In support of the above contention see Catherine Hoskyn, *The Congo Since Independence: January 1960–December 1961*, (London: Oxford University Press), published for the Royal Institute of International Affairs, 1965, p. 201; and Andrew Tally, *CIA The Inside Story* (New York: Morrow), 1962, pp. 220–222.

[15]See, U.N., SCOR, Supplement for October, November, December, 1960, S/4557 (November 2, 1960), 7–34, *passim*. Consider also a speech given by Harlan Cleveland, the Assistant Secretary of State for International Organization Affairs, U.S. Department of State Press Release No. 34 (January 17, 1963), 34.

[16]For details of Lodge's speech see, U.N., SCOR, S/PV873 (July 1960), 15 and 42–43.

endorsed the Security Council resolution that called for "energetic measures" to expel the Belgians at the time that the Congolese Parliament reconvenes. (At this time Washington was forced, because of the general atmosphere, to come closer to the position of the more militant Afro-Asian states who resented Belgian presence in the Congo.)[17]

4. A general policy of limited liability and risk in Africa. That is, in the case of the Congo, no unilateral military intervention by the United States forces. A belief that the American responsibility for African security should be also shared by other states (those that were friendly to United States).

This American attitude was revealed some two years after the Congo operation stated in a speech made by Harlan Cleveland U.S. Assistant Secretary of State for International Organization Affairs. He commented: "Should the Congo chaos be tackled by hastily assembled international peace force; or should we send a division of United States Marines, or should we just sit on our hands and wait for our adversaries to exploit the situation?" "We wisely decided," he continued, "not to wish a confrontation of nuclear powers in the center of Africa." "We believed," he added, that a United Nations force would serve "the national interest of the United States and the majority of other United Nations Members."[18]

5. In the face of a severe and persistent Soviet attack on the Secretary-General, a strong effort to support and strengthen the office of the Secretary-General and reinforce his authority in the Congo.

Apart from supporting several resolutions supporting the Secretary-General in the face of mounting Soviet criticism, the United States Government developed what its European allies called the "American Plan." This plan was in part meant to bolster the prestige of the Secretary-General as well as the United Nations mission in the Congo as a whole. The Plan included four major elements: (1) That all Congolese troops be neutralized by the ONUC. "This disarmament . . . or limitation of arms . . . should be accomplished by negotiations if possible, but by force if necessary." (2) That all foreign interference in the Congo outside the frame of the United Nations be halted. (3) That if the neutralization proved to be effective, all political prisoners, including Lumumba, be released and be allowed to participate in domestic politics. (4) That subsequently a broadly based government under the authority of Kasavubu and representing all major factions in the Congo be established.[19]

---

[17]See U.N., SCOR, S/PV941 (February 20, 1961), 16–17.

[18]See U.S. Department of State Press Release 34 (January 17, 1963), 34.

[19]For details of this plan see Adlai E. Stevenson's presentation during a Security Council debate. U.N., SCOR, S/PV934 (February 15, 1961), 12–13.

Gratification of American aspirations

1. The net impact of the United Nations presence in the Congo was to support a moderate government representing all major factions in the country, against the secessionist aspirations of Tshombe on the one hand, and against the claims of Lumumba on the other—a result consistent with the United States objective.

2. The United Nations mission frustrated efforts by the Soviet Union to support the Stanleyville regime with direct military and technical assistance when except for United Nations aircraft it closed the airports to all traffic, including Soviet aircraft—an action consistent with the United States objective of preventing Communist interference.

3. The United Nations operation also helped to blunt the Afro-Asian charges of Western neocolonialism against the United States and, in general, it enhanced the American prestige among the moderate as well as militant Afro-Asian member states—an outcome the United States aspired to achieve.

4. The United Nations helped to eliminate the Katanga secession and thereby ended one of the major challenges to the unity and territorial integrity of the Republic—an outcome desired by the United States.

United States support of the United Nations mission

Similar interests and objectives between the United Nations mission in the Congo and the United States provided the basis for a generous and consistent American support throughout the entire period of the mission. Without strong United States support in all areas—political, financial, moral, and logistical—the operation would probably never have been authorized. Even if the authorization is conceivable, it certainly could neither have been made operational in such a short time, nor survived over the four years of turmoil without continued American support. More specifically, the United States provided the following financial and logistical supports:

1. Out of the total cost of the United Nations operation in the Congo from July 1960 to June 1964, which amounted to approximately $411 million, the United States provided $170 million through both assessments and voluntary contributions. This figure amounts to approximately 42 percent of the total expenditure.

2. The United States was also the largest single purchaser of United Nations bonds that largely resulted from a debt incurred because of the nonpayments of the peacekeeping assessments on the part of several countries. In fact, it bought $100 million in bonds on a matching basis with other member states with the explicit understanding that yearly payments of the interest and principal for the next 15 years would be included in the regular United Nations budget.

3. The United States logistical support of the Congo operation throughout its period was also unmatched by any other member state. By June 30, 1964, the Defense Department had transported 118,091 troops for duty with the ONUC and other related United Nations activity, and 18,596 tons of cargo into and out of the Congo. It also, by this date, had airlifted 1991 troops and 3642 tons of cargo within the Congo. See Figure 1 on page 266.

case study 2
The United Nations and the Cyprus Crisis: Law Observance Through the Role of the Secretary-General

Background to the United Nations involvement in Cyprus

One can go far into history to seek explanations of the underlying problems that led to an outbreak of violence in the Republic of Cyprus in December 1963, and resulted in the creation of the United Nations Force in Cyprus a few months later. But for our purpose the outbreak of hostilities stemmed largely from the friction and animosity between the two ethnic groups on this small island—the Greek Cypriots who are in the substantial majority, and the less populous Turkish Cypriots. Both groups of inhabitants over a long history had managed to perpetuate a strong and rich different cultural heritage that continued to make assimilation extremely difficult.[20] This became quite apparent at the time of independence from the British rule in 1960 when the Greek Cypriots demanded a union with Greece and the Turkish Cypriots demanded a partition of the island. Consequently, the recent cause of tension can be attributed to the 1960 national constitution of this island republic that was written under the explicit premise that neither of the above two demands will be met.

Cyprus attained its independence in 1960 according to the provisions of the Zurich Agreements of February 1959. These Agreements were signed by the United Kingdom, Greece, and Turkey, and were accepted by the representatives of both the Greek Cypriots and the Turkish Cypriots. The provisions of these agreements were subsequently embodied in an interrelated series of treaties, as well as in the body of the Constitution itself.[21]

[20]For a good historical background of the Greek-Turkish Cypriot differences see T. W. Adams and A. J. Cottrell, "The Cyprus Conflict," Orbis, 8 (1) (Spring 1964).

[21]The treaties signed were (1) the Treaty of Alliance, signed by Greece, Turkey, and the Republic of Cyprus; (2) the Treaty of Guarantee, signed by the United Kingdom, Greece, Turkey, and the Republic of Cyprus; (3) the Treaty Concerning the

Figure 1. *United States contributions to the Congo operations as compared with the contributions of other states.*

Note: The following data was compiled from United Nations financial reports, and cited by Ernest W. Lefever in his study.

All 12 governments that made voluntary contributions (in addition to the United States) were *Western oriented* and received varying satisfaction from the outcome of United Nations intervention in the Congo. In fact, with the exception of Austria, Finland, Ireland, and Sweden, all were militarily allied with the United States.

United States Contributions: 1960–1964

1960		$ 3,900,000
1961		15,305,596
1962		11,400,800
1963		1,768,479
1964		704,111
	Total	$33,078,986

All Contributions: 1960–1964

Note: Only the United States contributed before 1963.

		1963	*1964*	*Total*
1.	Australia	92,000	36,500	128,500
2.	Austria	25,000	9,900	34,900
3.	Denmark	37,000	13,286	50,286
4.	Canada	173,000	90,000	263,000*
5.	Ireland	5,053	2,947	8,000
6.	Japan	81,927	33,425	115,352
7.	Netherlands	57,000	22,694	79,694
8.	New Zealand	22,916	9,002	31,918
9.	Norway	28,000	10,000	38,000
10.	Sweden	75,000	37,500	112,500
11.	Finland	18,635	8,244	26,879
12.	United Kingdom	410,000	175,000	585,000*
13.	United States	1,768,479	704,111	33,078,986*†

*This figure identifies nations making available initial air transportation services amounting to $11,487,622. This includes the United States, $10,317,662; Canada, $650,000; and the United Kingdom, $520,000. Note that these amounts were in addition to the total amount authorized for the initial period.

†The total United States voluntary contributions including the initial airlift of United Nations troops in 1960, which cost $10,317,662, was $43,396,648.

Approximately three years after the passage of the Constitution, the Greek Archbishop Makarios, the Republic President, proposed 13 constitutional changes that, for example, would have eliminated many of the rights of the separate Turkish community; and reduced significantly the Turkish representation in the armed services, police forces, and the civil service. His proposal would have also eliminated the restrictive Turkish veto, and provided in the House of Representatives a greater measure of unity.[22] The reaction of the Turkish minority to this proposal was prompt and violent. As the communal friction grew into an open conflict between the two ethnic groups, the matter was thrown into the laps of the Security Council by the Cyprus Government, who charged Turkey with agression.[23] The Council briefly met, but no action was taken because the matter was already in the hands of the guarantor powers who quickly established a joint peacemaking force of their own. The Force was only partially successful in restoring peace and stability. At this time the United Kingdom also took the initiative in calling for a conference of interested parties in London with the hope of arriving at a more lasting solution in Cyprus. The conference, which was also attended by a United Nations observer, produced two resolutions; both were rejected by Archbishop Makarios.[24]

United Nations involvement and differences among the interested parties

The question of Cyprus was again referred to the United Nations on February 5, 1964. The British representative requested the Security Council for an early meeting on Cyprus.[25] But the Cyprus representative asked for an emergency meeting of the Council, arguing that there is a grave

---

Establishment of the Republic of Cyprus. See *American Foreign Policy Current Documents 1959*, United States Department of State Publication 7492 (Washington, D.C.: U.S. Government Printing Office), 1963, pp. 765-775, for a complete text of the first two treaties. However, under the provisions of the Treaty of Alliance, common defense arrangements were established between Greece, Turkey and the New Republic; under the provisions of the Treaty of Guarantee, the United Kingdom, Turkey and Greece assured the independence and territorial integrity of Cyprus; and, under the provisions of the same treaty they also guaranteed the basic articles of the Constitution—which in addition to defining the basic laws of the republic, provided somewhat generous and broad rights to the Turkish minority in communal matters and an absolute veto on any important governmental legislation.

[22]J. K. Gordon, "The U.N. in Cyprus," *International Journal* (Toronto) (3) (Summer 1964), 336–347.

[23]U.N. Doc. S/5488 (December 26, 1963).

[24]For details see, "U.N. Peace-Keeping Force in Cyprus," *United Nations Review*, 11 (4) (April 1964), 6.

[25]U.N. Doc S/5543 (February 15, 1964).

danger of Turkish aggression against his republic.[26] The Council met on February 17 to review the entire situation in Cyprus.[27] By this time the intensity of terror and bloodshed was so high that there was a real danger of Turkish intervention in support of Turkish Cypriots. There was some consensus in the Council on at least two points at this time: that some sort of United Nations force should be dispatched to the island to stop the bloodshed and that some mediator should be appointed to help the involved parties reach a negotiated settlement of their differences. But beyond this point there were conflicting positions taken by various members of the Council. At this time, in fact, the British were still arguing in favor of a NATO force under a United Nations umbrella to be sent to Cyprus. They also had the American support in their favor. The Cyprus Government did not want to have anything to do with a NATO force, which it felt, and perhaps quite correctly, would impose a settlement upon the Greek Cypriot majority—a settlement basically favorable to the Turkish Cypriot minority. It was, however, too late for the British and American suggestion to materialize, for a consensus seemed possible only on a 100 percent international force of the UNEF and ONUC type.

There were other strong differences among the Council membership. For instance, a clash developed on the validity and significance of the Treaty of Guarantee. This brought the Americans and the British in conflict with the Russians. The Soviet position was simple. It argued that no treaty signed by several states can deprive a sovereign nation of its right to ask the United Nations for protection from an outside threat to its territorial integrity. The British tried with little conviction to sidetrack the issue of threat by saying that this Treaty provides sufficient protection to the Republic from outside intervention. The United States, in its desire to support its ally against the Soviets, argued poorly that no treaty could be abrogated, nullified, or modified by the Security Council unless all the signatories agreed. Obviously, the Russians were not suggesting anything related to the abrogation of the Treaty at all. Their argument was a simple one and a strong one, which later forced the British and Americans to change their position. After much debate the Council was able to break up the deadlock and on the initiative of six nonpermanent members (Bolivia, Brazil, Czechoslovakia, Ivory Coast, Morocco, and Norway), on March 4, 1965 voted unanimously to adopt a resolution setting up the United Nations Force in Cyprus (UNFICYP).[28]

Notice, however, that despite a unanimous vote on the resolution, the

[26]U.N. Doc. S/5545 (February 15, 1964).

[27]Security Council *Official Records*, 19th year, 1095th-1102nd Meetings (February 18–March 4, 1964).

[28]Security Council Resolution 186 (1964) (March 4, 1964) U.N. Doc. S/5575.

Soviet Union and several other states still had some reservations concerning certain procedural aspects of the United Nations peace-keeping operation in Cyprus.[29] The critical issues were apparently taken care of in the clauses in the Preamble. These two clauses were:

> *Considering* the positions taken by the parties in relation to the Treaties signed at Nicosia on 16 August 1960; *Having in mind* the relevant provisions of the Charter of the United Nations and its Article 2, paragraph 4, which reads: "All Members shall refrain in their territorial relations from the threat of use of force against the territorial integrity or political independence of any State, or in any other manner inconsistent with the purpose of the United Nations. . . ."

Powers of the Secretary-General

The resolution, providing a go-ahead signal for the creation of the Force for three months, gave broad powers to the Secretary-General. He was given the sole responsibility for establishing the Force, for selecting its military commander, for issuing specific operational instructions to the United Nations Force in Cyprus (UNFICYP), and for submitting periodical reports of progress to the member states contributing troops and to the Security Council itself. Once more, in an area where counsels were divided on the role of the force, and they would easily become more divided, the way out was found by giving a greater degree of responsibility to the International Executive. Not all members of the Council were satisfied; for instance, France, the Soviet Union, and Czechoslovakia wanted the Council to direct the Force itself and the Force to be directly responsible to the Council, but an increased authority to the Secretary-General U Thant was the only compromise that seemed possible at the time.

The Secretary-General was also given the freedom to determine the size and the composition of the UNFICYP, in consultation with, of course, the governments of the United Kingdom, Cyprus, Turkey, and Greece. He also had the freedom to accept any voluntary contributions made by any member state toward financing the UNFICYP.[30] He was also authorized by the Security Council to name a mediator, in consultation with the guarantor powers and Cyprus, to help promote a peaceful solu-

---

[29]These reservations became apparent when the Soviet Union requested a separate vote on paragraph 4 (the main operative paragraph establishing the Force) and on which the Soviets, French and the Czechs abstained.

[30]In view of the past financial difficulties of peacekeeping operations, the voluntary method of financing was the only method to which all the members of the Council could agree. For details on the debate of finances for the UNFICYP, see *Security Council Official Records,* 19th year, 1095th-1103rd Meetings (February 18–March 13, 1964). See also U.N. Doc. S/5764 and Add. 1 (June 15, 1964).

tion and mutual settlement of the disputes between the two ethnic groups in Cyprus.[31] As a result of these broad powers U Thant was able to anticipate the needs of the Force, and the machinery to create the Force was set in motion almost immediately. Only two days after the passage of the resolution he informed the Council that a goal of 7000 troops had been set up for the UNFICYP and the discussions with the potential contributing states were in progress.[32] Despite the difficulties of conducting extensive and detailed negotiations with the contributing states and despite the reservations of some states with regard to the feasibility of voluntary method of financing the Force, the Canadian and British troops of the UNFICYP became operational in Cyprus on March 27, 1964. They were joined by the advanced troops of Swedish and Finnish contingents the following day and by April 30, 1964 the UNFICYP had a strength of over 6000 troops from seven different countries.[33] Early in the process of force buildup the Secretary-General was able to conclude agreements with the Cyprus government concerning the status of the Force.[34] This minimized the possible misunderstandings that existed during the operations of UNEF and ONUC with the Egyptian and the Congolese Governments.

In fulfilling his broad functions, the Secretary-General in the early stages of the operation also prepared and circulated to the states concerned an aide-memoire providing general guidelines for the conduct of the Force. He outlined the manner in which UNFICYP would accomplish its objectives: (1) to prevent the recurrence of fighting, contribute to the maintenance and restoration of order, and to contribute to a return to normal conditions; and (2) to assist in achieving a long-term settlement that would contribute to the maintenance of international peace and security.[35] These guiding principles clarified the role of the Force and the authorities of the Secretary-General in this regard for all interested parties in the Council or elsewhere.

On the basis of a report submitted by the UNFICYP Commander in Cyprus, after the incident of St. Hilarion Castle, the Secretary-General further exhibited his broad powers by assigning the Force a more active role and by notifying the Council that he was going to institute a 10-point program for the restoration of order on the Island.[36] He also appointed one

[31]See the March 4, 1964 Council Resolution, U.N. Doc. S/5575. It may be noted that U Thant appointed Finnish Ambassador Tromioja as the U.N. mediator to Cyprus. See U.N. Doc. S/5625 and Corr. 1 (March 26, 1964).

[32]See U.N. Doc. S/5579 (March 6, 1964).

[33]See U.N. Doc. S/5679 (May 2, 1964), 1.

[34]U.N. Doc. S/5634 (March 31, 1964).

[35]U.N. Doc. S/5653 (April 11, 1964).

[36]Here are the 10 specific goals that the Secretary-General sought: (1) the achievement of freedom of movement on all roads in Cyprus; (2) the achievement of

of his top-level political officers to work closely with the Force Commander and the local communities to negotiate agreements between them.[37]

To relieve the anxiety of those member states who contributed troops to the UNFICYP, with regard to the nature of the specific task of the Force in Cyprus, the Secretary-General issued them copies of the above 10 points and also communicated them to the Force Commander for his guidance. But beyond communication of these 10 points to the contributing states he made it very clear to them that:

> It was not his intention to negotiate instructions which he proposed to issue to the Commander with any Government either directly concerned in the situation of or contributing contingents to the Force. . . .[38]

Turning to the question of raising money for the operation, U Thant estimated a cost of $6 million for the first three-month operation. Because of the earlier intense controversies among the members on the question of peacekeeping finances, the Secretary-General was given broad powers to solicit voluntary contributions. On the basis of this authorization, he was able to get the United States to pledge $2 million; Great Britain, $1 million; Greece and West Germany, $500,000 each; Italy, $250,000; Australia, 112,000; Belgium, the Netherlands, and Turkey, $100,000 each; Denmark and Switzerland $75,000; Norway, $50,000; New Zealand, $42,000; and Luxemburg, $5,000. These were the contributions pledged initially as of April 1964.[39]

Despite the encouraging report made by the Secretary-General on the

---

freedom of movement for all communities in Nicosia and other cities; (3) progressive evacuation and removal of all fortified positions with priority for Nicosia; (4) examination of the problems arising from the division of the Cyprus police between the Turkish Cypriot and the Greek Cyproit members, and negotiation for their progressive reintegration; (5) the progressive disarming of all civilians other than the regular police gendarmerie and the Cyprus army, by the Cyprus government and the Turkish community. UNFICYP, as requested, would assist in facilitating and verifying the disarming and storage of arms under conditions of security; (6) the control of extremists on both sides; (7) the formulation of appropriate general amnesty arrangements; (8) the arrangement of security measures and other conditions to facilitate the return to normal conditions and particularly economic activity; (9) the facilitation of the return of the Turkish Cypriot civil servants and government officials to their duties, including public services such as the postal service, telecommunications, and public works; and (10) the normal functioning of the Judiciary. See U.N. Doc. S/5671 (April 29, 1964) Annex 1.

[37] See U.N. Doc S/5691 (May 11, 1964).

[38] For details see, U.N. Office of the Public Information Note No. 2917 (March 17, 1964).

[39] See Rosalyn Higgins "Basic Facts on the U.N. Force in Cyprus," *The World Today* (August 1965), 347–350.

general situation in Cyprus on September 10, 1964, the conditions were still far from good, especially when viewed from the point of view of the March 4, 1964 resolution.[40] There was a great gap between the beliefs of the two communities concerning what, for instance, constituted the "return to normal conditions," as the UNFICYP mandate specified. The Turkish Cypriots argued that the Force was duty bound to restore constitutional supremacy to the governing of the island, by force of arms if necessary. The majority view of the Greek Cypriots held that the constitution was not at all acceptable without revision and they would fight to prevent a return to the preconflict legal order. As the fundamental differences between the two groups remained unresolved, the Secretary-General once again took the initiative and declared that he would not accept either of these positions. He further argued that the Council never intended to establish the Force as an arm of the Cyprus Government, and he was going to make every effort to maintain objectivity, fairness, and justice, by relying on his own independent judgment. Note that during the early months of its operation, the major effort of the UNFICYP was to eliminate hardships imposed by the Cyprus government on its Turkish communities by imposing numerous economic sanctions and restrictions.

With the date of the expiration of UNFICYP'S three-month mandate approaching, the Secretary-General recommended to the Council a further three-month extension of the Force. He also informed the Council that it had been suggested that a further clarification was needed on the Force mandate, and he had decided to proceed on the assumption that (1) the Council intended the force to have "complete freedom of movement"; (2) to prevent fighting, the force is entitled to remove positions and fortified installations where these endanger peace, and may take all necessary measures in self-defense if attacked in performance of this duty; and (3) the force commander may demand separation of opposing armed forces at reasonable distances to create buffer zones in which the armed forces are prohibited. The entire membership of the Council accepted his proposal without any objections. There were three extensions of the Force later on.[41]

In conclusion, the dynamic role played by the Secretary-General in establishing and dealing with the various aspects of the UNFICYP was extremely significant and even authoritative at times. Furthermore the wide differences between the conflicting parties on the one hand and the interested parties on the other made it possible for the Secretary-General to exercise a great deal of discretion in the Cyprus crisis. Suspicion of each

[40]See U.N. Security Council, S/5950, p. 62.
[41]U.N. Security Council, S/6102 (December 12, 1964).

other's motives among the various parties forced them to compromise by giving greater power to the Chief Executive who possessed a certain amount of their confidence.

case study 3

The United Nations and the Crisis in Lebanon: Law Observance Through the Role of the Secretary-General

Background to the United Nations involvement in Lebanon

During the spring of 1958 when it became clear that the pro-Western President Camille Chamoun of Lebanon might attempt to change the national constitution to allow himself to run for the second six-year term as the president of the country, the opposition elements became alarmed, and it was suggested that they demand his resignation. But when a newspaper publisher, who had been critical of Chamoun's negative attitude toward the United Arab Republic and President Nasser, was assassinated, riots and fighting broke out in Tripoli between the pro- and anti-Chamoun elements. In only a few days the entire country was involved in civil strife. The opposition was now demanding President Chamoun's resignation. Throughout May the situation deteriorated rapidly. When it became clear that the Government of President Chamoun might be forced out of office by mounting opposition, the Government officially charged the United Arab Republic with training the rebellious elements in Lebanon and providing them with military weapons, supplies, and moral support. With this accusation, Lebanon brought the matter to the attention of the Security Council.[42]

In response to the Lebanese request the Council met briefly to hear Lebanese charges, but it postponed any substantial discussion of them to provide the Arab League with an opportunity to solve the conflict on a regional basis. The League met four times and finally produced a compromise draft resolution that was acceptable to the United Arab Republic and Lebanese representatives; it was sponsored by countries such as Libya,

[42]Note that on May 22, 1958 a letter was presented to the President of the Security Council by the Lebanese representative asking him to convene an urgent meeting of the Council to consider Lebanese complaints against the United Arab Republic. The essence of the complaint was that the United Arab Republic had been intervening in the internal affairs of Lebanon and if it was not stopped the situation was Likely to endanger international peace and security. For details, see U.N. Doc. S/4007 (May 22, 1958).

Sudan, Saudi Arabia, Iraq, Jordan, and later Yemen. But just before it was scheduled to be signed, the Lebanese government rejected the resolution without much explanation.[43] The more popular speculation of the reasons behind Chamoun's rejection of the resolution has been that Chamoun wanted to stay in office at almost any cost. He was not so much interested in solving the conflict with his number one enemy Nessar but, rather, in internationalizing the crisis through United Nations involvement. A solution provided by the League was simply not significant enough. A United Nations involvement, President Chamoun thought, would provide him with an opportunity to continue in office behind the cloak of a kind of national emergency.

United Nations involvement and differences between the interested parties

When the Arab League failed to settle the dispute, the Council met again on June 6 to pursue the matter further. This time the Lebanese representative made these formal charges against the United Arab Republic.

1. There has been and there still is massive, illegal, and unprovoked intervention in the affairs of Lebanon by the United Arab Republic.

2. This intervention aims at undermining and in fact threatens the independence of Lebanon.

3. The situation created by this intervention that threatens the independence of Lebanon is likely, if continued, to endanger the maintenance of international peace and security.

The Lebanese delegate further asserted that these charges were based on six facts.

1. The supply of arms on a large scale from the United Arab Republic to subversive elements in Lebanon.

2. The training in subversion on the United Arab Republic territory of elements from Lebanon and the return of these elements to Lebanon to subvert the Government.

3. The participation in subversive and terrorist activities in Lebanon by United Arab Republic civilian nationals residing in or passing into Lebanon.

4. The participation of United Arab Republic governmental elements in subversive and terrorist activities and in the direction of rebellion in Lebanon.

5. The violent and utterly unprecedented press campaign conducted by the United Arab Republic against the Government of Lebanon.

[43]U.N. Security Council, *Official Records*, Thirteenth Year, 823rd Meeting (June 6, 1958), p. 24.

6. The violent radio campaign conducted by the United Arab Republic against Lebanon.[44]

The United Arab Republic argued that the Lebanese charges were false and were drummed up by President Chamoun to create an air of emergency in his country that would justify his staying in power beyond his term of office for the sake of national interest. Failing to do that, he had then attempted to internationalize a domestic conflict to enlist international support.[45] The Council meeting was marred by charges and countercharges between the two nations. Finally, the Council became divided, so that no action seemed possible. The United States, the United Kingdom, France, and China supported the Lebanese charges. Iraq also joined in support of Lebanon. The Soviet Union supported the United Arab Republic and argued that the United Nations should not get involved in a domestic conflict. The Soviets further charged that Lebanese complaints were drummed up to prepare the way for a direct intervention by the Western powers.[46] With the American troops landing in Lebanon later on, the Soviet fears seem to be borne out.

The position of other Council Members—Canada, Columbia, Japan, Panama and Sweden—can be described as neutral. Finally, when it became apparent that the Council was deadlocked, the Swedish delegate presented a compromise draft resolution, giving a great deal of authority to the Secretary-General in solving the crisis. The content of the draft was vague and broad. It simply reflected the Council's concern for the continued independence of Lebanon, without implying that the Council had made a decision that the Lebanese charges were necessarily valid. The draft resolution further called for the dispatch of an observation group to Lebanon to "ensure that there is no illegal infiltration of personnel or supply of arms or material across the Lebanese borders." It farther authorized the Secretary-General "to take the necessary steps to that end" and direct "the observation group to keep the Security Council currently informed through the Secretary-General."[47]

The draft resolution was accepted by both the United Arab Republic and Lebanese delegates and subsequently adopted by the Council with a 10 to 1 vote; the Soviet Union abstained.[48] In explaining his abstention

---

[44]For further details on the Lebanese charges see Security Council *Official Records*, Thirteenth Year, 823rd meeting (June 6, 1958), 3–4.

[45]*Ibid.*, p. 32.

[46]U.N. Security Council, *Official Records*, Thirteenth Year, 824th Meeting (June 10, 1958).

[47]For details of the Swedish draft resolution see, U.N. Doc. S/4023, (June 11, 1958).

[48]See U.N. Doc. S/4022 (June 11, 1958).

the Soviet delegate made it quite clear that in his opinion it was a mistake for the United Nations to get involved in the domestic affairs of Lebanon even if the Lebanese government wanted it, and that the only reason he did not veto the resolution was because neither of the two parties objected to it.[49]

Powers of the Secretary-General

As pointed out earlier, the resolution adopted was a compromise resolution and, consequently, an extremely short and a vague one. It left all the responsibility of specific action to the Secretary-General, and provided him with a great deal of authority for the general conduct, mandate, and the operation of the United Nations Observation Group in Lebanon (UNOGIL). Its vagueness was intended to make it acceptable to all of the conflicting parties. This meant that it was open to several interpretations. Particularly, at the time of the American troop landing in Lebanon, there was a great danger that the mandate of the UNOGIL may be misunderstood and confused with the purposes of the United States adventure in that country. It was the Secretary-General who took the initiative during the first meeting of the Security Council since the passage of the June 11 resolution and made it very clear to the Council membership as to how he proposed to interpret the resolution. In general, he took the narrow interpretation of the resolution contending:

> The Security Council, in deciding to dispatch to Lebanon "an observation group," defined not only the character of the operation but also its scope. It did so by linking the observation to illegal traffic in arms and infiltration. . . . In taking this stand, the Council defined the limits for authority delegated to the Secretary-General in this case.[50]

There is, however, very little doubt that had the Secretary-General wanted to broaden the UNOGIL's functions he could have done so by virtue of an entirely different interpretation. His decision to interpret the resolution narrowly was predicated on his conviction, as he later explained it, that because of the situation in Lebanon it was not possible to interpose a United Nations force between the conflicting groups without letting the force become a party to internal conflicts among the nationals of Lebanon.[51] As the conflict developed further in that country, it became

[49]See Security Council *Official Records*, Thirteenth Year, 825th Meeting (June 11, 1958), 17–18.

[50]See Security Council *Official Records*, Thirteenth Year, 825th Meeting (June 11, 1958), 17–18.

[51]See U.N. Doc. A/3943, para. 151.

apparent that the Secretary-General was right. Implicit in the Secretary-General's decision to restrict the UNOGIL to strictly "observation" duties was his desire that the United Nations should not be party to any coercive action that might force it to make judgments on the rights and wrongs of the various issues that were purely domestic in nature. Consequently, UNOGIL restricted its operation only to take "all steps necessary for an operation, covering illegal traffic in arms infiltration, as effective as it could be made as a tool towards ensuring against such traffic or infiltration with its basic character of observation maintained."[52] The interpretation expressed by Hammarskjöld was consistently reflected in almost all the reports the UNOGIL made to the Security Council.[53]

There were other areas of the resolution where the Secretary-General had a great deal of freedom of interpretation. For instance, he had the freedom to expand the Observation Group without asking for an additional mandate from the Council. United Nations records show that in this respect Hammarskjöld broadly interpreted not only the resolution, but also cut his own powers. Speaking before the Council on July 15, he clearly stated that UNOGIL "has and will have as many observers as it has asked or might ask for." In fact, he told the Security Council that his decision on "the size, scope or mandate of the Observation Group" was determined "exclusively by the attitude taken by the Group itself."[54] As the situation in Lebanon grew worse with the passage of time, President Chamoun, still holding on to his office, called for direct military intervention by the United States, which the Americans, of course, were happy to provide. It was in the American national interest to help bolster the political fortunes of a man who had been strongly pro-American in the past. The American troops landings divided the Americans and Russians in the Council even more. As the Security Council convened on July 21, both the Soviet Union and the United States submitted rival draft resolutions. The Soviet draft resolution called for the withdrawal of American troops immediately,[55] while the American draft resolution called for the dispatch of United Nations military units to that country.[56] Both resolutions failed to get the necessary votes, and once again it appeared that the Secretary-General was to be given still broader powers to implement a settlement of the crisis at his own initiative. A draft resolution, sponsored by Japan, stated in part that the Secretary-General should be re-

[52]*Ibid.*, para. 63.

[53]See especially, First Report of UNOGIL (U.N. Doc. 4040), para 11 and also the Fifth Report of UNOGIL (U.N. Doc. S/4114), para. 26.

[54]Security Council *Official Records*, Thirteenth Year, 827th Meeting, July 15, 1958, p. 13.

[55]U.N. Doc. S/4047/Rev. 1.

[56]U.N. Doc. S/4050/Rev. 1.

quested to take any measures that he deemed necessary, in addition to those envisaged in the first resolution, to:

> fulfill the general purposes established in that resolution [of June 11], and which will, in accordance with the Charter of the United Nations, serve to ensure the territorial integrity and political independence of Lebanon, so as to make possible the withdrawal of United States forces from Lebanon.[57]

On the request of the Canadian delegate, Hammarskjöld explained that should the Council decide to approve the Japanese draft resolution, he would take immediate steps to strengthen the Observation Group so that it "could adequately do the job of ensuring against infiltration and the smuggling of arms." The Group was to be expanded to the maximum capacity rendered possible in the circumstances.[58] The Japanese draft resolution was vetoed by the Soviet Union after an unsuccessful attempt to amend it to require the immediate withdrawal of the American troops. Note that the draft resolution was not defeated because it gave more freedom of action to the Secretary-General. Following its defeat, Hammarskjöld reminded the Council that since it had failed to take action in an emergency situation, the responsibility of the United Nations under the Charter, to make all efforts to live up to its principles remain and, consequently, he would take whatever steps were necessary without any guidance from the Assembly or the Council to "fill any vacuum that may appear in the systems which the Charter and traditional diplomacy provide for the safeguarding of peace and security."[59] It can be concluded here that by this declaration of intention the Secretary-General took a great deal more responsibility upon himself. In fact, he extended his area of discretion with regard to this particular peacekeeping operation even farther than the Japanese were proposing in their draft resolution. Nobody in the Council, not even the Russians, challenged the Secretary-General's decision to assume greater powers. The strengthening of the UNOGIL was subsequently carried out as seen fit by the Secretary-General himself.

Right after the passage of the first resolution establishing UNOGIL, the Secretary-General immediately went to work to organize the Group. He initially borrowed several observers from the United Nations Truce Supervision Organization (UNTSO), and only two days after the passage

---

[57]U.N. Doc. S/4055/Rev. 1.

[58]Security Council *Official Records*, Thirteenth Year, 835th Meeting (July 21, 1958), 17.

[59]Security Council *Official Records*, Thirteenth Year, 837th Meeting (July 22, 1958), 3.

of the resolution, United Nations military observers were conducting the reconnaissance work. Almost immediately, the Secretary-General also took the initiative to outline the methods of operation that UNOGIL followed.[60] By September 20, regular military headquarters were in operation in Lebanon to coordinate and conduct the operations of the Group. By November, the UNOGIL's maximum strength had been reached.

The Secretary-General also took the initiative in concluding an agreement with the Lebanese Government on the status of immunities of UNOGIL in Lebanon. He invited representatives of Brazil, Canada, Ceylon, Columbia, India, Norway, and Pakistan to accept the membership in an Advisory Group that he created for consultations. When the Americans militarily intervened in Lebanon, he told the Security Council that the landing of United States troops and their international repercussions are irrelevant as far as the mandate of UNOGIL is concerned. Despite a great deal of pressure from some quarters, especially from Lebanon, he refused to change the character of the observation group to one of a police force.[61]

In conclusion, the above brief analysis of the major aspects of the Secretary-General's role in the Lebanon crisis again indicates that in those conflicts where there is a great deal of disagreement among United Nations membership, a way out is usually found by giving greater powers to the Secretary-General. This was the case in Lebanon.

[60]The methods of the operation were as follows: (1) all accessible roads were patrolled regularly and frequently from dawn to dusk, primarily in border districts and in the areas adjacent to the zones held by opposition forces. The observers traveled in white jeeps with United Nations markings that were equipped with two-way radio sets. (2) Permanent observation posts were set up where groups of military observers were stationed. These posts were in continuous radio communication with headquarters in Beirut, with each other, and with the patrols. (3) An emergency reserve of experienced military observers was formed at headquarters and at the main observation posts. The observers were available for making inquiries on short notice or could be detailed to places where instances of smuggling of arms might be reported. (4) An evaluation team was set up at headquarters composed of specialized observer personnel with responsibility for analyzing, evaluating, and coordinating the information received from observers and other sources. (5) Observation by helicopters and planes was established. These planes and helicopters were outfitted with aerial photography devices and radio sets to enable them to communicate with headquarters and military observers in the field. (6) A procedure was established to use the information that the Lebanese Government might secure regarding suspected infiltration. See U.N. Security Council, S/4040 (July 3, 1958).

[61]See U.N. Security Council, *Official Records*, Thirteenth Year, 82nd Meeting (July 15, 1958), para. 36.

A concluding remark

Inferences may be drawn from the preceding three case studies. The first case study attempts to establish the relationship between a nation's important interests, their satisfaction by the forces of international law and order (the United Nations peacekeeping mission), and the support of these forces by this nation. There seems to be little doubt that in the Congo crisis the United States was on the side of the forces of international law for reasons that definitely included the satisfaction of American national interests. How else can we explain the persistant American support of the United Nations mission in this central African country?

Concerning the case studies of Cyprus and Lebanon, similar conclusions emerge, although in a somewhat different way. Apart from the satisfaction of national interest as a measure of international law observance, the exceedingly important role played by the Secretary-General in the *divided* councils of the United Nations during international crises and, more importantly, the predisposition of the states to allow him to play this role is an indication of the states' trust in him and in the role of international law as a last resort.

chapter 13
why nations violate
international law

The general observance of both classic and current international law does not preclude the fact that all nations have violated the law at one time or another, and will probably violate it again in select situations. The observance of law is usually a rational choice and has advantages that may not be clearly understood during an international crisis. But states are *not always known to act rationally* or to their *best advantage.* This is partly true because of the nature of the international system in which a good deal of foreign policy, as indicated earlier, is a by-product of the many pressures and cross-pressures that are put on decision makers. These pressures may not always give the leader much of an opportunity to act with proper deliberation and from a careful calculation of the costs and rewards involved in following one alternative as against another. There are also instances when nations are drawn into unexpected positions, resulting in involuntary law violations; or law violations on the basis of "no choice available." Moreover, there are always cases where international law was violated *incidentally* because it conflicted with an extremely important foreign policy goal. In such cases a foreign policymaker is aware of the law violation, but deliberation on the "legal aspect" of the policy in either minimized or simply preempted by an overwhelming concern with the goal itself. Occasionally, an international legal norm might be violated because of a *genuine uncertainty* on the specific applicability of law in a specific situation. More frequently, laws are violated because their *norms are susceptible to multiple interpretations* and because the legal advisors of foreign offices' have the ability to make a "legal case" in most law-violation situations, knowing fully well the faulty reasoning involved but nonetheless insisting that the law is being "observed."

In this chapter, however, we are more urgently concerned with deliberate international law violations, where time for reflection was available to the policymaker, and where apparently (on the basis of circumstantial evidence) a decision to violate the law was made after explicit weighing of all relevant considerations. In such circumstances a nation chooses to violate the law because the cost of observing the law appears to be too high and the cost of law violation temptingly low. The cost-reward weighing by the policymaker may be, on the one hand, based on this kind of reasoning: "Oh, well, the law will probably never be enforced; most countries have broken this law, why should not we; chances are there will be no widespread consequences, etc." On the other hand, this reasoning may be influenced by strong domestic forces of public opinion or special interest groups, pressing for law violation and thus making it easy for the leadership to violate the law. After all, public support, however manipulated or extracted by providing less than completely true information on an international issue, is gratifying to a leader, because it provides an air of legitimacy to his otherwise lawless behavior in an international crisis. The leadership in democracies where public opinion is held in a relatively higher esteem is particularly susceptible to this folly.

Advantages of lawless behavior

In those situations where international law and dictates of national interests do not coincide perfectly, a state is always under some temptation to act illegally because international law, by its very definition, attempts to constrain state behavior by restricting the choices available to it. Sometimes the temptation is too great to overcome and thus the legal norms, other agreements, or treaties, for example, may be deliberately violated because a state expects to gain some advantages, and because, after careful consideration, a state has already decided that the advantages outweigh the cost of law violation. There are instances, of course, when a state makes an error in its judgment as a result of faulty information concerning the reaction of the "other side," or the world community in general. In other words, it may overestimate the benefits it expects to derive from its lawless behavior, or the benefits simply may turn out to be unattainable or unretainable for any appreciable length of time.[1]

Obviously, as any student of politics will readily point out, there are many advantages to armed aggression in violation of international law, that is, if a nation is sure of victory. By committing aggression a nation

[1]A few examples of "lawlessness does not pay" are the Anglo-French invasion of Egypt in 1956. It resulted in no particular advantage to England and France. After losing face in the world, both countries were obligated to withdraw from the Suez area. Another example is the American involvement in Vietnam, which has brought no honor to the United States at home and abroad and no real advantages that can be readily observed. Still another example is the illegal nationalization of Anglo-Iranian Oil Company by the Iranian government, where for some time after the law violation Iran was not able to market the oil.

may hope to attain the classic gains of territory, wealth, greater security, more resources, prestige, power, and influence, in world affairs. On the other hand, it may be interested in contemporary goals that are frequently couched in the language of "reasonableness," such as: "All we want is North Vietnam to leave South Vietnam alone," said President Lyndon B. Johnson as he escalated the war after the passage of the Gulf of Tonkin resolution in the United States Congress in 1964. Or, "Pakistan can make a contribution to peace in the sub-continent by withdrawing its troops from 'Bengla Desh,'" said Mrs. Gandhi in India, as the lady prepared to order her armed forces into East Pakistan and subsequently succeeded in dismembering an old foe.

An armed aggression has other secondary advantages. It may provide an attacker with a battleground for the testing of its latest weapons on live targets. It may provide a justification of sorts for the high expenditures for new armaments that it has been incurring for "defense." Moreover, there are some who have pointed out rather eloquently that possession of material resources for developing new weapons and an ever-renewed commitment of these resources to a continued arms buildup not only makes armed aggression a physical possibility, but it also figures significantly among the factors that make war a political probability. To put it simply, a commitment to develop and possess an ever-growing variety of newer weapons produces trigger-happiness. Armed aggression may provide professional soldiers with the psychological gratification that they may badly need to justify their professional existence and their role in life, especially during times of peace. For example, an aggression may be committed simply to gratify the ego of a leader who is determined to "punish" an adversary at all costs for its "alleged" crimes against a friendly nation, or he may be interested in "bombing the enemy back to the conference table."

There are other forms of international law violations that fall short of armed aggression. For instance, a state may deliberately violate international law by using illegal modes of gathering intelligence concerning a potential enemy's state of preparedness or intentions to make war. For example, it may conduct reconnaissance flights over another nation's territorial airspace and then publicly defend this illegal act in the name of national security, as President Eisenhower did in the case of F. Gary Power's U-2 flight over the Soviet Union where he was shot down. By unlawful seizure of foreign property, popularly called "nationaliaztion," a state may improve its economic conditions, or "prove" to itself and to its people that "we are masters of our own destiny." In some instances, however, there may be a real opportunity to use the funds thus obtained to invest in developmental projects, *if* development was indeed the main reason behind the nationalization of foreign property. Usually, however, the so-called naionalizations have turned out to be purely symbolic acts for a nation's gratification and as such no substantial economic benefits have resulted for the general population. Nonetheless, these are powerful temptations to violate the norms of international law. Violation of the provisions of a treaty can be very gratifying if it was an "unequal" treaty or if it was a treaty signed by a leadership that was violently overthrown by popular will. In such a circumstance the violation itself is viewed not as an "illegal" act but as an act of exercising for example, political sovereignty, fair-mindedness, and equality.

We have just given a few of the more obvious, immediate, and visible examples of advantages that a state may acquire through law violations. Against such advantages, the cost of law violation is not always clearly perceived, and even when a decision maker is able to assess it, he may disregard it as insufficient or indecisive. The many advantages of law observance that are available for the states to enjoy tend frequently to be long term, slow in coming, and sometimes difficult to measure in terms of specific gains. The so-called hard-boiled "realist" (not necessarily an advocate of unlawful behavior by his government) generally found in key positions in foreign offices finds it hard to accept the difficulties involved in demonstrating national advantages to upholding legal norms, *especially* when the "other" side may not be showing much regard for law observance in a conflict situation.

When getting ready to commit deliberately a law violation, a national leader may rationalize his act as follows: "Well, order, stability, and predictability are nice objectives that international law pursues, and I am for them all the way. But I need more immediate and more tangible results to show my people that I am not a softy, and to show to my adversary that I mean business. Besides, just how much order is there anyhow? Will one more violation really jeopardize it? The whole world knows our record of law observance is better than any other country anyway. However, what I am going to do is not all that illegal. Let us ask our law experts if they can figure out a way to make it legally look good." In the contemporary international system where the supremacy of politics frequently prevails over other considerations, such traditional concerns as honor, statesmanship, personal honesty, and gentlemen's agreements in upholding international law or a duty to act legally when a strong national interest suggests taking the other route, may be regarded as unpatriotic and may get a leader in deep trouble.

The cost of a law violation may be further played down by a nation that no longer considers its moral duty to uphold the law. In the absence of a moral obligation the case for law observance is damaged somewhat, although it is difficult to pinpoint or measure what role moral norms play in the observation of legal norms. What is being implied here is that when a decision maker accepts the proposition that law violations are not necessarily immoral, the private ethics of the decision maker himself can be easily put to rest under the conclusion, "I have no right to sacrifice my country's national interest to my private ethics." A particular law violation may in fact appear "just" or "moral," when viewed in the context of the development or relevance of that specific law. A nation that has recently acquired its independence from a foreign rule may find an international legal norm unjust, unfair, or outdated and thus may consider that it has a sacred duty to disregard that law. In such a circumstance, it may find it easier to dismiss world public opinion as prejudiced or irrelevant and, according to some points of view, it may in fact enhance its prestige, forcefulness, and decisiveness through law violation; for example, Egypt's nationalization of Suez Canal was hailed by many poor countries as an act of courage and forcefulness.

These reasons and arguments reflect some of the common attitudes of decision makers in most countries, even in democracies. They help to explain why nations find it advantageous to violate international law. They further help us to understand why the broad advantages of being lawful are not always clear to policymakers in all situations and, therefore, law fails to prevail. Even given the clarity of advantages, law observance may not follow, because in some cases the advantages may be very minimal or practically nonexistent. In the contemporary international system the spokesmen for the creation of a lawful world have an obligation to measure their interest against many other interests available in the international arena that run counter to the notion of a lawful world or are simply thought to be more urgent. It is true, for instance, that after the Second World War there was a strong interest in abolishing war and creating a more lawful world, and a promise was made to the present generation for more law and order but never kept.[2] But, at that time there were other strong, persuasive interests too, some of them clearly more persuasive than the interest in a more lawful world, at least for those states who espoused them. For example, for the nations of Africa and Asia the goal with the highest priority was the achievement of independence from colonialism. For nations of Western Europe, with their economies shattered by the war, just as strong, if not stronger, was the interest in a rapid economic recovery. For the Soviet Union, it was a unique opportunity to broaden its influence in Eastern Europe, subscribe to the spread of Communism, and consolidate its gains by developing what later came to be known as a "Communist bloc" of nations, dominated by the Soviet

[2]See the eloquent remarks on this broken promise, made by Stanley Hoffmann in "introduction" in L. Scheinman and David Wilkinson (eds.), *International Law and Political Crises—An Analytical Casebook*, (Boston: Little, Brown), 1968, pp. xviii–xix.

Union. For the United States, there were too many other concerns born out of its sudden and generally unsought-after thrust to the leadership of the free world. To be sure, none of these American concerns ran counter to the notion of a lawful world but in retrospect, some of them can be said to have a higher priority for the United States, for example, the recovery of Western Europe, the commitment to decolonization and, within a few years after the war, a strong commitment to contain the spread of Communism. The United States also had a general desire to prove to itself and to the rest of the world that it could successfully meet the challenge to its leadership in any field that was created by the emergence of the Soviet Union to prominence.

Even today, not all nations are equally committed to the notion of a lawful world. If some states have a special interest in the observance of law as it stands today, others may have very little, for several reasons; for example, they may be interested in changing the status quo for the purpose of creating a new legal order. If the United States and the Soviet Union may appear on one day determined to uphold the law in a particular instance because of strong domestic public opinion, on another day they might find themselves being congratulated for violating the law by the same public. The nature of the competition for world leadership between the Soviet Union and the United States and yet, at the same time, a strong desire to coexist if all else fails, may at times compel them to observe international law religiously, and disregard it completely on other occasions, as was true with Russia in Hungary in 1956 and with United States in the Dominican Republic in 1965. Fear of condemnation by world opinion, in the United Nations, and among friends apparently meant very little to the People's Republic of China when it illegally gobbled up Tibet and invaded India, to India when it gobbled up the States of Hydrabad, Junagarh, and Goa and later succeeded in dismembering Pakistan, to Pakistan when it let loose its armed forces on the insurgent civilian population in the Eastern province, to South Africa, and to Portugal. Other examples in this area are too numerous to cite.

Immediate and specific cost of law violation, if any, to be paid by a country may be further minimized, since the victim may lack powerful friends, or the violation may be so isolated and removed from world attention to invoke any significant public concern, or the victim may learn to live with it because it has no choice but to continue "friendly" relations with the law violator. On the other hand nations are no longer in a habit, if they ever were, to engage in armed conflict in flagrant violation of international law in response to *minor provocations*. There are many other instances in which they do not choose to violate law in the *first instant*, such as mistreating each other's private citizens and diplomats, by burning each other's embassies or by violating treaties, or by breaking up economic relations. One kind of law violation that is on the rise today and is considered to be a violation with supposedly high rewards and low costs *takes place quickly and accomplishes its goal in a relatively short period of time.* It presents a *fait accompli* before the international community has a chance to grasp the violation and reflect on it. Often it is difficult to undo the violation, because the purpose of the violation has been achieved and thus its advantages may be difficult to take away. There may be some condemnation of the action through one or more United Nations resolutions or through expressions of outrage by others, especially by those who were somehow affected adversely by the violation. The United Nations may invoke sanctions or take other enforcement measures. *But these measures in themselves do not automatically increase the cost of law violations,* as indicated by the case studies that follow, unless, of course, the United Nations intervention could result in the *success of its mission.* The cost of such a law violation could increase only if the violation is serious enough to lead to a war or to a significant escalation of an existing conflict. Circumstances that usually lead to this kind of violation are usually extraordinary and the violator, *after the fact,* whether he denies or admits the violation, in his statement generally implies good behavior in the future by emphasizing the uniqueness of the incident. A good example of this is the Israeli armed attack on the commercial airliners at the Beirut International Airport a few years ago.

In the remaining part of the chapter we shall answer some pertinent questions concerning the behavior of nation-states vis à vis international law, and provide detailed examples of law violations, some of which we have discussed thus far hypothetically. This task will be accomplished in analytical case studies. These cases are analytical accounts of political conflicts where international law and international politics met head on. An analysis of these cases may help us understand how international law is in fact employed in situations of political crises and to what effect? The main contribution of this part of the chapter, is to reveal the *actual practice* of law in the international system. Such a concern should help us balance the contributions of those standard textbooks that have usually conceded, as indicated earlier, either too much or, *a priori,* too little to the role of international law in its confrontations with international politics.

In the selection of these brief case studies, it was deliberately decided not to use a set of abstract judicial decisions. Instead, it was felt that some recent cases of international crisis situations, embedded in a historical context of the "coming of the crisis," may be useful for our purposes. In all of these case studies, as was true with the studies in the last chapter, the United Nations was involved in one way or the other. Once again the United Nations represented the forces of law and order and the states represented the political concerns based on their national interests. Unlike the situation in the last chapter, in the various conflicts here the temptation to violate legal norms by the states directly involved was *too great to resist*. In these cases, states involved were signitories to the United Nations Charter; they recognized the relevance of international law as well, but they were caught in a situation where they apparently felt strong national interests justified law violation. In some instances, they went as far as to accuse the United Nations or the "other" side of what they perceived to be law "violations" by them.

case study 1
The United Nations; the Soviet Union, and the Hungarian Crisis

Background to the United Nations involvement

The violence in Hungary was erupted when students, workers, and soldiers demonstrated against the much-feared and much-hated Hungarian Security Police (AVH) that opened fire on the seemingly unarmed demonstrators. The four days that followed the October 23, 1956 demonstrations saw the fighting increase in strength and momentum as it spread throughout the country. The Russians had already intervened in Budapest with tanks and machine guns, and by the time the Hungarian Premier ordered a general cease-fire, the ill-prepared demonstrators were being badly beaten back by the Soviets and the AVH. About the same time the United States, France, and the United Kingdom requested an emergency meeting of the Security Council charging that an outside power was ruthlessly suppressing the civil rights of the Hungarian people that were guaranteed by the Treaty of Peace signed by the Associated and Allied powers along with the Government of Hungary.[3] Despite the Hungarian protest and the Soviet negative vote, the Council decided on October 28 to put the question of Hungary on the agenda.[4] For a brief time it seemed that the Hungarians

---

[3]For details of American and French and British charges in the United Nations, see *United States Participation in the United Nations, Report by the President to the Congress for the Year 1956* (Washington, D.C.: Government Printing Office, 1957), p. 83.

[4]The vote was 9 to 1 with the Soviets voting against and the Yugoslavs abstaining. The essence of the Hungarian protest was that this is essentially a domestic conflict and, consequently, United Nations intervention is not called for.

were going to work out a settlement among themselves. Imre Nagy was installed as the new Premier of the country during the first two days of the conflict. By the end of October he was able to restore some measure of peace in the country by meeting many of the demands of the rebelling population that wanted a mixed government of both Communist and non-Communist leaders; a negotiated withdrawal of all Soviet troops from the Hungarian soil; an end of the one-party political system and the secret police; and so on. Briefly, it seemed the Russians were going to accede to these demands because they had begun to move out of Budapest.

About the same time the Anglo-French and Israeli invasion of Egypt started, and world attention shifted to the Middle East. About this time also the Russians returned to Hungary with a greater force, and by November 4 they were systematically attacking all the major cities in Hungary and any other place where they met resistance. The official Hungarian reaction to the Soviet move was almost immediate. Nagy's Government declared Hungary to be neutral in the East-West struggle and withdrew from the Warsaw Pact. It also appealed not only to the United Nations but also to the Western great powers to help Hungary defend its neutrality. An appeal was also made to the Council directly to instruct the Soviets and the Hungarians to start immediate negotiations on the Soviet troops withdrawal. An emergency Council meeting was called, the Americans attempted to push through a resolution calling for the withdrawal of Soviet troops and banning any further Soviet military intervention in Hungary. It was vetoed by the Soviets. It was proposed that the matter should be referred to the General Assembly under "Uniting for Peace" resolution. The Council approved it by a vote of 10 to 1. The Soviets voted against it.

United Nations involvement in the Hungarian crisis and the frustration of its missions

As soon as the Security Council referred the Hungarian question to the General Assembly under the "Uniting for Peace" resolution, it met almost immediately to consider the situation. This time the United States was able to get a resolution passed by the Assembly. The essence of the resolution was a call on the Soviet Union to stop attacking the Hungarian people and withdraw its armed forces from that country without delay; it also asked the Secretary-General to appoint his representatives to investigate the situation in Hungary with an intention to make recommendations to the General Assembly concerning the proper methods of eliminating foreign intervention in the country and, finally, it called on the Soviet Union and Hungary to permit United Nations observers to enter and travel freely in Hungary to make their own assessment of the situation in order to report to the Secretary-General.[5] In the meantime a new government was installed in Hungary. The foreign office of the new Russian-backed Premier Janos Kadar informed the Secretary-General that the former Premier's request for an intervention by the United Nations in Hungary's internal affairs had no legal status and therefore must be considered void.[6] With the new pro-Soviet government in office, the door was closed in the United Nations face. Further requests by the Secretary-General to admit United Nations observers were made later on to the Hungarian Government. All of the requests were promptly denied by the authorities of that country.[7]

In the face of Hungarian opposition, the task of the Three-man Observation Group amounted to a mere examination of material available to the United Nations Secretariat, which of course was very little[8] and, consequently, the Group was rendered useless. Two further resolutions were passed by the Assembly in much stronger terms, urging the entry of the Observers in Hungary.[9] These resolutions further requested the Secretary-General to consider dispatching the Group to the other nearby countries as well, if it helped the investigation. The text of the resolution was communicated to the Soviet Union, Austria, Rumania, and Czechoslovakia, and it was only Austria that agreed to facilitate the Group's task.

In view of the failure of the Three-man Observer Group to perform its assigned task, the General Assembly passed still another resolution setting up a Special Committee on the Problem of Hungary on January 10, 1957.[10] This committee was to serve as an organ of the Assembly and observe the developments in Hungary over a longer period of time for the purpose of reporting to the General Assembly periodically. In other words, the Committee had explicit instructions "to investigate, to establish and maintain direct observation in Hungary and elsewhere, taking testimony, collecting evidence and receiving information."[11] The essence of the Committee's mandate, as seen by the Committee itself, was to determine: (1) the extent of the effects on and the circumstances of the Hungarian

[5]See U.N. General Assembly Resolution 1004 (ES-11), November 4, 1956. The vote was 50 in favor with 8 against and 15 abstaining.

[6]U.N. General Assembly, A/311 (November 4, 1956).

[7]U.N. General Assembly, A/3341 (November 12, 1956).

[8]U.N. General Assembly, A/3403, (November 30, 1956).

[9]U.N. General Assembly Resolution 1128 (XI), November 21, 1956, adopted by 57 in favor and 8 against and 14 abstentions; and U.N. General Assembly Resolution 1130 (XI) (December 4, 1956) 54 to 10 with 14 countries abstaining.

[10]General Assembly Resolution 1132 (XI), adopted by 59 to 8 with 10 countries abstaining. Note that the individuals who served on the Committee represented Australia, Ceylon, Denmark, Tunisia, and Uruguay.

[11]Ibid.

people in October and November to regain their civil rights; (2) the exact factors that led to the Soviet military intervention; and (3) most importantly, the consequences of the Russian suppression of this uprising on all of the Hungarian people, and on the capacity of Hungary as a state to fulfill its international commitments.[12] The statement of the Committee's main concern in part reads:

> The Committee will attempt, in particular to clarify the nature of the relations between the USSR and its representatives in Hungary with the Nagy Government, the origin and significance of the communications addressed by the Government to the United Nations, as well as the role of the USSR in connection with the removal of that Government and the setting up of the present regime.[13]

With the establishment of the new Committee the Hungarian Government was once again requested to cooperate. A similar request was also made to the government of neighboring Rumania. Both refused cooperation, saying that the establishment and the purposes of the Committee violated the Charter of the United Nations and undermined the interests of international cooperation; and consequently, they wanted nothing to do with it. In the face of strong opposition from the Government of Hungary and its neighboring states who could have proved helpful, the Committee's task was reduced to interviewing influential Hungarian refugees who fled their country when trouble came; monitoring reports of official Hungarian broadcasts; and analyzing the documentary information made available by such Western countries as the United States, United Kingdom, France, Italy, Belgium, and the Netherlands.[14] A study made by the International Commission of jurists was also included in the Committee's report. Despite the obvious fact that the Committee's report was one-sided, it did shed considerable light on the events in Hungary. Notice that when the Secretary-General requested the names of these refugees who testified in front of the Committee, his request was denied by the Committee chairman. To protect these persons, the Chairman had made a personal promise that he would not reveal their names to anyone. The Committee submitted three reports.[15]

Discouraged as it was, much of the United Nations membership was still not willing to let matters rest in Hungary. On September 14, 1957 the General Assembly passed still another resolution (sponsored by the United States) that noted the reports of the Special Committee and con-

[12]U.N. General Assembly, A/3546 (February 20, 1957), 4–6.

[13]Ibid., p. 6.

[14]U.N. General Assembly, A/3592 (June 12, 1957), 1.

[15]U.N. General Assembly, A/3546; A/3592; A/3849.

demned the Soviet and Hungarian Governments for their acts that were "confirmed" by the findings of the Committee. The resolution further called on them to desist their repression of the Hungarian people, respect their freedom and their rights, and make provisions for the return of Hungarian citizens who were deported to Russia.[16] It further requested the Assembly President, "as the General Assembly's special representative on the Hungarian problem, to take such steps as he deems appropriate . . . to achieve the objectives of the United Nations . . . to consult as appropriate with the Committee . . . and to report and make recommendations . . . to the General Assembly."[17] The Assembly President Prince Wan of Thailand reported back to the Assembly some three months later that his efforts on (1) the return of deportees; (2) the humanitarian treatment of the Hungarian people; (3) withdrawal of Soviet troops; and (4) free elections in that country, *were a failure because of the noncooperation of the Hungarian government.*[18] When Prince Wan was succeeded by New Zealand's representative as the President of the General Assembly, a new resolution was adopted by the Assembly, appointing him to report either "to Member States or to the General Assembly on significant developments relating to the implementation of the Assembly resolutions."[19] His subsequent reports did not add much to what was already known to the United Nations on Hungary;[20] however, his summary report on that country was a comprehensive one that covered the entire four-year period of the Hungarian issue. His final report also noted that concerning:

Certain developments within Hungary which bring the situation within the country more in line perhaps with the Assembly resolutions on the observance of fundamental human rights and freedoms, though not in other respects . . . no change has taken place in the basic situation which has prevailed since 1956—the denial to the Hungarian people of the elementary right of self-determination as a result of the past use and through the continuing pressure of a foreign army.[21]

By the end of 1963, the Assembly resolved to abolish the position of the United Nations Special Representative on Hungary, and also requested

[16]General Assembly Resolution 1133 (XI) (September 14, 1957) adopted by 60 to 10, with 10 nations abstaining.
[17]*Ibid.*
[18]U.N. General Assembly, A/3774 (December 9, 1957). (Italics added)
[19]General Assembly Resolution 1312 (XIII).
[20]U.N. General Assembly, A/4304 (November 25, 1959); A/4606 (December 1, 1960; A/4996 (December 1, 1961).
[21]A/5236 (September 25, 1962).

the Secretary-General to "take any initiative that he deems helpful in relation to the Hungarian question."[22]

A concluding remark

The voting records in the General Assembly on the various resolutions passed concerning the situation in Hungary clearly showed that much of the United Nations membership was shocked and angered by the brutal and ruthless Soviet military intervention in that country. But there was not too much the United Nations peacekeeping machinery could have done short of provoking a major conflict with the Soviet Union. Since the Russians had made a strong commitment to maintaining their control over Hungary and since the Russian-backed Hungarian Government wanted no part of the United Nations and its inquiry in its internal affairs, the possibility of the United Nations playing any meaningful role in solving the Hungarian crisis was eliminated. Because of strong Soviet interests in keeping Hungary under its control and because of the inability of the world body to prevent it, the probable rewards of law violation for the Soviets far exceeded the cost of violation.

The experiences of past United Nations peacekeeping operations have indicated that in those international crises involving two or more roughly equal conflicting states (e.g., fighting on a border dispute), usually one of the states would agree to admit a United Nations force or United Nations presence in general in its territory. But in those cases where the area of conflict is within one country and that country is not predisposed to a United Nations intervention, or if that country is militarily controlled by another stronger power that feels a United Nations intervention would run counter to its interests in that country and, consequently, is opposed to such an intervention, it is likely that in the face of such opposition the forces of law and order, even their efforts to investigate or settle a conflict, will largely be unsuccessful. *This was true in Hungary.* The Hungarian authorities, under pressure from the Soviet Union, refused to allow a United Nations presence in their country or to cooperate with the United Nations investigations of the Hungarian crisis in any way, under the time-worn phrase "it's an intervention in the internal affairs of a sovereign state."

Also, one of the several lessons that can be learned from the United Nations peacekeeping encounter with the Hungarian crisis is that a country will cooperate with the United Nations efforts, even to the point

---

[22]U.N. General Assembly Resolution 1857 (December 20, 1963) adopted by 50 to 13, with as many as 43 countries abstaining.

of giving up part of its sovereignty, *only* if it is convinced that the United Nations presence in its country is in its national interest.

case study 2

The United Nations, Portugal, and the Angolan Crisis

Background to the United Nations involvement

The fight for freedom against the Portuguese suppressive rule in Angola had been going on for some time before the widespread violence and general rebellion erupted in the early part of 1961. During the first weeks in February of that year there were several attacks on police stations and prisons in the colony's capital by the nationalists. The purpose was to free their imprisoned national leaders and to create international sympathy for their cause of freedom.

As the violence and rebellion increased in the middle of March, so did the determination of the Portuguese government to suppress the aspirations of the inhabitants for self-rule by massive force. In the midst of this conflict, the Angolan plight was brought to the attention of the Security Council by Liberia under Article 34 of the Charter. In the meantime attempts were also made by Liberia, the United Arab Republic, and Ceylon to get a draft resolution adopted by the Security Council, setting up a subcommittee to look into various aspects of the Angolese crisis and report back to the Council. The resolution failed to receive the necessary vote for approval.

With the Security Council undecided on the question of Angola and with an increase in Portuguese atrocities committed against the natives, the matter was placed on the General Assembly Agenda on March 20 by some 40-odd member states. An identical draft resolution was proposed by 36 Afro-Asian nations with one additional feature, that is, the proposed Sub-Committee would consist of five members appointed by the Assembly President. The resolution was adopted on April 20, by a roll-call vote of 73 to 2 with 9 nations abstaining.[23]

United Nations involvement in the Angolan crisis
and the frustration of its mission

By this time the nationalist element in that colony had further stepped up its drive for freedom, and was now in control of several major areas in

[23]General Assembly Resolution 1603 (XV).

Northern Angola. The reaction of Portuguese to the natives' success at home and in the International Organization was violent, primitive, and typical of the worst of the colonial mentality. Some reportedly 20,000 armed troops were introduced in the Colony to eliminate systematically all traces of the drive for independence around the middle of May. Increased fighting and brutality led the Security Council to consider again the situation in Angola in June. A resolution was passed reaffirming the Assembly's resolution; and requesting the Sub-Committee to implement its mandate without delay. Most importantly, the Council resolution also called on the Government of Portugal to stop its repressive measures against the people of Angola and provide every facility to the Sub-Committee in the performance of its task expeditiously. The Sub-Committee was now to report both to the General Assembly as well as the Security Council at the earliest possible date.[24]

The essence of the Sub-Committee's mandate was to inquire as fully as possible into the situation in Angola. This was interpreted to mean an examination of the various statements made by Portugal before the Assembly with regard to that colony; an examination of all relevant documents; and most importantly, conducting such inquiries that the Sub-Committee may deem necessary.[25] This meant, according to the own convictions of the Sub-Committee, three concerns: the disturbances and conflicts in the colony since February 1961; the background of the entire situation; and its repercussions from the perspective of international peace and security. A further resolution by the General Assembly on January 30, 1962 further defined its terms of reference as: "To study ways and means to secure the implementation of the present resolution and to report thereon to the Security Council and to the General Assembly."[26]

Backed by the various United Nations resolutions and mandates, the Sub-Committee decided to investigate the conduct of Portuguese authorities in Angola with regard to its repressive measures and atrocities committed by its armed forces against the natives of that land; check the extent of reform measures carried out; and examine various ways and means of securing implementation of United Nations resolutions concerning Angola. The Sub-Committee was convinced from the very beginning that it could not possibly make any significant progress in its work without the full cooperation of the Government of Portugal, for its mandate required a visit to Angola with the purpose of on-the-spot investigations. Consequently, it sought Portuguese permission for a visit and attempted to make several informal and formal contacts with that government. The

[24]Security Council Resolution S/4835.
[25]U.N. General Assembly, A/4978 (November 22, 1961), 19.
[26]U.N. General Assembly Resolution 1742 (XV), operative para. 6.

Portuguese response to all this was that the Sub-Committee and its mandate was illegal and the United Nations was guilty of violating the provisions of the Charter by interfering in purely domestic affairs of a member nation. The request to visit Angola was, of course, denied. However, the Portuguese Government felt that the chairman of the Sub-Committee could come to Lisbon "in a personal capacity" to receive the *official* Portuguese report of the events in Angola.

In the face of Portugal's opposition to the work of the Sub-Committee, the whole inquiry was reduced to whatever outside sources of information could be found. The Sub-Committee's representatives visited the Congolese Republic and interviewed the Angolan refugees there. Furthermore, the Sub-Committee gathered all the information it could through reports of United Nations specialized agencies and material provided by the Portuguese Government. On the basis of various sources of its information the Sub-Committee attempted to fulfill its mandate and submitted its first report to the United Nations.[27]

After the Sub-Committee's mandate was renewed in early 1962, it made a series of further attempts to seek Portuguese cooperation in the performance of its functions, but was consistently ignored by the Portuguese Government. Although it continued to examine various reports and testimony from various groups in neighboring countries and the testimony of the victims of the Angolan conflict who were able to flee from Angola, the fulfillment of the main part of its mandate, as defined in the Resolution 1742 (XVI), was completely prevented because of the noncooperation and hostility on the part of Portugal, who also challenged the integrity of the Sub-Committee's first report. The Sub-Committee's second and last report was submitted to the United Nations on November 14, 1962 and was just as inconclusive as the first one.[28]

A concluding remark

Once again the voting records in the General Assembly clearly showed that much of the United Nations membership had already condemned Portugal through several resolutions for the atrocities it committed against the natives of a land who aspired to be free. There is also no doubt that a United Nations presence in Angola, even for the purposes of inquiry or observation, would have been detrimental to Portugal's colonial ambitions in that territory. Also, at the height of conflict, the Portuguese committed

[27]U.N. General Assembly A/4978.
[28]U.N. General Assembly A/5286 (November 14, 1962).

20,000 of its armed troops to eliminate systematically all rebellious elements in Angola. In view of this, it was not surprising to see Portuguese promptly branding the United Nations concern in that country as an intervention in Portugal's "domestic affairs." Once again, because of the Portuguese refusal to let United Nations observers in Angola or to cooperate with the United Nations investigations in any way, the United Nations peacekeeping activities in Angola were rendered no more effective than they were in Hungary.

In the face of Portuguese opposition an intervention by a United Nations peacekeeping force would have meant a direct confrontation with Portugal.

case study 3

The United Nations, South Africa, and Crisis in Southwest Africa

Background to the United Nations involvement and the frustration of its mission

The United Nations has been concerned with the racial problems of South Africa almost since the international organization was formed. As early as 1946 the General Assembly placed the question of the treatment of Indians (after 1947, Indians and Pakistanis) on its agenda. Almost every session since 1946 has seen a debate on the question of racial discrimination in South Africa. In 1952, the United Nations also included the question of discrimination against the entire colored population in that country because of the new and stringent apartheid laws established by the white ruling minority. At a still later date the question of South African discrimination in South-West Africa was also added.[29] South African opposition to any United Nations peace observation commission set up to look into the question of discrimination against the Indo-Pakistan ethnic groups and the rest of the colored population in that country, has made it impossible to have any on-the-spot check and investigations in South Africa.

South African refusal to cooperate with any of the United Nations committees, comissions or observer groups is based on the same old Charter provision that says the United Nations has no authority to interfere in

[29]The territory of South West Africa was placed under the administrative authority of the South African Government by virtue of a League of Nations mandate.

the domestic affairs of a member nation.[30] Nevertheless, in view of the significance of the racial strife in that country and in its administered territory, the United Nations General Assembly voted to establish a special commission, as early as 1952, to look into the South African publicly stated practice of systematically denying millions of its nonwhite citizens the basic human rights. Three years later the Assembly asked the Secretary-General to designate a personal representative of his to investigate the violations; and still later, in 1962 the Assembly set up another special committee to intensify its work of dealing with the racial problem there. The main objective of the Committee was defined by the Secretary-General, to review constantly South Africa's atrocities committed against its nonwhite population under its apartheid laws and to report to the International Organization. Despite South Africa's refusal to recognize the United Nations' competence to intervene in this area and its active opposition to all the United Nations investigatiaons, the Committee obtained information from outside sources and learned about South African practices from the victims who fled to neighboring countries. On the basis of the Committee's reports, the United Nations was able to censure that country. But it was unable to do more than that.

On the question of South-West Africa, the South African Government, ever since World War II, had refused to negotiate any agreement with the United Nations. Fully realizing the weaknesses of the United Nations peacekeeping machinery, and ensured of support by several European colonial powers, the South African Government has repeatedly refused to place the territory of South-West Africa under the trusteeship system of the United Nations. Despite an International Court's ruling that the United Nations had competence to exercise the supervisory functions previously held by the League of Nations, the South African stand remains unchanged. Once the Government did invite the chairman and vice-chairman of the Committee to visit South-West Africa briefly. It was the first on-the-spot observation, but since the Government officials escorted the two visitors everywhere they went and since they were allowed to see only those areas authorized by the Government, the validity and reliability of the report of the Committee stands suspect.

In conclusion, once again the United Nations was unable to influence the international problems that occur either within a country whose government is unsympathetic to United Nations intervention, or if they occur in a country controlled by force by another nation, that does not want any part of the United Nations intervention in that country.

[30]See Article 11 (7) of the United Nations Charter.

case study 4
The United Nations, United Arab Republic, Saudi Arabia, and the Crisis in Yemen

Background to the United Nations involvement

On September 26, 1962 the despotic rule of the Imam of Yemen was abruptly brought to an end through a coup led by an official of his palace. The events that followed the coup saw a civil war in that country, and it also saw an intervention by outside powers that eventually brought the United Nations presence to this rather obscure land. The republican nature of the coup was welcomed in many countries of the world, for it provided some hope for social reforms that were badly needed. To the United Arab Republic, particularly, it meant another republican ally against the waning kingdoms of the Middle East. Consequently, the United Arab Republic was one of the first countries to recognize the new regime and promise support. The Russian and the American recognition also followed almost immediately.

The coup apparently did not have the wholehearted support of the entire population and the civil war that followed instantly threatened the survival of the new regime. There was a confrontation between the republican faction that for obvious reasons did not want to go back to the despotic rule of the Imam and the royalist faction that seemed determined to return the country to the previous status quo. In view of the Saudi Arabian active support of the royalists, the United Arab Republic, fearing the collapse of the new regime, introduced its troops in Yemen in an attempt to crush the royalist opposition. President Nasser, however, underestimated the military support he would be required to provide to keep the republican regime afloat (which later turned out to be extremely weak) when he first committed U.A.R. troops.[31]

As the tempo of the civil war increased, crystallizing the aims and efforts of both sides, thousands of Egyptian soldiers were poured in the country and so increased the Saudi Arabian military aid to the royalist faction. The matter was soon brought to the attention of the Secretary-General who dispatched Ralph Bunche to Yemen on a fact-finding mission as his personal representative. The Secretary-General, it seems, was encouraged to take the initiative in this crisis by the parties in conflict themselves. As it turned out later, the implicit understanding was that they shall all welcome

[31]For a fine background study of the Yemeni crisis, see Harold Ingrams, *The Yemen* (London: John Murray), 1963.

a United Nations intervention. Just about the same time, the United States Government dispatched its own representative Ellsworth Bunker to the Middle East to attempt to persuade both the United Arab Republic and Saudi Arabia to refrain from giving aid to the warring factions in Yemen. The essence of Bunker's approach was that Arabs should not have to fight other Arabs. Interestingly enough, he was able to get all the three parties—the United Arab Republic, Saudi Arabia, and the Government of the Republic of Yemen (Royalists were ignored)—to agree on a disengagement plan. This plan specified a timetable for the withdrawal of all U.A.R. troops from Yemen on the understanding that Saudi Arabia would halt all aid to the royalists immediately. The United Nations was expected to supervise the implementation of this disengagement agreement.

On the basis of Bunker's recommendations and Bunche's findings (incidentally, both were Americans) the Secretary-General first confirmed the terms of the agreement with the representatives of the countries involved and then submitted a detailed report to the Security Council on April 29, 1963.[32] Just about the same time he also asked Major General Carl Von Horn, the UNTSO's Chief-of-Staff in Jerusalem, to negotiate the details relating to the nature and functioning of United Nations observers in implementing the disengagement terms, with the three powers involved in conflict.

In a second report to the Security Council on May 27, 1963, the Secretary-General spelled out the details of the findings made by General Horn on his behalf.[33] He further stated that because of the urgency of the situa-

[32]The essence of the Secretary-General's report was that the three countries involved in the conflict favor a United Nations intervention in the Yemen crisis and have agreed that (1) the Saudi Arabian Government should immediately cease to provide any aid or support to the royalist faction in Yemen. It should further ensure it that the Saudi Arabian territory is no longer used by the royalist leader. (2) The United Arab Republic should immediately start the withdrawal of its troops from Yemen and conclude the withdrawal according to a previously announced time schedule. Its forces should refrain from attacking the Saudi Arabian territories and suspend all punitive measures against the royalists who fought with them before the cease-fire went into effect. The United Nations was to provide impartial observers to check that the terms of the disengagement agreement were properly observed The Secretary-General's report also pointed out that the Saudi Arabian Government and the Government of the United Arab Republic have both shown a strong desire to "co-operate with the representative of the United Nations Secretary-General or some other mutually acceptable intermediary in reaching an agreement on the modalities and verification of disengagement." For details, see U.N. Security Council, S/5298 (April 29, 1963).

[33]The details of the findings of the Secretary-General's staff with regard to the Yemen crisis were: (1) United Nations observers in the Saudi Arabia-Yemen area are vitally necessary and could be the decisive factor in avoiding serious trouble there. All parties concerned desired their presence. The need was urgent, and they should be sent without delay. (2) The terrain and climatic conditions in parts of the area are

tion in Yemen and because all the three nations involved in the conflict were eager to cooperate with the United Nations effort in that country, he was going ahead with the establishment of the operation. The Secretary-General's announcement came to some of the Members as a surprise, because there had been no authorization by the Security Council of any United Nations presence in Yemen and it was not clear under what authority the International Executive was proceeding to send a mission there. Two weeks later, the Secretary-General submitted a third report stating that Saudi Arabia had agreed to pay approximately half the cost of the United Nations operation for the period of two months (this was the amount of time U Thant thought would be required to complete the mission), and it is very likely that the Government of the United Arab Republic would pay the other half. He also reminded the Council that in a few days the United Nations observation group would be operating in Yemen.[34]

Several states, as pointed out earlier, were surprised over the extent of U Thant's initiative in preparing to initiate a United Nations mission without a resolution of any kind either from the Security Council or the General Assembly. The Soviet Union was particularly perturbed and took the initiative in reminding the international executive that although each of the three states involved in the conflict was eager to have a United Nations mission, he should not forget that it was the Security Council that was responsible for the maintenance of international peace and security under the Charter and not the Secretary-General per se. It further asked the Secretary-General to call a meeting of the Security Council to discuss the Yemeni question.[35]

---

difficult, and considerable danger might be encountered. Although problems of movement and logistics would be great, stationing of observers could be accomplished. (3) Personnel required for the mission would not exceed 200, including a small number of officer-observers; a ground patrol unit of about 100 men, carrying only arms for self-defense, crews for about eight small aircraft for reconnaissance and transport; and personnel for such supporting services as communications, logistics, medical aid, transportation and administration. (4) The observation function was estimated to require no more than four months. (5) Some of the personnel required for this observation operation could be recruited from UNEF, UNTSO, and possibly UNMOGIP (United Nations Military Observers Group in India and Pakistan), subject to clearance with the governments concerned. General Von Horn would be designated Chief of the Yemen Mission. (6) The total cost of the Yemen Observation Mission was estimated at less than $1,000,000. The Secretary-General hoped that the two parties principally involved would bear the costs of the mission. He was sure the parties would agree to bear at least part of the costs, in money or in other forms of assistance.

[34]U.N. Security Council, S/5325 (June 7, 1963).

[35]For details of the Soviet Union's note to the Secretary-General, see U.N. Security Council S/5236 (June 8, 1963).

United Nations involvement in Yeman and the establishment of UNYOM

The civil war broke out in Yemen in September 1962, but it was almost a year later on June 10, 1963 that the Security Council began considering the question of sending the observers in that country. All of the previous reports submitted by the Secretary-General were reviewed. U Thant, after sensing Soviet indignation over his past initiative with regard to proposing to send observers without an authorization from the Council, and fearing a Soviet veto, pleaded with the Council that if the observers were not sent right away the terms of disengagement earlier agreed to by the conflicting parties would become void, creating new problems for the international organization.[36] A draft resolution was submitted by Ghana and Morocco to send the United Nations observers to Yemen right away. The Soviet Union once again reminded the Council that the aggressors must pay for the cost of the operation.[37] The resolution was adopted by a vote of 10 to 0 with the Soviets abstaining.[38] Two days after the adoption of the resolution, headquarters for the United Nations Yemen Observation Mission (UNYOM) were set up in the capital of Yemen, and less than two weeks later the United Nations operation was fully functioning. The essence of the June 11 resolution was that UNYOM was to observe, certify, and report the violations of the disengagement agreement. It had no mandate to mediate or concilate between the parties and, as it proved later, this was the single major weakness of the UNYOM. There were problems of logistics and the shortage of personnel and other facilities that were aggravated because of the harsh climate and the ruggedness of terrain. It has been suggested that one of the major reasons for the resignation of General Von Horn as the Commander of UNYOM was the lack of proper support of this mission by the Secretariat.[39]

Irritated by the press criticism of his handling of UNYOM, U Thant sent General Rikhye, his military advisor, and another officer to Yemen for a tour of inspection. Their report was: "despite personal hardships, difficulties in supplying fresh rations and unavoidable lack of amenities, the morale of Mission personnel is indeed very high . . . ration stock never

[36]See U.N. Security Council S/5236 (June 10, 1963).

[37]U.N. Security Council S/PV1038 (June 11, 1963), 11–12.

[38]U.N. Security Council Resolution S/5331 (June 11, 1963).

[39]See the first report of the Secretary-General on the activities of UNYOM, U.N. Security Council, S/5412 (September 4, 1963), 3. There was elaborate press coverage on the so-called neglect of UNYOM by the U.N. Secretariat and the reasons for General Von Horn's resignation. See, for instance, reports published in the August 31, 1963 issue of *Washington Post*, and the September 1, 1963 issue of *New York Times*.

reached a critical stage."[40] The main implication of their report was that General Horn, in his desire to do an effective job, had taken it upon himself to go beyond the UNYOM mandate by investigating violations and thus straining the modest resources of the Mission.

Analysis of UNYOM performance and the extent of the United Arab Republic and the Saudi Arabian cooperation—some law observance

For the purpose of analysis, the United Nations presence in Yemen can be divided into two phases. The first phase of the operation began with the establishment of UNYOM on June 11, 1962 and ended just prior to the appointment of Pier P. Spinelli, Under-Secretary and Director of the United Nations European office, as a Special Representative of the Secretary-General in Yemen, on November 4, 1963. The second phase of the operation began with his appointment and ended with the termination of United Nations presence in that country.

First phase of the operation. The first phase of the operation was marked by only a partial and selective cooperation of the United Arab Republic and Saudi Arabia with the United Nations effort in Yemen. For instance, an analysis of the Secretary-General's first report submitted to the Security Council on the Yemeni operation indicates that some significant aspects of the terms of disengagement agreement were not being implemented by either of the two major parties. It was further pointed out that UNYOM observed the departure of thousands of U.A.R. troops from that country, but apparently some fresh troops were also introduced, although in much smaller numbers. For security reasons United Arab Republic was unwilling to provide the specific details of its troop movements to the United Nations observers. The report also indicated that there were significant reductions in the arms supplies to the royalist faction from Saudi Arabia, but again these were not completely halted. The report concluded by praising the courage and persistence of the United Nations personnel in that country for being able to do a good job under most difficult climatic conditions and in an area marked by rugged terrain.[41] The main implication carried in the report was that despite the selective cooperation of both sides, the extremely limited mandate of the mission made it easy for the contesting parties to violate the terms of the disengagement agreement because UNYOM simply would not be able to check.

The second report of the Secretary-General was also discouraging. It was

[40]U.N. Security Council S/5412, p. 3.
[41]For details see, U.N. Security Council S/5412 (September 4, 1963).

presented to the Council toward the end of the second two-month period of the operation. The Secretary-General observed that "There has been no decisive change in that situation in the subsequent two months."[42] The report also indicated the current positions of the two contesting nations in Yemen. The Saudi Arabian position was that it had completely stopped giving arms to the royalist faction and, furthermore, charged that because U.A.R. troops not only had not been withdrawn from that country but had increased in numbers, the unilateral observation of the disengagement Agreement by Saudi Arabia could not be taken for granted indefinitely. The United Arab Republic's position was that even if it were to accept the Saudi Arabian contention that arms shipments to the royalists had now been halted, the stockpile of previous shipments was so enormous that the royalists could conduct a war against the Republic for some time without Saudi Arabia's assistance. Besides, the United Arab Republic argued, once its troops had pulled out of Yemen, there was no guarantee that Saudi Arabia would not resume its aid to the royalists. In view of the political nature of the conflict, and the limited nature of UNYOM mandate, the conclusion of the Secretary-General's second reports was that he did "not believe that the solution of the problem, or even the fundamental steps which must be taken to resolve it, can ever be within the potential of UNYOM alone—and most certainly not under its existing limited mandate."[43]

In view of the above somber conclusion, the United Nations Secretariat prepared to withdraw all United Nations personnel from Yemen, not because of the noncooperation of the parties involved, but primarily because of the limited mandate and resources of the mission and, *most importantly*, because of the fact that UNYOM was not allowed to mediate between the conflicting parties to seek a political solution.

Both the Saudi Arabia and the United Arab Republic were disturbed by U Thant's implied decision to withdraw UNYOM. Both countries offered to pay the full cost of the operation and requested an extension of the mission for another two-month period. There were no objections to that, and the mission was extended.

Second phase of the operation. Since both the United Arab Republic and Saudi Arabia had previously cooperated only partially with UNYOM, it is interesting to analyze their reasons for asking the Secretary-General to continue with the United Nations presence in Yemen. The most plausible explanation is that by this time there was a stalemate in the conflict. The republican regime of Yemen proved to be extremely weak, and there is

[42]U.N. Security Council, S/5447 (October 28, 1963), 1.
[43]*Ibid.* p. 7.

little doubt that a general pullout of the U.A.R. soldiers would have meant an end of the brief republican era in that country. The whole responsibility of running the country was thrown in the laps of the U.A.R. military High Command—a job they neither wanted nor cared for once they became involved in it. While the U.A.R. troops controlled the cities and the valleys, the mountain tribes supporting the royalists controlled the hills.

At this time all the conflicting parties realized that a clear military victory was not possible and that, to save face, a solution had to be found through negotiated settlement with the help of the United Nations.

Thus, began the second phase of the United Nations operation that saw the appointment of Pier Spinelli by the Secretary-General as his personal representative to Yemen. Apart from running the UNYOM, Spinelli was also authorized to initiate and encourage negotiations between the parties with a hope of reaching some accord. Interestingly enough, the appointment was enthusiastically welcomed by all parties. Since Spinelli's appointment, the presence of the UNYOM was extended three times for two-month periods in March, May, and July 1964, while the United Nations attempted to solve the conflict.[44]

The next two reports of the Secretary-General were discouraging. For instance, in his March 3, 1964 report he indicated that extensive fighting had taken place between the U.A.R. troops, which were now estimated to be around 32,000, and the royalist faction, which was receiving huge shipments of arms possibly from the South Arabian Federation, which was not a party to the Disengagement Agreement. U Thant, however, saw some hope of a settlement because of a recent conference of Arab states in Cairo in January 1964.[45]

The last two reports of the Secretary-General were more encouraging. They indicated that the mission had helped to open doors for negotiated settlement and had lessened the danger to the international peace and security. The Secretary-General felt that direct negotiations between the Arab leaders would be more fruitful. On September 4, 1964 the mandate of the mission was terminated. The last report of the Secretary-General indicated the military situation had significantly improved and no military

[44]See U.N. Security Council A/5681 (May 4, 1964); S/5794 (July 2, 1964); and S/5927 (September 2, 1964).

[45]U.N. Security Council, S/5572 (March 3, 1964). The Arab Summit Conference referred to in the Secretary-General's report took place in Cairo in January 1964. It was decided that Algeria and Iraq were to help mediate between the conflicting parties by attempting to accomplish two major objectives: (1) restoration of normal relations between the United Arab Republic and Saudi Arabia, and (2) persuasion of Saudi Arabia to accept some sort of a "mild" republican form of government in Yemen. It was hoped that accomplishment of these two objectives would provide a basis for the withdrawal of U.A.R. troops and the end of Saudi Arabian shipments of arms to the royalists.

supplies were discovered reaching the royalists. There was also a reduction in the U.A.R. troops in Yemen. The essence of the final report was that during its 14 months in Yemen, the UNYOM exercised important moderating and restraining influence over the conflicting parties.[46]

A concluding remark

It is obvious from the analysis of over half a dozen successive reports of the Secretary-General submitted to the Security Council with regard to the situation in Yemen that none of the conflicting parties cooperated with the UNYOM throughout its stay in Yemen. But it must be admitted that in those areas and periods of time, the powers involved did cooperate fully when they were convinced that such a cooperation was in their interests. It is submitted that the United Nations presence, even with selective and partial cooperation of the parties, was able to get the Saudi Arabian Government to reduce the shipments of arms across the border, and was able to persuade the United Arab Republic to stop bombing the depots and supply trains inside the Saudi Arabian territories. In conclusion, it can be said that UNYOM was able to function effectively only in those areas and again only when the three states cooperated.

General conclusion

A brief analysis of these four international crises conducted in this chapter provides significant evidence in support of our main proposition concerning incentives to violate law. The first three crises indicated the ineffectiveness of the United Nations intervention because of the non-cooperation and even hostile opposition of the parties involved toward the United Nations effort. In each case this hostility was generally based on the belief that a United Nations intervention would definitely work against their interests. Concerning the fourth and the last crisis, the analysis revealed somewhat different results, but with the same conclusions. The United Nations presence in Yemen was welcomed by all the parties concerned for somewhat different reasons that were based on their own national interests. Whenever the parties were convinced that a United Nations presence would contribute to their interests, their cooperation on a *selective and partial basis* was extended to UNYOM. And, most importantly, the suc-

---

[46]U.N. Security Council S/5927 (September 4, 1964).

cess and the effectiveness of the United Nations intervention was possible only because this cooperation was provided.

From the above analysis it becomes clear that the forces of law and order will find it difficult to be effective and fruitful unless they have the willingness and cooperation of the countries involved. It is also clear that those countries who stand to gain significantly by law violations will be tempted to violate the law. On occasions national interests will prevail over the dictates of legal norms.

In the face of noncooperation, all that the United Nations can do is to proceed with the assigned task of its mandate as best it can until it has acquired the capacity and determination to implement its resolutions and mandates *fully*, and by force if necessary, against the will of those members who stand in the way. Such a time may be long in coming.

chapter 14
international lawmaking and unmaking

Process of international bargaining and consensus formation prior to deliberate law development

The literature in the field of international law more than adequately reflects the concern that legal scholarship has exhibited on the indentification and elaboration of *formal* sources (outlined earlier) of international law evolution and development. Within this concern, special attention has been paid to *treaties and formal agreements* as one of the most important sources of law. Consequently, a great deal of energy is spent in analyzing, interpreting, and reinterpreting the provisions of these treaties and agreements. Some treaties have been specifically singled out as "lawmaking" treaties, suggesting that as a consequence of these treaties new laws have developed. Several older treaties have been characterized as "unequal treaties," implying that the provisions of such agreements do not recognize the sovereign equality of signatory states, or that they are in some other way unequal, unfair, or prejudicial to the interests of specific parties to the treaty; therefore any laws that might subsequently be developed out of such treaties will also be unequal or unfair. There is no doubt that a concentration on the formal sources of law development, evolution, and modification is desirable, if for no other reason than simply to assist the international lawyer, whose professional emphasis makes him more concerned with what the law presently is and how it can be applied to a particular situation, instead of with the *broader social, psychological, economic, and political factors responsible for the lawmaking and unmaking behavior of the states*. The social scientist on the other hand is more deeply and fundamentally involved in understanding these factors. He is, for instance, interested in probing the very roots of human behavior to arrive at satisfactory answers to such basic questions as: Why are legal norms developed? Whose will do they actually represent? And precisely how are they developed?—in addition to the more traditional question: What are the legal norms? The concerns of the social scientist in this area can be justified if only because of the generally accepted weakness of the formal sources of international law as adequate explanations of lawmaking and law evolution. These sources themselves still need further explanations. For instance, to this day this weakness of formal sources of law is reflected in an old debate that goes on unabatedly concerning whether these sources are really *sources* or mere *evidence* of international law?

The number of legal treaties signed or other formal agreements instituted in the contemporary international systems has never been higher; thus much of the legal scholarship continues to be focused on this area of easily observable evidence concerning the nature of contemporary international law This particular source of lawmaking is certainly more easily researchable, more conclusive, and less subject to scholarly arguments than are many other sources of which "custom" is one. Most treaties provide explicitly stated information for legal interpretations and comments by the scholar. More importantly, from the point of view of a social scientist, treaties provide other useful information too. For example, provisions of international treaties and agreements, at any period of history of international affairs, provide *tangible bases* for the identification, analysis, and measurement of sociopolitical, economic, and military variables present in the international relations of states that were signatory to the agreements at the time of their formulation and acceptance.[1] Moreover, analysis or comparison of various treaties can help us understand the dynamics of the law-politics relationship of that time, and also the degree of interdependence, integration, mutual respect and trust, or mutual fear and distrust that prevailed among the signatories. These are the important relations to which international law of the time is not indifferent and neither can the legal scholarship afford to be. Furthermore, treaties can help the student understand the "applied" aspect of international law much better, for they help him ascertain the dimensions of a state's foreign policy. He can, by closely studying some of the important treaties to which a particular state is signatory, develop what is now being called a *treaty profile* of the international relations of that state. He can further empirically observe and quantitatively measure a state's attitudes in the international

---

[1]In support of this proposition see the works of J. F. Triska and R. M. Slusser, *The Theory, Law and Policy of Soviet Treaties* (Stanford: Stanford University Press), 1962; and P. H. Rohn, "Institutionalism in the Law of Treaties: A Case for Combining Teaching and Research," *Proceedings, American Society of International Law* (1965), 93–98.

system by systematically analyzing its treaty commitments with other nations in just about every aspect of international life.

However, the major theme of this chapter is that the important and justifiable concerns as indicated above in the study of the formal sources of international law and particularly the study of treaties and other formal agreements *should not* be allowed to take attention away from an equally important task of legal scholarship, for example, *the actual, observable process of treaty making and treaty evolution that results in lawmaking and law evolution.* In other words, we need to know a great deal more about the *various processes of international bargaining and consensus formation prior to deliberate law development through treaties and other formal agreements.* To a certain degree, this task is already being done by social scientists and law scholars who have attempted to "reinterpret" the norms of existing international treaties: (1) by analyzing the changed circumstances of states signatory to the treaties and by observing their present behavior concerning the norms of these treaties; (2) by studying the pertinent decisions of national and international courts and drawing inferences from them concerning law evolution; (3) by analyzing the role played by various international arbitral tribunals in this field and; (4) by looking at the politics of international lawmaking and unmaking in appropriate international organizations, including the United Nations. But here too, as seems true with general descriptive commentary on the formal sources of law, or even on the text of treaties, the scholarly emphasis remains on the *"outcome" (output)* aspect of the whole process of law development or law changes. *The "input" aspect and the actual "process" aspect* of bargaining and decision making (including all those factors that are well articulated by bargaining and decision-making theorists that go into this process) are generally neglected.

The politics of international lawmaking

To focus on the input aspect (prebargaining stage) of international negotiations leading to law development, we need to identify and operationalize various sets of independent and intervening variables that are responsible for various sets of expectations concerning future laws by states and, consequently, do influence the outcome (output) aspect of law development. We need to develop appropriate dynamic models of international bargaining that can help us explain the *process* of lawmaking and thus fill some gaps that exist in our knowledge in this area of inquiry—models that will account for the linkage of internal and international systemic variables that contain differential lawmaking elements. Before we address ourselves to the actual task of model building, several things should be kept in mind. The politics of international lawmaking in the contemporary international system can be viewed from various dimensions. Today, it can be regarded as the by-product of domestic and international forces. The *domestic* forces can be described in two categories: (a) the pertinent background factors of each nation that are instrumental in the formulation of those broad and long-term foreign policy objectives that nations like to pursue and that are instrumental in determining the kind of laws that a state feels best suited to follow. These background factors, it appears, are always present when a nation sits down to bargain for the development or modification of international law. (b) The *specific* national foreign policy goals that a state has articulated and firmly believes will be best served with the presence of certain kinds of international norms and with the eradication of others. These international forces can be described in terms of the environmental situational factors available in the international arena that are usually given and that most states generally tend to accept. These environmental and situational factors may, at different occasions in different issues, help the position of one or more states in their efforts to develop the kinds of laws they prefer because they are most suited to the pursuance of their foreign policy goals during a particular period of history.

The politics of international lawmaking at any given time is also influenced by certain special forces that happen to be prevalent in the international system at that time. These forces succeed for several reasons in finding their way into the heart of the international system and thus into the lawmaking process. These forces, while leaving a more stable and durable mark on the law, tend to lose their significance with the passage of time. As the international system changes, these forces disappear or are replaced with other forces expressing more contemporary concerns with law development. Given the dynamics of contemporary international politics, it is indeed difficult to evaluate systematically their impact on lawmaking or law evolution, but the task is not impossible if carried out as a major project in itself, and no great claims of precision are made on behalf of its findings. Two examples of these special forces found in the present international system will help clarify what is being suggested. Consider, for instance, the role of (1) new nations in the formulations of new laws and (2) the need for national security through arms control and disarmament.

The new states. The attitudes and the behavior of the new states concerning international law and its observance have already been discussed. At the present only a brief remark is warranted with regard to the present role of these new states in lawmaking and unmaking. Today, many of these states along with several other states (some of them from the Communist bloc) are expressing dissatisfaction and restlessness toward some of the norms of the current international legal system. Most of the reasons for the present dissatisfaction are well known, the main one being the law's Western origin and character that is out of step with the needs and aspirations of some areas of a largely non-Western world. The situation is further aggravated because, whether a state likes it or not, one of the most cherished maxims of international law is that each new state must accept the existing laws of the international society when joining the family of nations. Just how closely this maxim is followed in reality by the new members of the international society is subject to debate. One thing seems clear; most of the new nations have taken exception to some norms without particularly invoking the wrath of the international society as a whole. If this was not true, how else could international law be modified, changed, or discarded in favor of new laws. Despite the sanctity of the maxim, the practice seems to reveal that it has been more enthusiastically supported by states that are comfortable with the status quo. In reality, international legal patterns have been continually modified to accommodate the changes in the system. In some instances there have been some radical changes in the law, initiated by these new and dissatisfied states.[2]

Many of these new states have been active in the process of law development, modification, and law codification inside and outside the United Nations. Their participation in this activity represents their particular self-interest that can be best served by a more lawful international society. They have been interested in anticolonialism, principles of nonintervention in the domestic affairs of other states, sovereign equality under law, and territorial integrity, for example. Increasingly, their interest in international law has broadened to cover such areas as management of international conflict, economic development, and international welfarism. Their participation in the process of lawmaking today can be appropriately called a manifestation of revisionist if not radical political orientation. Despite the sometimes harsh criticism of some legal norms, it is clear they are not antilaw or indifferent to the law These states, on the contrary, are among the states most committed to the ideals of a lawful world.

It is difficult to assess accurately the long-term influences of these new members of the international society on the character and role of international law. However, some trends are unmistakably clear. For instance, all of these states are at various stages of economic and political development; many of them generally reject Western commercialism as inappropriate for their settings for several reasons (not all of them quite rational)

[2]See, for instance, R. L. Friedheim, "The 'Satisfied' and 'Dissatisfied' States Negotiate International Law: A Case Study," *World Politics*, XVIII (October 1965), 20–41; see also J. Castaneda, "The Underdeveloped Nations and the Development of International Law," *International Organization*, XV (Winter 1961), 38–48.

yet they very much wish to Westernize (i.e., industrialize). They violently protest and also violate the principles of international law that they feel are unjust relics of the colonial past, yet they not only support but actively work for a world law that will give them equality, justice, and protection from the whims of the more powerful. I believe it is in the nature of their style and processes of economic and political development that they shall continue to try various political models and espouse different ideologies, and thus seemingly contribute to the principle of the supremacy of politics over law. However, in the long run, the author is convinced that international law has a compassionate friend in them because by using the language of law they stand to gain more toward equality, prosperity and, above all, the *international welfarism* that they desire most, than by using the language of force that, given their relatively modest capabilities, will impress no one, particularly the rich and powerful nations.

National security. One of the most important objectives of contemporary international law is to provide a reasonable degree of security to a state from the threats or acts of aggression by other states. At least at the super-power level, the acquisition of new and more sophisticated weapons have not provided a corresponding amount of greater security. It is generally accepted by most observers of the arms race today that the way to improve one's national security is to move toward mutual disarmament and arms control, coupled with foolproof inspection systems against possible violations of disarmament treaties, and followed by new sets of international law prohibiting rearmament and the spread of weapons in new areas, for example.

In the past decade several major treaties have been signed in the field of arms control. As a result of these treaties, new laws in this area are now in the process of development. The need for greater security through arms control and disarmament is providing new incentives to develop internatinoal law in this area. Law, of course, can help provide security to states in other ways too. For instance, international law will continue to defuse the highly explosive instances of interstate conflict, but with new laws the job can be more effectively done. There are some formidable obstacles in the way of this task. For instance, the main entity responsible for a nation's security remains the so-called "sovereign state" and as long as security remains a state's responsibility, the state and its agents cannot shirk that responsibility, given the nature of contemporary international politics.

There are other important forces that can be simply enumerated: (1) the role of international consensus exhibited through the resolutions of the United Nations or elsewhere in mobilizing the international system or portions of it to the development of much needed new international laws.

Currently, there appears to be a great deal of public concern for the development of international laws curtailing terrorism and skyjackings. (2) Emergence of new units of international power and politics in the international system other than the nation-states and their impact on current lawmaking units such as, blocs, political groupings, regional international organizations, whether economic or military. (3) A growing sense of international welfarism in the world that suggests that poor countries have a legitimate right to expect and receive various types of assistance from rich nations in their efforts to modernize.

Before we proceed further, a word of caution is necessary. We should be keenly aware of the close relationship between international law and the patterns of international politics over *a specific period of time*. Therefore, periods of political stability, predictability, and common value systems, for example, (as was true somewhat in the eighteenth- and nineteenth-century Europe) produce periods of stable expectations concerning law and, thus, uniform and less conflict-prone development of law may follow. Accordingly, periods of widespread conflict, political unrest, socioeconomic discontinuities and multiple sets of value systems (as is true in the twentieth century) are also periods of legal turmoil, currently called "crises in international law." In the context of this observation our main task here is to identify and discuss the processes of lawmaking, law evolution, and law codification. A great deal of speculation has surfaced in the last decade concerning the *process* of what is called "law codification", that is the *need* for new law foundations; the absolute necessity to *limit* further a state's right to be sovereign; the emerging role of the *new* subjects of international law such as private corporations and individuals in lawmaking. All of these considerations and there are many more have merit because all of them try in one way or the other to deal with the *nature of the contemporary processes of law development*, but these factors need to be put together in some sort of a conceptual framework. The immediate task here is what is commonly called "putting the pieces together."

The approach or "putting the pieces together." Only through systematic studies of states' attitudes and beliefs, their ideological preferences and the disparate value systems that they invariably introduce into the international bargaining process prior to consensus formation, can we *first* learn how mutual consensus on legal norms is arrived at and agreement is reached on treaties that subsequently lead to law development on the contemporary international scene. *Second*, such studies in the long run can also help us to asecrtain what states are most likely to violate or uphold what kinds of international laws and under what political circumstances. What is being suggested here is that the purpose of our analysis should not be limited to the mere attainment of some new insights into the study of progressive and pragmatic development of new laws per se, but we should also make some assessment, tentative as it may be with regard to their future effectiveness as impartial arbiters of international disputes. In our task of analyzing law development through politics, we should be concerned particularly with the specific forms of state behavior with unique features that can be identified as impinging on the process of international lawmaking. These unique features are to be found in the international actions that Raymond Aron once apty called a state's "diplomatic-strategic" behavior.[3] It is a kind of behavior that is highly competitive, often conflictive, and almost always takes place under an implicit or explicit threat of violence. Since the competitive-conflicting nature of this diplomatic-strategic state behavior obliges the actors to calculate their motives and decisions through not always well-defined and well-articulated national interests, it can best be understood only if we study it both by reference to *actions oriented toward values and goals* and by reference to *instrumental state actions.*[4]

In short, there is a great need for new conceptualizations, approaches, and models that can help us identify and analyze several crucial and thus far neglected sets of variables responsible for the dynamic relationship between international politics and international law, particularly *the variables that play a significant part in the process of lawmaking.* Only in this manner can we make the study of international law more relevant, both to the social scientist and the student in the classroom.

The relevant variables can best be identified and their relationships analyzed through a *social-psychological approach* to states' behavior in various international bargaining situations, leading eventually to the formulation of accepted international conventions and the subsequent development of international law. Such an aproach can effectively assist us in integrating, for instance, important factors prevalent in a state's diplomatic-strategic behavior: for example, (1) the background social and cultural factors of a state and the limitations that these factors pose in the international arena; (2) the military, technical, and industrial position of a state *vis-à-vis* other states; (3) national goals and "other" motives that a state brings to the bargaining table; (4) the process of negotiations that itself involves moves, countermoves, and various types of communications; (5) the nature of the international climate under which negotiations are conducted; and (6) the outcomes and the degree of satisfaction and dissatisfaction with them.

---

[3]*Peace and War: A Theory of International Relations* (New York: Praeger), 1968 ed., pp. 580–585 and 591–600.

[4]See E. M. Schur, *Law and Society: A Sociological View* (New York: Random House), 1968.

Acceptance of an international legal norm by states, binding them to certain prescribed patterns of behavior, is *contingent on a consensus of a set of broader value systems underlying that norm*. The broader value system held by a state in a given period of history is essentially the product of crucial sets of social-psychological, political-cultural, and military-industrial variables that should be identified and their impact assessed, both on the formation of a state's national objectives and on the process of international bargaining and consensus development, prior to lawmaking. Only in this manner can we be in a position to identify the crucial relationship between international law and international politics, and reach some tentative conclusion with regard to future state behavior vis à vis specific international lawmaking.

The significance of these variables on the development of consensus on the broader value system (which must underlie legal norms if laws are to be effective) can partially be ascertained by an analysis of present trends toward "lawlessness" and breakdown of traditional patterns of "law and order" in some communities in the United States today. For instance, one can argue that the new social and political awareness on the part of the black American community, coupled with its increasing demands for more physical and psychological gratifications, has brought home at least one important fact—the traditional consensus that we once took for granted on the broader value system underlying some of our laws can no longer be said to exist.[5] On the international scene also, a comparable situation is developing; with the emergence during the past two decades of many new sovereign states with different value systems and foreign policy objectives, some of the so-called cherished principles of international law of the past (based on Western character and representing primarily Western values) are under heavy attack. These "laws" are often violated by the countries of the Third World, which took no part in their development.

"Law" ideally functions as a restraining force on uninhibited state behavior only when it is considered by *all* parties to be an impartial arbiter of disputes. If today's international law and the institutions created to provide a structural framework for its formulation fail to impart this image, they cannot hope to function effectively as a restraining force on uninhibited state behavior. To achieve this impartial and, therefore, effective framework it seems necessary to obtain the required consensus for future laws by creating a *community of interests* among states. Perhaps only in this manner can we still have a chance of reaching the end goal of a world of law.

First, it seems desirable to reemphasize the true nature and role of con-

[5]Fortas, *Concerning Dissent and Civil Disobedience* (New York: World Publishing), 1968.

temporary international law. In the broadest sense, the function of law, both municipal and international, is to serve the interests of its citizens by normalizing, that is, standardizing, their relationships with one another. In a social sense, law aims to foster a community of interests and values by providing the maximum satisfaction of desired ends for a large majority with a minimum of inconvenience, sufferings, or deprivations for the minority. Economically law attempts to limit the choice of alternatives available, along with the scope and intensity of conflicting interests of nations in the competitive pursuits of their national goals. Most importantly, international law, in a political sense, performs these crucial functions: as suggested earlier, it enhances cooperation among states through standardizing techniques and patterns aimed at limiting interstate conflict; that is, it attempts to serve an impartial framework for the process of international decisions. In a decentralized and heterogeneous world, it serves as an instrument of communication by providing a common language and a joint frame of reference. In the making of foreign policy, it frequently serves as a tool since states do indeed use legal arguments to protect or enhance a particular position. All of this is essentially done by using law as a means of putting pressure on an adversary through mobilization of international support and, thus, internationalizing a national interest. But, at the same time, the inherent ambiguities of international law in other situations enable policymakers to dismiss international law altogether as irrelevant, as if it were neither a guide nor a restraint.

In the international arena attention inevitably focuses on the impact of nonsatisfaction of state demands on international lawmaking; for states are under no obligations voluntarily to accept deprivation or frustration of their national objectives. Thus, in the actual process of lawmaking we *must* entertain various notions of bargaining as a part of their diplomatic-strategic behavior and their incentive to compete and even conflict. Within this wider framework we must also take into account characteristics unique to states' behavior as a result of the disparate broader value systems that they interject in the process of negotiations. One cannot afford to ignore the international environmental factors either, within which the process of law development must take place and that, in fact, subsequent laws must reflect. For instance, factors such as the impact of the most recent weapons of mass destruction in international politics; a general desire to disarm mutually as the initial Soviet-American Salt Agreement has indicated; a strong willingness to keep these weapons out of such areas as outer space and the ocean floor, as the relevant treaties point out; the significant role of the emergent states in world politics; the United States-Soviet detente; and perhaps, most importantly, the role of supranational and international organizations that have introduced in the international environment new dimensions that future lawmaking and laws cannot ignore. With growing membership and with an ever-increasing *functional* complexity, some of these international organizations have become a revolutionary force in world affairs.[6] Their proliferation represents an effort on the part of nation-states to reach for new organizational forms of cooperation to improve their economic health. These organizations have meant the creation of new and important problem-solving capabilities in the international system.

While the notion of "state sovereignty" remains intact, the so-called impermeable nation-state is now frequently penetrated by the activities of either these organizations or other states belonging to such organizations. This statement is true of all nation-states that belong to various functional international organizations regardless of their size or relative powers. Relations among them are no longer confined, for practical purposes, to those involving formal government-to-government contact. This process of international integration through functional organizations, however modest it may seem at the present, has great significance for future international lawmaking. It tends to foster both a broader value system among states, and a general consensus on the "rules of the game" at the bargaining table.

Along with the above considerations in lawmaking, we must also not neglect certain other characteristics unique to the international arena that hinder this process. First, world authority is decentralized. There exists no supranational institution with absolute authority that could use its centralized position to mitigate and inhibit trends toward international conflict. Second, the nation-state remains the supreme actor. Given this fact, the trend exists, without any possibility of substantial change in the near future, that states will continue to define their supreme interests in national instead of international terms. Generally, states still find security within their own societal orders and perceive and project images. The inherent mistrust of elements external to their own order is still rather strongly and widely held. Third, at an international level "law" does have an impartial character. Not only is there a lack of effective institutions that can serve as impartial arbiters of interstate disputes, but law itself has become tainted with valueladen overtones. Many scholars such as Mc-Dougal, Burke, Goldie, and Lauterpacht conceive of law as "reasonableness." Yet reasonableness to one nation generally does not mean reasonableness to other nations. Thus, law is cloaked in the values of the historically stronger nations, values that a majority of the weaker, newer nations of today simply do not share. Consequently, if a state is not satisfied with a legal interpretation of its rights and obligations under a

[6]Jack C. Plano and R. E. Riggs, *Forging World Order: The Politics of International Organization* (New York: Macmillan), 1967; and D. W. Bowett, *The Law of International Institutions* (New York: Praeger), 1963.

particular law, it proceeds to choose definitions that it considers "morally" justified in professing. Consider, for instance, current states' actions with regard to the doctrine of the continental shelf: Chile, Ecuador, Peru, Panama and Costa Rica claim a continental shelf area up to 200 miles from their national borders; the United States and all North Sea states also find justification for expansion of their national jurisdictions. Thus, in this situation, as indeed in many other new areas, one is faced with a lack of consensus on both the *procedure* and *substance* of law. Fourth, one must accept that the interests of states will naturally overlap and even conflict. This is so because the complexities of the modern world and the growing interdependence of nations mean more state activities, both in scope and intensity, beyond the confines of national borders.

In constructing an approach aimed at understanding the development of international law through politics, one must consider more than the prevailing conditions of the international environment. What must somehow be done is to investigate whether there is a possibility for states to build into the international system conditions by which they can identify meaningful alternatives to conflict for greater flexibility in pursuing their foreign policy objectives. To achieve this condition, aside from building into the framework calculations based on perception of the strength of state interest in an issue, one must consider alternative means by which to achieve areas of consensus on values, because a consensus on values is a prime factor in reducing misjudgments and in creating voluntary obedience to law. Several writers have suggested, in this regard, that some standardization of values can be achieved by relying on the language (and values) of a technological elite—values such as "efficiency," "competition," and "stability." These "values" are said to be impartial because of their relationship to the laws of science. Yet as recent events in Vietnam, the Middle East, and Czechoslovakia have demonstrated, one must create as a preliminary step the necessary cross-national contacts for such "standardized" values to have enough impact on foreign policy considerations, the latter of which may be said to blend functional rationality with social, psychological, and cultural, as well as political variables. Conceivably, to a certain extent, this desired impact (a standardization of values) might already have been achieved because the values of technocrats and expertise are already standard (e.g., stability, efficiency, and order) and since anything that is perceived as a threat to these values frequently meets a common reaction from all quarters. In this case, we need to expand the commonality of these values to the realm of international law as far as that is now possible. However, the perception of specific values to be promoted in international law in terms of *priorities* may vary from nation to nation to such an extent that the desired impact may be minimized. For example, the value of "competition" might be promoted actively by nation

X, which then translates this value objective into a policy of expansion of its foreign trade market that the international law may be required to reflect. Nation Y, on the other hand, may perceive "stability," that is, a lack of competition, as its first priority. Its policy objective may be to strengthen its own position by having international law reflect norms prohibiting entry of others into the foreign market that it controls.

Despite the above kind of difficulties, substantive cross-systemic contacts, cross-national trade ties, mutual regional development pacts, and memberships in various functional organizations can best lead to common perceptions of value and similar interpretation and analysis of "issues" for purposes of law development. While not precluding an area of *exclusive* interest, the above also does not preclude an area of *common* interest—or the feeling that an "issue" has some modicum of mutual interest in several countries, that there are parameters to these interests, and that somewhere within these parameters, there are areas of mutually perceived accommodations that may result in the development of new international laws of consensus.

What has not been mentioned in the above references to cross-systemic contacts is common, or lack of common, *ideology*. The types of cross-systemic contacts described up to this point—especially those that provide the depth of contact necessary to have an impact on policy considerations—may generally exist among states with similar ideologies. They may not exist, at least in any large measure, among states that possess conflicting ideologies. However, for a variety of reasons this may now be changing. In most nation-states today there is a predictable and measurable gap between the public espousal of whatever widely held ideology a nation may have and its *actual* translation into public policy, including foreign policy. In fact, it has become recently quite fashionable for many international and national actors, particularly in the emergent states, to espouse consummatory ideologies primarily for psychological gratifications, their own and those of their masses. This *seemingly* makes international compromises on "issues" (i.e., future international laws) more difficult to achieve. But in *reality*, these states find no conflict whatsoever in developing foreign policy goals that are significantly free of professed ideological constraints and more attuned to the pragmatic needs of their nations. To the extent that this new pragmatism has become a significant force in the international arena today, it may well continue to widen the gap between ideology and policy, thus making compromises (necessary for consensus formulation and subsequent law development) among nations holding conflicting ideologies *much easier* to attain.[7]

The above process has already begun. Recently both super-powers have

[7]Fred C. Ikle, *How Nations Negotiate* (New York: Praeger), 1967 edition.

shown a predisposition to close an era of "confrontation," and enter into a decade of "negotiation," regardless of their ideological differences. Several important international treaties recently signed by these two nations and subsequently ratified by many other countries indicate this predisposition. Recent treaties on strategic arms limitation and on keeping the seabed free of weapons of mass destruction can also be cited as indications of more pragmatic forms of cooperation. In terms of changing public attitudes, too, one can discern the emergence of faint signs that may be replacing notions such as "better dead than Red," "right or wrong my country," and the "President knows best" with expressions such as "friendly Communist nations," "you can do business with the other side," and "mutual survival." The emergence of more bureaucratic, businesslike, and technologically oriented elites in the Soviet Union and the modernizing military elites in the developing countries may also be regarded as helpful signs in this evolution.

The emphasis on "state" as a proper unit of analysis for our approach seems logical simply because, despite the persistent attempts of various functional and other world organizations to introduce some measure of international integration, the nation-state has remained the most significant operating unit in the international scene. All attempts to extend the realm of international jurisdiction have been usually greeted with traditional arguments in support of "state sovereignty" and the supremacy of "national interests." Thus, it is the complex interrelationship of these states across their national frontiers that gives the fields of international politics and international law both their form and substance. Generally, while the discipline of international politics is the study of those patterns of behavior that accompany state activities across state boundaries, international law may be regarded as an attempt to organize and structure these patterns of behavior into an orderly framework designed to enhance cooperation among states through standardizing techniques and patterns aimed at limiting interstate conflict to certain generally accepted forms and levels of overt and covert international violence. In a strict legal sense, international law may be considered an attempt to serve as an impartial frame of reference for the process of international claims and decisions.

The model

Our model is concerned primarily with conceptualizing the intricate process of international negotiations and bargaining that precedes the consensus formulation necessary to the development of new international laws. It assumes that most international laws of the future will be consensual norms developed as a result of international treaties agreed on through negotiation and bargaining. The participants in these negotiations clearly act as representatives of their respective governments instead of as individuals. Their freedom of action is restricted, depending, for example, on the significance of their status within the decision-making hierarchy of their own countries. Even those negotiators who come with practically no instructions at all and, who consequently, possess a significant freedom to explore any new oportunities presented at the bargaining table still operate under powerful constraints and stresses.[8]

The presence of these constraints and stresses in international negotiations is certainly one of the more significant characteristics in contrast to other situations, in which the participants may be free to interact and react spontaneously. It is also one of the most neglected factors in our analyses of international negotiations. Given this situation, the model attempts to raise such questions as: What forms and directions does the interaction take? How are the processes and outcomes of the negotiations influenced by the conditions under which these negotiations are conducted, under limited information or under conditions of stress? What effects do the preexisting mutual images of the negotiating countries, the personal characteristics of the negotiators and their domestic systemic inputs (i.e., background factors and national objectives), have on the negotiating process and its outcomes? What latitude exists for accommodation even when all the constraints and stresses have been considered? What role do interpersonal factors of the negotiators play in determining the course of interaction?

The model conceives negotiations on international law making, a process through which two or more sovereign states interact to develop potential agreements that will provide legal guidance and regulation of their future international behavior. Within the context of this interaction, the focus of the model is on social-psychological variables. This is certainly not to suggest that a lack of consensus among states results only because of misperception and misunderstanding. On the contrary, a lack of consensus may well result from a clear incompatibility of national objectives. However, the model assumes that even such obvious conflict of interests may be sharpened or perpetuated indefinitely by various social-psychological factors and that these may influence its eventual outcome.[9]

---

[8]See J. David Singer (ed.), *Human Behavior and International Politics: Contributions from the Social-Psychological Sciences* (Chicago: Rand McNally), 1965, particularly Part 2.

[9]In support of this position see R. C. Snyder, "Some Recent Trends in the International Relations Theory and Research," in A. Ranny (ed.), *Essays On the Behavioral Study of Politics* (Urbana: University of Illinois Press), 1962, pp. 103–171;. F. C. Ikle, *How Nations Negotiate*; and J. Bernard, "Some Current Conceptualizations in the Field of Conflict," *American Journal of Sociology*, 70 (1965), 442–452.

In its initial formulation our model is composed of six interdependent components: (1) *preexisting background variables* of national-cultural traditions, value hierarchies, ideological preferences, and politicomilitary relations between negotiating parties. (2) *National objectives* that a state brings to the bargaining table. These objectives, of course, play an important role in the formulation of a state's position vis à vis other states, because they require that the outcome of negotiations result in the satisfaction of these objectives; in the present case, the development of a complimentary and supportive set of laws. These objectives are generally responsible for originally motivating a state to enter into negotiations and then to keep them going. (3) *The international environmental forces* that are generally accepted as given. (4) *Specific situational conditions* under which negotiations are conducted. (5) *The process of negotiation* itself, which involves communications, bargaining for direct and side effects, formulation of various strategies and tactics for negotiations, various moves, bluffs, threats of negative sanctions, and promises of rewards. (6) *The outcomes*, which are translated into formal treaties prior to law development, and their assessment in terms of cost and reward. The six components and their relationship with each other are further explained in the first part of the model in Figure 1.

At the beginning of any international negotiation, it is useful to conceptualize the setting by using four major elements: (a) the parties to negotiations; (b) the alternative actions that might be taken by each party; (c) the various outcomes (decisions, treaties, laws, etc.) expected to result from their combined action; and (d) the utility that each state ascribes to each of the various outcomes. Such a formulation, originally derived from game theory, can prove useful for both theory building and empirical research dealing with international bargaining. Four elements are placed in a decision matrix of outcomes and utilities that constitutes the second part of our model. See Figure 2.

In Figure 2, each of the two nations (U.S. and U.S.S.R., for instance) can alternatively decide to restrict their freedom of action in the international arena to a compromise level, by developing new international law, or by "holding out" at the present no restriction level. Current international negotiations on the question of the exploitation of the ocean floor for economic and military purposes and, hopefully, the subsequent development of new laws of the sea through a treaty may be an appropriate example in this context.

In this illustration involving restrictions on the use of area for military and economic purposes, each of the two states can take certain actions independently of the other or jointly. However, there are four possible outcomes as indicated in the four cells of the matrix: (a) both nations may retain the present situation of no restrictions at all, and consequently no laws of the sea; (b) only the United States' freedom of action may be

Background Factors

1. Social, economic, political, and cultural variations
2. Value hierarchies
3. Ideological preferences
4. General relations among parties, etc.

National Objectives

1. Community of objectives
2. Specificity of objectives
3. Long- and short-term objectives
4. Priorities among goals

Process of Negotiation

1. Communications
2. Bargaining
3. Strategies (alliances, etc.)
4. Tactics (e.g., bluffs, threats, rewards)

Outcome

1. Clarity of outcomes
2. Degree of consensus
3. Development of treaties, etc.
4. Estimation of cost/reward by each state, for short- and long-terms

International Environmental Forces

1. Conflict
2. Claims and demands
3. Actions of deviants
4. Activities of private persons and groups
5. Past acts or precedents

Current Situational Factors

1. International climate (mood)
2. Timings
3. Need for results
4. Stresses on negotiators

Figure 1. *Interdependent Components.*

Alternatives for the Soviet Union	Hold out for no international restrictions on the state exploitation of the ocean floor for national military and economic purposes.	Laws of the sea developed as a result of compromise between the two states.
Alternatives for the United States		
Hold out for no international restrictions on the state exploitation of the ocean floor for national military and economic purposes.	*Outcome (A)* No laws of the sea (no restrictions on state activities in the area) *Utilities* 0 for U.S. 0 for U.S.S.R.	*Outcome (C)* Discriminatory laws developed restricting only U.S.S.R.'s freedom of action in the area. *Utilities* + 10 for U.S. − 5 for U.S.S.R.
Laws of the sea developed as a result of compromise between the two states.	*Outcome (B)* . Discriminatory laws developed restricting only U.S. freedom of action in the area. *Utilities* + 10 for U.S.S.R. − 5 for U.S.	*Outcome (D)* Development of laws restricting both countries' activities in the area. *Utilities* + 5 for U.S. + 5 for U.S.S.R.

Figure 2. *Exemplary matrix of outcomes and utilities when each of the nations may alternatively give up its freedom of action by agreeing to a particular set of laws of the sea* OR *"hold out" for status quo, that is, "no laws."*

restricted; (c) only the Soviet Union's freedom of action may be restricted; or (d) both superpowers may agree to restrict their freedom of action by agreeing to a treaty halting the spread of military hardware on the seabed or economic exploitation of the area for national self-interest.

Let each of the four outcomes have a certain utility for each country as shown in this figure. The status quo of "no laws" in this instance may be taken as a reference point, so that its continuing existence has a zero utility for each party. The utilities of other outcomes are shown as incremental amounts over the utility of status quo; the negative utility for a state, when it alone decides to restrict its activity, represents a worsening of situation over the status quo. The sum of the utilities for the two countries involved is higher for some outcomes than for others. That is, the matrix represents a nonconstant-sum or nonzero-sum situation, as is usually true in most international bargaining. In such international bargaining situations, as in the example under discussion, the utility of various outcomes can be assessed by the judgmental evaluation of policymakers in each country concerning whether any law of the sea that a nation eventually agrees on will facilitate or frustrate the achievement of its national interest both now and in the future. In the present negotiation matrix, the best outcome for either nation occurs when it retains its freedom to use the area as it pleases while the other nation's freedom of action is restricted.

In this matrix it is also assumed that the international situation has reached the point at which status quo, which allows each nation to choose its own course of action independently, is *not desired* by either party. When choices are made jointly rather than independently, it is useful to regard them as being made among several outcomes (four in the present situation) rather than between (two) alternative actions. Thus, a decision

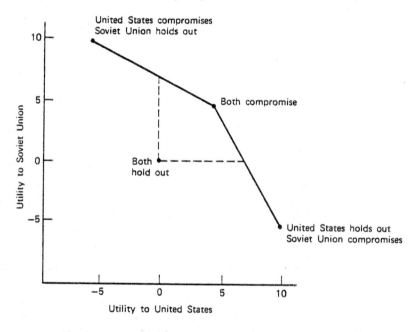

Figure 3. *Graph of utilities for four possible outcomes when each of two negotiating parties has the alternative of "compromising" and of "holding out."*

matrix of independently chosen alternatives may be constructed with a negotiation graph of jointly selected outcomes. The four outcomes under discussion are plotted in a negotiation graph in Figure 3, according to the utilities that each outcome poses for the United States and for the Soviet Union.

A tentative concluding remark on the model

Perhaps with more optimism than is really warranted, I hope that the accumulation of empirical findings resulting from the employment of such social-psychological models of observation in the analysis of the actual process of contemporary international lawmaking, will enable us to make the study of law more relevant to the social scientist and the student in the classroom. Such an approach may also provide a basis for the development of an integrative theory of international negotiation that will eventually help in specifying all of the critical elements of negotiations and their causal relationships. The model also suggests that some coherence may be provided to specific findings that we have now reached in dealing with particular failures of various international negotiations.

For the present, however, such a model, even in its rudimentary and simplistic form, does accomplish three things: (1) it provides a useful mode of identifying and organizing several social-psychological and other variables associated with international negotiations and bargaining prior to lawmaking; (2) it suggests certain significant relations among them; and (3) it helps us develop a framework that tends to accommodate various types and levels of negotiations and bargaining. Identification of these variables, as enumerated in the first part of the model, is by no means an exhaustive list; but it is a start.

By using systemtic notions the model emphasizes that analysis of international negotiations on future international law development must consider, not only the process of bargaining *on* the table but also *around* it, *before* it, and *after* it. Distinctions among these various aspects of negotiation permit their essential differentiations. For instance, background factors and national objectives can be regarded as systemic *inputs*, situational and environmental factors, along with the process of negotiation itself, as *decision making* or the *conversion process*, and the outcomes and their estimation of cost and rewards in terms of the negotiating party's preferences as *outputs*. This type of systemic sequence, now fairly widely used in the analysis of other political processes at least does suggest some general direction of influences that future international lawmaking and subsequent laws will reflect. From this general direction of influence, we someday may be able to identify more specific causal inferences.

International law codification attempts

On several occasions it was pointed out that one of the reasons it has been relatively easy for states to twist, misuse, and abuse parts of international law was because not all laws are explicitly stated in unmistakable terms. It contains loopholes and ambiguities that allow a state to use it as an instrument of its foreign policy at one time and ignore it completely, as if it never existed, at other times. Its multiple interpretations have been a commonplace in some of its areas. The ambiguities and uncertainties of international law, at least in part, are responsible for some of the current disillusionment with its role in the international system. For instance, states continue to shy away from trusting the dictates of law for the settlement of their more important disputes. Political solutions for most international disputes continue to be favored by almost all states as compared with legal solutions.

Some of the more derogatory charges against international law are certainly not valid because they neglect the tremendous effort put in by various legal institutions to make international law work in the resolution of present-day international disputes. For instance, international courts, arbital tribunals, and other legal bodies have been generally successful in finding a legal basis for the settlement of most disputes brought to them. They have attempted to fill gaps in the law by using analogy and citing general principles of international law. However, some criticism of the weaknesses of international law in this area is justified.

In response to this criticism, it is here that nations have developed the concept of international law codification. Codification is a process by which various states get together and formulate multilateral treaties after lengthy discussions and compromises. These treaties restate in clear, and to a degree, in *current*, systematic terms the primary rules of international law. Scholars have sometimes stretched this concept of law codification to mean "agreements to draw up *new* international law." Others have challenged this interpretation of the process of codification.[10] Nevertheless, because there are multiple sources in the development of international law, some of them as old as the oldest norms of law themselves, and not all states accept all of these sources, it appears that codification is a unique and useful technique to arrive at international consensus on the *specific* meaning of laws. The process of codification may have been used at one

---

[10]See, for instance, Jennings, "The Progressive Development of International Law and its Codification," *British Yearbook of International Law*, 24 (1947), 301–329; Lauterpacht, "Codification and Development of International Law," *American Journal of International Law*, 49 (1955), 16–43; see particularly United Nations, *Yearbook of International Law Commission*.

time to develop what appear to be "new" laws, but not too much importance should be read into this, because the process has generally attempted to clarify, organize, and systematize existing international norms instead of revamp the entire legal system of the international society. It is not, and should not be considered a cure-all for political disagreements, because technical codifications do not usually result in political consensus concerning, for example, the great questions of international law and its place in world politics or concerning the utilities of its norms in crisis situations, or problems of its enforcement.

Some of the earliest efforts in international law codification were made in the two famous Hague Conferences of 1899 and 1907. However, they appear very small in view of the successful efforts made in this area at Geneva in 1949. In these Geneva conferences a great deal of clarification and codification of international law took place concerning such topics as foreign occupation and treatment of prisoners of war. There were other major breakthroughs as we move to more contemporary periods. Consider, for instance, law codification in the 1958–60 Geneva Conferences on the Law of the Sea; in the 1961 Vienna Conference on the Diplomatic Privileges and Immunities, and in the 1963 Conference on the codification of laws concerning consular relations.

A quick look at the United Nations Charter reveals that the General Assembly was charged under the provisions of Article 13, paragraph 1, part 1, to promote specifically the codification of international law. In response to this provision the Assembly established the well-known International Law Commission in 1947. The consensus in the literature is that the Commission has been fairly successful in its task. Since its very inception, it has worked endlessly in drafting various conventions and articles on many topics of international law. Several of its draft conventions have been formally adopted by the General Assembly and are in force now. But even the draft articles developed by the Commission have served rather well to eliminate the ambiguities in segments of international law. They have provided help to international and national courts as well as to the governments in defining and elaborating on the accepted rules of law currently in force, whatever their source of development.

Despite some of the difficulties encountered in its work, the process of international law codification goes on. It is a slow, painstaking, but necessary process because it continues to clarify and thus contribute to the growing body of legal norms.

section V
Conclusion

chapter 15
some tentative conclusions

A look at international law at the present time clearly indicates that it has not only survived but managed to broaden its scope and influence. Such a conclusion is arrived at in the midst of dire predictions concerning its present and future health by law cynics and well-meaning law critics. Although bruised by a considerable misrepresentation of its actual and potential role in the international system by those who mean well, it has also managed to live through the claims that exaggerate or underrate its influence in international politics. Its present level of fairly widespread observance also is proof that it has survived successive international crises that have threatened the stability of the international system. It has managed to live through the claims of many propagandists (some of whom are serious students of law and politics) that breaches of old treaties, disregard of some of the customary international legal norms, and specific law violations, frequently in "the heat of crisis," show the failures of *international* law, rather than the failures of *states*. On the other hand, it has survived the onslaught of those well-meaning idealists, who have claimed that an era of world government through a world legal order is at hand and all that is needed to be done is to develop appropriate norms and force the members of the international society to accept them. If there was no alternative to a choice between the cynics and the idealists, I would probably be more inclined to accept the idealist position, for the simple reason that at least they do not challenge the reality of international law. In other words, they do less damage to the purpose of their inquiry than the cynics or the so-called hard-boiled realists. The cynics have not limited their criticism to the more vulnerable portions of international law, for example, laws of power that they say merely serve an ideological mask to cover the requirements of international political strategy to satisfy a state's hunger for more power. Their criticism has often been directed against the whole gamut of law and the very fabric of the law of nations as a whole. By way of contrast, the idealist, partly because driven to extremes in their defense of law by the charges of the cynics and partly because of their own temperaments, have made exaggerated claims on behalf of international law—claims that defy dispassionate inquiry. They might have done better and still could do better by adopting an attitude of "wait and see."

In any case there is an alternative to the choice between the two schools—between the world of the cynics where the law never existed and the world of the idealist where the law perhaps can never be. This is the world of the social scientists and the world of a dispassionate inquiry where the biases are made known to all concerned. In spite of their radically opposing observations, the cynics and the idealists have a few things in common, the most important of which is a fundamental methodological deficiency. Neither side has paid sufficient attention to the important *social realities* underlying the law-politics relationship in the international society. They have generally failed to take into account all the dynamics and peculiarities of the contemporary international system, its needs for radical changes, even for revolutions and civil wars, yet for stability and predictability too. Although the cynics have badly underestimated the present role of and the future possibilities left for international law even in a system of power politics, the idealists have ignored the inherent limitations imposed by this system of power politics on the role of international law. *Any comments, therefore, on the future of international law—its observance, its further development, and the prospects for its teaching and research in the future .—must equally attempt to avoid the "realism" of the one school and the "idealism" of the other.*

This text has attempted to sensitize the student to the dynamics of international law, international politics, and all of its ramifications for law as well as politics. It has suggested that while the concept of nation-state remains important for its functional utility in our understanding of law-politics relationships, in some areas its utility has fallen in disrepute. For instance, a state is no longer the sole repository of legal power, and its most important symbol, the notion of absolute sovereignty, has increasingly become a target of the very inhabitants of these states who have made demands in economic and in many other activities that no state (regardless of how well off) can provide in splendid isolation from the rest of the world. Consequently, a considerable success has been achieved in the redistribution of power, authority, influence, and legal and socioeconomic competence of the traditional state, among other members of the international system. This has been accomplished generally without violence and in most instances with the consent of the state itself. Interestingly enough this development is taking place in the middle of what we shall call "reverse trends"; for example, the apparent triumph of nationalism in certain parts of the world, supported by the emergence of consummatory ideologies, particularly in the Third World countries; the dark shadows that weapons of mass destruction continue to cast on this globe; and the continued, in some cases worsening, social and economic inequalities in the world. On the more *positive* side consider the following observations.

1. The internationalization of economic activity and the now rapid development of many transnational activities, particularly in the business world (symbolized by the presence of modern and huge transnational corporations) are successfully challenging the legal, political, and economic monopoly of the nation-state.

2. There is an increasing growth of an international welfare philosophy, and the emerging concern seems to be toward assisting the common man and protecting his human rights. This concern is now being extended to include the members of poor countries. As part of this emerging welfare philosophy, the richer nations have accepted a vague responsibility to help the poor through various foreign assistance programs.

3. The emerging international organizations, many of them functional in nature, have not only helped broaden the role of international law but have also contributed to law development and law codification. These organizations continue to reflect the most recent expressions of worldwide interest in international cooperation, survival, preservation and, most importantly, development of a generally more content world.

4. The broadening of the international system (horizontal extension) in which the participants are no longer a handful of European states. This has meant that international law now has an opportunity to be relevant to the needs of *all mankind*, a direction in which it is unmistakably moving.

5. Along with this significant horizontal expansion, there is the important vertical expansion of law; that is, its growing role in many new areas of universal concern, and its regulations in the far-reaching aspects of interstate relations.

6. Emergence of a new consciousness for the need of peaceful coexistence, prompted by the potential horrors of a possible war of massive destruction at the upper levels of the international hierarchy. This has resulted in the greater stabilization of the international system.

7. Newly realized threats to the world environment, its resources, and the deeply felt need for new international legislation to protect the environment, to conserve the resources, and to control the population explosion.

International law has not remained indifferent to these and many other developments in the international system. Consequently, international law has developed deliberately and in some cases rapidly to meet the challenges of today and to satisfy the needs of the international society at regional as well as universal levels. Along with the development of what can properly be called the international law of *consensus, cooperation,* and *coordination,* law observance has improved not because of the fear of sanctions or even out of habit *but because of the mutual expectations of cer-*

tain needs satisfaction. Consider, for instance, these developments in international law.

1. Development of international administrative law in recognition of the legal needs of international civil servants, bureaucracies, administrative relations of various international organizations, both internal and external.

2. Development of international criminal law, admittedly still in its infancy, but nonetheless attempting to assimilate many overlapping and often conflicting principles of national jurisdiction over criminal matters.

3. Development of universal constitutional law as a result of the initiative taken by the office of the United Nations Secretary-General and the United Nations membership. The main source of this law is the United Nations Charter and the constitutions of its many functional agencies. Some of the international constitutional law is also developed by highly successful regional international institutional arrangements, particularly in Western Europe.

4. Development of international labor law, as a result of several conventions adopted by the International Labor Organization. This law has also benefited from many recommendations and suggestions made by several labor movements of national origins.

5. Development of international commercial law, as a result of an unprecedented number of business transactions between states, between states and public international organizations, between states and private or semipublic business corporations, and between any combination of these entities.

6. Development of international economic development law, as a result of the growing relationships between the governments of the Third World countries who wish to modernize and the multinational and large national corporations, investors, and various public development aid institutions. International economic development law regulates the legal relationship of these entities in the control of natural resources, the protection of foreign investments against arbitrary "nationalization," the principles of conpensations, rules concerning management of investment and the character of agreements concerning concessions. The point to remember here is that this law is quite different from international laws that regulate the commercial relationships and foreign investments between the *industrial* societies.

7. Development of international corporation law, as a result of the activities of transnational public, semipublic, or private corporations, such as dredging of canals, building of harbors and dams, and trading in arms.

8. Development of international antitrust law, particularly in the context of various European economic communities, and as a result of work done by a special committee of the United Nations in the development of international antitrust principles.

To the above list of various types of international law, one can easily include many more, for example, international human rights and environmental laws. Perhaps one of the most important factors concerning the current role of international law in general is not so much whether it offers its followers an alternative to power politics, but that in many instances it does succeed in limiting the role of power politics by modifying the traditional relations between the role of force and the role of international law; that is limiting power politics to forms of pressures short of the application of brutal physical force.

The outlook for future law observance

Apart from new developments in the international system and in the body of international law, all of the evidence suggests that most states generally honor their international obligations. Moreover, with the above stated new developments in the law-politics relationship can anyone deny that the prospects for future international law observance are indeed good? The encouraging implications of this observation, however, should never be taken to mean all is well for the future. Out of professional necessity we must also subject the other side of the picture to scrutiny. I believe that good prospects for future law observance are indeed partly dependent on the future international behavior of the major powers, particularly the two superpowers. As long as the major powers do not frequently become guilty of major infractions of international law, the present legal system is *explicit* and *extensive* enough, *pursuasive* and *attractive* enough to command observance by most states in most instances. Yet the sad part of law-politics relations has been that the major and superpowers have frequently attempted to hold themselves above the law. They have used their powers to escape the sanctions of the law, either those applied through the United Nations actions or through any other direct action by other states. This has encouraged some lawlessness at the smaller powers level, especially when important national interests are involved. But there are indications, as we have pointed out, that the present state of affairs is changing for the better, because with each passing year there is clearly a greater need for reliance on international law by *all* states.

The prospects for international law observance within the framework of the United Nations also remains promising despite some setbacks suffered by the United Nations in its peacekeeping activities. From a legal point of view the United Nations has ample authority to more than encourage law observance. In terms of legal principles, when compared with the provisions of the Covenant of the League of Nations or even with the provisions of the Kellogg Pact, the United Nations Charter is an obvious improvement. For instance, it is now of little or no consequence under the Charter whether a state simply resorts to the limited use of armed force, or whether it intends to resort to a declared large-scale war in the full meaning of the term. Any threats to use force or its actual use, including reprisals and other coercive meansures against any country by any other country are simply *illegal*. Again, speaking from the perspective of the Charter, the so-called "inherent right of individual or collective self-defense" is also subject to the scrutiny of the Security Council.

Politically the United Nations has a better prospect in the future for the encouragement of law observance. There are several reasons for this. For instance, the emerging Soviet-American detente will have some spill-over effect on the United Nations since both countries are slowly moving toward an analogous position on certain issues there. For instance, on certain occasions both have joined together as "have" nations to alert the "have not" nations in the United Nations not to expect a great deal of financial support for every project that the poor countries "vote in" because of their majority in the General Assembly. Since the United States no longer exerts the kind of influence it did in the General Assembly in the 1950s and early part of the 1960s, it has shown some inclination to move the "action" back to the Security Council where it has a veto and where the Soviet Union always wanted it for the same reason and where it legally belongs, at least for a *binding decision* on peace and security issues. The Soviet Union in recent years has been warming up to the United Nations because it believes that it will no longer be in a minority position and that the United Nations *can* occasionally serve Soviet interests. Concerning the American attitude toward the United Nations it is certainly reasonable to hope that after the sad, bitter and, indeed, tragic experiences of direct military involvement in Indo-China types of conflicts, the United States will consider it wise to let the United Nations intervene instead. Most assuredly, the recent cuts in the American contributions to the United Nations finances is a healthy sign for this organization, since it means that the United Nations could no longer be dominated by the United States because of financial dependence. This may make the other nations realize that the financial support of the United Nations is *their* responsibility too. All of these signs in the United Nations, along with the fact that it now has a more dynamic Secretary-General, appear favorable for future law observance.

Furthermore, in assessing the future outlook for law observance we should not overlook the important fact of the probable extent of homogeneity in the international society, as a result of the further development of international political culture and multiple movements toward greater degree of international communication and integration. It is difficult to assess accurately the weight of all of the forces that are at work presently and that tend to make the outlook for law observance more promising. But, the forces are there, and they are intertwined in the present patterns of the law-politics relationship.

The outlook for future law development

The future development of international law will have to proceed in the general context of three sets of separate yet not mutually exclusive important systemic variables. These are: (1) variables representing the limitations imposed by domestic or internal considerations. These are social, economic, political, military, or any other limiting factors that may at a given time influence a policymaker's perceptions, expectations, and attitude toward the desirability (or lack of) of new law. (2) Variables representing the limitations imposed by the foreign or international considerations. These are a multitude of states' actions, reactions, and interactions, not the least among them, of course, consideration arising from patterns of power relationships among states and between states and other international actors such as organizations, groups, individuals, and other significant entities. (3) Variables representing the limitations imposed by what are *unique* challenges and opportunities in the contemporary era. Both law and politics must consider them if life is to continue on this globe not only as it has in the past with frequent outbreaks of man's inhumanity to man, but with radically different concerns, among them a wider distribution of economic and social goods and services, a more effective control of international violence and of population explosion and a better use of world resources (a shift from guns to butter) along with a real concern for the protection of world ecology, to list just a very few.

Within the limitations of the above stated three sets of variables, the development of contemporary international law is already in progress. Law is steadily expanding its domain and depth. New subjects and new areas of concern are constantly being added to its present body of norms. Much of the present law development is deliberate and is the expression of an ever-growing number of common interests that the international society, or portions of it, have acquired through elements of commonality in one or more of these three sets of limitations described above. As is true now, much of the newly developing international law of the future will probbaly continue to be somewhat less than universal in scope and nature, at least at the beginning. Almost all of it will continue to emerge through a deliberate process of lawmaking rather than through the slow evolution of custom or judicial interpretations. This lack of universality certainly does not apply to all of the new law. The status of international law in terms of its scope is indeed very closely related to the specific subject matter at hand. In some subjects the new law tends to be universal, as is true of laws of commerce and transportation, and in others it may reflect only regional international concerns, as is true of laws of labor.

The outlook for future law research and teaching

Today as we look at the future of scholarly research in the field of international law, we cannot help but notice that the many challenges confront the researcher. On the methodological level alone there are difficulties, all too well known to the social scientist, of building analytical and functional models and conceptual framework with the help of pertinent variables that can be meaningfully related and operationally specified in appropriate categories to broaden our understanding of the dynamics of law-politics relationship in a variety of contexts. Also, then there is the problem of data collection. The validity and reliability of data may not be easy to attain because of the nature of the subject, yet data collection is necessary to test these models and develop more specific testable hypotheses.

The main task for future research (from a methodological perspective) is to combine the knowledge of legal norms and legal procedures that the lawyers have so richly provided us, with the tools, concepts, and concerns of the modern social science. After all, today, perhaps for the first time, the scholar has both the historical records and also a variety of analytical concepts and tools with which to identify and to evaluate the *functions* of international law in the midst of international politics. What is more, he is capable of integrating multiple approaches to the study of law and social sciences so that a probing of the pathology of international relations and national behavior can be made possible. Such a probing in the study of international law should start with the *social process*, which is the *interaction* between law and politics.

On the more substantive level, there is the need to clarify exactly what we are trying to find out about international law? What should be the proper area of our research concern at the present time? In the substantive field of international law today a scholar faces some peculiar difficulties. These include, for instance, the bewildering complexity and the scope of the law *subject matter* at this time, represented by hundreds of international conventions, declarations, treaties, and other formal agreements. It may concern international copyright law or patent law. It may regulate labor behavior under collective labor agreements or may define international medical law. The need for research at the substantive level today seems to be toward accumulating a great deal more knowledge about the *role that international law plays in the international society*. In the process of accomplishing this task, the other important need is to construct *medium-range* theories about its *development*, *functions*, and *effects* in the international system.

What is being suggested is that research, at least for the present, should not be concentrated so much on the already existing legal norms and their enumerations, elaboration, and description, nor even on the "pros" and "cons" of a given action by a state with regard to an international crisis, for example, whether the act was legal or illegal? *Instead, the present need for research is on the specific and related question of what the international law has actually done in the past, what it does at the present time, and given the changes in it and in the conditions of the international system, what it is most likely to do?* The secondary need for further research is in the field of *prescriptions*, that is, what should international law do or how we can move it to that ideal position where it will perform the functions that we wish it to perform? In other words, the main concern of research should be on the analysis of the functions of international law in an appropriate theoretical framework with emphasis on brief description, a great deal of evaluation, and some prescription, in that order.

Many scholarly publications in the field of international law continue to devote too much time either to what the existing international norms are, or to what internatinal law as an "effective system of law" should look like. This is being done at the expense of what we should be doing, for example, *building a science of the functions of international law.* It is too obvious to deny that to do anything with international law the student must first know what actually are the legal norms. Admittedly, he cannot comprehend the functions of international law without knowing what the law is? But the task of the scholar must not finish here. Also, there is nothing inherently wrong in approaching the study of international law from a prescriptive framework. This will leave the student with the knowledge that "things in the world of law and politics could be better." But again, the responsibility of the scholar does not stop here. The teaching of the *functions* of international law must also be carried out in the context of the study of its *relationship with the international society.*

There are several but not enough scholars who in their writings on law attempt to carry out this function. Their work has been fruitful and, slowly but surely, as more and more scholars join their efforts, the outlook for law teaching will continue to improve even more. Here are the names of some of these scholars that readily come to mind: William D. Coplin, Robert Friedman, Wesley Gould, Michael Barkun, Thomas Hensley, Peter Rohn, and Martin Jarvard. Also, there are Richard A. Falk, Wolfgang Friedman, Harold Lasswell, Myres McDougal, and Stanley Hoffmann, among others. Teaching of international law in the classroom should be closely integrated to the concerns that exist in the field of research. For techniques of teaching, it will certainly be fruitful to borrow the recent experiments from the field of international relations, for example, simulation techniques of small groups experiments. As the emphasis on research increases along the lines described in this text and as the entire field of law is analyzed in its relations with politics, the teaching of international law will become more relevant, imaginative, and perhaps somewhat more controversial, all of which are healthy signs.

bibliography

1. Ahluwalia, Kuljit. *The Status, Privileges and Immunities of the Specialized Agencies of the United Nations and Other International Organizations.* The Hague: Martinus Nijhoff, 1964.
2. Alexandrowicz, Charles Henry. *World Economic Agencies.* New York: Praeger, 1962.
3. Anand, R. P. *Compulsory Jurisdiction of the International Court of Justice.* New York: Asia Publishing House, 1961.
4. ———. "The Role of the New Asian-African Countries in the Present International Legal Order," *American Journal of International Law,* LVI (1962), 383–406.
5. ———. "Attitude of the Asian-African States Toward Certain Problems of International Law," *International and Comparative Law Quarterly,* XV (1966), 55–75.
6. Aron, Raymond. *Peace and War: A Theory of International Relations,* translated by Howard, Richard and Fox, Annette Baker. Garden City, N.Y.: Doubleday, 1966.
7. Aubert, Vilhelm. "Courts and Conflict Resolution," *Journal of Conflict Resolution,* XI (1967), 40–52.
8. Baade, Hans W. (ed.). *The Soviet Impact on International Law.* Dobbs Ferry, N.Y.: Oceana Publications, 1965.
9. Barkun, Michael. "Conflict Resolution Through Implicit Mediation," *Journal of Conflict Resolution,* VIII (1964a), 121–130.
10. ———. "International Norms: An Interdisciplinary Approach," *Background,* VIII (1964b), 121–129.
11. ———. "Bringing the Insights of Behavioral Science to International Rules," *Western Reserve Law Review,* XVIII (1967), 1639–1660.
12. ———. *Law Without Sanction.* New Haven: Yale University Press, 1968.
13. Bloomfield, Lincoln P. *The Peaceful Uses of Outer Space.* New York: Public Affairs Committee, 1962.
14. Boczek, Boleslaw Adam. *Flags of Convenience: An International Legal Study.* Cambridge: Harvard University Press, 1962.
15. Bowett, D. W. *Self-Defense in International Law.* New York: Praeger, 1958.
16. Castenda, Jorge. "The Under-developed Nations and the Development of International Law," *International Organization,* 15 (1961), 38–48.
17. Chiu, Hungdah. "Communist China's Attitude toward Internationl Law," *American Journal of International Law,* 60 (April 1966), 245–268.

18. Clark, Grenville, and Sohn, Louis B. *World Peace Through World Law.* Cambridge, Mass.: Harvard University Press, 1964.

19. Clawson, Marian (ed.). *Natural Resources and International Law.* Baltimore: The Johns Hopkins University Press, 1964.

20. Cohen, Maxwell (ed.). *Law and Politics in Outer Space.* Montreal: McGill University Press, 1964.

21. Consultative Council of the Lawyers Committee on American Policy Toward Vietnam. *Vietnam and International Law,* 1967.

22. Coplin, William D. "International Law and the Assumptions of the State System," *World Politics,* XVII (1965), 615–635.

23. ———. *The Functions of International Law.* Chicago: Rand McNally, 1966a.

24. ———. "The World Court in the International Bargaining Process," in Gregg, R., and Barkun, M. (eds.), *Functions of the United Nations System.* Princeton: Van Nostrand, 1968.

25. D'Amato, Anthony. "The Inductive Approach Revisited," *Indian Journal of International Law,* IV (1966), 509–514.

26. Edwards, Richard W. "Electronic Data-Processing and International Law Documentation," *American Journal of International Law,* LXI (1967), 87–93.

27. Falk, Richard A. *Law, Morality and War in the Contemporary World.* New York: Praeger, 1963.

28. ———. "The Adequacy of Contemporary Theories of International Law: Gaps in Legal Thinking," *Virginia Law Review,* L (1964a), 231–265.

29. ———. *The Role of Domestic Courts in International Law.* Syracuse: Syracuse University Press, 1964b.

30. ———. "World Law and Human Conflict," in McNeil, Elton (ed.), *The Nature of Human Conflict.* Englewood Cliffs, N.J.: Prentice-Hall, 1965, pp. 227–249.

31. ———. "New Approaches to the Study of International Law," *American Journal of International Law,* LXI (1967), 447–492.

32. ———. "Janus Tormented: the International Law of Internal Wars," in James Rosenau (ed.), *International Aspects of Civil Strife.* Princeton: Princeton University Press, 1964.

33. ———. "The Shimoda Case: A Legal Appraisal of the Atomic Attacks Upon Hiroshima and Nagasaki," *American Journal of International Law,* 59 (1965), 759–799.

34. ———, and Mendlovitz, Saul H. *The Strategy of World Order,* New York: World Law Fund, 1966.

35. Fisher, Roger. "Bring Law to Bear on Governments," *Harvard Law Review,* LXXIV (1961a), 1130–1140.

36. ———. "Factionating Conflict," in Fisher, Roger, *International Conflict and Behavioral Science.* New York: Basic Books, 1964.

37. Friedheim, Robert L. "The 'Satisfied' and 'Dissatisfied' States Negotiate International Law: A Case Study," *World Politics,* XVIII (1965), 20–42.

38. Friedmann, Wolfgang. *The Changing Structure of International Law.* New York: Columbia University Press, 1964.
39. ———. "The Uses of 'General Principles' in the Development of International Law," *American Journal of International Law,* 57 (1963), 279–299.
40. Gross, Leo. "Problems of International Adjudication and Compliance with International Law," *American Journal of International Law,* LIX (1965), 48–59.
41. Haas, Ernst B. *Beyond the Nation-State.* Stanford: Stanford University Press, 1964.
42. Harvard Law Review Symposium. "A Symposium: Social Science Approaches to the Judicial Process," *Harvard Law Review,* LXXIX (1965–66), 1551–1603.
43. Higgins, Rosalyn. *The Development of International Law Through the Political Organs of the United Nations.* New York: Oxford University Press, 1963.
44. Hoffmann, Stanley. "International Systems and International Law," *World Politics,* XIII (1961), 205–237.
45. ———. *The State of War.* New York: Praeger, 1965.
46. Hoyt, Edwin C. "The Contributions of the International Law Commission," *Proceedings of the American Society of International Law* (1965), 2–8.
47. Hudson, Manley O. *The Permanent Court of International Justice.* New York: Macmillan, 1943.
48. Ikle, Fred Charles. *How Nations Negotiate.* New York: Harper and Row, 1964.
49. I.C.J.: *International Court of Justice Reports.*
50. I.C.J.Y.B.: *International Court of Justice Yearbook.*
51. Jarvad, Ib Martin. "Power Versus Equality: An Attempt at a Systematic Analysis of the Role and Function of the International Court of Justice, 1945–1966," paper presented at the Conference of the International Peace Research Association, 1967. Mimeographed.
52. Jenks, C. Wilfred. *International Immunities.* Dobbs Ferry, N.Y.: Oceana Publications, 1961.
53. ———. *The Prospects of International Adjudication.* Dobbs Ferry, N.Y.: Oceana Publications, 1964.
54. Jessup, Philip C. *Transnational Law.* New Haven: Yale University Press, 1956.
55. Kaplan, Morton A., and Katzenbach, Nicholas De B. *The Political Foundation of International Law.* New York: Wiley, 1961.
56. Katsarov, Konstantin. *The Theory of Nationalization.* The Hague: M. Nijhoff, 1964.
57. Kelman, Herbert C. "Social-Psychological Approaches to the Study of International Relations: Definition of Scope," and "Social-Psychological Approaches to the Study of International Relations: The Question of Relevance," in Kelman, Herbert C. (ed.), *Interna-*

tional Behavior: A Social-Psychological Analysis. New York: Holt, Rinehart and Winston, 1965, pp. 3–42 and 549–565.

58. Kunz, J. L. "Natural Law Thinking in the Modern Science of International Law," *American Journal of International Law,* 55 (1961), 951–958.

59. Lador-Lederer, J. J. *International Non-governmental Organizations and Economic Entities.* Leiden: A. W. Sijthoff, 1963.

60. Landheer, B. "Contemporary Sociological Theories and International Law," *Recueil des Cours,* XCI (1957), 1–95.

61. Langrod, George S. *The International Civil Service: Its Origins, Its Nature, Its Evolution.* Dobbs Ferry, N.Y.: Oceana Publications, 1963.

62. Larson, Arthur. *Design for Research in International Rule of Law.* Program of Research No. 3. Durham: World Rule of Law Center, Duke University, 1961a.

63. Lauterpacht, Hersch. *The Development of International Law by the International Court.* New York: Longmans, Green, 1958.

64. ———. *The Function of Law in the International Community.* Oxford: Clarendon Press, 1933.

65. Lee, Luke T. *Consular Law and Practice.* New York: Praeger, 1961.

66. Lissitzyn, Oliver J. *International Law Today and Tomorrow.* Dobbs Ferry, N.Y.: Oceana Publications, 1965.

67. ———. "International Law in the Missile Age," *International Conciliation* (542) (1963).

68. McDougal, Myres S. "International Law, Power and Policy: A Contemporary Conception," *Recueil des Cours,* LXXXII (1953), 137–258.

69. ———. "Some Basic Theoretical Concepts about International Law: A Policy Oriented Framework of Inquiry," *Journal of Conflict Resolution,* IV (1960), 337–354.

70. ———, and Burke, W. T. *The Public Order of the Oceans.* New Haven: Yale University Press, 1962.

71. ———, Lasswell, Harold D., and Miller, James C. *The Interpretation of Agreements and World Public Order.* New Haven: Yale University Press, 1967.

72. McWhinney, Edward. "Peaceful Co-Existence and Soviet-Western International Law," *American Journal of International Law,* LVI (1962), 951–970.

73. ———. "Soviet and Western International Law and the Cold War in the Era of Bipolarity," *Canadian Yearbook of International Law,* I (1963), 40–81.

74. Merrillat, H. C. L. *Legal Advisers and Foreign Affairs.* Dobbs Ferry, N.Y.: Oceana Publications, 1964.

75. Niemeyer, Gerhart. *Law Without Force: The Function of Politics in International Law.* Princeton: Princeton University Press, 1941.

76. Nørgaard, Carl Aage. *The Position of the Individual in International Law.* Copenhagen: Einar Munksgaard, 1962.

77. Parel, Anthony. "The Relevance of International Legal Theories to World Politics." University of Calgary, 1967. Mimeographed.

78. *Proceedings of the American Society of International Law.*
79. Pruitt, Dean G. "Foreign Policy Decisions, Threats and Compliance to International Law," *Proceedings of the American Society of International Law,* (1964), 54–60.
80. Ramundo, Bernard A. "The Socialist Theory of International Law," Institute for Sino-Soviet Studies. Series No. 1. Washington: George Washington University, 1964.
81. Rohp, Peter. "Institutionalism in the Law of Treaties: A Case of Combining Teaching and Research," *American Society of International Law Proceedings,* LIX (1965), 93–98.
82. Röling, B. V. A. *International Law in an Expanding World.* Amsterdam: Djambaten, 1960.
83. Schacter, Oscar. "The Enforcement of International Judicial and Arbital Decisions," *American Journal of International Law,* LIV (1960), 1–24.
84. Schubert, Glendon A. *Quantitative Analysis of Judicial Behavior.* Glencoe, Ill.: The Free Press, 1960.
85. Schwarzenberger, George. *The Frontiers of International Law,* London: Stevens, 1962.
86. ———. *The Inductive Approach to International Law.* London: Stevens, 1965.
87. Shukri, Muhammad Aziz. *The Concept of Self-Determination in the United Nations.* Damascus: Al Jadidah Press, 1965.
88. Singer, J. David. *Human Behavior and International Politics.* Chicago: Rand McNally, 1965.
89. Skubiszewski, Kizypztof. "Forms of Participation of International Organizations in the Law-Making Process," *International Organizations,* XVIII (1964), 790–805.
90. Sperrazzo, Gerald (ed.). *Psychology and International Relations.* Washington: Georgetown University Press, 1965.
91. Stanger, Roland J. (ed.). *Essays on Espionage and International Law.* Columbus, Ohio: Ohio State University Press, 1962.
92. Stoessinger, John G., et al. *Financing the United Nations System.* Washington: The Brookings Institution, 1964.
93. Stone, Julius. "Problems Confronting the Sociological Enquiries Concerning International Law," *Recueil des Cours,* LXXXIX (1956), 66–177.
94. ———. *Law and the Social Sciences in the Second Half Century.* Minneapolis: University of Minnesota Press, 1966.
95. Syatauw, J. *Some Newly Established Asian States and the Development of International Law.* The Hague: M. Nijhoff, 1961.
96. United Nations. *Yearbook on Human Rights.*
97. United States Arms Control and Disarmament Agency Publication 4, General Series 3. *Blueprint for the Peace Race.* Washington, D.C.: Government Printing Office, 1962.
98. U.N.T.S.: *United Nations Treaty Series.*

INDEX